The Might that was Assyria

THE MIGHT THAT WAS
ASSYRIA

H. W. F. Saggs

Professor Emeritus of Semitic Languages
University College, Cardiff

SIDGWICK AND JACKSON, LONDON

ST. MARTIN'S PRESS, NEW YORK

First published in Great Britain in 1984
by Sidgwick and Jackson Limited,
1 Tavistock Chambers, Bloomsbury Way, LONDON WC1A 2SG.
First published in the United States of America in 1990
First Joint Edition Reprint (SMP, S&J) 1990

LIBRARY OF CONGRESS CATALOGING-IN-PUBLICATION DATA

Saggs, H.W.F.
  The might that was Assyria / H.W.F. Saggs.
    p. cm. – (Great civilization series)
  Reprint: Originally published: London : Sidgwick and Jackson 1984.
  Includes bibliographical references.
  ISBN 0-312-03511-X (St. Martin's Press)
    1. Assyria—History. 2. Assyria—Civilization. I. Title.
II. Series.
DS73.2.S23   1989   89-10786
935'.03—dc20   CIP

Picture research by Deborah Pownall

ISBN 0-283-98961-0 (Sidgwick and Jackson, HB)
ISBN 0-283-98962-9 (Sidgwick and Jackson, SB)
ISBN 0-312-03511-X (St. Martin's Press)

Printed in Great Britain
by Bookcraft (Bath) Ltd

Contents

List of Maps · *viii*

List of Plates · *ix*

Preface · *xi*

PART ONE

1 ASSYRIA: BACKGROUND AND BEGINNINGS · 2
The Geographical
    Framework · 2
Before History · 6
The Dawn of History · 16
Growth of Towns and
    Cities · 20

2 EARLY KINGS OF ASSYRIA · 23
The Assyrian King List · 23
The Third Dynasty of Ur · 27
Ashur and Trade · 27

**3 HURRIAN INTERLUDE: THROUGH VASSALDOM TO
INDEPENDENCE** · 35
The Kingdom of Shamshi-
    Adad I · 35
Hurrian Immigrants · 37
The Kingdom of Mittanni · 39
Assyrian Independence · 41
From Kingdom to Empire · 43

4 ASSYRIAN EXPANSION · 46
Adad-narari I · 46
Shalmaneser I · 48
Tukulti-Ninurta I · 51
The Silence of Decline · 55

5 THE MIDDLE ASSYRIAN EMPIRE · 58
Assyrian Renewal · 58
Aramaean Immigration · 65

6 THE GROWTH OF THE NEW ASSYRIAN EMPIRE · 70
Military Security and Economic
    Development · 70
Ashur-nasir-pal II, the Imperial
    Strategist · 72
Urartu, a Rival Kingdom · 79
Weak Kings and Over-mighty
    Governors · 82

7 IMPERIAL PRIME · 85
Administrative Reform · 85
Policy towards Vassal States · 86
Expansion under Tiglath-
    Pileser III · 87
The Accession of Sargon · 92
Sennacherib · 98

8 ZENITH AND COLLAPSE · 104

The Royal Succession · 104
Ashurbanipal · 109

The Downfall of the
Empire · 117

PART TWO

9 ASSYRIAN SOCIETY AND CUSTOMS · 124

Assyrians: a Nation, not a
Race · 124
Social Classes · 130
The Agricultural Basis of
Assyrian Life · 131
Poor Peasants, Serfs and
Slaves · 134

Childbirth and Infant
Mortality · 138
Marriage · 140
Sexual Life · 144
Education · 146
King and Court · 147

10 THE DOMESTIC SCENE · 152

Clothing · 152
Footwear · 154
Jewellery · 155
Hair and Headgear · 156

Household Furnishings · 156
Storage Equipment · 160
Water Supply · 160
Weights and Measures · 161

11 AGRICULTURE, ANIMAL HUSBANDRY AND TRADE · 162

Agriculture · 162
Animal Husbandry · 166

Trade · 170

**12 MASTERY OVER THE ENVIRONMENT:
THE ASSYRIANS AND NATURAL RESOURCES · 180**

Chemical Technology · 186
Town Planning · 187

Animal Power and Land
Transport · 195
Water Transport · 197

13 THE SUPERNATURAL WORLD · 200

Polytheism · 201
Incipient Monotheism · 203
The Temples · 204

Astrology · 220
Witches and Wizards · 225

14 ASSYRIAN MEDICINE · 226

The Assyrian View of
Disease · 227

The Physician in Practice · 229
Medicinal Materials · 231

15 ASSYRIAN ART · 233

Bas Reliefs · 233
Sculpture in the Round · 239

Carved Ivories · 239
Cylinder Seals · 241

16 THE ASSYRIAN ARMY · 243

Antecedents of Assyrian
Militarism · 245
Psychological Warfare · 248

The Army on Campaign · 250
Assyrian Motivation, Drive and
Achievements · 264

CONTENTS

17 ASSYRIAN WRITING AND LITERATURE · 269

Assyrian Royal
  Inscriptions · 271
Limu Lists · 273
Astrological Reports · 274
Oracles · 275
Letters · 275
Economic Documents · 277
Laws · 277

Texts Directly Borrowed from
  Babylonia · 278
Omen Texts · 282
Scribal Education Texts · 283
Rituals and Incantation
  Series · 283
Myths and Epics · 285
Wisdom Literature · 287
Other Classes of Texts · 288

18 THE REDISCOVERY OF ASSYRIA · 289

Travellers' Tales · 291
Decoding the Inscriptions · 294
Botta, Layard, and Rawlinson:
  the Fathers of
  Assyriology · 298

Place and Rassam · 317
International Expeditions · 320

Bibliography · 324

Indexes · 329
Proper Names · 330
General Index · 336
Biblical References · 340

List of Maps

Assyria and Babylonia   4

Prehistoric Sites   10

Ancient Routes from Assyria to Cappadocia   32

Boundaries to North and East, *circa* 1220 B.C.   53

Aramaean Migrations   67

Expansion under Ashur-nasir-pal II   76

Growth of Assyrian Control in the West, 883–727 B.C.   90

Sargon II: major Urartian and Babylonian campaigns   96

Assyrian Empire: maximum control claimed   110

List of Plates

Between pages 20 and 21

1A   Hair-style and dress of an Assyrian lady
1B   Late eighth-century limestone slab carved to represent a carpet
2A   Detail from banquet of Ashurbanipal after defeat of the Elamites
2B   Ancient representation of ziggurat on a cylinder seal
3A   Assyrian troops on campaign in the marshes of south Babylonia, carrying prisoners in local reed-built boats
3B   Carved ivory plaque of a cow and calf
4A   A seeder-plough depicted on a stone monument
4B   King Sennacherib on an armchair throne at the siege of Lachish in Palestine
5A   and 5B   Two types of footwear
5C   Irrigation machines on a bas relief
6A   Cult functionary wearing a mask
6B   Moving a colossus in the late eighth century
7A   Bronze weight in the form of a lion
7B   Quay wall at Nimrud
8A   Typical *tell* (unidentified), near Mosul
8B   Nineveh today

Between pages 84 and 85

9A   The modern remains of the ziggurat of Calah (Nimrud)
9B   Representation of a worshipper revering a sword on an altar as the symbol of a god
10A   Drawing of *keleks* on the Tigris in the mid-nineteenth century A.D.
10B   Drawing of Sennacherib's ships, from a bas relief
11A   Drawing of soldiers inflating and using goatskin floats, from a bas relief
11B   Phoenician-type galley, on a bas relief
12A   Armlet and bracelet of an Assyrian king
12B   Detail from the bronze gates of Balawat: the carving of a statue of Shalmaneser III
13A   Detail from the bronze gates of Balawat: prisoners in neck-yokes

13B   Detail from the bronze gates of Balawat: a sacrifice at the source of the Tigirs
14A   Seventh-century scene from a lion hunt
14B   Ninth-century statue of King Ashur-nasir-pal II
15A   Bas relief showing King Ashur-nasir-pal II on each side of a stylized 'Sacred Tree'
15B   Seventh-century scene from the hunt of wild asses
16A   Ashurbanipal's defeat of the Elamites
16B   Detail from 16A, showing the capture of Teumman, King of Elam, and his son

Between pages 148 and 149

17   C. J. Rich's plan of Nineveh
18   Five cylinder seal impressions:
      A   A god and a winged bull hunting a dragon
      B   Suckling goat beside tree
      C   Stag amongst trees
      D   Lion-man in combat
      E   The Assyrian king in a 'Sacred Tree' scene
19A   Vulture carrying off entrails of those killed in battle
19B   Lion colossus
20A   A woman's face in ivory – the so-called 'Mona Lisa of the Well'
20B   Carved ivory showing a Nubian bringing a monkey and an antelope as tribute
21A   Drawing from a late eighth-century bas relief of officers' tents in camp
21B   Watering and grooming horses, on a bas relief
22A   Artist's reconstruction of façade of temple at Khorsabad
22B   Seventh-century bas relief with a three-stage representation of a lion being released and killed
23A   Restored wall painting of King Sargon, from the throne room at Khorsabad
23B   Carved ivory plaque embellished with gold and precious stones
24A   Prisoners in Assyrian camp
24B   Deportation in comfort – transport provided for women and children
24C   Soldiers drawing carts, from a bas relief

Preface

It is customary to offer a prefatory justification for a book of this kind. The reason for the writing of this one is simple. Over more than half my life I have studied the Assyrians, and I should like the privilege of sharing with others some of the interest I myself have found in that people.

The reader will soon notice that I actually like the Assyrians, warts and all: I make no apology for this. Though the Assyrians, like the people of every other nation ancient and modern, were sometimes less than kind to their fellow humans, I feel no compulsion to be continually advertising my own rightmindedness by offering judgement upon their every action or attitude in terms of current liberal orthodoxy.

I am well aware that there are many topics omitted which might have been discussed. I have notebooks of material which would make up a book more than twice the size of this one, but there had to be a limit. In my selection of what to discuss, I have concentrated upon matters for which the evidence is clearest, areas which touch the modern world most nearly, and topics which seem the most interesting. Obviously, these three criteria do not always coincide, and I have sometimes had to sacrifice one or other.

It may be helpful to say a word about dating. Other writers may be found to offer dates which for the first millennium B.C. differ from mine by a year or two, for the second millennium by a decade or more, and for the third millennium by up to a century. Such differences derive from the way in which the total evidence is dovetailed, and there can seldom (dating from astronomical phenomena excepted) be absolute certainty. As I see it, exact dating is of little importance, provided the relative sequence of events is clear, but dates provide a useful framework and it is for this purpose that I offer them fairly freely. Those *au fait* with the discussion of Mesopotamian chronology will notice that I have used the system associated with my revered former teacher, Sidney Smith; I wish I had mastered the subject as well as he did, but no one could. All dates given in relation to ancient Assyria are to be understood as B.C. without specific indication. Occasionally I refer to a date in our own era, when, if there is the slightest chance of confusion, I supply the letters A.D.

I should not like to conclude this preface without recording my thanks to my wife, whose unfailing cheerfulness, enthusiasm and practicality have enhanced the enjoyment, interest and value of many a journey to and in Assyria which we have made together over the years.

Harry Saggs

Part One

1

Assyria: Background and Beginnings

Most readers in the Western world will have first met the Assyrians in the Bible. There they are found as the imperial power which destroyed the kingdom of Israel, taking the so-called 'ten tribes' into captivity. A generation later they attacked Jerusalem, capital of the sister kingdom of Judah. It is this latter attack which inspired Byron's poem beginning:

> The Assyrian came down like the wolf on the fold,
> And his cohorts were gleaming in purple and gold.

Largely in consequence of the Bible and of Byron's poem, the Assyrians have a reputation in the English-speaking world for ruthless barbarity. They have been maligned. Certainly they could be rough and tough to maintain order, but they were defenders of civilization, not barbarian destroyers.

The Jerusalem episode occurred within a century of the final disappearance of the Assyrians as a distinct people. But most of what gave the Assyrians their significance in world history had its roots in the thousand years and more of national identity which already lay behind them when they swept through Palestine.

The Geographical Framework

The Assyrian empire at its furthest extent was vast. For a short time, during the period in which we meet it in the Bible, it stretched from Egypt on one side to Persia (Iran) on the other. By contrast, the central Assyrian homeland, from which so much of the ancient Near East came to be controlled, was a very small country. It was no bigger than East Anglia, or Wales, or Palestine, or the state of Connecticut.

Basically Assyria was the land along the middle Tigris. Its northern limit was just north of Mosul, where the foothills of the mountains give way to plain. Southwards it extended to roughly a hundred and thirty miles north-west of Baghdad, in the region where the Tigris breaks through a range of hills called Jebel Makhul west of the Tigris and Jebel Hamrin to the east. The Tigris itself cuts Assyria down the middle. To the west of the Tigris is an extensive plain (more precisely, a low limestone plateau), the Jazirah, with a mountain range called Jebel Sinjar at its northern end. The Jazirah stretches, with no significant east–west interruption, as far as the Habur river. In this plain, open to nomads from the Syrian desert, the extent of Assyrian control at any time depended upon Assyrian military strength and determination. In the south-eastern part of this region, alongside the Tigris, lay the city Ashur, the most ancient capital.

To the east, the Tigris is fed within the region of Assyria by two major tributaries, both bearing the name Zab. The Lesser (or Lower) Zab joins the Tigris just north of the Jebel Hamrin, whilst the Great (or Upper) Zab makes its junction some twenty-five miles downstream of Mosul. High mountain ranges, in which the two Zabs rise, form a rough quarter-circle east and north of Assyria.

Thus, whilst there is a single plain west of the Tigris, eastern Assyria is cut into three. One sector is the plain between the Great Zab and the northern mountains; for this, Nineveh was always the most significant city in ancient times, as nearby Mosul still is today. The second sector is the area between the two Zabs, centred on Erbil. These two sectors were always, from the time that one can speak of a country Assyria, elements of it. The third sector is the country south of the Lesser Zab as far as the Jebel Hamrin; this area includes Kirkuk, now best known as the centre of a great oilfield, in ancient times the city Arrapkha. Assyria at its most limited did not control this region. Arrapkha, Erbil and Nineveh, with Ashur on the west bank of the Tigris, were the only major cities, for Assyria was predominantly a land of country towns.

Comprising these four main divisions, Assyria is far from being one uniform geographical unit; significant differences both of terrain and of climate exist between one part and another. But on the other hand, the constituent parts are sufficiently alike to make the whole region recognizably a single country in its own right, and to set it apart as distinct from what lies to the south of it. In most of the land rainfall is sufficient for agriculture without irrigation, at least in good years, although in the extreme south of Assyria the situation does become marginal, with crop failures in bad seasons. Further south still, beyond the latitude of Jebel Hamrin, the rainfall becomes definitely too low for cereal growing without recourse to irrigation. It is in much the same latitude that there is a change of soil; the mainly gravelly plains of Assyria here give way to alluvium laid down by the Tigris. These two features combine to create a geographical boundary between Assyria and the neighbouring land to the

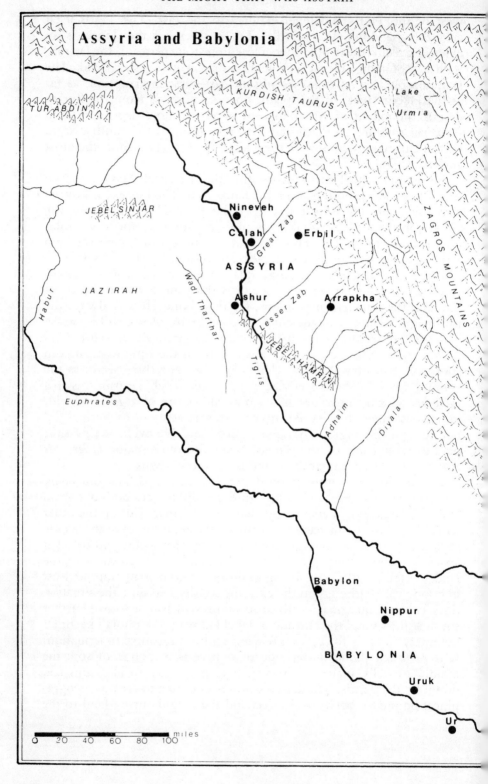

south. In the first and second millennia B.C. that southern land was known as Babylonia, and earlier still as Akkad and Sumer (its northern and southern halves). The political demarcation between Assyria and Babylonia in ancient times did not of course necessarily at all times follow the natural boundary, but shifted back and forth according to the fortunes of the two states.

The geographical distinction between Assyria and Babylonia remains quite evident today. A journey in spring from Baghdad, the capital of modern Iraq and within the area of ancient Babylonia, to Mosul, which is near several old Assyrian capitals, takes the traveller into what is manifestly a different country. In the region of Baghdad and southwards the predominant vegetation is palm trees. Except where carefully nurtured in parks and gardens, grass cover is lacking. The terrain is flat to the horizon, and for most of the year its sun-parched earth is arid and dead wherever irrigation ditches do not reach. Approaching Mosul the traveller finds a striking change. The flat terrain gives way to undulating plains, in spring green with pasturage or cereal crops and gay and scented with flowers and clover. The rolling plains are cut with wadis, aflow after spring rains, with higher ranges of hills on the horizon. The traveller has reached Assyria.

The primary strength of ancient Assyria lay in its fertile corn lands. In every region of Assyria there are small patches of corn land to be found, but there are two large areas in particular which are conspicuously productive. They always have been so. One is the Erbil plain, described as 'probably the best wheat-producing region of Iraq', and the other is the plain of Mosul. West of the Tigris there is another major belt of good corn land in the Jazirah south of the Jebel Sinjar; in favourable years one sees barley growing in this plain – though becoming sparser and more stunted the further south one goes – to approximately the line joining Hatra and Qal'ah Shergat (site of the ancient capital Ashur).

The origin of the kingdom of Assyria is referred to, if only very briefly, in the Bible. Genesis 10: 10–11 reads: '[Nimrod's] kingdom in the beginning consisted of Babel, Erech, and Akkad, all of them in the land of Shinar. From that land he migrated to Ashur [Assyria] and built Nineveh . . . and Calah.' Few Assyriologists would be prepared to defend all the details of this statement, but so far as Assyria is concerned, the basic implication agrees with what we learn from archaeology. 'Shinar' is usually accepted as a variant form of 'Sumer', which was the ancient name of the southernmost part of Iraq, watered by the two great rivers Euphrates and Tigris. It was in Sumer that the first civilization began, at about 3500. We know very little about where the Sumerians came from (if they were

THE MIGHT THAT WAS ASSYRIA

indeed immigrants and not indigenous), but a good deal about their early civilization in south Iraq. One of their earliest and most important cultural centres was called Uruk, and the biblical Erech is simply another form of this name. Nineveh and Calah were Assyrian capitals at different times, the former much the older city; their supposed founder, Nimrod, presents a puzzle. The name Ashur (which may also be transcribed Asshur or Ashshur or Assur) could apply to the country as a whole, or to its oldest capital city of all (or to its principal god), though in the biblical passage quoted it clearly denotes the country. Sumerian civilization spread up the Euphrates and Tigris, and the biblical statement about the migration from Shinar to Ashur is a reflection of the fact that Assyrian civilization largely derived from Sumer.

Note the qualification 'largely'. The geographical conditions were too different between the two regions for Sumerian civilization to be transplanted unchanged to Assyria. Other factors also came into play. West of Assyria there was an easy link by way of the Habur valley with Syria, and with the Mediterranean and Anatolia (central Turkey) beyond. At all times this route has opened the way to interaction between Assyria and other parts of the Near East, and these had their cultural consequences. We now know that there were notable developments in civilization at an early period in north Syria, well placed to influence Assyria. Also, the foothills and mountains surrounding Assyria to the north and east were neither empty of population nor complete barriers to communication with the lands beyond (now known as Turkey and Iran). Assyria was thus open to influences of various kinds from those directions also.

Before History

The regions to the north and east of Assyria have a major importance in human history as a whole, apart from their bearing on the history of Assyria. Their importance in the wider context concerns the beginning of villages and agriculture.

For any period before 10,000, it is meaningless to talk of villages in or around Assyria or indeed in any other part of the world. In the first place, humans were still rare creatures. In the foothills they were probably a good deal less common than wild sheep or goats, whilst in the plains of Assyria humans would scarcely have been seen at all, except possibly on hunting expeditions in pursuit of the wild asses that grazed the plains until the beginning of the twentieth century A.D. Secondly, such humans as there were lived by hunting animals and gathering wild plants, seeds and fruits, so that there was nothing to tie them closely and permanently to a particular spot. This is not to deny that these people may well have had seasonal bases in the form of caves or open-air sites; palaeolithic cave-dwellings are actually known from near Sulaimaniya and Rowanduz, whilst an open-air site has been traced east of Kirkuk. In any case, the absence of agriculture does not in itself absolutely rule out permanent settlements; there is a site on the bank of the Euphrates in Syria where permanent settlements had been established before man began to practise either agriculture or animal husbandry.

The first steps towards agriculture – the biggest change ever made in the human way of life – began at around 9000. Evidence about the early stages of this development is accumulating fast from sites excavated in Palestine and Syria, and in areas north and south of the Taurus and along the western side of the Zagros. Across this region there grew various plants which, in their domesticated forms, are still basic to the diet of the Western world today. Particularly important amongst these were wild wheat, wild barley and various legumes. In the same area roamed wild sheep and goats. Gradually the people in the foothills developed the cultivation of the food plants; the original wild species of wheat and barley still grow in some remote parts of the foothills, and plant geneticists are able to trace the changes from the wild forms to the forms found in excavated sites. Domestication of wild sheep and goats reached a significant stage at around the same period, though not necessarily among the same group of people. It was probably not a sudden innovation. It is likely that hunters had, in the course of millennia, learnt to regulate the movements of the flocks and herds they hunted and to restrict the boundaries within which they ranged. Deliberate extension of this to bring the flocks and herds under closer control would begin the process of domestication, and culling – either the killing off or the release to the wilds of the less controllable beasts – would in effect produce selective breeding in favour of a more easily managed type of animal.

These developments in control of food supplies are, because of their momentous importance, often referred to as the Neolithic Revolution. But the time-scale makes the term 'revolution' inappropriate. These changes spread over millennia; cattle rearing and cereal cultivation did not replace older sources of food in decades or even centuries. Indeed, for a period to be numbered in thousands of years rather than hundreds, hunting remained of considerable importance in augmenting the food supply. Relics of this are reflected in the fact that hunting remained an important ritual activity of the Assyrian kings right to the end of the empire, whilst of course

7

fishing (as distinct from fish breeding) is a form of hunting which is still a major source of food.

However, food production did eventually become the predominant way of life in the foothills fringing Assyria. Once this had happened, inevitably there were further consequences. Paradoxically, these consequences involved two opposites, settlement and migration. On the one hand, agriculture (though not sheep and goat herding) tied the particular individuals concerned in it to a particular area of land. As a result, permanent settlements – villages first and, later, towns – grew up. On the other hand, the new domestication techniques meant that to rear sheep and goats one was not limited to their native habitat in the hills; they could be fed and bred wherever suitable pasturage could be found. Similarly, corn crops could be grown far from the original settlement, wherever there was soil with adequate rainfall. Thus people were no longer tied to a particular type of terrain, and colonization of the Assyrian plains became possible. In this way there came into being the first villages of that region.

These changes had a considerable effect, both on human habitat and on human social organization. Man could now considerably extend his range, and even more so once irrigation had been developed. A given area of land could support more people, giving potentially a much larger population over the total area of settlement. Denser population in individual settlements would necessitate a more elaborate social organization, whilst proximity of a number of such settlements would bring about some kind of superstructure regulating rules of conduct between them, to minimize conflict. Once families, or settlements consisting of groups of families, owned stores of grain and herds of animals, they had to be able to defend them against other human groups less well provided, who might cast a hungry eye on those possessions. This would lead to social organization for defence and war. By such means the domestication of plants and animals modified and dictated the forms of early society.

Other changes followed. Vessels were now needed for storing food reserves. For this various materials were available, ranging from stone, which might be laboriously hollowed out, to plaited reeds. But a more convenient material was to come into general use as soon as it was discovered that when clay was exposed to fire it became hard, waterproof and durable. Fire had been used by man from high antiquity, long before the domestication of food plants and animals, but we do not know how its application to pottery first came about. Probably the discovery was made through the accidental burning of reed or wickerwork containers lined with clay, and with this the era of pottery began. Further consequences were to follow from this. The need for controllable firing to produce good pots led to the development of kilns capable of producing high temperatures, and this gave a means by which later generations could smelt metal ores.

The earliest evidence of these developments in our region comes from the sites of Zawi Chemi and Shanidar. The former site, fifteen miles north-east of Aqra and about thirty miles from the Mosul plain, has been dated by radio-carbon analysis to around 9000. Its dwellings were rough circular huts with walls built of river boulders. Stone tools show that some plant products were ground for food, though at present we have no means of knowing whether these were cereals, acorns, walnuts, or other nuts native to the area. Hunting was still the most important source of food, though the remains of a sheep with bone-form implying domestication shows that animal husbandry had already begun.

Shanidar, near Rowanduz, is a cave of the same period as Zawi Chemi; there is, indeed, the possibility that the two sites were directly linked, for Shanidar could well have been the winter quarters of people who spent the summer at Zawi Chemi. The site is important for us in giving a hint of contacts further afield. Obsidian – a hard attractive volcanic rock useful for tools – was found there, and as there is no source of this stone nearer than the Lake Van area, more than a hundred miles to the north over difficult mountain terrain, some sort of trading links between these areas must already have begun.

We can follow the developing process of controlling food supplies from sites of a slightly later period. On the outer fringes of Assyria, at Jarmo, north-east of Kirkuk, there was a settlement of three to four acres, occupied from about 7000 onwards. Archaeologists tend to be rather cavalier about time and would think of this as 'soon' after the beginnings of agriculture, but we need to notice that in absolute years the period for this development was about as long as from the time of Christ to the present. Jarmo was a small permanent village of twenty or so houses, with a population estimated at about a hundred and fifty people. Two early types of wheat (known as emmer and einkorn) and one of barley were cultivated there. Evidence has been found of domesticated goats and possibly pigs and dogs at Jarmo, but strangely – in view of the earlier evidence from Zawi Chemi – there were no domesticated sheep. If the absence of such evidence is not a mere accident of discovery, the contrast with Zawi Chemi shows there must have been several separate starts at the domestication of the various food animals, with the Jarmo people lagging in the case of sheep.

9

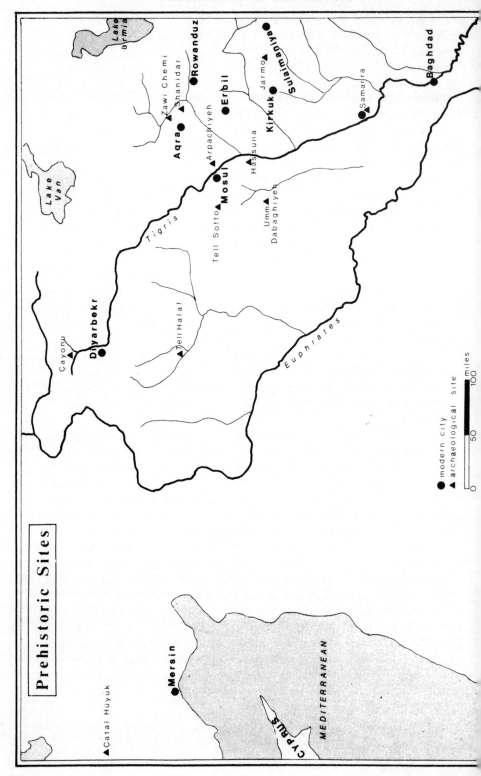

Prehistoric Sites

Earliest villages

The earliest type of settlement yet found in the Assyrian plains is named from the site Umm Dabaghiyeh, fifteen miles west of Hatra and so on the extreme southern limit of the area where rainfall agriculture is possible. Whether or not this was basically an agricultural settlement is in dispute. Remains of houses prove that the site must have been occupied regularly, though possibly not from year's end to year's end. But the main factor in the Umm Dabaghiyeh settlements may still have been hunting, with the principal quarry the wild ass. Several pieces of evidence point in that direction. Wall paintings in the houses show hunting scenes; the buildings include rows of storage blocks suitable for hides (though that actual use is not proved); and nearly seventy per cent of all animal bones found at the site were bones of wild asses, most of the rest being gazelle, though there are some bones of domesticated animals. An indication of one hunting technique which must have been employed there is the presence of thousands of baked clay balls, which were for slings. Possibly, therefore, the site Umm Dabaghiyeh was not so much an agricultural settlement as a hunting base. If so, it was presumably set up by people still centred on the foothills, who wanted to exploit the wild asses which then (and until we finished them off in the twentieth century) abounded in the Jazirah.

Other sites of the Umm Dabaghiyeh culture have been found further north, towards Jebel Sinjar. Unless Umm Dabaghiyeh itself is taken as a farming settlement, it is one of these, Tell Sotto, which marks the earliest known farming culture on the Assyrian plains, with its first phase dated by its Russian excavators to around 6000. The Tell Sotto type of settlement – a small village – was well behind some developments elsewhere, such as Çatal Hüyük in Anatolia, where a substantial town of thirty-two acres had grown up, or Jericho in Palestine.

The first settlements at present known in Assyria were ante-dated by two thousand years or more by villages in Palestine, along the middle Euphrates, and in Anatolia and Iran. But there may have been older or more advanced villages in Assyria than those of which we have evidence, for it has to be remembered that our information is often limited by modern constraints upon archaeological investigation. For example, the city of Erbil is situated in a well-watered plain which is now the best corn-growing area in Iraq, only a day's walk from where wild cereals can still be found growing, and it is a reasonable guess that Erbil was one of the very earliest of all permanent agricultural settlements. But Erbil was so very successful that it has been continuously occupied since its first foundation,

11

with the result that a huge mound – still lived on – has developed there, so deep from the top of the mound down to virgin soil that excavation of early levels has so far been impossible.

Archaeologists normally name an assemblage (to use the jargon archaeologists prefer when they mean 'cultural stage') after the site at which it was first identified. This convenient practice can be misleading to the layman, as it fosters the impression that that cultural stage had some particularly close link with the site after which it was named. But often the name-site was a quite minor settlement within a very large area. Thus, as we now go on to refer to Hassuna and Halaf cultural stages, we must not think of them as necessarily first developing at the sites bearing those names.

Hassuna

After the beginnings typified by Tell Sotto, the earliest major type of farming settlement known from the Assyrian plains is that named Hassuna, after a small mound twenty-two miles south of Mosul. Sites of this cultural stage, at present dated to a few centuries after 6000, have been excavated from the Jazirah to east of Erbil.

In the Hassuna assemblage, agriculture was certainly a major activity, with cultivated forms of barley and of several kinds of wheat. Typical utensils found at Hassuna sites also point to the large-scale use of grain; a peculiar kind of flat dish, with a corrugated inside surface, must have been used for separating grains of cereal from husks. Domesticated animals – their presence proved by bones – included sheep, goats, pigs and cattle. The presence of spindle whorls points to cloth production. Long-distance trade is established by the presence of obsidian and certain semi-precious stones, since the nearest source of some of these materials is about two hundred miles away over mountains; whether they were carried by travelling merchants or passed on from settlement to settlement, we have no means of knowing. Contacts of either kind are likely to have contributed to the spread of knowledge of technology, such as pottery production, building methods, irrigation and copper working. The last-mentioned certainly reached Hassuna settlements from further north. As far as we know at present, the first use of copper – cold hammered from native copper for small tools – was between 7500 and 6500 at Çayonu near Diyarbekr in south-eastern Turkey, within reach of the Assyrian plains and near later Assyrian sources of copper. The smelting of copper from ore is first attested at Çatal Hüyük, further west in Turkey, perhaps a thousand years later. The use of copper, including smelting, has now been found, though only on a very small scale, at one of the Hassuna sites, and as there is no source of copper ore anywhere near the site concerned, Assyria must have gained this introduction to the metal age from contacts with people further north in the Taurus foothills.

We know very little about Hassuna society. But one thing we can confidently say is that their social structure was based on the family: we deduce this from the fact that their houses were small individual dwellings, not communal buildings. We also know that they had the concept of private property, since they used stamp-seals, of which the primary function is always to mark ownership.

Hassuna settlements were limited to areas with sufficient rainfall for growing cereals. However, just to the south, where rainfall becomes inadequate, were other people who had developed primitive irrigation. This assemblage is known as Samarra; archaeologists differ as to whether or not this was totally distinct from Hassuna. One of its sites, Tell el-Suwwan, has given a radio-carbon dating (or 'determination', as the archaeologists like to call it, as they recoil from allowing anyone to suppose they are offering an absolute date) of about 5500 for its earliest stage. There was considerable eventual development, and one late Samarran settlement was so extensive that it might properly be called a small town.

Halaf

The Hassuna assemblage, virtually restricted to north Iraq, was in part overlapped by another culture, much more widespread, known as Halaf. The spread of Halaf was wide not only geographically but also in time, for it covered nearly a thousand years from the mid-sixth millennium onwards. Archaeologists divide it into Early, Middle and Late Halaf phases, and point to significant developments from one phase to the next. This has some relevance for our present purpose. It indicates that the Halaf culture in its developed form was not brought in fully-formed from elsewhere; the settlers gradually built up their way of life on the spot. That Halaf settlements were not offshoots of Hassuna or Samarra is confirmed by marked differences in their pottery. Additional evidence of the independent origin of the Halaf culture is provided by an architectural feature; a characteristic Halaf building comprised a beehive-shaped structure on stone foundations, a form found in no other prehistoric culture. The function of these buildings is uncertain, though some scholars plausibly interpret them as shrines. But whatever their function, their uniqueness shows that the first Halaf people were newcomers into Assyria. In confirmation, some Halaf settlements appear on virgin soil.

The best-known Halaf site in Assyria is Arpachiyeh, on the out-

13

skirts of ancient Nineveh and now part of east Mosul; but this assemblage as a whole came to stretch from approximately Mersin in Cilicia, across Syria and Assyria to around Sulaimaniya in Kurdistan, and north to Diyarbekr and Lake Van. One possible interpretation of this expansion is that it reflected a successful agriculture, and a consequent rise in population; as all the good farming land around a particular settlement came to be taken up with the rise in population, off would go the landless to found new settlements elsewhere. Thus the settlers on the Assyrian plains became part of an extensive interrelated group of peoples. But this is hypothesis, not proven fact, and the widespread common culture may instead have been primarily a matter of trade links over this considerable area.

There are features in the later Halaf settlements reflecting a distinct rise in the quality of life. For instance, the decorated pottery has considerable beauty, and there are amulets, plaques and beads skilfully cut from stone. Copper working was developing. There were efficient bread ovens in the houses. Arpachiyeh had a network of cobbled streets, to the advantage of its villagers in wet weather. It also had a workshop for potters, indicating development of craft specialization, a social landmark. Some scholars think that Arpachiyeh may actually have been a specialist potters' village, manufacturing its goods for a major town already in existence at nearby Nineveh. At present this remains a guess with no specific evidence to support it, but there is certainly the possibility that there may already have been large towns in Nineveh and elsewhere (perhaps Erbil) during the Halaf period.

We have already noticed trade, alongside efficient agriculture, as a possible factor in Halaf prosperity, and the trading connection of the Halaf people could go back to the time before they entered Assyria. One suggestion is that the area from which the original Halaf settlers came was between the Assyrian plains and Lake Van, and that there they were already traders in obsidian, of which there is a major source west of Lake Van. On this hypothesis, the Halaf people who settled in the Assyrian plains could then have retained their trading links with the north, thereby becoming wealthy as middlemen in the obsidian trade. Another possible factor in Halaf prosperity could have been trade in textiles; this suggestion arises from the presence on Middle Halaf pottery of motifs which seem to have derived from textiles patterns. If textiles were indeed a significant part of Halaf commerce, this may have permanently affected the way of life of the area, and contributed to the considerable importance of the textile trade in later Assyria.

What was the significance of these early cultural stages for what eventually became known as Assyria? It would be absurd to call the peoples of Umm Dabaghiyeh, Hassuna and Halaf the first Assyrians. On the other hand, it would be almost equally absurd to suppose that these peoples vanished from the face of the earth leaving no trace of posterity or cultural legacy. Thus the probability is that these first settlers were among the many strands that went to make up – however remotely – the later Assyrians, and that some aspects of the way of life they had introduced continued.

Ubaid

After Halaf, a new type of pottery begins to appear in Assyria, as well as in other parts of the Near East.

An immediate apology is necessary for beginning a new topic by talking about pottery instead of about people. But, dull as bits of broken pots may appear, we have to use the evidence of pottery because it is the most readily interpreted mark of the presence of particular cultural groups. The new culture (or 'assemblage'), marked by a new type of pottery, is known as Ubaid; without doubt, both the pottery and the associated culture first developed in south Iraq, in an irrigation economy. The number, size and grouping of mounds marking ancient settlements show that at this time there was a considerable increase in the population of south Iraq, due in part to immigration, and in part to natural population increase consequent on the flourishing agriculture made possible by efficient irrigation. The Ubaid culture, of which pottery was the marker, eventually spread very widely, from the Persian Gulf to Syria. Whether this came about mainly by cultural diffusion, or whether it was accompanied by actual migrations, we cannot certainly say, although an overlap of Halaf and Ubaid pottery at some sites favours the former view.

Who were the Ubaid people? This is a controversial question. In south Iraq they formed one link in a chain of cultural stages some-times known as Eridu, Hajji Muhammad, Ubaid, Uruk, and Jemdet Nasr, although the current tendency amongst archaeologists is to regard the first two of these as early phases of Ubaid, and Jemdet Nasr as a later phase of Uruk. This simpler terminology is used here. The Uruk period was certainly linked to the Sumerians of historical times, and it is in this period that we find such striking innovations as the beginning of cities, monumental architecture and writing. However, here we come upon a crux. Was the Uruk culture actually the result of the arrival (or self-assertion) of the Sumerians as a new ethnic group with strong innovating tendencies, or did it merely represent a spectacular jump forward in a continuing development? In the latter case, the peoples of the preceding stages in south Iraq, Ubaid in all its phases, could be thought of as proto-Sumerians.

The evidence of population increase associated with Ubaid admits the possibility of the influence of some new ethnic group, even in the latter case. It seems certain, from the most ancient surviving place names in south Iraq, that a language other than Sumerian – predominant by the beginning of the third millennium – was spoken there before 3500. This points to the Sumerians being either actual newcomers in the fourth millennium or at the least a distinct group who first began to make their cultural influence felt then. Altogether, there is a good deal of evidence in favour of the view that a particular ethnic group played a major part in the creation of what we know as Sumerian culture, although this sticks in the gullet of many younger archaeologists, who have been politically conditioned to regard it as wicked even to consider the possibility that one race or ethnic group may be more able than another.

Whether or not the Ubaidians were proto-Sumerians, their eventual arrival on the Assyrian plains (or alternatively the spread of their cultural influence) brought important developments, particularly in trade. The disappearance of the Halaf culture must certainly have been accompanied by a breakdown in their widespread trading network – and may even have been caused by it. Extensive trade contacts – significant for the pattern of life that was to characterize later Assyria – developed again in the late Ubaid period. This particularly involved links with north Syria for timber and with the mountain regions for copper, which – with the evolution of casting techniques – was beginning to play an important role. Mesopotamian dependence upon those raw materials from those particular regions was later to be an important factor in Assyria's economic and military strategy.

The Dawn of History

Developments within Assyria during the Ubaid and succeeding periods – say, 4500 to 2500 – are not as clear as we would wish. The abundance of contemporary material from further south only highlights this. In south Iraq, the periods following Ubaid – known archaeologically as Uruk and Early Dynastic – show new developments of the most striking kind. We meet the beginning of the complex societies we call cities, with massive temple buildings, highly developed craft specialization, and writing – that is, all the features associated with the Sumerians. These developments soon began to affect places well outside south Iraq. For example, at a site called Habuba Kabira, on the Euphrates in Syria, there are ruins of a major city of before 3000, showing unmistakable links with the Uruk period in south Iraq. The Uruk and Early Dynastic developments also spread up the Tigris, although, with some exceptions, their full effects were not generally felt in Assyria for several centuries. Because of this time lag, we have to be careful in our reconstruction. We are not justified in filling out our rather scanty evidence about Assyria during this time from the much fuller information – which towards the end of the period includes written documents – that we have for Sumer.

Yet we can see some of the directions in which things were developing in Assyria during these two thousand years. Settlements were gradually growing in size, becoming substantial towns, some of them guarded by fortification walls. The obvious deduction is that there was the risk of organized attack from outside, which makes it clear that warfare had become a feature of life. This has further implications for social structure. Fortification works involved tactical and strategic planning, and these presuppose the rise of war chiefs capable of giving appropriate leadership, and everything that that means in terms of social organization and class stratification. A seal from this period has been taken as depicting an aspect of warfare, namely, a file of prisoners. The taking of prisoners of war would represent the beginning of the institution of slavery, with a social group possessing no rights. However, this interpretation of the seal is not beyond question. None the less, there are other probable indications of the development of differentiated class structure. Thus, large secular buildings begin to make their appearance, and at least some of these are likely to have been the residences of a minority marked out by wealth or political power, or both. Graves give a similar picture, since a few of them contained much more elaborate burials than the many.

Developments in religious buildings are often a pointer to developments in the society as a whole. Thus it may be significant that at most Assyrian sites during this period, temples show only a very modest increase in wealth and size. This is in marked contrast with the situation in contemporary Sumer. There, imposing temple structures developed, such that by the late fourth millennium they had clearly become the focal points of Sumerian economic as well as religious life. But despite this general contrast, there were some places within the area of Assyria where Sumerian influence did have its effect in temple building. Two such are Tell Brak on the upper Habur and Tepe Gawra north-east of Nineveh, with series of elaborate temples closely resembling those in the south, and obviously directly influenced by them. But these remain exceptions; in general, the temples in the towns of Assyria during this period were less prominent than the citadels. There are two possible explanations for this. One is that the secular leaders were superior in the social structure to the priesthood. The other is that the leaders in secular affairs and the priesthood were identical, and that the members of this ruling class used the secular buildings as the basis of the social and economic administration; there would then have been no incentive for the conspicuous growth of temple buildings.

Trade continued to develop. This is shown by the very common presence in graves of imported objects, such as cowrie shells from the Indian ocean, or of objects made from imported materials, such as carnelian, amethyst, or lapis lazuli, the last originating far away in Afghanistan. There is other possible evidence for developing trade. Stamp seals of the Uruk period from Tepe Gawra show affinities with those from two contemporary settlements in Iran, and it is argued that this demonstrates cross-influences. Since the primary purpose of seals was to mark goods, this is a strong indication of merchants travelling between Assyria and Iran. The argument is strengthened by the fact that Tepe Gawra declined in importance in the late Uruk (Jemdet Nasr) period, with a simultaneous break in occupation at one of the Iranian sites mentioned, Giyan; both these facts could be attributed to interruption to the trade route which had given those two places their importance.

Evidence from Tell Brak suggests that professional sculptors and goldsmiths were attached to the temple, an indication of the beginning in Assyria of a more widespread pattern of craft specialization. However, caution is required in our conclusions from this evidence; as Tell Brak was subject to direct influence from the Sumerian south, it was not necessarily typical of the rest of Assyria.

In order to see how the next stage of development in Assyria came about, a brief summary of events in south Iraq during the first half of the third millennium is needed.

Developments in Sumer

With the creation of cities, there developed in Sumer, mainly along the Euphrates and to some extent along the Diyala, a number of city-states, independent but closely related. Hereditary dynasties arose, and the richer and more powerful states, such as Kish and Uruk (Erech), came to wield some form of overlordship over the others, their rulers taking the title 'king' (literally, 'Great Man'). The time when this form of political organization was at its height is known as the Early Dynastic period (with various sub-divisions).

18

During the Early Dynastic period people of another ethno-cultural element gradually made their presence felt alongside the Sumerians. This was the Semitic-speaking group whom we know as Akkadians. Their place of origin was the Syrian desert west of Mesopotamia, and they probably arrived by a long process of gradual immigration (perhaps beginning in the period before we can speak of Sumerians) rather than by a sudden warlike invasion.

The Dynasty of Agade

Early in the twenty-fourth century, one of these people of Semitic background, known to us as Sargon, originally in the service of a king of the Fourth Dynasty of Kish, asserted independence and built himself a capital, Agade (Akkad). Sargon eventually defeated all other local rulers and became king of all south Mesopotamia. We may put his reign at 2371–2316, although some other scholars would differ by several decades, on the basis of different assumptions in the calculations.

The importance of all this for Assyria is that Sargon showed himself the first imperialist. The last of the major Sumerian dynasts had made a foray far up the Euphrates and possibly reached the Mediterranean; Sargon followed this up by widespread conquests across Syria as far as the Mediterranean and the Amanus mountains, and possibly beyond, deep into Asia Minor. Not content with this, he also attacked and conquered another region called Subartu. This apparently meant the northern lands east of Syria, so that its central part must have been what we call Assyria. Ashur certainly became part of the Agade (Old Akkadian) empire. This can be established by an inscription on a copper spear-head discovered at the city which reads: 'Manishtusu, King of Kish: Azuzu his servant made this dedication to the deity.' Manishtusu was Sargon's grandson and the third ruler of his dynasty, and his title 'King of Kish' implied approximately 'emperor'. Azuzu was evidently one among many vassals ruling by courtesy of Manishtusu.

Nineveh, one of the other major cities of Assyria, was also controlled by the Agade dynasty. We know this from the finding there of a bronze mask of one of the kings of Agade. Further, Nineveh had a specific link with Manishtusu, proved by an inscription of a later king, recording that the temple he was then restoring at Nineveh had originally been built by Manishtusu. Thus, at least in the reign of Manishtusu, and possibly during much of the period of the Agade empire, Ashur and Nineveh were parts of a single political framework, a situation which may well have marked the initial step towards a unified kingdom of Assyria, with these two cities serving as southern and northern power centres.

Growth of Towns and Cities

Apart from this evidence of links with the Agade empire, very little is known definitely about Assyria before the very end of the third millennium, although archaeology is gradually filling out the picture. For instance, we now know that a number of substantial towns were developing in Assyria in the mid-third millennium. There was one such at Tell Taya, excavated in 1967 and later by Dr Julian Reade of the British Museum. This flourishing centre, just south of the Sinjar range, comprised 120 acres of dense urban development, with houses of both stone and mud brick, an outer wall, streets, and a central citadel. The excavator estimates the population at a minimum of ten to fifteen thousand. But many problems about third millennium Assyria still remain. There is, for example, the basic question about the very existence of an entity that we could call Assyria. As we have seen, there was a period at which Ashur and Nineveh were linked by both being controlled by Agade; but this relationship was imposed from outside and was not an organic unity. When was there first a single, independent native, political unit corresponding to Assyria in the later sense – that is, the triangle based on the three major cities Nineveh, Ashur and Erbil? How far had the culture of the country a distinctive native element, and how far was it borrowed from the south or (in view of what we are beginning to learn about early civilization in Syria) from the west? What was the ethnic composition of the country; was it uniform or were there distinctive areas related to earlier migrations of particular groups? What languages were used?

Some of these questions can at present only be answered tentatively and some not at all. The fairly abundant textual evidence from further south only serves to make our ignorance seem worse. There are, however, pointers offering answers to at least some of these questions. A look at the site of Ashur may give some indication of what sort of people first settled there, and why. It is built on a sandstone cliff right up against the west bank of the Tigris. The rainfall is almost marginal for farming in that area without irrigation; and crop failure is frequent. The only reasonable conclusion is that the area was first settled by people who wanted a defensible base with a permanent water supply, within reach of grazing lands, but who were not much concerned with agriculture. This points to their being pastoralists from the Jazirah who were in a sufficiently

1A   Hair-style and dress of an Assyrian lady. Carved ivory panel from Nimrud (British School of Archaeology in Iraq and Sir Max Mallowan, *Nimrud and its Remains*, Collins, 1966)

1B   *Below*: Late eighth-century limestone slab carved to represent a carpet (V. Place, *Ninive et l'Assyrie*, Paris, 1867–70)

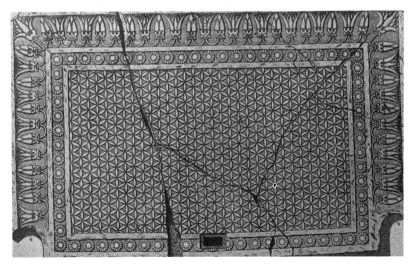

2A Detail from banquet of Ashurbanipal after
defeat of the Elamites. Here minstrels are playing
and birds are singing in the garden. Note the head
of the Elamite King Teumman hanging on a tree
(British Museum, photo H. W. F. Saggs)

2B Ancient representation of ziggurat on a
cylinder seal (Staatliche Museen zu Berlin)

3A   Assyrian troops on campaign in the marshes of south Babylonia, carrying prisoners in local reed-built boats (*c.* 700) (British Museum, photo H. W. F. Saggs)

3B   Carved ivory plaque of a cow and calf (H. W. F. Saggs)

4A A seeder-plough depicted on a stone monument (British Museum)

4B King Sennacherib on an armchair throne at the siege of Lachish in Palestine. The king's face has been mutilated, perhaps deliberately (British Museum, photo H. W. F. Saggs)

5A and 5B   Two types of footwear
(*c.* 700) (British Museum, photo
H. W. F. Saggs)

5C   *Below*: Irrigation machines on a
bas relief (British Museum)

6A   Cult functionary wearing a mask (British Museum)

6B   Moving a colossus in the late eighth century (A. H. Layard. *Discoveries in the Ruins of Nineveh and Babylon*, 1853)

7A   Bronze weight in the form of a lion (British Museum, photo H. W. F. Saggs)

7B   Quay wall at Nimrud (British School of Archaeology in Iraq and Sir Max Mallowan, *Nimrud and its Remains*, Collins, 1966)

8A Typical *tell* (unidentified), near Mosul (H. W. F. Saggs)

8B Nineveh today. The edge of the mound of Kuyunjik is in the foreground, with the River Khosr at its foot and Nebi Yunus in the background (H. W. F. Saggs)

organized state of society to need a permanent main base. That the first settlers came from the Jazirah is shown by Ashur's being west of the Tigris; settlers would stop at the point where they reached the major river.

By contrast, Nineveh is on the east bank of the Tigris, further north in sight of the foothills of the Taurus. This suggests it was originally settled by peoples emerging from the hills in the north-east. Erbil's position suggests a similar origin, and the religious tradition also seems to link Nineveh with Erbil but to dissociate it from Ashur. The deity predominantly associated with the two northern cities was the goddess Ishtar – Ishtar of Nineveh and Ishtar of Erbil are mentioned on innumerable occasions as two of the leading national deities. But the deity predominantly associated with the city of Ashur was the male god bearing the same name, Ashur.

We do not yet know very much about the early history of any of the three major Assyrian cities – Ashur, Nineveh and Erbil – although they had all certainly been long established by 2500 and their mounds doubtless contain the evidence by which we could track these developments in Assyria, given time and money. Unfortunately, Erbil remains virtually unexcavated, and though there has been considerable archaeological activity at both Ashur and Nineveh, technical difficulties have so far very much limited the information provided on the earliest periods. Nineveh has been intermittently excavated since 1842, but the greatest part of such activity has always concentrated on the palaces of the Assyrian imperial period in the first millennium. The main exception was a deep sounding dug by M. E. L. (later Sir Max) Mallowan in 1932, which reached virgin soil at ninety feet below the top of the mound. But whilst this gave a pottery sequence back to prehistoric times and showed that the site was already inhabited by 5000, it provided little specific information on growth from the first settlement into a major city.

Early Ashur

Our main information about early Ashur comes from a temple dedicated to the goddess Ishtar, attested from soon after 2800. Clearly, by that time Ashur was already a major religious centre with monumental buildings, albeit made of mud brick, with religion occupying a major place in the social and economic structure. This does not, however, make it necessary to infer a religious power structure separate from the civil; in the light of the religious titles and functions of Assyrian kings that we meet later, the two could always have been interlocked.

21

Finds in the archaic temple tell us a little about life in the third millennium. Amongst these are a number of terracotta models of houses, and although they obviously had some religious function, it is reasonable to assume that they were models of a real type of dwelling. What they show is a flat-roofed house, mostly two-storied at the front and one-storied at the back. This suggests that the typical dwelling was basically a single-storied structure with what the Bible calls an 'upper chamber' built on top at the front. One model, of the same basic form, actually shows three stories, that is, a single 'upper chamber' on top of a two-storied building.

In the archaic temple there are also statues which are typically Sumerian of the Early Dynastic period. This does not require us to suppose that the ruling group in Ashur at the time were Sumerians, but it does show that there was strong Sumerian cultural influence.

A painted gypsum relief was also found, showing the goddess, elaborately bejewelled as to her ears and neck but naked at her emphasized breasts and navel, lying on a bed. This shows, at one and the same time, the existence of a sexual cult in honour of the goddess and, more prosaically, establishes that beds were in use; the bed in question appears to be a flat pallet without legs.

Some further information about early Ashur is provided by its name. In addition to its usual name, it is quite often referred to as Baltil. This latter name, although it was afterwards given a Sumerian interpretation by folk-etymology, is no more Sumerian in origin than it is Semitic; in fact, it belongs to a language of an older population stratum which used a name-element *il* at the end of some place names – such as Babil (Babylon), Arbail (Erbil), Kurbail. (Later folk-etymology explained this *il*, wrongly, as the Semitic word for 'god'.) This non-Sumerian and non-Semitic old alternative name for the city Ashur suggests that a settlement existed there before either Sumerians or Semites had become ethnically predominant in the area.

2

Early Kings of Assyria

Prehistory ends and history begins when we have written sources; for Assyria this stage is reached in the second half of the third millennium, more than half a millennium later than for Sumer further south. Archaeology, queen in the realm of prehistory, is no longer supreme, though it continues to play a vital part by yielding the inscriptions upon which the systematic reconstruction of history rests. For this period, and for the whole of the subsequent millennia, these texts, diverse as they may be in content or language, have one thing in common: they are all written in the wedge-shaped writing known as cuneiform. This may be impressed into small tablets of clay or engraved on large monuments of stone or occasionally metal objects; in content it may be economic, religious, historical, lexical, or one of many other genres; and as to language, though the Semitic Akkadian is the most usual, there are several others in which the text may prove to have been composed. But all these texts eventually have their roots in the achievements of ancient Sumer, where writing was invented shortly before 3000.

The Assyrian King List

Some of these cuneiform texts, such as inscriptions on objects dedicated in temples, relate directly to the time at which they were written; others, more sophisticated, preserve information on events well before their date of composition. There is one document of the latter type which at its face value would seem to ease considerably our task of constructing the framework for earliest Assyrian history. The document in question, usually known as the Assyrian King List (extant in several copies), comprises names of rulers from the third millennium down to the late eighth century. Working back from datable kings and making reasonable assumptions about average lengths of reigns, this would appear to give us an unbroken list of kings way back to around 2500. But there are reasons why we cannot use it in this simple manner.

The first major king of Assyria known from extensive inscriptions of his own is Shamshi-Adad I (1813–1781). It is this king who provides the earliest fixed point for Assyrian chronology, since he overlapped Hammurabi of Babylon, whose dates are known. Before Shamshi-Adad, the Assyrian King List names thirty-eight kings or supposed kings. These are set out in groups, the first seventeen being summarized as 'kings living in tents', with the next ten presented as 'kings who were ancestors'. After this follow two groups of six each, and then Shamshi-Adad.

The observant reader will notice that the numbers in the lists of kings before Shamshi-Adad add up to thirty-nine, although it has just been stated that the kings named before Shamshi-Adad amount to thirty-eight. This discrepancy arises from the fact that the same name occurs at the end of each of two of the groups – a coincidence which hints that the structure and origin of these lists deserve further examination.

The first group – the 'seventeen kings living in tents' – is a straightforward list in chronological order, in which the last and latest two kings are named Ushpiya and Apiashal. But the second group – the ten so-called 'kings who were ancestors' – is arranged quite differently. The latest in the line are named first, each king being followed by his father and then his grandfather, in this way:

> Aminu son of Ilu-kabkabi,
> Ilu-kabkabi son of Yazkur-ilu,
> Yazkur-ilu son of Yakmeni,

and correspondingly for Yakmeni and six further generations before him, of which the earliest in time was

> Apiashal son of Ushpiya.

Thus in this second group the 'kings' are listed from last to first. But Apiashal again, as in the former list, brings up the rear, though here this makes him the earliest of the group. By this device, Apiashal is made to serve as a link between the two lists, although the difference in form of the two lists suggests that originally they had no connection.

This composite and manifestly artificial arrangement raises suspicions about the nature of the Assyrian King List for the early period. We therefore return to solid ground and see what the document says about Shamshi-Adad. For most kings there is very little circumstantial detail, but we find that for Shamshi-Adad the Assyrian King List gives an exceptionally detailed build-up in describing the immediate antecedents of his rise to power. The relevant part reads:

Shamshi-Adad son of Ilu-kabkabi. In the time of Naram-Sin [an earlier king of Ashur], he went to Karduniash [i.e. Babylonia]. . . . He came up from Karduniash; he seized the town Ekallatu; he stayed in Ekallatu for three years. . . . He went up from Ekallatu; he removed Erishum, son of Naram-Sin, from the throne; he seized the throne.

Thus it is not concealed that Shamshi-Adad gained the throne of Ashur by removing the representative of an existing dynasty. This, with four successive kings named before Erishum, was undoubtedly the native Assyrian dynasty, so that the plain fact is that Shamshi-Adad was a usurper. The question then naturally put, by his contemporaries as much as by ourselves, is: what was Shamshi-Adad's background? The answer the Assyrian King List gives is that he was a son of Ilu-kabkabi. But we have met Ilu-kabkabi earlier in that List; he was the father of Aminu, the first named but the latest in time of the ten 'kings who were ancestors'. So the further question – ancestors of whom? – can be given a credible answer; they were ancestors of Shamshi-Adad who had been cleverly incorporated into a traditional native Assyrian list of rulers for the purpose of legitimating the usurper Shamshi-Adad. By linkage via Apiashal to the earliest Assyrian kings of all, before the line of the dynasty he had supplanted, Shamshi-Adad could be presented as inheriting an ancestral right to the throne of Assyria, long prior to the supplanted dynasty.

We may turn briefly to the earliest group of supposed rulers in the Assyrian King List, the 'seventeen kings living in tents'. We have a list of the ancestors of king Hammurabi of Babylon, a contemporary of Shamshi-Adad, and in Hammurabi's list twelve of the names correspond with the first twelve of the 'seventeen kings living in tents' from the Assyrian King List. Now, the families of both Hammurabi and Shamshi-Adad were of Amorite origin, the Amorites (Amurru) being a Semitic people who came into Mesopotamia from the western desert shortly before and after 2000. Thus the twelve names common to the Assyrian and Babylonian lists must represent chieftains of the nomadic period, before the Amorites split into separate groups and settled in Mesopotamia; and Ilu-kabkabi, Shamshi-Adad's father, is linked to this line through Apiashal son of Ushpiya. By this means Shamshi-Adad is represented as direct descendant from the even older line of nomadic desert chieftains of primeval times.

A word is needed about the five names unaccounted for in the group of 'seventeen kings living in tents'. Some of these may have been actual earlier rulers of Ashur. One who almost certainly was is Ushpiya, father of Apiashal, since a tradition independent of the Assyrian King List makes him the builder of one of the earliest temples in Ashur. This joining in one group of nomadic Amorite chieftains supposedly ancestral to Shamshi-Adad, and actual rulers of Ashur of remote times, served to give Shamshi-Adad's line a link (albeit a bogus one) with Ashur as far back as any traditions of Ashur's real rulers extended.

Thus we cannot take the Assyrian King List at its face value as a straightforward list of all the kings of Assyria before Shamshi-Adad. This brings us to the question of who actually were the earliest rulers of Assyria. In tackling this problem, we need to notice that much of our early evidence relates to the city Ashur rather than to Assyria more broadly, and that though in the Akkadian language the same proper name is used both for the city Ashur and the country Assyria, geographically the two were not identical. The territory ruled from the city Ashur was certainly at times much less than what we understand by the country Assyria.

Besides including some early persons who can never have been rulers of Ashur, the Assyrian King List omits others who provably were. The first of these so far known to us was a certain Ititi, identified in a brief inscription on a fragment of alabaster, datable from its script and other indications to the Old Akkadian (Agade) period, *c.* 2400–2200. It reads: 'Ititi, the Ruler, son of Inin-laba, dedicated this to the goddess Innin from the booty of Gasur.' Gasur was the old name of a city that we later know as Nuzi, near Kirkuk. This inscription thus tells us that at this time the Kirkuk region was not part of the kingdom of Ashur but constituted a separate and hostile city-state. This separateness was not basically a racial matter, since texts found at Gasur show that, to judge by personal names, in the Old Akkadian period (though not later) the majority of the population of that city was Semitic, just as the population of Ashur was. Since Gasur was still independent, one may reasonably infer that the two major Assyrian cities, Nineveh and Erbil, both further away than Gasur, were likewise not at this time part of a kingdom based on Ashur.

In Chapter 1 we noticed the control of Ashur and Nineveh by the Dynasty of Agade (twenty-fourth to twenty-third centuries). When the Agade empire eventually collapsed, under attack by peoples from the Zagros mountains called Guti, Ashur also suffered, as we know from the destruction of its buildings, revealed by archaeology.

The Third Dynasty of Ur

Just before 2100, another empire emerged in the south, to rule all Mesopotamia for a century. Known as the Third Dynasty of Ur, it was less extensive than the Agade empire but more tightly organized, with its main centres under transferable governors rather than local vassals. An inscription of one such governor from c. 2040 establishes that at that date Ashur was under the control of Ur. Erbil also was intermittently held by the Third Ur Dynasty, as we know from several economic documents dated 'in the year Urbilum [the old form of 'Erbil'] was sacked', and from a Sumerian inscription of the time which names Ur's military governor of Urbilum.

The rich bureaucratic empire governed from Ur, the last manifestation of Sumerian political power, finally broke up in 2006 under the pressure of the Amorites, thrusting across the Euphrates from the Syrian desert. But that empire had begun to disintegrate some decades before its final collapse, allowing Ashur to recover a measure of independence. We infer this from a tradition that a certain Kikkiya built the walls of Ashur. Kikkiya can be approximately dated, as he occurs in the Assyrian King List shortly before two kings from whom we have inscriptions. As these inscriptions enable us to date those two kings to soon after 2000, Kikkiya's reign cannot have been much before 2000. But excavation shows that the original building of the walls of Ashur had been undertaken centuries before this. Yet the tradition that it was Kikkiya who built these walls must have had some basis. Most probably it reflected a rebuilding of the walls by Kikkiya at a time when he was able to assert himself as an independent ruler. This can only have been when the Third Dynasty of Ur was already contracting and crumbling.

Ashur and Trade

Up to the time of Kikkiya, Ashur, though strategically important as a stronghold on the middle Tigris, was not otherwise of major international significance. This position now starts to change. Inscriptions of kings of Ashur become more common, and show an extension of Assyrian influence abroad. One of these kings, Ilushuma, from just after 2000, twice refers to establishing 'the freedom of the people of Akkad' (meaning Babylonia in south Mesopotamia), and mentions some of the cities of Babylonia as far south as Ur, nearly four hundred miles from Ashur. Clearly this king must have undertaken some kind of intervention there. The exact sense of the expression about establishing freedom is obscure, but one thing which is certain is that it would be an anachronism to try to tie it to modern ideas of political freedom. The Akkadian word translated 'freedom' often has reference to an ancient city's exemption from taxation, and very likely this is the sense here, indicating that Ilushuma established the right of those cities to engage in trade with Ashur, without being mulcted by the southern rulers. Ilushuma's son, Erishum I, used the same word when he said that in his city he established the 'freedom' of silver, gold, copper, tin, barley, wool, bran and chaff; and here the term must certainly have had an economic reference, meaning that he exempted transactions in such commodities from tax. There is another obscure phrase in one of Ilushuma's inscriptions which may be relevant here. Speaking about the people of Babylonia, he says 'I washed their copper'; this may mean that he sold the Babylonians refined copper.

This all indicates that these early native Assyrian kings were very much concerned about trade, understandably, since trade brought not only political influence but also increasing economic prosperity. This growing economic prosperity is reflected in more ambitious building projects inside Ashur; and we have inscriptions of Erishum I in which he describes how he had increased the size and splendour of the temple area, and extended a wall built by his father.

Cappadocian merchant colonies

The dearth of political information about early Assyria gives our gleanings about its trade added importance. In fact, we know far more about the trade of Ashur between 2000 and the time of Shamshi-Adad I than we do about its politics. Most of this information comes, however, not from Ashur itself but from a source hundreds of miles to the north. The greater part of the evidence in question consists of clay tablets found at a site named Kultepe (ancient name Kanesh), north of Kayseri in Asiatic Turkey, in the region often called Cappadocia. These tablets were the archives of several generations of an Assyrian merchant colony living there at the beginning of the second millennium. There were at least a score more settlements of this kind in Anatolia, as place names in these texts tell us, but so far only one or two have been identified by tablets found at their sites. We do not know how long Assyrian merchants had been operating in Anatolia. The earliest date of the Assyrian records from Cappadocia does not necessarily fix the earliest date of the merchant colonies. There may have been colonies in Cappadocia, still unexcavated, before the one at Kanesh; or even at Kanesh itself there may have been earlier mercantile activity under commercial procedures not requiring documentation on clay tablets. According to a later tradition, Sargon, the first ruler of the Agade empire, was called into Cappadocia to protect merchants there as early as the twenty-fourth century. If this is based on fact, it puts the origin of the merchant colonies several centuries further back. But there is the possibility that this tradition was a later invention, reflecting the situation in Cappadocia at the beginning of the second millennium.

The site Kultepe, the buried corpse of the ancient city Kanesh, comprises a large mound where the palaces stood, and a residential area at its foot. It is from the residential area that the Assyrian business archives come. Those so far known amount to some 14,000 tablets, although barely a quarter have been published. The basic picture these texts give is that business houses in Ashur had representatives (often the principals themselves) in Cappadocia, organizing trade in Kanesh or other cities. At the heart of this trade were ass-caravans taking shipments of tin and textiles from Ashur to Cappadocia.

Who benefited from these Assyrian merchant colonies? One group must have been the local rulers, or they would not have permitted the settlements to continue. Yet the primary motivation for the original settlements must have been the advantages they secured for the Assyrians themselves. From Ashur to Kanesh – or, in current terms, from Qal'ah Shergat in Iraq to near Kayseri in central Asiatic Turkey – is no easy journey even today, with all the advantages of motor transport. The distance as the crow flies is about five hundred miles, but any practicable land route involves over seven hundred miles at least. Even today some of the roads may be no more than gravel tracks; the Taurus, a mighty mountain chain, has to be crossed, and in parts security is bad. In 2000 all these adverse factors applied with much greater force. One may accept that once the tradition of trading caravans across this area had developed it could continue by its own inertia, facilitated by a system of posting stages which grew up around it. However, it still needs to be explained why such a system ever began in the first place.

The colonies in Cappadocia were not the only Assyrian merchant colonies known. There is evidence, though on a much more limited scale, of merchants from Ashur operating in the Kirkuk district rather earlier than the period for which we have written evidence from Cappadocia. This, of course, was much nearer home, but it does illustrate the general concern of Ashur with trade. If Ashur was to be in the mainstream of the civilization stemming from Sumer, trade was vital, for (like Sumer itself) Assyria lacked two vital raw materials, timber and metals.

The Assyrian commercial expansion into Anatolia could originally have been in quest of metal supplies. Assyria needed copper and

Anatolia was able to provide it. But this is not a full solution, as there are Anatolian sources of copper much nearer than Cappadocia. However, the Assyrians did not mine the copper themselves, and it is possible that the native Anatolians, who did, centred their mining operations in Cappadocia.

A further problem is whence the Assyrians obtained the tin with which they traded. There is no source of tin in either Assyria or Babylonia, and in absence of solid evidence we have to guess that it was imported into Assyria from the Zagros or Iran. But not only are we in the dark as to the exact source of the tin; we also know nothing about the mechanism by which that metal reached Assyria. Possibly, corresponding Assyrian trading colonies existed in Iran or the Zagros to obtain the tin, but on this we have no evidence.

Even the word *annaku*, which we translate as 'tin', offers a problem. Controversy long raged over whether the word meant tin or lead, with opinion now settling for the former. Even so, it is by no means assured that the term denoted pure metallic tin. It may well have been some form of tin ore; the most recent suggestion at the time of writing is that *annaku* was a mixed ore containing variable amounts of tin and arsenic. Its use was, of course, to produce bronze from copper or copper ore, and arsenic as well as tin can alloy with copper to give a form of bronze.

Alongside 'tin', the other main trading goods of the Assyrians were textiles. The ultimate source of these also presents its problems. We know that the best quality came from Babylonia; but were they made commercially in workshops or were they the product of cottage industries? There are other unanswered problems. Who were the local consumers of these products in Anatolia? How were the goods distributed within Anatolia? What was the system of native government in Anatolia and the relationship of the Assyrian merchants to the local government? The threat is never far distant of one of these problems, or others of like nature, festering into a Ph.D. thesis.

There are, however, some things which we do know about the Assyrian trade with Anatolia, at least in general outline. We know quite a lot about the transport procedures. The goods were collected in Ashur, presumably by import from further east in the case of tin, and certainly from Babylonia for some of the textiles, and were then sent on to Anatolia by donkey.

At present we do not know how many donkeys there might have been in a caravan. Our texts mention numbers up to about twenty, but these represent only the animals carrying the goods of a particular merchant. Judging by procedures of every other time and place in the Near East, we would expect a number of merchants to have grouped together in a large convoy for mutual assistance and protection. That this did happen is put beyond doubt by the fact that some documents even mention a single donkey, and no one was likely to have embarked solo with one donkey laden with valuable goods on a 750-mile trek over difficult mountains.

A donkey's total load, including harness, would be near to two hundredweight (100 kilos). Tin was usually carried in a pair of panniers, balanced one on each side, with textiles on top. To prevent pilfering on the way, the packs of tin were sealed with a clay *bulla*; it was an offence to open them. The textiles, done up as rolls, were also sealed in some way, though how is uncertain. They were mainly bales of woollen cloth, although there were also made-up garments; as to size, one text specifies a complete textile as measuring about thirteen and a half feet by twelve. There can hardly have been looms weaving to such a width at this period, and so the finished textile must have been made by joining narrower strips, as was still the practice until at least the 1950s with the handmade cloth of Kurdistan.

The ass-caravan, loaded with its tin and textiles, set off for Anatolia, accompanied by documentation against which the consignments were checked on arrival. Of several different routes available, we cannot trace any with complete certainty, but it is likely that the usual way led across to the Habur, then to the Balih, and thence on towards Anatolia via the Elbistan plain. This could be a hazardous journey, which, covering up to seven hundred and fifty miles, would occupy about two months, and texts mention donkeys dying en route. Towns along the way, with colonies of Assyrian merchants, facilitated progress, and there was one place about halfway where fresh donkey-drivers were often hired. There are hints that security arrangements sometimes failed, for there are cases of kidnapped merchants having to be ransomed. A journey during winter might bring additional dangers to the caravan both from bad weather and from wolves. If the merchant escaped the wolves there was always the tax-collector, for taxes, amounting to ten per cent of the value of the shipment, had to paid en route, with an additional tax on arrival at Kanesh. It is not unlikely that smuggling was sometimes resorted to in an attempt to escape some of the customs charges, and certain passages in some texts have been taken as referring to this, since they mention 'the smugglers' road'. But this interpretation is not beyond question. There is one text which is a contract for the activity interpreted as smuggling, and this should give us pause. One hardly expects a written contract for performing an illegal act, which the authorities would penalize rather

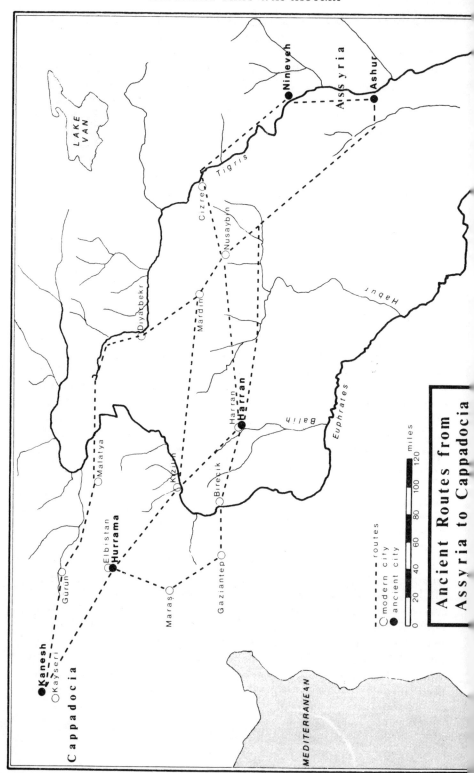

Ancient Routes from Assyria to Cappadocia

than enforce. Probably, therefore, 'smugglers' road' was just a term implying 'by-road'.

The body organizing the trade at Kanesh and other commercial centres was known as the *karum*, a word which literally means 'quay'. A basic problem is whether the merchants constituting the *karum* were private capitalists or government agents; the texts strongly suggest the former. Once the goods arrived in Kanesh, they were registered and taxed in the *karum*, after which they could be sold. Goods were mostly sold against silver or (less commonly) gold, but payment could be made in copper or wool, which was subsequently resold against precious metals. The gross profits on a caravan were substantial. They seem to have amounted to about 100 per cent on tin and perhaps more on textiles, but out of this the taxes had to be paid, as well as the expenses of the journey. The merchants in Anatolia sent the silver back to their agents in Ashur (in some cases a wife), and there are a number of instances in which they instructed the Ashur agents to spend half of it on tin for the next consignment and half on textiles; possibly this was a fairly general practice. The principals could remain in Anatolia for many years, and make local marriages, even if they already had a wife back in Ashur.

We have little more definite information about how the Assyrian commercial colonies in Anatolia ended than about how they began. Excavation has shown four levels of occupation at Kanesh, but so far the two deepest (and thus earliest) have not yielded any texts. Most of the tablets come from the third period of occupation, which ended in some catastrophe marked by a general fire. Possibly the place was attacked and gutted. Eventually, after between about thirty to fifty years during which the site lay waste, Assyrian traders resumed occupation, and documents appear again, the earliest datable within the reign of Shamshi-Adad (1813–1781). The period of non-occupation puts the end of the earlier and main group of documents at somewhere between about 1860 and 1840. They cover some sixty to eighty years, which would take in the reign of Erishum I (forty years spanning 1900); this chronological result fits well with the fact that Erishum is the earliest Assyrian ruler mentioned in the Kanesh texts. We have previously noticed this king's commercial intervention in Babylonia, and so it is not unreasonable to assume that he likewise gave active support to trade with Cappadocia. Some have suggested that Erishum actually established the Assyrian merchant colonies in Kanesh and other places as a deliberate act of policy. This seems unlikely. The considerable infrastructure involved in this trade could hardly have been created suddenly by a political decision; it must have grown up by gradual extension of contacts over a long period of time.

3
Hurrian Interlude: Through Vassaldom to Independence

The Cappadocian connection is the aspect of Assyrian history about which we have most detail for the beginning of the second millennium. But other things were happening, destined to have a considerable effect upon Assyria. For a couple of centuries the Semitic people known as the Amorites had been on the move, pressing out of the Syro-Arabian desert, and settling in the fertile lands around. Pressure from them had indeed been the main factor in the collapse of the Third Dynasty of Ur, with groups of Amorites settling along the Euphrates and in Babylonia, to form local dynasties. Erishum I's incursion into Babylonia may have been prompted by Amorite dislocation of trade there, and the reference of his father Ilushuma to establishing 'the freedom of the people of Akkad' may reflect such an intervention.

The Kingdom of Shamshi-Adad I

Although Assyria – screened by cities such as Mari along the middle Euphrates – did not suffer to the same extent as Babylonia from the earlier waves of Amorite pressure, it could not remain insulated indefinitely. In the middle Euphrates area, the head of one Amorite clan, a certain Ilu-kabkabi (mentioned in the Assyrian King List, see page 25), had carved out a petty kingdom for himself. He had a son, Shamshi-Adad, who spent some time in Babylonia, possibly sent there as a vassal of the current king of Ashur to deal with threats to Assyrian security. From Babylonia Shamshi-Adad returned, full of ambition. He first seized a fortress, Ekallatu, commanding the region east of Tigris, and then, after three years, Ashur itself, in 1813. Installed as king of Ashur, he quickly extended his control to the middle Euphrates area from which he had originated. There the major city and kingdom was Mari, which he succeeded in annexing.

From this point we have, for a generation, almost an embarrassment of information. A little of it comes from official inscriptions left by Shamshi-Adad, the great bulk from archives found at

Mari. Mari, strategically placed on the middle Euphrates, had a network of links with Babylonia and Syria, and the archives, containing clay documents amounting to tens of thousands, reflect this. Shamshi-Adad himself, although apparently regarding Ashur as his formal capital and receiving tribute there, made his main residence at Shubat-Enlil further to the north-west, where he was close to political currents in Syria. For control of the middle Tigris and middle Euphrates areas he installed his older son as sub-king in Ekallatu and his younger, Yasmakh-Adad, in Mari. Correspondence found at Mari between Yasmakh-Adad and his father and brother and other persons gives us a considerable amount of detail about events of the time. A small group of texts of the same period, from the site Shemshara, near Rania in Iraqi Kurdistan, shows that Shamshi-Adad's kingdom extended as far east as the Zagros.

Up until this time, there is no evidence that the three major cities of Ashur, Nineveh and Erbil were all normally united in one kingdom. With the coming of Shamshi-Adad this situation changed, and these cities became without question part of a single domain. We find the king rebuilding a temple in Nineveh and recording his conquest of 'all the fortified cities of the land of Erbil'. He also controlled the region of Arrapkha (modern Kirkuk), so that all Assyria in the widest sense was in his reign one kingdom. The region directly controlled by Shamshi-Adad and his sons extended well beyond Assyria, stretching from the foothills of the Zagros to the Euphrates, and from the Adhaim river to the approaches to the Anatolian plateau, or nearly three hundred miles each way. Shamshi-Adad's influence by way of diplomacy and economic activity went further still. The Assyrian merchant colonies in Cappadocia saw renewed activity, and Shamshi-Adad claimed to have set up his steles (stone monuments) on the shores of the Mediterranean. And it is clear that contemporary Amorite rulers regarded Shamshi-Adad as a major power.

How did Shamshi-Adad succeed in making Assyria the most prominent kingdom of his time? There are two factors in particular which need to be taken into account: his administrative efficiency and his political skill. His extensive extant correspondence shows that Shamshi-Adad kept a close watch on all matters, small as well as great, connected with the efficient running of his kingdom. (The same could be said of Shamshi-Adad's equally successful near-contemporary, Hammurabi of Babylon.) He set up an efficient network of administrative officials – 'I installed my governors everywhere', he says – and beneath the governors was an efficiently organized chain of administrators, couriers, census officials, etc. Politically, Shamshi-Adad succeeded in allying himself, either by treaty or by dynastic marriage, with many other ruling princes, particularly in Syria.

But part of the success of Shamshi-Adad was undoubtedly due to his use of military power. In parallel with his claim to have installed governors everywhere, so also he 'established garrisons everywhere'. To supplement the permanent garrisons, troops were conscripted temporarily for particular campaigns, in one instance as many as sixty thousand men being involved. Siege warfare, which used to be thought to owe its development mainly to the Assyrians of the early first millennium, reached a high degree of efficiency, including the use of siege engines.

The extended kingdom of Shamshi-Adad diminished after his death almost as rapidly as it had come into being. The Assyrian King List credits his son Ishme-Dagan with a reign of forty years, but his rule was limited to Assyria itself – the region based on Ashur, Nineveh, Erbil and Arrapkha (Kirkuk), with doubts about the last; the wider possessions of Assyria, along the middle Euphrates and in north-east Syria, and even his father's favourite residence of Shubat-Enlil, were quickly wrested from his hands.

After the light which shines on the period of Shamshi-Adad and his sons, we find ourselves again in one of the shaded valleys of history. For the next three centuries, inscriptions and archives of Assyrian kings are scanty at best, sometimes non-existent, though the Assyrian King List indicates an unbroken sequence of kings of Ashur. The authority of the king of Ashur during this period may often not have gone far beyond his city, and could not effectively have extended north to Nineveh and Erbil.

Hurrian Immigrants

In concentrating upon the achievement of Shamshi-Adad, we paid little attention to the ethnic situation in the area he ruled, apart from mentioning the Amorites. In fact, other racial movements were under way, destined to have major consequences for Assyria. The most important group in this connection were the people we know as Hurrians. These spoke a language markedly different from both Sumerian and Akkadian, so that Hurrian personal names are very distinctive and usually constitute an easily recognizable marker for persons of Hurrian origin. Such evidence shows that there were Hurrians in south Mesopotamia as early as the Agade period and, towards the end of that period, short-lived petty states in the Habur region with rulers bearing Hurrian names. Soon after, in the period of the Third Dynasty of Ur, many Hurrian personal names are found in the region north of the river Diyala.

The indications are that these Hurrians were coming into Mesopotamia from further north, probably from a homeland in highland Armenia. A few dissenters from this view argue that the Hurrians were the original inhabitants of Assyria, pushed out to the foothills in the third millennium by immigrating Semites. But this theory is mainly based on a very dubious analysis of early place-names as Hurrian.

By the time of Shamshi-Adad, Hurrians had become widespread in northern Mesopotamia, with areas west of the Tur Abdin ruled by Hurrian princes. There was a strong Hurrian element in the Zagros also, and a grandson of Shamshi-Adad actually married a princess from a powerful tribe there, which, to judge by the personal names, was Hurrian. Over in Syria, less than a century after Shamshi-Adad, Hurrians were an important element in Alalakh, a city on the Orontes, well known from a mass of clay tablets excavated there.

It looks as though two racial movements had been taking place simultaneously, the Hurrians coming into Mesopotamia and Syria from the north-east at the same time as the Amorites were moving in from the Syrian desert; with some give-and-take the Euphrates largely formed the boundary between them. Along the middle Euphrates the Amorites were predominant but further north it was the Hurrians who eventually became the most important element, and it was there, and particularly in the region of the Upper Habur, that major Hurrian power structures afterwards developed. Whereas further south the Amorites had considerable influence on Babylonia, in Assyria during the middle of the second millennium it was the Hurrians who culturally, and to no little extent politically, dominated.

The Hurrians were not the only people to emerge as a new political and cultural force during the second millennium. In Anatolia, neighbouring on Hurrian territory, were the Hittites, a group of peoples speaking Indo-European languages. They had entered Anatolia from the north, beyond the Black Sea, not later than the beginning of the second millennium. Establishing a kingdom in the region of the Halys (Kizil Irmak) river, they gradually spread their control southwards as far as the Euphrates, north Syria and Cilicia. This brought them into close contact with the areas in which Hurrians were culturally and politically dominant, and both political competition and mutual cultural influence developed between Hittites and Hurrians.

The Kingdom of Mittanni

By the middle of the seventeenth century, Hurrians were well enough organized to attack the Hittite kingdom to their north-west; an inscription of a Hittite king records a dangerous attack on his kingdom by a people alternatively designated 'Hurrians' and 'Hanigalbat'. We shall meet the latter term again later. Another text about military activities at this period names four 'kings of the Hurri-people'; this plurality shows they were still a confederation and not yet a unified kingdom. By soon after 1550 a major Hurrian-based kingdom, known as Mittanni, had developed east of the Euphrates; other similar states existed in Syria, Cilicia, and north of Mittanni. Mittanni was by far the most powerful Hurrian kingdom, and it negotiated – and at times fought – on equal terms with both the Hittites and Egypt, the two other main powers of the mid-second millennium. At about 1472 one of the Mittannian kings clashed with Tuthmosis III of Egypt, who claimed control of Syria and had penetrated with his army as far as the Euphrates. This check upon Mittanni was welcomed by other Near Eastern states, and Assyria, in company with Babylonia and the Hittites, sent Tuthmosis congratulatory presents, which the Egyptians, to enhance their own prestige, chose to represent as tribute.

We have few details about how Mittanni arose, and this lack is not likely to be made good until major Mittannian archives are discovered. That archives did exist is beyond reasonable doubt. A few letters from Mittanni, in the form of clay tablets inscribed in cuneiform, have been found at El Amarna in Egypt, and there are other indications of correspondence between Mittanni and its neighbour states. The gap in the evidence has been richly filled with speculation. One hypothesis, now largely discounted though it held its ground for many years, explained Mittanni as a kind of symbiosis of races. According to this, the state of Mittanni arose when a horse-and-chariot-owning Aryan (Indo-Iranian) aristocracy, left behind from the main Aryan migration from south-east Europe to India in the early second millennium, imposed itself on the Hurrian masses. It was left to a clear-sighted Russian scholar to demolish this finally. He pointed out that the sole basis for this hypothesis is the presence, within texts running into tens of thousands, of five occurrences of Indo-Iranian numerals, two or three terms connected with horse-training, four Indo-Iranian god-names in Hurrianized form, and about a score of personal names of uncertain origin which superficially look as if they might be Indo-Iranian.

The main importance for Assyrian history of the powerful Hurrian kingdom of Mittanni was that, as it expanded, it began to move eastwards into the territory of what we normally understand as Assyria, eventually reducing it to vassaldom. A substantial part of Assyria was still independent in the second half of the sixteenth century, since just after 1550, if a chronicle is to be trusted, a minor Assyrian king was able to make a boundary treaty with Babylonia. A further indication of a measure of continuing Assyrian independence is given by the present sent by Assyria to Egypt after the clash of the latter with Mittanni in 1472. But it must have been very shortly after the latter date that the Mittannian king Saustatar annexed Assyria.

The annexation of Assyria

It is recorded that Saustatar looted Ashur of a door of silver and gold with which he enriched his own palace at Washukanni. This in itself could have been a matter of a quick raid, but other evidence indicates a Mittannian presence at Ashur over a long period. The kings of Ashur were now vassals of Mittanni, and rulers only in name. Legal texts found at Ashur from the fifteenth century mention officials with Hurrian names, and two later officials left monuments indicating that their forebears had served the king of Hanigalbat, which is an alternative name for Mittanni. The Assyrian king Ashur-uballit, writing at about 1360, speaks of the king of Hanigalbat as though a direct predecessor of his of several generations before. Mittannian control extended right across Assyria as far as the Zagros, and south-east to include the Kirkuk region.

Under Mittannian suzerainty Assyria was so insignificant that for six reigns down to about 1420 there are no extant Assyrian royal inscriptions at all. Such evidence of Assyria as we have for this period comes mainly from the archives of towns in the region of Kirkuk, most of them from a site named Nuzi. The documents concerned give us some interesting insights into the social and economic life of the Nuzi area, and show that Hurrian cultural influence was very strong. There is, however, nothing to suggest that the Nuzi area, normally only peripheral to Assyria politically and culturally, had become of greater importance than usual, and an apparent emphasis on the region at this time is probably a mere accident of archaeological discovery.

One thing the Nuzi documents do show us about Assyria generally is that during Mittannian domination, Assyria – as we normally understand it in its wider sense – was not a single kingdom, even as a vassal. The Nuzi area, based on Arrapkha (Kirkuk), was certainly treated as a sub-kingdom with its own petty king, administratively separate from Ashur; three kings of Arrapkha are known by name. There was a strong Mittannian presence there: we find many persons mentioned there described as Hanigalbatian, (i.e. Mittannian), some of them apparently settled and receiving rations, others temporarily present as officials or messengers. References to Hanigalbatian chariotry prove the presence of Mittannian military units. Elsewhere in Assyria, Erbil and Nineveh are likely also to have been centres of separate administrative areas, though the evidence for that has not yet appeared.

Assyrian Independence

By the very end of the fifteenth century we have indications of the beginning of Assyrian revival. There was re-building of the walls of Ashur – significant, since an ancient Near Eastern capital with strong walls was potentially independent – and once again a boundary treaty was made between Assyria and Babylonia. By about 1400 a king of Assyria was sufficiently his own man to correspond with the king of Egypt and to merit a present of twenty talents of gold, a fact mentioned by his second successor, Ashur-uballit I (1365–1330).

A Mittannian king tells us of the circumstances, though not the precise year, in which Assyria finally and decisively threw off Mittannian control; the information comes from a treaty (extant in two copies) made between Mittanni and the Hittites. Basic to the situation was the existence alongside Mittanni of a second Hurrian kingdom, known as Hurri, with rivalry between the two dynastically related rulers. When border friction developed between Mittanni and the Hittites, the pro-Hittite stance of Hurri allowed the Hittites to invade Mittanni. Crisis ensued in Mittanni. The Assyrians and another kingdom, Alshe (probably in the Tur Abdin), took advantage of the situation to seize Mittannian territory. The Assyrian king concerned is not named, but the chronology makes it likely that it was Ashur-uballit's father, Eriba-Adad (1392–1366).

Ashur-uballit, writing to the king of Egypt soon after 1365, was clearly free of the last vestige of Mittannian control. He felt able to speak to him as an equal, addressing him as 'my brother'. Not everyone accepted this new independence of Assyria. The king of Babylonia complained to the Egyptian king about his countenancing overtures from the Assyrians, whom he claimed as his own vassals: 'Why have these Assyrians, who are my subjects, . . . come to your country? If you love me, do not let them get what they want. Send them off empty-handed.' But the Babylonian king's claim that the Assyrians were his subjects was no more than the reflection of an ambition beyond his grasp – to seize control over his northern neighbour, now that the Mittannian sway over Assyria was at an end.

Assyria was certainly growing rapidly in international importance during the reign of Ashur-uballit. We know that he had dynastic links with Babylonia, and he was both able and willing to intervene in the succession there. A text known as the Synchronistic History, recording encounters between Babylonia and Assyria, tells us this. It reads:

> In the time of Ashur-uballit king of Assyria, the Kassite troops rebelled against Karahardash king of Karduniash [Babylonia], son of the lady Muballitat-Sherua daughter of Ashur-uballit, and they killed him. . . . Ashur-uballit went to Karduniash to avenge his grandson. . . . He placed Kurigalzu the younger . . . in the kingship.

Links with Egypt

As already mentioned, Ashur-uballit was in correspondence with the king of Egypt, and we have two of his letters. One of them may usefully be quoted in full. It reads:

> To the king of Egypt, say, thus says Ashur-uballit king of Assyria. May it be well with you, your household, your land, your chariots, and your troops. I have sent my envoy to you, to see you and to see your land. I have entered into communication with you today as up to this time my forefathers never entered into communication. I have had sent you a fine chariot and pair and a jewel of real lapis lazuli as presents to you. Do not detain my messenger whom I have sent to see you. He is to see you and come back. Let him be apprised about you and your land and then let him come back.

We see it emphasized that the envoy was not intended to remain in Egypt, but to return to Assyria promptly after informing himself about Egypt and the Egyptian king. It is clear that Ashur-uballit was not thinking in terms of becoming a client of the Egyptian king; rather, he intended to use links with Egypt to the advantage of Assyria.

The presents that Ashur-uballit sent deserve comment. They are called *šulmanu*; in such a context this term implies gifts to initiate friendly relations, with the expectation of something in return. That is, a *šulmanu*-gift was seen as the prelude to a commercial as well as political relationship. This ties up with Assyria's long tradition of international trade, exemplified by the earlier link with central Anatolia.

The hoped-for link with Egypt was duly opened up. This appears from the second letter from Ashur-uballit in the Egyptian archives, which refers to messengers from Egypt being 'entertained with all due honour' at the Assyrian court. Trade had also begun, or was actively in prospect, since Ashur-uballit had sent further 'presents' and was asking for an adequate quantity of gold in return, for the decoration of a new palace he was building. He was insistent about the gold; he emphasized that the quantity so far sent was not only less than had been sent to certain earlier kings, but even insufficient to pay the expenses of maintaining the Egyptian link. This explicit reference to the profit-and-loss aspect clearly brings out the commercial element in these negotiations.

From Kingdom to Empire

It is to Ashur-uballit that we can trace back the beginning of the Assyrian empire. Assyria did indeed, after this era, experience reversals, but these gave no permanent check to its rise to overall dominion in the Near East. Other states had their phases of expansion, but none matched Assyria in its centuries-long bid for supremacy beyond its own national borders.

Ashur-uballit himself gives no details of his military campaigns, but that there were such campaigns we learn from allusions by his descendants. These indicate that he initiated a thrust northwards. This was natural enough under an energetic monarch, in an Assyria recently freed from foreign domination. One of the problems of Assyria was always the mountain regions beyond Nineveh and Erbil to its north and east, from which fierce hillsmen could raid into the Assyrian plains. These regions were also important as sources of raw materials – metal ores, timber, semi-precious stones – and contained important horse-breeding areas. As soon as Assyrian kings begin to write inscriptions giving detailed accounts of their campaigns, military activity in the northern and eastern mountains is a constantly recurring theme. Unfortunately, the areas concerned – border regions of Iraq, Syria, Turkey and Iran – are still politically sensitive, which has restricted the possibility of surveys, and left considerable doubt about the identification of places mentioned in Assyrian inscriptions.

Ashur-uballit's great-grandson said of him that 'the security of his kingship was firmly established as far distant as the mountains', and attributed to him successes against 'the forces of the wide-spread land of the Subarians' and a land called Musri. 'Subarian' is a problematic term, with different meanings at different periods. Its constant element is that it always denotes people to the north of the speaker (so that, indeed, it may well have been a pre-Sumerian word for 'northerner'). This usage makes the term 'land of the Subarians' at the time refer to somewhere north of Mosul. There is also dispute about the precise fixing of Musri, but, taken together, these two terms probably indicate that Ashur-uballit pushed north-westwards to control part of the Tur Abdin plateau; we subsequently hear a great deal about this area, known in the Assyrian sources as Kashiari.

When we present the second half of the fourteenth century as marking the beginning of a new era for Assyria, this is more than a convenient modern device for splitting history into manageable slices. The Assyrian kings themselves saw it this way, a fact reflected in royal titles. Although we have been speaking of Assyrian 'kings' from the time of the native rulers of the third millennium, only one ruler of Assyria used the title 'king' in his official inscriptions before the fourteenth century. Underlying this was a reason which we might call theological. From the point of view of the pious Assyrian, it was the god Ashur who was king, the ruler being his human representative. Royal building and dedication inscriptions were in origin religious documents intended to bring the ruler's pious deeds to the notice of the gods, and so it was proper that in such documents the king should refer to himself by terms which we translate as 'governor, regent' or 'overseer, supreme judge'. An innovation came in the later official inscriptions of Arik-den-ili (1319–1308), who boldly gave himself the title 'mighty king, king of Assyria', a change suggesting a deliberate decision to introduce more grandiloquent terminology. In one respect, indeed, Arik-den-ili had been fore-stalled by his grandfather Ashur-uballit, who did call himself 'king of Assyria, great king' in correspondence with the king of Egypt, and identified himself as 'king of Assyria' on his seal; this, however, was not quite the same as using the same terminology in official inscriptions formally intended for the eyes of the gods. Arik-den-ili's son Adad-narari went one better than his father, calling himself by the title 'king of the universe'.

It was not only the north that was affected by the beginning of Assyrian expansion. We have already seen that the murder of a king of Babylon who was a grandson of Ashur-uballit had led the Assyrian king to intervene in the Babylonian succession. The resultant tension continued after Ashur-uballit's death. His successor, Enlil-narari I (1329–1320), is described by his grandson as 'the one who slew the hosts of the Kassites', a term here denoting

Babylon, which since 1600 had been under a Kassite dynasty from the Zagros. A chronicle mentions an Assyro-Babylonian battle at a place twenty miles south-west of Erbil; and it looks as though the king of Babylonia had invaded Assyria in an attempt to assert the sovereignty over Assyria claimed half a century earlier in correspondence with the king of Egypt. But another epithet bestowed upon Enlil-narari I was 'the one who widened borders and boundaries' – pointing to an attempt on his part to extend, or at the least to consolidate, the expansion under Ashur-uballit.

The next Assyrian king, Arik-den-ili (1319–1308), according to his son further extended Assyrian borders. An Assyrian chronicle agrees, but with details which show that Arik-den-ili's military activities were not mere expansionism, but a fight for national survival. The chronicle mentions the repelling of an enemy from only a few miles north of Nineveh; evidently Assyria's very heartland must have been threatened by invaders from the Taurus foothills. Arik-den-ili surmounted this threat, and thrust northwards into the eastern Taurus, where dwelt the widespread people called the Qutians, and then north-westwards to capture Kadmukh, the plain west of the Tigris bounded by the Tur Abdin plateau.

4

Assyrian Expansion

We now enter a period much richer in historical inscriptions. The king concerned is Adad-narari I (1307–1275). Earlier we have credited Ashur-uballit with taking the first steps which were to lead to the rise of the Assyrian empire; Adad-narari's achievements were such that some historians would cast him in the role of founder. The point is debatable, but certainly Adad-narari I was a major figure in Assyrian expansion.

Adad-narari I

Adad-narari described himself as 'defeater of the ferocious ones – the hordes of the Kassites, the Qutians, the Lullumeans and the Subarians'; 'Kassites' usually meant Babylonians at this time (probably here with special reference to Assyria's south-eastern border), and the others were the mountain peoples of the Zagros and eastern Taurus from south Kurdistan to north-west of Assyria. Elsewhere Adad-narari defined his conquests in territorial terms, as 'from the town Lubdi and the land Rapiqu to Eluhat'. Lubdi, near Kirkuk, was a fortress marking the boundary between Assyria and Babylonia east of the Tigris. Rapiqu, on the Euphrates, marked the corresponding boundary to the west. Eluhat is not indisputably identified; some have sought it north of Diyarbekr, but it must have been well to the south of that. Diyarbekr is north of the rugged Tur Abdin plateau, whereas at least three identifiable towns named by Adad-narari in this connection were certainly south of the Tur Abdin. This suggests that Adad-narari was treating the Tur Abdin as his boundary of control. Now the south side of the Tur Abdin plateau rises very sharply from the plain, and at the western end of its southern edge there is a strikingly prominent hill fortress, now called Mardin, guarding a pass. For their own security any strategically minded people occupying the plain south of the Tur Abdin would attempt to hold Mardin. Thus it is very probable that the boundary point Eluhat, mentioned by Adad-narari, was Mardin.

Adad-narari's conquests south of the Tur Abdin included several old Mittannian cities, among them the former Mittannian capital

Washukanni (Ushukani). The tables between Mittanni and Assyria were now completely turned, with the rump of the Mittannian kingdom, now referred to as Hanigalbat (or Haligalbat), being claimed by the Assyrians as·in their sphere of influence. When Hanigalbat's king showed hostility, Adad-narari had him arrested. He was brought to Ashur, put under oath as a vassal, and obligated to send annual tribute. But vassaldom chafed, and it was to be long before Hanigalbat finally ceased resistance to Assyria. The next king rebelled and sought to buy military assistance from the Hittites, the major power in the area. But on this occasion the Hittites remained neutral, allowing Adad-narari to overrun all of Hanigalbat and annex it to Assyria. Emboldened by the Hittite neutrality, Adad-narari made political overtures to the powerful Hittite king, and spoke of brotherhood. The Hittite king, unimpressed and not yet envisioning Assyrian imperial greatness, rebuffed Adad-narari with a smart snub: 'Why should I write to you about brotherhood? Were you and I born of the same mother?'

With Hanigalbat in his possession, Adad-narari now controlled the whole region up to the great bend of the Euphrates, a major natural boundary; to the west and north of this lay the Hittite empire. Thus the whole block of western and northern territory bounded by the Euphrates and Tigris was now under Assyrian control, as far north as where those two great rivers came closest. The rivers themselves made these borders defensible. But they also gave the area another significance. Because the rivers dictated the main trade routes in the ancient Near East, Assyria now had a large measure of control over these routes – always assuming that the sections of them running west of the Euphrates to the Mediterranean and Asia Minor were in friendly hands. That the situation might sometimes be otherwise was a prime reason for later Assyrian expansion right through to the Mediterranean.

In the south, east of the Tigris, there were three possible natural boundaries between Assyria and Babylonia; from north to south, these were constituted by the three tributary rivers, the Lower Zab, the Adhaim, and the Diyala. This border saw innumerable clashes throughout Assyro-Babylonian history, and the line it took at any particular time reflected the current relative status of the two kingdoms. After border clashes, Adad-narari was able to dictate a settlement with a boundary line following the Diyala from the Zagros foothills to the Tigris. An epic – one of the first native Assyrian literary works – was composed to celebrate the Assyrian victory.

But Babylonia too had achieved a victory, and one long to endure. From this time there was a significant increase of Babylonian cultural influence in Assyria. Enlil, a god who enjoyed in the Babylonian pantheon a supremacy which in Assyria belonged to Ashur, became prominent in Assyria, so that both Adad-narari and his son Shalmaneser I gave themselves, as their primary title, the epithet 'governor of the god Enlil'. The writing of the first Assyrian epic just mentioned is another mark of Babylonian influence. So also is the use of Babylonian dialect (not Assyrian) for the Assyrian royal inscriptions which became so numerous from the time of Shalmaneser I.

Shalmaneser I

Shalmaneser I (1274–1245), Adad-narari's son, introduces us to an area destined to play a considerable part in Assyrian affairs for the next five centuries. We meet in his inscriptions the term Uruatri, later spelt Urartu. In the early first millennium, Urartu denoted a powerful kingdom centred on Lake Van in eastern Turkey, able at times to challenge the Assyrian empire itself; but in Shalmaneser's reign it was still a federation of peoples in the Armenian highlands, for Shalmaneser names eight mountain lands as comprised in the wider term Uruatri. Though not yet consolidated into a single kingdom, they must have been to a large extent a settled population, since Shalmaneser speaks of destroying fifty-one of their 'towns' – as we translate a term which might cover anything from a substantial village to a major city.

According to the best modern translation, Shalmaneser says that he attacked these Uruatri people because they 'rebelled', a translation which would imply that Shalmaneser already thought of these people as his subjects. But the verb is frequently used in the more neutral sense of crossing a border. It seems more likely that this is what the term means here; some of the Uruatri people were trying to push southwards into what Shalmaneser claimed as Assyrian territory, and Shalmaneser set out to check them in the interests of national security.

Significantly, Shalmaneser tells us that he enlisted some of the young men of Uruatri into his service. This reflects a new phase in Assyrian policy. From this time Assyria began to shift conquered populations around on a scale which eventually became very large indeed. This practice demands explanation. One well-favoured suggestion is that the main object of the Assyrians was to lodge conquered populations of rebellious tendency where they would be unable to give further trouble, usually among an alien ethnic group. This may well have been one element in the policy, but can hardly be a complete explanation. Had military security been the main consideration, the Assyrians – not a squeamish people – could have achieved this end more simply by mass slaughter. It therefore seems that the main motive for large-scale deportation must have been economic.

With expansion into Hanigalbat (the rump of the former Mittanni), Assyria had acquired extensive new territories with not only a prosperous agriculture but also thriving towns and cities. The latter presupposed the flourishing of various crafts – metal-working, wood-turning, building, the making of jewellery, and so on – and the city craftsmen constituted a pool which could be used for the benefit of Assyria. The additional manpower which became available as Assyria conquered further areas to the north permitted the wider exploitation of the very productive Assyrian agricultural land. Implementation of such measures necessitated large-scale movements of population, and Shalmaneser I himself speaks about deporting 14,400 people from Hanigalbat. It may be added that he mentioned blinding these deportees, but presumably they were only blinded in one eye, otherwise they would have become economic liabilities rather than assets. Shalmaneser does not say what he did with these particular captives, but administrative documents from the period of Shalmaneser or his successors give a clue to what happened to prisoners of war from other areas. These texts list such matters as rations of grain and wool, the latter intended to provide workers with the raw material for making their own clothes. A text dealing with wool rations from 'the palace' (meaning 'administrative headquarters'), itemizes the recipients. There were 720 people from the land Shubru, in four gangs each under an Assyrian foreman with an overseer responsible for the whole, 99 people from the land Nairi, and 174 from Kadmukh under two Assyrian officials. These lands were all in the northern territories; Kadmukh was a region between the Tigris and the Tur Abdin, Shubru was probably within or north of the Tur Abdin, and Nairi lay north of the Tigris and west of Lake Van. Though we are not directly told what work these people were engaged in, we can infer it. Later in the text there are listed further wool rations (on a more generous scale) for several Assyrians designated 'builder'. This involvement of Assyrian 'builders' makes it a reasonable guess that they were architects supervising building operations, with the foreigners as labour gangs. It is instructive to note in passing, as an instance of Assyrian precision in organization, that the total of foreign workers plus the seven Assyrian officials in charge of them amounts to exactly one thousand.

Returning to political history, we find that during Shalmaneser's reign there was a re-play of the troubles in Hanigalbat; again that land rose under its vassal king, and Shalmaneser swept over the region in the manner of his father. But now there was a new factor in the situation, in that we hear of a people called Akhlamu giving support to the Hanigalbatians. These Akhlamu were associated with the Aramaeans, a new wave of Semites coming from the desert in the late second millennium and destined to make a major impact on the Near East.

On this occasion the rebels of Hanigalbat received assistance from the Hittites, assistance which was not limited to troops but even included economic sanctions against Assyria. In a treaty, the Hittite king prescribes for a vassal state, Amurru in Syria, 'No merchant of yours shall go to Assyria, and you shall allow no merchant of theirs into your land.'

The Hittites were still the major international power, but the growing importance of Assyria was now internationally recognized. Despite friction, both Shalmaneser and his successor Tukulti-Ninurta engaged in diplomatic exchanges with the Hittite monarch, as extant fragments of their letters show, and the Hittite king no longer snubs his Assyrian counterpart as at the time of Ashur-uballit but addresses him as an equal, 'brother'.

Developments under Shalmaneser provide us with an opportunity for touching upon the nature of Assyrian kingship. From the beginning we have spoken of the Assyrian rulers as kings, but the persons we so designate often used other titles and thought of themselves as both more and less than kings. The true king of the land was the god Ashur. Theologically the human ruler was only the divine king's deputy, yet because of that his power was more than human, inasmuch as he acted for the god. We find this consciousness of being the god's representative particularly marked with Shalmaneser. His expansion into the northern and north-eastern mountains led him to think of himself as the divinely appointed shepherd elevated by the gods over civilized mankind; he had himself called 'Shepherd of the assembly of human settlements' and 'True Shepherd', the former a title unique to him, the latter used by many of his successors.

On the human level, Shalmaneser's activities on the northern frontier seem to have been matched by a new concern with the great northern city of Assyria, Nineveh. Texts of Shalmaneser deal with the restoration of a temple there, as well as with the temple of a deity called 'the Ninevite goddess' (that is, Ishtar as venerated at Nineveh) inside the capital Ashur itself. Business tablets found at Tell el-Rimah, some thirty miles west of Nineveh, datable to late in the reign of Shalmaneser or early in that of his successor, attest to a flourishing trade in the northern sector of Assyria, including trade in tin with the land Nairi, well up into Anatolia. We hear later that, doubtless to protect this trade, Shalmaneser garrisoned two cities on Nairi's borders; these were subsequently taken by Aramaeans. Though it was not until well into the first millennium that Nineveh became the official capital of Assyria, its strategic and economic importance came to surpass that of Ashur as soon as Assyria's northern and western expansion got under way, and Shalmaneser's involvement with Nineveh reflects this.

Tukulti-Ninurta I

The momentum of Assyrian expansion continued under Shalmaneser's son Tukulti-Ninurta I (1244–1208), a conqueror whom some have sought to identify as the original of Nimrod, the 'mighty hunter before the Lord' of Genesis 10: 8. There is much in common between Tukulti-Ninurta's exploits and those of his father and grandfather – not surprisingly, since the problems Assyria had to deal with had not basically changed. But Tukulti-Ninurta went further than his predecessors, not only in distance, but also in exploitation of the regions within Assyria's orbit. Assyrian penetration was becoming more thorough. Tukulti-Ninurta was able to be more specific about the lands his armies invaded, within the wide area of the northern mountains which he called 'the land of the Qutians', and the information he gives shows that he had closer acquaintance than his predecessors with the organization of the people of this area. He specified the principal kingdom as Uqumeni (or Uqumani, later Qumani), and was able to name its king. He knew that the social structure of the kingdom was a loose federation under princes. But it was socially advanced, for it had walled cities, and its forces were well organized. This very fact, however, led the highlanders into a tactical error. Instead of relying on guerilla warfare in their rugged mountainous terrain, which would have given them an advantage over an invading army, they committed their forces in a set battle. In such an engagement they were no match for the powerful well-trained Assyrian forces. Tukulti-Ninurta became 'master of the extensive land of the Qutians'. He took the princes of Uqumeni prisoner to Ashur, put them under oath of allegiance, and then allowed them to return to their land as Assyrian vassals. Here again we see the economic aspect of Assyrian conquests, for those vassal princes were made subject to the levy, which in this instance meant that they had to provide workers to fell and transport timber. Thus Tukulti-Ninurta began the exploitation of the forests of the eastern Taurus for his building projects in Assyria. The princes also had to deliver a heavy tribute annually at Ashur; regular visits of this kind provided a channel by which

Assyrian cultural influence would increasingly affect the people of Uqumeni. We also find personnel from Uqumeni in receipt of rations as workers in Assyria at this time.

Tukulti-Ninurta summed up his conquests with a geographical description of his boundaries – the whole semi-circle of mountain lands from the Lower Zab to the Euphrates. The precise interpretation of his summary depends upon the identification of the places named, which are not free from obscurities, but one possible interpretation of his boundaries is on the map opposite.

With the north stabilized, Tukulti-Ninurta now turned to his southern neighbour, Babylonia. Boundary clashes had long been a feature of Assyro-Babylonian relations, but what happened now was an altogether more serious matter, developing into a successful full-scale invasion of Babylonia. A major Assyrian epic was composed to celebrate the victory. According to this epic – manifestly from the Assyrian viewpoint – it was the Babylonian king, Kashtiliash, who first violated the peace by raiding into Assyria. The peace-loving Tukulti-Ninurta patiently sought to resolve the dispute by diplomatic means, until finally the arrogance of the Babylonian king left him with no option but to declare war. Invasion and the sack and looting of Babylon and its great temple followed. The Babylonian king was deposed and Babylonia was ruled for seven years through governors.

All this had a religious dimension. Babylonia was not a land of barbarians that could be invaded at will like the regions beyond Assyria's northern borders; it was the source and centre of civilization and its capital, Babylon, was a religious shrine of the highest sanctity. To sack Babylon in the ancient world was like sacking the Vatican or Jerusalem or Mecca in our own time. The Tukulti-Ninurta epic had the function, besides feeding national pride in victory, of providing theological exoneration for the offence against piety. Tukulti-Ninurta had only done what the divine powers intended him to do. The epic relates how the gods of Babylonia, with Babylon's tutelary deity Marduk at their head, had themselves first indicated their disapproval of Kashtiliash by refusing him favourable omens for his resistance to Tukulti-Ninurta, and had then deserted him totally and withdrawn from their cities. Marduk's theological abandonment of his city Babylon was represented physically by Tukulti-Ninurta taking the image of the god away to Ashur, where, despite the early recovery of Babylonian independence, it apparently remained for the greater part of a century.

Ironically, the conquest of Babylonia by Tukulti-Ninurta probably had more long-term effect upon Assyria than upon Babylonia itself. By the consequent extended cultural contacts, Assyria was

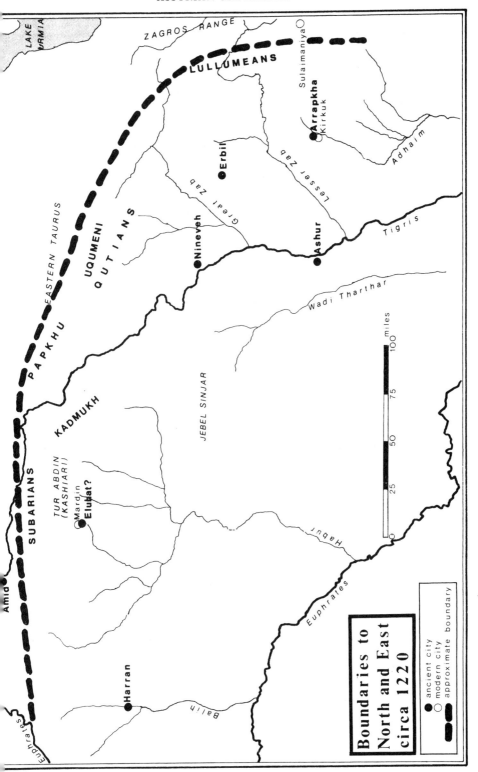

Boundaries to
North and East
circa 1220

● ancient city
○ modern city
▬ ▬ approximate boundary

laid wide open to Babylonian influence, both religious and political. In addition, prisoners taken to Ashur – the defeated Babylonian king among them – must have had a significant impact upon Assyrian society. Within seven years there was a revolt in Babylonia; this marked a turning-point for Tukulti-Ninurta.

In two inscriptions from the end of his reign, Tukulti-Ninurta states that at the very beginning of his rule he carried off to Assyria 28,800 Hittites from beyond the Euphrates (i.e. from north Syria). This is puzzling, because nothing is said of such an event in inscriptions of earlier years. We know from extant letters that earlier in his reign Tukulti-Ninurta had been attempting to enter into good political relations with the Hittites; could it be that he had therefore censored his own early public inscriptions to save Hittite sensibilities? This seems improbable. Any major attack by Tukulti-Ninurta on Hittite territory would have soured relations irrespective of whether or not Tukulti-Ninurta chose to record the fact. In any case, his father Shalmaneser's inscriptions, referring to the slaughter of Hittite armies, were already deposited at Ashur, so that a corresponding statement by Tukulti-Ninurta would hardly in itself have occasioned coldness between the two states. It seems more likely that Tukulti-Ninurta's later claim of victory over Hittites was a gross exaggeration, based on some minor raid, and was introduced into his inscriptions to boost his image when things began to go badly with him after the successful revolt of Babylonia. With his prestige then on the wane, the situation demanded a success against a major power to counter the effects of his recent reverse.

Over the centuries, a number of Assyrian kings changed their capitals, Tukulti-Ninurta among them. The kings who so acted are not explicit about their reasons, but two distinct factors seem to have operated in varying degrees. One was strategic: the old capital might not be the best centre of government in the current situation. But a second possible factor was tension between the citizens and the central government. In the cities of great antiquity, the citizens enjoyed traditional rights, including exemption from some forms of taxation as well as hereditary rights over land. Building projects in the capital might trespass upon the latter, or the needs of the treasury might induce the king to seek to trim the old tax-privileges of the citizens. Either would generate friction, and to eliminate this the king might eventually find it desirable to shift his capital. This Tukulti-Ninurta did, building in the latter part of his reign a new capital, Kar-Tukulti-Ninurta, on the opposite side of the Tigris to Ashur, to serve as his centre of government from the time of his Babylonian campaign to the end of his reign.

Tensions within Ashur, a probable major factor in the building of this new capital, eventually became so marked that they brought Tukulti-Ninurta's reign and life to an end. Within seven years of the conquest of Babylonia, a rebellion there brought the legitimate Babylonian successor to his ancestral throne, with independence from Assyria. The ancient Near Eastern theology of kingship now worked against Tukulti-Ninurta. Any successful rebellion was a threat to a monarch's rule, calling in question the gods' approval of his reign; and it would be particularly dangerous when it occurred in Babylonia, in view of the high international prestige of Babylon and its gods. So it proved for Tukulti-Ninurta. According to a chronicle, the Babylonian recovery of independence was followed by a palace conspiracy in Kar-Tukulti-Ninurta:

> Tukulti-Ninurta, who had brought his hand for evil upon Babylon – his son Ashur-nasir-pal and the nobles of Ashur rebelled against him, removed him from his throne, imprisoned him in a building in Kar-Tukulti-Ninurta, and killed him with a weapon.

An assassination in which a royal prince was implicated must have created some confusion in the succession, and this confusion is reflected in our sources. The murderer may have temporarily gained the throne, but if he did so this was but a brief interlude, for the formally recognized successor was another son of Tukulti-Ninurta, Ashur-nadin-apli. The fact that he and his three successors had short reigns – twenty-eight years cover the four of them – points to a period of instability, a consequence of the internal tensions reflected in the conspiracy against Tukulti-Ninurta.

The Silence of Decline

Assyrian kings loved recording their exploits, not in the main for the benefit of humans but rather to ensure that they received due credit from the gods. Thus a period with few royal inscriptions is likely to be one in which the Assyrian king was short on major achievements. We now enter such a period. Inscriptions become sparse, reflecting the impotence which had stricken Assyria. From Ashur-nadin-apli the sole thing of interest we learn is that the Tigris changed its course at Ashur, though happily it was restored to its old bed by royal prayers to the gods, presumably with a helping hand from Assyrian engineers. This was not necessarily a trivial matter; a major shift of a river could be a death sentence upon a city depending upon it for communications and irrigation. Even a small change of course could have serious consequences, particularly upon the city's defence, either by undermining walls and causing their collapse or by leaving exposed sections formerly moated by the river; indeed, flooding made a major contribution to the final downfall of Assyria when its last capital Nineveh was under siege in 612.

Assyria had other problems during this dark period than a shifting river. Large-scale movements of peoples by sea and land in the eastern Mediterranean had brought the collapse of the Hittite empire and attempts at settlement along the Levant coast. These events had repercussions upon trade routes which must have affected Assyria adversely, while migrant peoples may have directly affected the westerly and northerly possessions of Assyria. Babylonia had – to judge by some fragmentary correspondence between the rulers of the two kingdoms – become, if only temporarily, politically in a position to intervene in Assyrian affairs. This is reflected in the Assyrian succession. The fourth of the minor kings following Tukulti-Ninurta, a certain Ninurta-apil-Ekur, was so remote from the current direct succession that he traced his descent back to a king two centuries before. There was clearly some irregularity in the succession, and the background to this becomes apparent when we learn that Ninurta-apil-Ekur seized the throne from a base in Babylonia after an Assyro-Babylonian clash; obviously this prince gained the throne with Babylonian support.

In the long term this Babylonian intervention served Assyria's interests. The rapprochement gave a basis for renewed internal stability, so that Ninurta-apil-Ekur's son, Ashur-dan I (1179–1134), had the longest reign in Assyrian history. A paucity of inscriptions at this period suggests that Assyria was quietly consolidating, without political or military adventures; a border clash with Babylonia is mentioned, but this may have been no more than a local incident, and need not imply a major aggression by either kingdom.

In fact, around the middle of the twelfth century it was neither Assyria nor Babylonia but a third power which dominated events in Mesopotamia. That power was Elam, in south-west Iran (Khuzistan), an area which, from the third millennium to the present day, has had a close, though intermittent, involvement with Mesopotamian culture and history. This cultural link is reflected in the Bible in the tradition that Elam was a brother of Ashur (Genesis 10: 22), although in language the Elamites were distinct from the Babylonians and Assyrians. In the early part of Ashur-dan's reign, when there was disruptive social disturbance in Babylonia, Elam attempted a westward expansion into south Mesopotamia. An Elamite ruler had already raided Babylonia in the thirteenth century, clashing there with Tukulti-Ninurta, but the Elamite expansion in the twelfth century was a more far-reaching affair. The Elamites overran the area along the Diyala – where there were important trade routes – and reached Babylon itself in 1160. The old Kassite dynasty came to an end; and much of north-east Babylonia was under Elam for about thirty years, until control of Babylonia proved too much for Elamite resources. This affected Assyria marginally, inasmuch as Elamite control northward extended towards the Lower Zab, in territory so often the subject of border disputes between Babylonia and Assyria. A long-term result was to emphasize to Assyria the strategic and economic importance of the area south-east of the Lower Zab.

In the ancient Near East, the main opportunity for public opinion to make itself felt was at the death of a king. In consequence, the end of a reign, particularly a long reign, was often marked by disturbances or even revolt, with rival princes putting themselves at the head of various factions. This happened at the death of Ashur-dan, when two of his sons, one supported by Babylonia, had reigns of no more than a year each, the first being driven out and the second probably murdered.

Political normality returned with Ashur-resh-ishi I (1133–1116). Economic normality had probably never been lost, as we may conclude from texts from this period recording delivery of sheep and cattle for the royal court from various provincial officials and giving detailed arrangements for their distribution in the capital. Agricultural production, and the humdrum but essential tasks of the Assyrian administrative network, continued little interrupted by military clashes abroad or power struggles at home.

5

The Middle Assyrian Empire

We now come to one of the major figures in Assyrian history, Tiglath-Pileser I (1115–1077). This brings us face to face with a recurrent problem. Periods in which Assyria was a vigorous state and its kings major figures seem to alternate with phases wherein both state and kings dwindle into insignificance. Thus the question arises: did able kings raise Assyria to power and prosperity by their innate ability, or did improved international circumstances for the Assyrian state invest its kings – the visible embodiment of the state – with an aura of purpose and might? The truth probably lies between these extremes. No king, however able, could raise Assyria to power and prosperity in the teeth of adverse international conditions. But when international circumstances favoured Assyria, only an able and resolute king could wring full advantage from this.

For the greater part of the twelfth century, circumstances had made any major advances by Assyria impossible. The Elamite factor has already been touched upon. But of more significance was the considerable ethnic movement which had taken place around the eastern Mediterranean, giving rise to the legend of the Fall of Troy, sweeping away the Hittite empire in Anatolia, bringing the settlement of new peoples – the best known being the Philistines – on the coasts of Syria and Palestine, and threatening even Egypt. The shock waves from these movements (to use a convenient cliché which serves to conceal our knowledge of details) must certainly have reached as far as the Euphrates, and dislocated trade along that river, and thus the trading patterns of Assyria itself.

Assyrian Renewal

Things began to improve in the final third of the twelfth century, which is when kings of some prominence appear once again in both Assyria and Babylonia. The inscriptions of Ashur-resh-ishi indicate that he was in a position to undertake marches into the arc of mountains east and north of Assyria, outside Assyria proper but claimed as falling within Assyrian control. Increasing prosperity facilitated the putting under way of overdue rebuilding projects, such as the repair of buildings damaged in an earthquake earlier in the century.

With Tiglath-Pileser I, son and successor of Ashur-resh-ishi, we have a clear instance of Assyrian renewal, made possible indeed by an improvement in the general circumstances, but owing much to the personality of the king himself. There is apparent a clear strategy by which Tiglath-Pileser tackled successively the problems facing Assyria, each step facilitating that which was to follow.

We have a last echo, with Tiglath-Pileser, of the mass movement of peoples in the eastern Mediterranean littoral and Asia Minor at about 1200. He tells us that at the beginning of his reign twenty thousand people called Mushki, who for fifty years had held territories to the north-west of the Tur Abdin, came and seized the land of Kadmukh, adjacent to Assyria to the north-west and regarded as an Assyrian province. The antecedents of the Mushki leave little doubt that they were one of the peoples engaging in a major migration in western Asia in the late second millennium.

A defensive war

There is no indication of any Assyrian action against the Mushki so long as they remained beyond the Tur Abdin. Tiglath-Pileser's actions here were in defence of Assyrian security, not predatory aggression, for the Assyrian intervention began only with the invasion of Kadmukh. Clearly this invasion was seen as a direct threat to Assyria, for Tiglath-Pileser made an immediate counter-attack. He records that he did not even wait to cover his rear; that is to say, he saw the situation as an emergency which brooked no delay for normal tactical procedures.

The initial attack was a success. Six thousand of the defeated Mushki were taken prisoner and then, settled in the land they had invaded, regarded as subjects of Assyria. Besides assisting agricultural production, they were useful to Tiglath-Pileser militarily, as they provided him with 120 chariots, teams of horses, and presumably also a substantial contingent of related skilled personnel.

The operation against the Mushki led Tiglath-Pileser further afield. Natives of Kadmukh, siding with the invaders, had crossed to the left (north) bank of the Tigris to defy the Assyrians from a fortress there. Pursuing the rebels, Tiglath-Pileser came into conflict with a people called Papkhu (apparently Hurrian-speaking, to judge by the names of their kings) who were widespread north of the Tigris; 'Papkhu' seems to be not an ethnic term but a Hurrian word meaning 'mountain folk'. After some minor skirmishes in the immediate neighbourhood of the Tigris, Tiglath-Pileser led a raid into Papkhu territory in the hinterland. Although he refers to burning cities and taking booty, the sparsity of details of place-names makes it clear that this was no more than an exploratory reconnaissance.

Tiglath-Pileser's prompt action against the Mushki in Kadmukh had its effects on adjacent areas to the west, where there were other groups of displaced peoples. One such was described as 'disaffected troops of the Hittite land', probably meaning organized groups that had shifted south-eastwards after the Hittite empire disintegrated. There is also mention of Kaska people, known to have lived along the Black Sea coast at an earlier period. Such peoples may well have welcomed the opportunity of being accepted as settlers by a stable power, and they submitted at Tiglath-Pileser's approach and were claimed as subjects by him. The extensive ethnic mix of the Assyrian empire was taking form.

Tiglath-Pileser in Anatolia

Tiglath-Pileser followed up his exploratory reconnaissance beyond Kadmukh by taking his chariotry and main army across the Tigris and northwards into Papkhu territory. Where the mountains were impassable for chariots, he tells us, he had his troops manhandle them along; as this was only an occasional necessity, there must already have been roads of a sort, usable by chariots, over a large part of the region. The Papkhu peoples attempted to stop the Assyrians by an engagement in the mountains, but failed, and Tiglath-Pileser went on to ravage a number of lands in Papkhu territory; that he was able to name these lands demonstrates his growing acquaintance with the area; and that many different lands are named proves that no single major kingdom had yet emerged there.

It is clear that Tiglath-Pileser's campaigns took him north of the Tigris into eastern Anatolia, but exactly where and how far he went remains very disputable. However, we do possess two definite pieces of information on this matter. One identifiable point in his northern advance is the city of Melid (represented today by Malatya), the taking of which is recorded. Another fixing is provided by an inscription which Tiglath-Pileser left on a rock in the Melazgirt area, north-west of Lake Van. It reads: 'Tiglath-Pileser, strong king, king of the universe, king of Assyria, king of the four quarters, conqueror of the land Nairi from the land Tumme to the land Dayenu, conqueror of the land Habha to the Great Sea.'

This text ought to give us some definite bounds for Tiglath-Pileser's campaigns, listing as it does five geographical terms. Unfortunately, none of these terms can be precisely delineated beyond dispute. Even for Tiglath-Pileser himself, Nairi was a quite vague term; it was the total territory associated with 'sixty kings of Nairi' whom he encountered and pursued in one of his campaigns. Tumme and Dayenu obviously meant something quite specific to him, pinning down exact areas within the more general term Nairi, but despite much that has been written on the location of these countries there is no certainty. All one may say is that Nairi was west of Lake Van and north of the Tur Abdin, with little certainty about the western and northern limits, and that Tumme and Dayenu were the south-eastern and north-western ends respectively of Nairi. From the context, Habha clearly meant the region between Nairi and the Great Sea, but the specific understanding of this will depend on what was designated here by 'Great Sea'. Usually it meant the Mediterranean. But another term for the Mediterranean was 'Upper Sea', with or without the additional phrase 'of the west', and complications arise from the fact that 'Upper Sea' (without the qualification 'of the west') could sometimes denote Lake Van. It is not impossible that 'Great Sea' could have had the same double usage as 'Upper Sea', and that in Tiglath-Pileser's inscription it meant Lake Van. The only possible interpretations other than this are either to understand 'Great Sea' here in its common sense of Mediterranean, which would not fit the geography at all, or to take it as the Black Sea. This last seems much too far for Tiglath-Pileser's penetration, although some scholars do accept that as the meaning here.

Whatever the exact geography of Tiglath-Pileser's northward expansion, it is clear that a major motive for it was economic. He records booty in the form of copper and bronze vessels, tribute of horses and cattle running into thousands, and herds of oxen and asses. The economic concern of Tiglath-Pileser is specifically mentioned in his inscriptions: 'I had the whole of the land of Assyria equipped with ploughs, and so increased the stores of grain above those of my forefathers. I built up herds of horses, cattle and sheep.' He was also explicit about the policy of increasing the effective territory of Assyria and its working population by deporting captured peoples. The military arm was developed, chariotry being increased above anything known before.

The Aramaean threat

Tiglath-Pileser's expansionist exploits were not limited to the north; on each of his frontiers there was activity, most regularly along the Euphrates, of which he says: 'I crossed the Euphrates twenty-eight times. . .in pursuit of the Aramaeans.' The Euphrates, a main artery of communication, has always known movements of nomadic peoples, often interfering with settled populations or with the central administration. At the time of Tiglath-Pileser I, this threat had grown to formidable proportions with the emergence from the desert of these nomadic Aramaeans. Their original home seems to have been in the hinterland of the Jebel Bishri area, the region between the Euphrates and the site which was later the great caravan city of Tadmor, alias Palmyra. The reason for the Aramaean thrust into the Euphrates area beginning at this time is not clear, but in the absence of solid evidence we may speculate. The Jebel Bishri, originally well wooded, was certainly bare before the Christian period, and it is a reasonable guess that this deforestation was due to the principal early inhabitants of the area, the Aramaeans in the second millennium. Deforestation would have resulted in rapid run-off of what had formerly been fertilizing storm-rains, with loss of soil by erosion and periods of drought. Once under way, this process would quickly have rendered the region unable to support its former population, and it would take no more than two or three exceptionally bad years to set a major migration under way.

According to Tiglath-Pileser, the Aramaeans had already managed to cross the Euphrates, into what was claimed as permanent Assyrian territory, settling along the whole length of the river from the Babylonian border region to Carchemish. Tiglath-Pileser drove them back, getting his own troops across the Euphrates on goat-skin rafts – probably the type of raft today called a *kelek* (see page 198).

Tiglath-Pileser recorded that the Aramaean nuisance was so persistent that he had to go after them twenty-eight times, 'twice in one year'. It is not certain how the last phrase is to be understood. Was it twice every year, so that the period of the twenty-eight expeditions was fourteen years; or did one show of force normally suffice, except for one particular year when the situation was so bad that Tiglath-Pileser had to undertake a second campaign? The sequel supports the view that Tiglath-Pileser meant twice every year, and that after fourteen years of this the Aramaeans laid off Assyrian territory for the time being. Well before the end of his reign of thirty-eight years, Tiglath-Pileser was able to penetrate to the Mediterranean coast not only by way of north Syria through former Hittite territory but also via Tadmor, which meant that he was marching through the heart of the Aramaean territory. Had the Aramaeans until nearly the end of Tiglath-Pileser's reign been a sufficient threat along the Euphrates to necessitate an annual punitive campaign, this would have been most unwise tactically, and Tiglath-Pileser was militarily no fool.

When Tiglath-Pileser eventually reached the Mediterranean coast, he suddenly showed himself human. He wanted a ride in a boat, and when in the boat must have tried his hand at a harpoon: 'I rode in ships of the city Arvad of the land Amurru, and made a successful trip of three double hours from Arvad. . .as far as Samuru. I killed at sea a *nahiru* which they call a "sea-horse".' He evidently recalled this adventure with pride, for elsewhere he records how he incorporated his achievement in the decoration of his palace entrance: 'I made replicas in basalt of the *nahiru*, which they call a "sea-horse", which with a harpoon, as an achievement of my own hand, I killed in the sea of Amurru-land at the command of. . .the great gods, my lords.' The identification of this 'sea-horse' has occasioned quite a spillage of ink, learned opinion varying as to whether it was a dolphin or some species of whale.

Tiglath-Pileser clearly has a marked interest in foreign animals. This was a feature of a number of the Assyrian kings, who welcomed strange animals – such as apes and crocodiles – as tribute and who in some cases – Tiglath-Pileser being one of them – established zoos in their capitals from such gifts and from animals they had captured themselves in the Syrian desert. There was much wild life in and around ancient Assyria, and the fauna was considerably richer than it is now, with many species of large mammal. Texts speak of hunting 'bears, hyenas, lions, tigers, leopards, deer and wild goats', all of these being species still present in Mesopotamia a century ago, although the great cats are now mostly extinct. Other large mammals present in or near ancient Mesopotamia included the bison, the water buffalo (indigenous as a wild animal, later re-introduced as a domestic animal after its extinction in the wild), the wild pig (still abundant), and several species of gazelle (some recently rendered extinct and the remainder in peril from Arab 'sportsmen' hunting them in the desert in four-wheel-drive vehicles with machine guns). There were also wild sheep, lynx, cheetah, and the wild ass or onager, still abundant in the Jazirah in the nineteenth century A.D. but extinct since 1927. One species which Tiglath-Pileser had sent from abroad by merchants and which he attempted to breed into herds was the two-humped camel. This is mentioned in the Broken Obelisk by his son Ashur-bel-kala (see page 65). This animal must have been brought in from beyond the Zagros, since the name by which it was known, *udru*, derives from the Indo-Iranian word for two-humped camel. Tiglath-Pileser mentions another animal, called *burhiš*, sent to him as tribute, and some scholars guess this to be the yak; but surely the yak is much too specialized in its terrain (the high mountains of Tibet) to have been accessible to Assyria by either tribute or trade. In fact, the word *burhiš* occurs alongside *udru* in the Broken Obelisk, and it is not precluded that it may be a name invented by the Assyrians when they first met the camel, since the word could mean 'with a knob', referring to the hump. Other large quadrupeds found close to Mesopotamia in ancient times included two that were very imposing: the wild ox, a powerful beast of which the bull stood six feet at the shoulder; and a species of elephant. These, like the lion, were both hunted by Assyrian kings, and it was probably their hunting excesses which rendered the two species extinct, although they were still found two centuries after Tiglath-Pileser. Another spectacular member of the ancient fauna was the ostrich, which the Assyrian kings found, hunted and decimated in the Syrian desert, though it survived and has occasionally been sighted there in the twentieth century A.D.

Lions were common enough to be a danger both to domestic animals and to humans in the open country. Assyrian kings mention battues in which they killed up to eight hundred lions at a time, and whilst these particular victims had probably been trapped and then released in a special hunting park (see plate 22B), the figures give some indication of the commonness of the animal. In the epilogue to the Flood story (see page 319), it is suggested to the executive god Enlil that instead of an indiscriminate general flood it would be a better scheme to use lions to diminish mankind – an indication that they were regarded as a very real threat to human life. From Mari on the middle Euphrates comes a report from the early second millennium that a lion had been caught on the flat roof of a house; evidently at that time a lion might come right inside a village.

Tiglath-Pileser I must have been a man of considerable energy and wide interests, and it is from his reign that we have an interesting collection of Assyrian laws, which were systematized compilations, probably at his instructions, from earlier laws. Arranged by subject-matter, one group deals principally with land tenure and another concerns women (see pages 140ff.).

The Babylonian frontier

We return from Tiglath-Pileser the naturalist and legislator to Tiglath-Pileser the military strategist, to see his attitude to Assyria's most politically sensitive frontier, that in the south with Babylonia. Here there were the usual border clashes, to which he eventually responded by pushing beyond the frontier to capture the northern cities, including the capital Babylon. But he made no attempt to establish himself as king of Babylonia, and this campaign seems to have been no more than a punitive raid to bring pressure for acceptance of a more southerly alignment of the Assyrian frontier. Once again, closer contact with Babylonia had the consequence of augmenting Babylonian cultural influence in Assyria; one instance of this was the beginning of the substitution of Babylonian month names for the original Assyrian ones.

The reign of Tiglath-Pileser also saw a further growth in the political importance of Nineveh, strategically vital for the control of the north. This city, apparently now recognized as the second capital of Assyria, was the scene of considerable building works, including the reconstruction of its wall.

International circumstances alone do not suffice to explain the vigour of Assyrian activity at the time of Tiglath-Pileser, and his reign represents a good example of the importance of the personal ability and drive of the ruler. There were later Assyrian kings who took Tiglath-Pileser as a throne-name – a reflection of the first Tiglath-Pileser's enduring reputation for success. But no later ruler took the names of the two sons who were his immediate successors, despite the impressive name of the second of them – Ashur-bel-kala, 'the god Ashur is Lord of All'. The name reflected the father's aspirations rather than the son's achievement.

Aramaean Immigration

After the reign of Tiglath-Pileser there was a rapid decline, associated with the ever-increasing prominence of the Aramaeans, against whom he had so persistently, and to immediate appearances so successfully, struggled. How we reconstruct the details of the manner in which the Aramaeans eventually turned the tide against Assyria depends in part upon how we understand a monument known as 'the Broken Obelisk'. Because this obelisk is broken, we lack a statement of the name of the king who wrote it, but it is now usually credited to Tiglath-Pileser's son and second successor, Ashur-bel-kala. The text has some odd features. It is composed partly in the third person and partly in the first, and it seems likely that the passages in the third person are speaking not of Ashur-bel-kala but of a predecessor. On grounds of piety alone, that predecessor is likely to have been Ashur-bel-kala's own father, Tiglath-Pileser, and when we find that the text records hunting and animal-collecting exploits agreeing in considerable detail with what Tiglath-Pileser tells us of himself, the matter seems beyond reasonable doubt. But whereas Tiglath-Pileser's inscriptions simply speak in general terms of his chasing the Aramaeans across the Euphrates (a matter also included in the Broken Obelisk), the Broken Obelisk adds references, dated to the exact month, about attacking 'a caravan of

Aramaeans' in various places. Some of these places are far from the Euphrates and deep inside Assyrian territory; for example, in the Tur Abdin, along the Tigris, near Harran, and along the Habur river. There is nothing to indicate whether the Aramaean caravans comprised traders, fighting units, or simply groups endeavouring to find places in which to settle, but clearly they were very widespread. At the same time they can have been neither powerful nor acting in consort, since the Assyrian king was able to mop up each group very quickly, in some cases dealing with two, three, or even four separate groups of Aramaeans in the same month. The conclusion from all this can only be that, despite Tiglath-Pileser's successful attempts to check the main body of Aramaeans attempting to cross the Euphrates from Jebel Bishri, many small groups were escaping his net and succeeding in infiltrating into Assyria. This boded ill for the ability of Tiglath-Pileser's successors to stand unaffected by Aramaean pressure.

Ashur-bel-kala (1074–1057) came to the throne after a brother who reigned less than two years. His annals speak grandiloquently of immediate action against the northern mountain areas. Military successes were claimed and presumably achieved, but what is significant is that, although there is mention of booty being taken by the Assyrians, there is no word of tribute being brought to Assyria by conquered vassals. The Assyrian armies could still ravage, but to no lasting purpose; under Ashur-bel-kala Assyria was no longer able to consolidate its military victories into more significant administrative arrangements for formal acceptance of Assyrian overlordship. Ashur-bel-kala also mentions campaigns against the Aramaeans, but his phraseology makes it clear that they were no longer a people whose main body could be whipped back over the Euphrates at will: the Assyrian king's statement that he 'continually plundered' them shows that the Aramaean problem had become endemic.

Assyro-Babylonian entente

In fact, the Aramaeans were becoming a serious threat to the whole of Mesopotamia, Babylonia as well as Assyria. The initial result of this was to bring Assyria and Babylonia together for mutual defence, a situation described in a chronicle: 'In the time of Ashur-bel-kala king of Assyria and Marduk-shapik-zeri king of Karduniash [Babylonia], they made an entente cordiale together.' This strengthened the Assyrian position, but did not dispose of the Aramaean pressure. At the death of the king of Babylonia, Ashur-bel-kala was now in a position to intervene in the Babylonian succession, and, according to the chronicle just quoted: 'He appointed Adad-apla-iddina, son

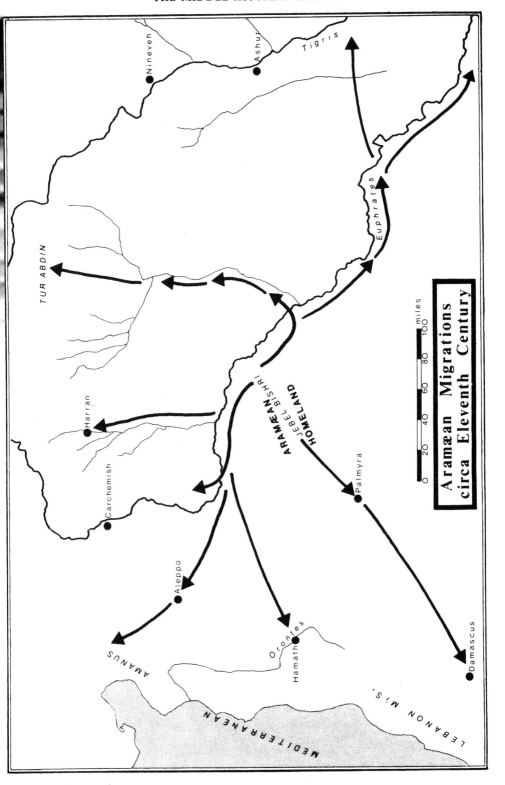

Aramæan Migrations circa Eleventh Century

of Esaggil-shaduni, son of a nobody, to the kingship over them.'
'Son of a nobody' shows that the new king's family was not of the
old Babylonian royal stock. We get a clearer picture of what was
happening when we find that another chronicle calls Adad-apla-
iddina (with a different name for his father to add to the uncertainty
about his origins) 'an Aramaean usurper'. It seems that Ashur-bel-
kala was now treading the path of diplomacy and dealing with the
Aramaean threat by accepting a leading Aramaean prince as vassal
and ally; he squeezed the maximum benefit from the situation by
marrying Adad-apla-iddina's daughter. As the chronicle puts it:
'Ashur-bel-kala king of Assyria married the daughter of Adad-apla-
iddina king of Karduniash and took her with her considerable dowry
to Assyria. The people of Assyria and Karduniash were mingled
together.' This sequence of events placed Assyria in a strong position
in Babylonia and at the same time, by gaining the allegiance of
a principal Aramaean leader, temporarily removed the Aramaean
threat.

The other side of the coin was that Assyria had shown itself to
be no longer able in the circumstances to pursue an independent
policy. At the same time, an alliance in which Assyria could interfere
in the Babylonian succession left Assyria equally open to Babylonian
intervention in its own domestic affairs. This duly happened. Ashur-
bel-kala's son and successor was removed after little more than a
year by his uncle, Shamshi-Adad IV, another son of Tiglath-Pileser,
who, as we learn from the Assyrian King List, took the throne from
a Babylonian base and so presumably with Babylonian support.

For the next century, covered by the reigns of six descendants of
Shamshi-Adad IV, our knowledge of Assyrian history is minimal
from lack of royal inscriptions, a clear indication of the debility of
the Assyrian state. A text from about 970 bears on this. The text in
question credits a provincial governor with building and canal works
in the Habur area; in the time of a strong Assyria such works were
the prerogative of the king, and for a local governor to carry out
public works of this kind indicates that at that time the central
administration of Assyria was weak if not non-existent.

Evidence from Babylon shows the serious disruption occasioned
by continuing Aramaean immigration at this time. In that city there
took place annually a religious festival, called the Akitu, which was
only foregone when political circumstances were so dire as to make
its central procession impossible. Chronicles recording such disas-
trous breaks with tradition mention that in 971 and 970 the festival
was abandoned because hostile Aramaeans threatened the immediate
neighbourhood.

Aramaean kingdoms

As the Aramaeans settled, they gradually coalesced into kingdoms, the earliest of which were in Syria; one of these Aramaean kingdoms, Zobah (Ṣupite in cuneiform inscriptions) was already encountered by King Saul of Israel just before 1000 (1 Samuel 14: 47), and it was shortly after this that the newly emergent Israelite kingdom expanded under David and Solomon to extend (albeit only briefly) as far as the Euphrates. That no encounter with Assyria is recorded – and indeed that expansion to those limits was possible at all – is another reflection of the impotence of Assyria at this time.

Why did the Aramaean situation reduce the Mesopotamian states to impotence and yet permit Israel to expand northwards as far as the Euphrates? This was largely a matter of how far particular groups of Aramaean nomads had gone in settling into stable kingdoms. With a federation of tribal clans, there tends to be no one central authority: as the biblical phrase puts it, in such a situation everyone does 'that which is right in his own eyes'. Generally there is no single ruler who can accept treaty terms and enforce them over the whole area; there is no one who can guarantee security for merchants, to ensure that their caravans are neither robbed nor subject to the extortions of any clan through whose territory they have to pass. Equally, there is no one who can speak for political relations for the whole area. In Syria the Aramaeans were well on the way to settling into stable kingdoms by 1000, whilst in Mesopotamia they were still migrating and settling for another two generations. It is this which explains why the kingdom of Israel could temporarily control the whole of Palestine and Syria as far as the Euphrates, at a time when Assyria east of the Euphrates remained powerless.

By the second half of the tenth century the Aramaean settlers in Mesopotamia were also, like those in Syria, becoming tamed into organized kingdoms. Assyria benefited from this; and from the reign of Ashur-dan II (934–912), Assyrian royal inscriptions again become plentiful, marking the re-emergence of Assyrian prosperity.

6

The Growth of the New Assyrian Empire

In his annals, Ashur-dan might almost be writing for the modern reader; as he records his own military activities, he glances back at the tribulations of Assyria during the preceding century, for which we are otherwise so ill-informed. One defeated people had, he tells us, been 'committing destruction and murder since the time of Shalmaneser' [II, (1030–1019)]. Aramaeans, whose cities he now burnt, had captured Assyrian territory in the time of Ashur-rabi [II, (1012–972)]. He speaks of 'the toil-worn people of Assyria who had left cities and houses from want, hunger and famine and gone to other lands', and assures us that he brought them back and re-settled them so that 'they dwelt in peace'.

Military Security and Economic Development

These comments of Ashur-dan confirm that, for the century before 934, the central administration in Assyria had virtually broken down, with resultant economic collapse. Correspondingly, Ashur-dan's activities were directed to economic development no less than to military security. He made no attempt to emulate the far-reaching military exploits of Tiglath-Pileser, but contented himself with establishing sound Assyrian control within Assyria's natural borders, from the near side of the Tur Abdin to the foothills beyond Erbil. His policy of resettlement of populations in Assyria is reflected in the passage already quoted. To counter the previous breakdown in the central administration, he built government offices in the provinces, and as a direct boost to the economy he emulated Tiglath-Pileser I in providing ploughs throughout his land, thereby producing 'more grain than ever before'. All this provided a sound base for further development and expansion, if subsequent rulers had the ability to use it.

It proved that they had. Ashur-dan was succeeded by four able kings in his direct line, and within a century from his accession Assyria was the major world power. These four rulers – particularly the third of them – narrate their exploits in considerable detail, and space does not permit more than a brief summary of the main trends of their reigns.

Ashur-dan's son, Adad-nerari II (911–891), campaigned to re-assert Assyrian control in the north-west, moving into the northern mountains beyond the Tur Abdin. Although severe military measures were taken against opposition, his activities were not senselessly punitive and predatory; his objective was to establish settled conditions that would bring the most productive use of resources and the greatest benefit to Assyria. As he puts it, in recording the conclusion of his campaign against the northern people Qumani, 'the rest of their troops, who had fled before my weapons but come back, I settled in peaceful dwellings'.

The most intractable problem was still the Aramaeans. South of the Tur Abdin, some of them had effected widespread settlement between the Habur and the western elbow of the Euphrates, and in the particular area of the headwaters of the Habur a confederation of Aramaeans, who had arrived after the reign of Tiglath-Pileser I, attempted to assert their independence. It took Adad-nerari six annual campaigns to subdue them; he finally did so by starving out the paramount chief in his fortified capital at Nisibin. A subsequent march along the Habur brought the formal submission of a whole series of Aramaean-controlled cities. Meanwhile Adad-nerari had received gifts, implying submission as a vassal, from a more distant Aramaean principality, Bit-Adini (the 'Beth-Eden' or 'House of Eden' of Amos 1: 5), on the elbow of the Euphrates.

In the south-east, Babylonia had once again, as often during periods of Assyrian weakness, seized the territory south of the Lower Zab; Adad-nerari took action, but although he gave himself the title 'conqueror of the entire land of Karduniash', his activities there were little more than a border skirmish to push the Assyrian frontier south to either the Adhaim or the Diyala river. The border agreement was cemented by a marriage alliance.

Tukulti-Ninurta II (890–884) continued the thrust to regain control of the northern and eastern mountain areas, and in the south pushed his boundary with Babylonia almost to where Baghdad now stands. Aramaean settlements along the Tigris, Euphrates and Habur were now mostly content to present tribute in token of acceptance of Assyrian vassaldom, with occasional recalcitrants requiring military action. One Aramaean tribe which was troublesome at this time, the Itu'a, must have had fighting qualities which won Assyrian respect, for later (when their loyalty was beyond question) they were used as shock troops for policing troublesome urban populations.

The type of tribute paid by some of the Aramaean tribes points to their wealth and the nature of their trading activities; besides gold and silver, bronze and tin, such tribute included myrrh (showing trading links with south Arabia, its nearest source), dromedaries (again pointing to links with the Arabian desert), ivory inlaid furniture (a mark of conspicuous wealth, probably of Syrian or Phoenician craftsmanship), textiles, iron (from Cilicia), cattle, sheep, asses, ducks and grain. There is no mention whatever of horses from the Aramaean tributaries; presumably they used only donkeys and camels for transport at this time. Tukulti-Ninurta did however receive horses by the thousands as tribute from the northern regions, and indeed began the large-scale use of cavalry by the Assyrian army.

Ashur-nasir-pal II, the Imperial Strategist

With the reign of Ashur-nasir-pal II (883–859), we come to one of the high points in the Assyrian empire. His records are voluminous and their scale reflects his achievements as the real founder of the final Neo-Assyrian empire.

Ashur-nasir-pal began with demonstrations of force along the arc of mountains running from east of Erbil to north-west of Nineveh, in modern terms northern Kurdistan. He had reached Kadmukh, the plain west of the Tigris north-west of Nineveh, when he was faced by trouble elsewhere. The nominally vassal state of Bit-Adini, in the Carchemish elbow of the Euphrates, was attempting to assert independence and to gain wider support, and at this moment won a diplomatic success. The major city in the area where the Habur river joins the Euphrates murdered its pro-Assyrian governor (incidentally a man whose name shows he was of non-Assyrian origin – the Assyrians were not racialists) and installed a nominee from Bit-Adini as king. Ashur-nasir-pal reacted swiftly. Marching southwards down the Habur, receiving en route the homage of the vassal cities that lined the river, he captured the rebel stronghold, vigorously crushing all opposition and placing the city once again under an Assyrian governor.

The wealth of the rebel city proved considerable, leading Ashur-nasir-pal to remark that its 'heavy spoil, like the stars of heaven, could not be counted'. The king does, however, list the main categories. These included, in addition to the kind of Aramaean tribute mentioned earlier, chariotry and horses, the first reference to these amongst Aramaean-controlled states. Obviously, the Aramaean groups in Mesopotamia were no longer simply half-settled nomads engaging in trade; they were well on the way to becoming fully-developed stable kingdoms with the organized military arm which that implied.

Kadmukh, which Ashur-nasir-pal had reached when diverted to the Habur region, is a key to the Tur Abdin (Kashiari) plateau and the regions north of the Tigris; the king now turned his attention back to this area. Several earlier Assyrian kings had claimed to conquer Kashiari, but the terrain makes this region very hard to police, and Assyrian control there was usually only temporary. It was when a vassal ruler in the area rebelled and attacked an Assyrian garrison town that Ashur-nasir-pal began his operations; he moved against the offender, killing, looting, burning, blinding, mutilating. Other petty kingdoms in the area made submission. After a demonstration against the lands north of the Tigris known as Nairi, Ashur-nasir-pal rebuilt an old city on the Tigris, Tushkhan, as a garrison against both Kashiari and Nairi. It was, indeed, more than a garrison; it was a major base and store city, settled with Assyrians and supplied with grain and other provisions from neighbouring areas so that in time of attack it could hold out indefinitely.

Ashur-nasir-pal had now created a powerful line of defence along his northern and western boundaries; he next acted to develop this into a complete security ring. In the east he moved into south Kurdistan, the region east and north-east of Kirkuk. Some Assyrian kings of the thirteenth and twelfth centuries had temporarily held this area, but otherwise it had not been under firm Assyrian control for nearly a thousand years. Ashur-nasir-pal represents his operation in the region as beginning with action against a rebel vassal, but his subsequent mention of places 'which no one had ever seen', or where 'no king among my forefathers had ever been', makes it clear that this was naked military expansion. Some of the peoples encountered were evidently quite strange to the Assyrians; of the inhabitants of one conquered land it is said that 'they do their hair [or possibly 'adorn themselves'] like women'. Subjugation of this region extended the Assyrian defence chain along the Zagros from the headwaters of the Diyala (boundary with Babylonia) to the headwaters of the Lower Zab.

Ashur-nasir-pal's early campaigns all used either Erbil or Nineveh as his main operational bases, even though his capital was Ashur much further south. Clearly, the needs of the empire demanded a northern capital. Ashur-nasir-pal had already found the value of cities such as Tushkhan (one amongst several of its kind) which were primarily garrisons, store cities and administrative centres, where the king could start virtually from scratch, without the constraints that a major old cult-centre or residential–commercial city would involve. He now built a new city, Calah (represented today by the great mound Nimrud), on the site of an old city founded by Shalmaneser I which had fallen into ruins. This site had the strategic importance not only of being in the north, but also of lying in the angle where the Upper Zab joins the Tigris. He provided his new capital with water by a canal from the Upper Zab, gave it splendid buildings with a sewage system, planted it with orchards settled it with peoples from various parts of his empire (making it a cosmopolitan city indeed), and inaugurated it with a week-long feast recorded in an inscription complete with menu. (For the latter, see pages 165f.).

We return to Ashur-nasir-pal's military strategy. There were further measures to be taken in the west. Moving due west across the Tigris from Calah, Ashur-nasir-pal reached the Habur, and marched down its length, receiving tribute, to the Euphrates. There he moved downstream as far as the Babylonian border, and captured a Babylonian border town. This represented what today might be called an exercise in brinkmanship; it did not result in all-out war with Babylonia but had considerable propaganda consequences, of which Ashur-nasir-pal was well aware. He tells us: 'The fear of my dominion reached as far as Karduniash [Babylonia]; the terror of my weapons overwhelmed Chaldaea [south Babylonia].' A subsequent insurrection in the border area was quickly crushed. Ashur-nasir-pal had nothing more to fear on that border; as he intended, all potential Babylonian opposition had been neutralized.

To the Mediterranean

With a ring of security – Babylonia, the Zagros, the eastern Taurus, the Tur Abdin, the Habur – encircling Assyria, Ashur-nasir-pal now began the second stage of his strategy. No Assyrian ruler had held the routes to the Mediterranean since Tiglath-Pileser I, two centuries before. Ashur-nasir-pal now pushed up the Euphrates from the Habur junction, mopping up opposition on the way, and incidentally hunting ostriches and wild bulls, still quite common in the Syrian desert at that time. This movement culminated in operations against the Aramaean state of Bit-Adini in the elbow of the Euphrates; the effective pacification of the whole area required several campaigns and the founding of two new cities – 'Ashur-nasir-pal's Quay' and 'Ashur's Crossing Place' – controlling crossings of the Euphrates. Bit-Adini formally became an Assyrian province early in his successor's reign.

With his rear secured, Ashur-nasir-pal was ready to push through to the Mediterranean, crossing the Euphrates by raft in the region of Carchemish. His previous crushing of all opposition ensured him the submission of all the kings of north Syria, who came to pay homage. As a safeguard he took hostages (probably their sons), keeping them with him against treachery on his route via the Orontes to Mount Lebanon and the Mediterranean coast, where he received tribute from as far south as Tyre.

Ashur-nasir-pal was now in firm control of the whole area from south Lebanon to south Kurdistan, with a looser suzerainty over a considerable expanse of the Taurus region. Subsequent campaigns were directed mainly to consolidation rather than to acquisition of new territories; one notable exception was the taking under direct Assyrian control of Amid (Diyarbekr), then as now the key to an extensive area of the foothills of the eastern Taurus.

Ashur-nasir-pal's son and successor Shalmaneser III (858–824) in the main continued and extended his father's policies, though with some significant new developments. The chronology is not of high relevance and the data will be discussed geographically.

Into the Old Testament minefield

First, the west. Here Shalmaneser followed his father in ensuring control of the Phoenician coastal area, and on his bronze gates (see pages 236, 320) we see the tribute of Tyre being brought by boats. But when he attempted to move into more southerly regions of inner Syria, he was resisted at Qarqar (853) by a powerful coalition of Syrian and Palestinian kings, including Hadad-ezer of Damascus and Ahab of Israel – both known from the Bible. Ahab brought a powerful cavalry force. Once the historian runs into biblical material, 'farewell the tranquil mind, farewell content'; religious partisanship raises its monstrous head. In the present instance, with an Israelite king involved, there is a tendency for the strategic issue of Assyrian policy to become swamped in the question of whether Assyria or Israel won the particular battle. The only direct evidence we have of the encounter is Shalmaneser's own record, and he claims to have defeated the coalition. But even if, as some scholars think, Shalmaneser exaggerated in his claim of success and the battle of Qarqar actually gave a significant set-back to Assyrian strategy in relation to Syria and Palestine, this was no more than temporary. By twelve years later the Assyrian empire had engulfed Palestine, and Ahab's usurping successor Jehu was an Assyrian vassal; we actually see him doing obeisance before Shalmaneser on an Assyrian monument.

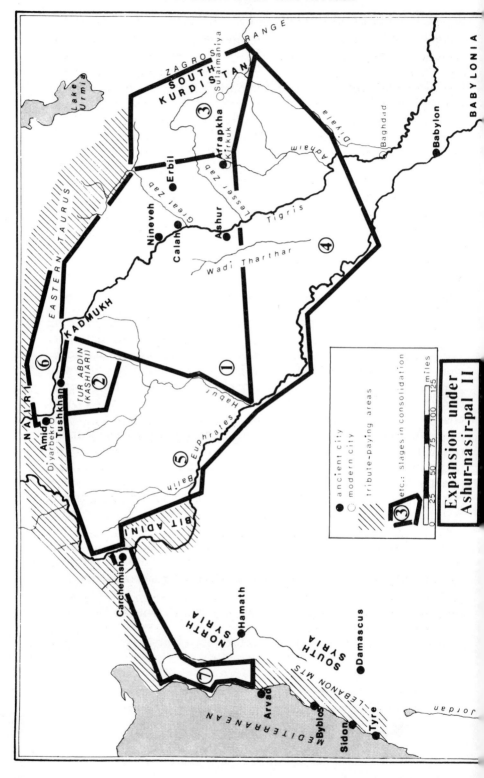

Expansion under Ashur-nasir-pal II

● ancient city
○ modern city
▨ tribute-paying areas
③ etc.: stages in consolidation

miles
0 25 50 75 100 125

Beyond the Amanus and Taurus

Strategically, Shalmaneser's most important achievement was the extension of Assyrian control to the north-west beyond the Amanus into Cilicia and towards central Anatolia. The significance of this was that Cilicia was the principal source of iron for the Near East and was also important for maritime trade with Cyprus and Greece, so that Assyria's economic links were markedly extended. In the south, Shalmaneser had to undertake a brief invasion of Babylonia to stabilize the situation there; the problem he faced was mainly in south Babylonia, where powerful Chaldaean tribes had established themselves, an indication of things to come. In the north-east there were other developments of long-term strategic importance. Peoples in the eastern Taurus had coalesced into what was becoming a powerful kingdom, Urartu, eventually based on Lake Van. For over a century it was to prove a major rival to Assyria, spreading westwards across Anatolia to north Syria and competing with Assyria for control of trade routes and major areas of metal production and horse rearing. Assyrian campaigns into the Taurus, which had mainly been operations against petty princedoms in regions known broadly as Nairi and Habha, now began to meet more formidable opposition from the state army of Urartu, backed by a series of fortresses.

Beyond the Zagros; Medes and Persians

Further east there was another new element in the situation. Shalmaneser crossed the Zagros from where Ashur-nasir-pal had campaigned in southern Kurdistan, and on the eastern side had his first encounter with the Medes and Persians. These associated peoples, Iranian tribes, had come into Iran from the north towards the end of the second millennium. The Persians, later to settle in south-west Iran, were still in the north-west. The Medes, eventually to make their capital at Ecbatana (modern Hamadan), and to prove such successful apprentices in Assyrian warfare that they would in the end lay victorious siege to the great Assyrian cities, were at the time of Shalmaneser simply a new client nomadic people, long referred to as 'the wide-spread Medes', and useful to Assyria, standing as they did across an ancient route which brought lapis lazuli to Mesopotamia from Afghanistan.

Civil war

The reigns of Shalmaneser III and his father together totalled sixty years, with a single consistent policy pursued by two strong-minded rulers. With little opportunity for the expression of public opinion, this was a situation in which discontent might build up, and it is hardly a matter for surprise that, despite the continuing imperial expansion, the end of the reign of Shalmaneser should have been marked by revolt. For several years before Shalmaneser's death there was a power struggle headed by two sons of Shalmaneser, and the victorious successor – Shamshi-Adad V – names twenty-seven cities as having revolted. These included, together with a number of provincial cities, the major Assyrian cities of Nineveh, Erbil, Ashur and Arrapkha. A notable exception from the list was Calah. Clearly, Calah remained firmly in the control of Shalmaneser and Shamshi-Adad V; so long-sighted and efficient had Ashur-nasir-pal and Shalmaneser been in the planning and organization of their new capital that it now proved that the ruler who held this city held the empire.

After civil peace had been restored in Assyria, Shamshi-Adad's activities were mainly concerned with the north-eastern frontier and with Babylonia, which Shamshi-Adad overran, removing two successive kings (c. 813–812). We have no solid evidence about the political background to this latter development. A possible reconstruction is that Shamshi-Adad received Babylonian help in securing his kingdom (deducible from fragments of a treaty between him and a Babylonian king), and that subsequent attempts by Babylonia to continue humiliating interference in Assyrian affairs led Shamshi-Adad to violent counter-action. The havoc Shamshi-Adad wrought in the cities of north Babylonia caused disruption which favoured the growth of Chaldaean influence.

A Queen Mother who became a legend

Shamshi-Adad V gives us a link with classical legend, for his wife was Sammurammat, who occurs in Greek tradition from Herodotus onwards, and indeed also in medieval tradition, as Semiramis. Diodorus of Sicily, a gentleman who wrote history in Greek in the first century B.C., has many pages of fanciful stories about this lady, represented as the embodiment of superwoman: pre-eminent in beauty, counsel, military ability, sexual prowess, administrative skill and ambition. This last trait led her, when left the widow of a king, to build Babylon and many other cities in Mesopotamia and beyond, whilst Armenian tradition even has her building a great city overlooking Lake Van in eastern Turkey – actually the capital built by an Urartian king contemporary with her.

The grain of truth behind all this is that Semiramis must have been a virago; she was unusually prominent for a woman in the reign of her son, Adad-nerari III (809–782), and some scholars even want to make her regent, though without conclusive evidence. Regent or not, her exceptional prominence is vouched for by a stone monument. Among finds in the old Assyrian capital Ashur were two rows of inscribed steles, memorials to various people. In one sequence all those commemorated were high officials, whilst in the other all but the latest three were kings. Of the three exceptions, one was for the queen ('Lady of the Palace') of Ashurbanipal, one for a lady (presumably queen, though the title is lost) of Sennacherib, and the third for Semiramis. Her monument reads:

> stele of Sammurammat;
> Queen [lit. 'Lady of the Palace'] of Shamshi-Adad,
> king of all, king of Ashur;
> mother of Adad-nerari,
> king of all, king of Ashur;
> daughter-in-law of Shalmaneser,
> king of the four regions.

The fact that the stele of Sammurammat was in the royal sequence, and that she alone of the three ladies included there was identified as the mother of a king, suggests that she held a special status in the reign of Adad-nerari. We may also note that the governor of Calah, in dedicating two divine statues, added an honorific inscription in which 'for the life of Adad-nerari, king of the land of Assyria, his lord' is linked with 'for the life of Sammurammat, Lady of the Palace, his lady'; this again points to an exceptional status for Sammurammat.

Urartu, a Rival Kingdom

Adad-nerari III had other problems than a dominant mother. To understand what was happening in the Assyrian empire in the first half of the eighth century, we need to look at what was happening to the north of it, in what is now eastern Turkey (formerly Armenia). Here there was a kingdom, Urartu, approximately bounded by three major lakes: Van, Urmia (otherwise Rezaiyeh) in Azerbaijan (north-west Iran), and Sevan in Armenian SSR (south Russia). This kingdom developed in the ninth century from a federation of peoples in and beyond the Taurus, whom the Assyrians had raided for several centuries. Although a form of the name Urartu (Uruatri) occurs in Assyrian inscriptions as early as the thirteenth century, it is very doubtful if it then meant anything more than a small peripheral part of what eventually became the kingdom of Urartu.

In a sense, Urartu – the major rival of Assyria – was the creation of Assyria itself. The constant Assyrian incursions into the Taurus and beyond; the taking of its princes as hostages, its working population for corvée, and its young men for the Assyrian army; and the presence of Assyrian administrators and scribes to control and record deliveries of timber, metals and horses to Assyria; all these must have familiarized the people of Urartu with much of the culture and infrastructure of a major kingdom. The link is reflected in the fact that the first surviving Urartian inscriptions are written in the Assyrian language, and most of them at all times in a cuneiform script based on Assyrian.

The effective beginning of Urartu as a significant kingdom may be placed in the time of Shalmaneser III. Shalmaneser not only described his campaigns against Urartu but also illustrated them, in the form of reliefs in bronze cladding on the gates of a city he built not far from Calah. We see the approach of Urartian infantry over steep mountains, an Assyrian cavalry charge, Assyrian archers in action, and the burning of Arzashkun, the first capital of Urartu. Arzashkun, though not identified, was probably not in the Lake Van area but further west or north-west. In a quest for security against further Assyrian raids, the Urartian king Sarduri I shortly after built a new capital Turushpa, in a highly defensible site on the south-eastern shore of Lake Van.

The internal troubles at the end of the reign of Shalmaneser III gave Urartu an opportunity to expand. Already under Shalmaneser the Assyrians had crossed the Zagros into Iran, probably mainly in quest of horses. South of Lake Urmia they encountered a people called the Mannai (Mannaeans), as well as the Persians (not yet in their final place of settlement in the south), and the Medes. Urartu now expanded southwards into the mountainous territory between Turushpa and Assyria, and eastwards and south-eastwards into fertile Azerbaijan as far as Lake Urmia. When Urartu attempted further expansion south from Lake Urmia, competition developed for the land of the Mannai, only resolved when Assyria finally overran the whole of Azerbaijan in 714.

Assyria's internal problems at the end of the reign of Shalmaneser III had also weakened control in the north-west, allowing Urartu to expand as far as the Upper Euphrates. This was an area of high importance to Assyria, as the river constituted the main natural route into Anatolia from Syria and Mesopotamia. When Urartu encroached on an important Assyrian tributary here, the state based on Melid (Malatya), this unsettled other vassals within the Assyrian orbit, in both north and south Syria. This was reflected in the widespread withholding of tribute from the area in the reign of Shamshi-Adad V.

Syria's economic importance to Assyria was manifold: it was a source of skilled manpower; it provided timber from the Amanus and Lebanon; it held the Assyrian routes to the Mediterranean; and it was the main supply line for metals and horses from Anatolia and Asia Minor. Adad-nerari III reacted to the strategic problem by campaigning mainly in south Syria, an easier target than north Syria, partly from the terrain, but principally because this would not directly involve Urartu. He began by attacking Arpad, north-west of Aleppo, but subsequently concentrated on recovering control of south Syria, receiving tribute from as far south as Tyre, Sidon and Israel (whose king Joash is mentioned by name). His main south Syrian target was the wealthy city of Damascus, from which Adad-nerari claimed to receive (taking the lower figures from variant accounts) some thirty tons of copper or bronze and twice that quantity of iron. From the Lebanon mountains he carried off 'a hundred mighty cedars needed for my palaces and temples'.

The part played by Syria as a source of manpower has been touched upon. Adad-nerari saw the need to develop his lands further, and in one text appends to his account of the south Syrian campaign details of a major resettlement project, apparently in the fertile region of the Upper Habur. It is a reasonable inference that the people for these new settlements came from south Syria.

In reaction to the Assyrian threat to Syria, the king of Damascus attempted to organize a coalition of all the states from Melid and Cilicia (Que) right down to Damascus, although some islands of allegiance to Assyria, such as Hamath, remained.

The resulting situation was that there was now a powerful state of Urartu controlling the whole region westwards from south of Lake Urmia to Melid, with states from Melid southward as far as Carchemish completely under Urartian influence, and further south a fairly solid coalition under the domination of an anti-Assyrian Damascus. All this adversely affected supplies to Assyria of essentials such as horses, metals, and timber, as well as luxury goods such as lapis lazuli from Afghanistan, which normally reached Assyria by a route through northern Iran, and spices from south Arabia which came up through Palestine and Syria.

Assyria under an able strategist would have been able to overcome these problems. With its rich corn plains stretching along the great river Tigris, with easy communications across the whole, it was much better placed geographically to be a major warrior state than was mountainous Urartu, which was difficult to weld into a unified state. Whilst the terrain of Urartu made it virtually impossible to conquer and subdue it as a whole, suitable direction could – and eventually did – ensure that Assyria would control those areas of Urartian influence which were strategically vital for Assyria. But at the moment, suitable direction in Assyria was not forthcoming. The problem in Syria was also not insoluble. The attempts of Damascus at a pan-Syrian coalition were only partly and temporarily successful; the resistance of Hamath has already been mentioned, and the Bible makes it clear that Jeroboam II of Israel, far from welcoming a Damascus coalition, benefited by the preoccupations of Damascus to seize some of its territories (2 Kings 14: 25–8), possibly as an actual ally of Assyria when the latter campaigned against Damascus in 773. Assyria would have preferred a strong Israel, which consti-tuted no threat to Assyria in the Syrian Euphrates area, to a Damas-cus-led coalition of Aramaean states, which undoubtedly did.

Weak Kings and Over-mighty Governors

Yet for three reigns and about forty years after Adad-nerari III Assyria showed no marked initiative. This does not imply that Assyria suddenly went soft. The year lists still mention campaigns – in the case of Shalmaneser IV (781–772) six against Urartu in eight years, and four against north Syria between 772 and 754 – but the indications are that these were either defensive actions by local governors or glorified raids or border clashes; they were not major attempts at further Assyrian expansion. A factor in this was the internal situation, with a shift in the power structure away from the central government to the provincial governors, a gradual develop-ment from the time of Shalmaneser III. The assertion by that king and his father of firm Assyrian control over such areas as the middle and upper Euphrates, and the regions north of the Tur Abdin, needed a provincial administration with considerable powers to safeguard the security of such fringe areas. This strategy of defending a greater Assyria within the borders of the Euphrates and the northern Tigris had considerable success. It permitted immediate action against any local insurrection, and governors in the proximity of Urartian forces could react quickly to any threatening move. But there was another side to this development. Governors in this situation could and did, in the absence of a forceful king, acquire a large measure of independence, becoming almost local dynasts. This is well illustrated by inscriptions of three different governors from this period recording their own exploits, such as military successes and the founding of towns – matters at most times confined to royal inscriptions. In one instance a governor – ruling a region along the middle Euphrates – dates his deeds by his own years of office without mention of a king, indicating that he was virtually an independent ruler. It may be added, though, that this particular governor did much more for humanity than many kings: he introduced bee-keeping to his province, which was manifestly his proudest achievement. He writes:

> I am Shamash-resh-usur, Governor of Suhu and Mari [on the middle Euphrates]. Bees which gather honey, which no one among my forefathers had seen nor brought down to the land of Suhu, I brought down from the mountains of Habha [eastern Turkey] and established in the town Gabbari-ibni [a town he had founded]. They collect honey and wax. I understand how to do the melting out of the honey and wax, and the gardeners also understand it. Any later person who appears, let him ask the old men of the country whether it is true that Shamash-resh-usur the Governor of Suhu introduced bees.

It is significant that Shamash-resh-usur says he obtained his bees from the north, for the Hittites are known to have kept bees in hives in the second millennium.

Under weak central government, with economic problems arising from interference with the supply of goods Assyria was accustomed to obtain from Syria or the north, tensions developed. From around 760 insurrections are reported from several cities. By the reign of the last king of this period, Ashur-nerari V (753–745), Urartu had made considerable political, and possibly military, gains in north Syria; his Urartian contemporary, Sarduri I, claimed that he had 'conquered the land of Ashur-nerari, king of Assyria', with no further specific details but mention of a place name which suggests that he was in Assyrian territory near Carchemish. Ashur-nerari was not in a position to make any firm military response – entries for five years out of the eight in his year list record 'in the land', that is, 'no campaign' – and it would appear that he attempted to protect Assyria's position in north Syria by diplomacy. We have the text of a treaty (possibly two, if another fragment comes from a different text), seeking to bind a north Syrian state to support Assyria against Urartu. This initiative had little permanent effect and Urartu continued its advance in north Syria.

In the end, the tensions within Assyria boiled over in a revolt in the capital, Calah. The governor of Calah, possibly a usurper but certainly of royal blood, came to the throne. His personal name was Pul, as recorded both in the Bible and in some cuneiform inscriptions, but he took Tiglath-Pileser as a throne name and an indication of the kind of expansionist policy which, following the first royal bearer of the name, he proposed to pursue.

9A The modern remains of the ziggurat of Calah (Nimrud) (H. W. F. Saggs)

9B Representation of a worshipper revering a sword on an altar as the symbol of a god (Staatliche Museen zu Berlin)

10A Drawing of *keleks* on
the Tigris in the mid-
nineteenth century A.D.
(V. Place, *Ninive et
l'Assyrie*, Paris, 1867–70)

10B Drawing of
Sennacherib's ships, from
a bas relief (A. H. Layard,
The Monuments of Nineveh,
London, 1849–53)

11A   Drawing of soldiers inflating and using goatskin floats, from a bas relief (A. H. Layard, *The Monuments of Nineveh*, London, 1849–53)

11B   Phoenician-type galley, on a bas relief (British Museum, photo H. W. F. Saggs)

12A   Armlet and bracelet of an Assyrian king (British Museum, photo H. W. F. Saggs)

12B and 13B   Details from the bronze gates of Balawat, depicting (*below*) the carving of a statue of Shalmaneser III and (*opposite*) a sacrifice, both at the source of the Tigris (British Museum, photos H. W. F. Saggs)

13A   *Above*: Prisoners in neck-yokes, also from the bronze gates of Balawat (British Museum, photo H. W. F. Saggs)

14A *Above*: Seventh-century scene from a lion hunt
(British Museum, photo Joan Saggs)

14B Ninth-century statue of King Ashur-nasir-pal II
(British Museum, photo H. W. F. Saggs)

15A   Bas relief showing King Ashur–nasir–pal II on each side of a stylized 'Sacred Tree'
(British Museum)

15B   Seventh-century scene from the hunt of wild asses (British Museum, photo
H. W. F. Saggs)

16A   Ashurbanipal's defeat of the Elamites. The detail enclosed in the rectangle at left is depicted below (Hirmer Fotoarchiv, Munich)

16B   Detail from plate above, showing the capture of Teumman, King of Elam, and his son (British Museum, photo H. W. F. Saggs)

7

Imperial Prime

Administrative Reform

The reign of Tiglath-Pileser III (745–727) introduced the century of
the greatest expansion of the Assyrian empire. The dramatic change
in the international situation followed in large part from administrative reorganization, which gave the king direct and almost immediate control over all the resources of his empire. In the old provincial
administration, some of the governorships held by noble families
had come to be thought of as hereditary possessions, with the
governor a semi-independent ruler. These were now split up and
manned by a hierarchy of officials appointed by and directly responsible to the king at the capital. A rapid and efficient communications
system – a network of posting stages afterwards taken over by the
Persians, together with the undeserved credit for devising it – was
organized across the empire, and provincial officials were required
to send reports to the capital regularly and promptly. The king had
his personal travelling inspectors to investigate the performance of
provincial officials right up to the top. In vassal states beyond the
directly-governed provinces, Tiglath-Pileser appointed representatives to safeguard Assyrian interests at court, in particular in matters
of trade and foreign policy. Local ruling families, so long as they
paid the tribute imposed upon them and accepted the direction of
the Assyrian resident in appropriate matters, were left substantial
independence and were assured of the backing of the imperial power
against internal revolution or external attack. Examples of this are
not hard to find. Thus, we have an Aramaean inscription of a
grateful Syrian vassal, king of Sam'al, some seventy miles north-
west of Aleppo, describing how Tiglath-Pileser had re-instated his
father after a rebellion and destroyed the opposition. Again, in the
Bible we see how Ahaz of Judah, when threatened by a hostile
coalition, appealed, not in vain, to his overlord Tiglath-Pileser (2
Kings 16: 7–9).
    An intelligence system was also built up. From this time there is
abundant evidence of Urartian spies in Assyrian pay – we have
mention of their reports in some cases – and it is not unreasonable
to assume that this was not limited to Urartu. By the time of

85

Sennacherib's attack on Jerusalem in 701, the Assyrian officials certainly knew – if the biblical narrative is to be believed – a good deal about internal developments in Judah.

What Tiglath-Pileser did in general is very clear; what he did in particular is less easily arrived at. His annals are particularly badly preserved, and detailed reconstruction of the chronology and geography of his campaigns continues to provide many happy hours of research for cuneiformists. Tiglath-Pileser's inscriptions have suffered in various ways. He wrote his annals on reliefs on the walls of his palace, and a successor took away these reliefs as material for decorating a new palace he was building, disarranging and damaging them as he did so. Then the earliest nineteenth-century excavator to come upon the slabs made things worse by cutting away some of the inscribed portions to lighten them and facilitate removal of the reliefs – O Art, what crimes are committed in Thy name! – although he tried to avoid loss of information by taking paper squeezes of the text. The squeezes in turn suffered damage, and some eventually disappeared, in the caverns of the British Museum. Furthermore, those who had access to the original texts and the squeezes on the whole published them badly. One factor underlying this final defect was that Tiglath-Pileser comes right into the thick of biblical history as known from the Books of Kings, so that the main concern of some scholars with Tiglath-Pileser's annals was not ancient Near Eastern history in its broader aspects, but confirmation of the biblical statements about Israelite history.

Policy towards Vassal States

Tiglath-Pileser extended the Assyrian empire. Ashur-nasir-pal and Shalmaneser III had treated the Euphrates as Greater Assyria's border in terms of direct provincial rule; west of that there were vassal states, tied to Assyria by treaty or military threat but still – if sometimes only nominally – independent. Tiglath-Pileser changed all that. In his reign a number of former vassal states beyond the Euphrates were taken over as directly-ruled provinces, a development which was extended in later reigns.

Was this the result of a new political strategy or was it no more than the consequence of former policy? The evidence points to the latter view. The Bible gives details of the annexation of the kingdom of Israel, and it is very clear that Tiglath-Pileser made several attempts to gain the co-operation of Israel as a vassal state; not until this failed did Assyria, under Tiglath-Pileser's successor, invade and take over Israel. Down in Judah, King Ahaz actually called on

Tiglath-Pileser for assistance, and this he would hardly have done had he supposed that this might lead to the annexation of his kingdom (which in the outcome it did not). A vassal in north Syria explicitly narrates the good relations of his father and himself with Tiglath-Pileser III:

> My father. . .grasped the hem of his lord, the great king of Assyria; then did he live and Y'dy [the name of the kingdom] lived. . . .My father ran at the wheel of his lord Tiglath-Pileser, king of Assyria, in campaigns from east to west. . . .My father. . .died at the feet of his lord Tiglath-Pileser, king of Assyria, on campaign, and all the camp of his lord the king of Assyria wept for him. And his lord, the king of Assyria. . .erected an image of him by the roadside, and brought my father across from Damascus. Then, because of my father's loyalty and my own loyalty, my lord Tiglath-Pileser set me. . .on the throne.

Manifestly this king had no reason to think that, so long as he remained a loyal vassal to Tiglath-Pileser, his kingdom would be annexed.

Assyria's main problem at the accession of Tiglath-Pileser was Urartu. Control of the Syrian routes was essential to Assyria for timber, metals and horse supplies. Urartu was equally determined to gain control of north Syria. With two major powers in the vicinity (and a third, Egypt, less powerful but briefly renascent at this time and by no means negligible), most vassal states eventually proved, from the point of view of Assyria, unreliable at critical moments. Assyria was thus forced, for the security of the routes on which it depended, to introduce direct provincial rule, and to weaken local scope for insurrection by the deportation of the leading classes.

So much for the principles of Tiglath-Pileser's expansion. Because of the state of his records, the details remain disputable at many points. The following reconstruction largely adopts the interpretation proposed by the Israeli scholar Chaim Tadmor.

Expansion under Tiglath-Pileser III

The endemic border disputes between Babylonia and Assyria have frequently been touched upon; it was no major break with tradition for Tiglath-Pileser's reign to begin with assertion of Assyria's rights along the disputed border with Babylonia, in the south-east. On this occasion Tiglath-Pileser was able, with a Babylonia weakened by internal troubles, to fix the border on the most southerly of several possible lines, along the Diyala from the Zagros to the Tigris. There was also some Assyrian penetration further south, where tribal peoples – Chaldaeans, already mentioned, and to be encountered as major opponents later – were disrupting Babylonia. He then turned to the region of his main problem, north Syria.

Here Urartu had made considerable recent advances, with a whole line of states west of the Euphrates – Melid, Kummukh, Carchemish – becoming Urartian vassals. Arpad, south-west of Carchemish, controlling the approaches to regions further south and important for Assyria's routes to the Mediterranean and nominally tied by treaty to Assyria, had also joined the anti-Assyrian coalition. In 743 Tiglath-Pileser attacked Arpad, which was being held by Urartian forces. A *Limu* List (a document giving a skeleton list of memorable events for chronological purposes; see page 273) in respect to this year records 'in Arpad, a defeat of Urartu was effected', but it required two more years of siege before the city was actually taken. This brought the submission, in the form of payment of tribute, of many states of north and south Syria, while Tiglath-Pileser was consolidating his position in north Syria. This was in 740, for which we have the year entry 'in Arpad', the city being used as a base for mopping-up operations against recalcitrant states.

Tiglath-Pileser now turned to deal with another Urartian vassal, the land Ullubu in the Dohuk-Zakho area, due north of Nineveh and too close to be comfortable in hostile hands, well illustrating the threat Urartu posed for Assyria. Tiglath-Pileser took the region – which must have been prosperous, as twenty-nine towns are mentioned – brought it under direct Assyrian rule, and resettled it with deportees from other conquered areas, presumably north Syria, giving another stir to the racial mixing-pot of the Assyrian empire.

Tiglath-Pileser's activities from his base in Arpad in 740 brought him tribute, implying formal acceptance of vassaldom, from a number of wavering states down to the borders of Palestine. At this point extant records are so fragmentary that different reconstructions are possible, and academic throat-cutting still continues on such trivial details as the exact date of the payment of tribute by Menahem of Israel, recorded in the Bible. However, it seems that some of the remoter states of south Syria and Palestine failed to send tribute, thereby giving notice that they were not loyal vassals. Therefore, in 738 Tiglath-Pileser made a demonstration of force into south Syria. It was probably on this occasion that Menahem of Israel paid tribute: 'Pul [Tiglath-Pileser] the king of Assyria came against the land; and Menahem gave Pul a thousand talents of silver, for his hands to be with him to confirm the kingdom in his hand. . . .So the king of Assyria turned back and did not remain there in the land' (2 Kings 15: 19,20).

The biblical verses preceding those just quoted mention that Menahem seized the throne of Israel late in the reign of Azariah of Judah. It is interesting that Tiglath-Pileser encountered, as a prominent figure in a Syrian coalition, a certain Azriyau of Yaudi, who had support as far north as Hamath. Some have identified this Azriyau with the king of Judah, assuming that Azariah had joined (or even forged) a south-Syrian coalition of anti-Assyrian states; but, interesting though it may be for biblical history, this has little bearing on the reconstruction of Tiglath-Pileser's strategy.

From 737 to 735 Tiglath-Pileser was engaged in counter-Urartu measures further east, as far as the land of the Medes, east of the Zagros in north-west Iran. The withdrawal of the main Assyrian army from Syria gave a misleading impression of Assyrian ability to maintain its authority. Anti-Assyrian coalitions were formed, notably between Damascus and states in Palestine, though Ahaz of Judah firmly stood out (possibly at the advice of the politically alert prophet Isaiah) and called on his suzerain Tiglath-Pileser for support. Tiglath-Pileser put down the trouble without difficulty, turning Damascus and outlying parts of Israel into provinces, though leaving the central part of Israel under a native king, Hoshea, installed in place of the rebellious Pekah. Far from bringing all conquered areas under direct provincial rule as a matter of policy, Tiglath-Pileser was still obviously endeavouring to retain vassal kingdoms wherever possible.

Trouble with Chaldaeans

Tiglath-Pileser now had problems in a fresh area. Passing mention has been made of Chaldaeans disrupting Babylonia. These were tribal peoples, having points of similarity with the Aramaeans. They had entered south Babylonia at around 1000, establishing their main settlements in the vast swamp areas in southernmost Babylonia – the famous Iraqi marshes. Subsequently they began to move up the Euphrates and to attempt to dominate some of the ancient cities. In 734 the paramount chief of the Chaldaean tribe of Bit-Amukkanni, a certain Ukin-zer, occupied Babylon and seized the throne. Babylonia was split in its allegiance. To the non-Chaldaean peoples, their northern neighbour represented the old stable order of things against the disruptive Chaldaeans, and when Tiglath-Pileser responded to the situation by sending military forces, much of the urban population of Babylonia, and even some of the non-Chaldaean tribal peoples such as Puqudu (Pekod, mentioned in the books of

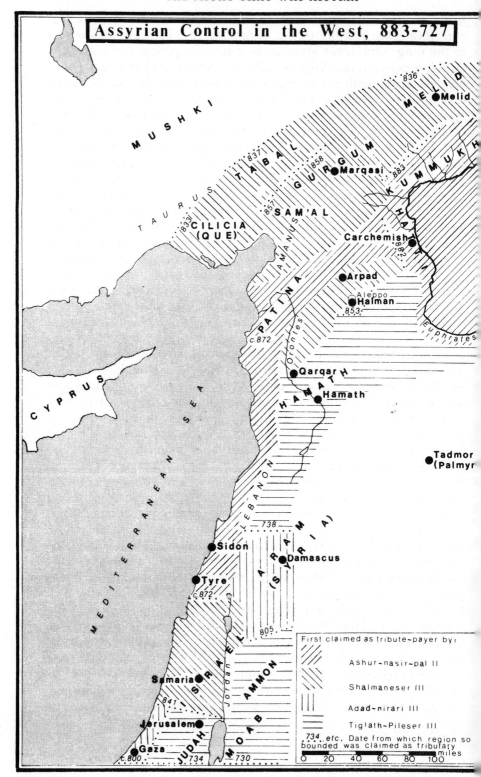

Assyrian Control in the West, 883-727

MUSHKI

MELID
●Melid *836*

TABAL *837*

GURGUM *858*
●Marqasi

TAURUS *833*

CILICIA
(QUE)

SAM'AL *857*

KUMMUKH *883*

Carchemish ●*882*

●Arpad

Aleppo
●Halman
853

AMANUS

PATINA
c.872

Orontes

Qarqar ●*H*

Hamath ●Hamath

A
M
A
T

Euphrates

CYPRUS

MEDITERRANEAN SEA

Tadmor
(Palmyr

LEBANON

A
R
A
M

(SYRIA)

738

●Sidon

●Damascus

●Tyre
c.872

805

I
S
R
A
E
L

AMMON

Jordan

Samaria●
841

Jerusalem ●

JUDAH

MOAB

●Gaza
c.800   *734*   N   *730*

First claimed as tribute-payer by:

/// Ashur-nasir-pal II

\\\ Shalmaneser III

||| Adad-nirari III

=== Tiglath-Pileser III

734. etc. Date from which region so
bounded was claimed as tributary

miles
0   20   40   60   80   100

Jeremiah and Ezekiel), welcomed this. We have some of the actual correspondence relating to the campaign, in which generals report to the king. One letter gives an account of a parley at the gates of Babylon between the Assyrian officials and the people within, with the Assyrians deliberately trying to appeal over the heads of the rebel leaders directly to the populace, in exactly the manner of the interview between the Assyrian Rabshakeh and the Jews at the siege of Jerusalem in 701, reported in the Bible (2 Kings 18: 17–36). But the Chaldaean position was so powerful that the settlement of Babylonia cost Tiglath-Pileser three years. The eventual Assyrian success owed as much to diplomacy as to military force. Amongst the royal correspondence from this period are several letters showing that Tiglath-Pileser was in touch with various Chaldaean leaders, including a certain Marduk-apil-iddina of the tribe Bit-Yakin, who was the Merodach-baladan mentioned as negotiating with Hezekiah of Judah in 2 Kings 18: 12 at a rather later period. The reaction of the prophet Isaiah to the latter incident shows that he did not trust Merodach-baladan. Isaiah had good reason: Merodach-baladan was a double-crosser. Extant Assyrian letters now show that, at the time of Ukin-zer's rebellion, Merodach-baladan was secretly accepting payment from Tiglath-Pileser to stab his fellow Chaldaeans in the back.

The Assyrian tactics in taking Babylon are known in some detail. The attack was directed from the province of Arrapkha (Kirkuk), the Assyrian army moving south down the east side of the Tigris and entering Babylonia by crossing the river somewhere near Baghdad. Loyal tribesmen guarded the routes while the Assyrian army moved westwards to the north Babylonian cities held by the Chaldaean rebels. Babylon was taken, and Ukin-zer fled south to his own tribal capital deep in the southern marshes. Thither an Assyrian army pursued him, devastating his territory and that of his tribal allies, though leaders such as Merodach-baladan who had come to terms with Assyria had their territories spared. When matters were settled, after three years, Babylonia was placed under Assyrian administrators. Subsequently Tiglath-Pileser 'took the hand of the god [Marduk]' (that is, escorted him) in the New Year (Akitu) ceremony at Babylon, thereby being formally invested with kingship over Babylonia, an office which no Assyrian king had held for more than four centuries. The priesthood ceremonially recognized Tiglath-Pileser as the gods' representative and the rightful king of Babylon by offering him a share in a sacramental meal of the gods. This was in 729. Tiglath-Pileser died two years later, leaving Assyria with an empire which (taking account of its vassals) extended from the Persian Gulf to the borders of Egypt and ran up through north Syria into Cilicia and Anatolia.

Assyrian campaigns under Tiglath-Pileser had gained control of the Palestine coast as far south as what in modern times we call the Gaza strip. This was a manifest threat to Egypt. Also, the Assyrians had interfered with Egyptian trade by placing an embargo upon the export of timber from the Lebanon to Egypt. These factors were behind Egyptian attempts to organize an anti-Assyrian movement in Palestine and south Syria in the following years. The most dramatic consequence of this was the Assyrian siege and capture of Samaria, the capital of what was left of Israel, well-known from the Bible (2 Kings 17: 3–5).

The Accession of Sargon

Sargon II, who claimed to be a son of Tiglath-Pileser, came to the throne after an insurrection in the ancient capital Ashur against his briefly reigning predecessor, Shalmaneser V (727–722), who had attempted to impose forced labour there, contrary to all precedent. The power of Assyrian kings had limits. In recognition of the support Sargon had received in reaching the throne, he confirmed freedom from certain taxes and obligations not only to the people of Ashur but also to all the temples of Assyria, thus imposing a substantial constraint upon the royal finances.

Not unexpectedly, the insurrection in Assyria awakened an echo in other parts of the empire, and Sargon was immediately faced with trouble in Babylonia.

Earlier we met the kingdom of Elam in south-west Iran. Late in the ninth century we begin to get mention of Elamites combining with Chaldaean tribes in clashes with Assyria; the fact that Elam's territories adjoined the Chaldaean area of southern Babylonia gave the two peoples a common interest. At the beginning of Sargon's reign, Merodach-baladan secured formal alliance with Elam, and with this backing seized the kingship of Babylonia in 721, which he claimed by right of descent from a grandfather who had made himself king earlier in the century. As on the occasion of the Ukin-zer rebellion, the Assyrian army moved down to Babylonia east of the Tigris, but this time their further advance was blocked by Merodach-baladan's allies, the Elamite army, at Der. Although Sargon claimed 'I smashed the forces of Humbanigash king of Elam', in fact any further major action against Merodach-baladan was checked for a decade.

Sargon was prevented from immediately devoting more resources by problems elsewhere. One such area was Syria, where Hamath attempted another anti-Assyrian coalition, in alliance with Arpad and Samaria. This was easily put down, Hamath being brought under direct provincial rule. The Bible also alludes to later operations by Sargon in the coastal areas of south Palestine (Isaiah 20: 1–6); though it should be said that, dramatic as these may have appeared from the Jewish capital, Jerusalem, they were of little significance to the imperial power.

The Urartian problem; the final solution

As with Tiglath-Pileser, Sargon's main problems were in the north. Urartu, still a rival for the trade routes through Cilicia and Anatolia, was now extending her control over the region south of Lake Urmia in north-west Iran (Azerbaijan), important to Assyria both for horse supplies and for the routes from further east. Letters from provincial administrators to the king at this time are full of references to clashes with Urartu, and attempts by Urartu to push southwards in the Zagros; some of these letters show the employment of Urartian spies, in a very efficient Assyrian intelligence system.

Sargon decided upon a raid into Urartu itself, a hazardous operation in view of the difficulty of the terrain. Frequent border clashes with Urartu culminated in a well-planned major campaign in the summer of 714, on which we have detailed information, from a report by Sargon in the form of a letter to the national god Ashur. Leaving his base Calah, Sargon headed east to cross the Upper and Lower Zab rivers and so into the Zagros. Either Sargon himself was a poet, or there was a scribe of poetic parts in his entourage, for the writer of the report distils into his verse a living echo of the awe with which he responded to the majestic scenery:

> High mountains, where trees of all kinds grew entwined;
> The midst of the mountains chaos, their passes stirring fear;
> Where over all stretched shade, like a forest of cedars;
> Where he who treads their paths sees no ray of the sun.

A poet might bow in wonder before the mountains, but Sargon ensured that he had sappers in his army to make them passable:

> I equipped my sappers with strong copper picks, and they shivered the crags of steep mountains to fragments as though limestone, and made a good way.

Although the text says 'copper', it probably meant its alloy, bronze.

Once east of the Zagros, Sargon headed for the Mannaean

country. He was now south of Lake Urmia. The poor Mannaeans (the Minni of Jeremiah 51: 27) were in the unfortunate position of being a buffer between two powerful neighbours, and had several times suffered, at a change of control of the area, from having accepted the prior regime. The Mannaean ruler at once submitted to Sargon, though his principal neighbour had thrown in his lot with Rusa, king of Urartu.

The approach to Urartu west of Lake Urmia was blocked by a powerful line of fortresses; Sargon therefore took his army up the eastern side of the lake to turn the main anti-Assyrian defences. By the time Sargon made contact with the main Urartian army, defending a mountain pass south of Tabriz, he was separated from his home base by about three hundred miles, including the whole of the Zagros, much of it very difficult terrain. His troops were near to mutiny, and he comments:

> The harassed troops of Ashur, who had come a long way, very weary and slow to respond, who had crossed and re-crossed sheer mountains innumerable, of great trouble for ascent and descent, their morale turned mutinous. I could give no ease to their weariness, no water to quench their thirst; I could set up no camp, nor fix defences.

Unable for the moment to rely on the discipline of his main army, Sargon in his battle-chariot led a furious charge with his household cavalry – whose commanding officer is mentioned by name – on one wing of the opposing forces. The enemy line gave. The main Assyrian army, given fresh heart by Sargon's spectacular attack, fell upon the Urartian coalition, breaking their lines and sowing panic. The Urartian general led his own force in a disciplined retreat, but the contingents of his allies, now a leaderless rabble, fled in disorder over the mountains, where great numbers perished from exposure. The defeat of the Urartian army was a shock to Urartian morale, and Sargon was able to move round the northern end of Lake Urmia, westwards into the Zagros again, and then penetrate, almost unopposed, deep into Urartian territory. Rusa abandoned his capital Turushpa (probably unnecessarily, as it was highly defensible and Sargon was ill-placed for a protracted siege) and took to the mountains. There, according to Sargon, he eventually died of grief, although a later (and probably less reliable) text of Sargon says he committed suicide.

The return line of Sargon's campaign is still a matter of much dispute. Some think he went right round Lake Van, others that he headed back for Assyria by one of several possible routes south of

Lake Van. What we are certain of, because Sargon explicitly tells us (or rather, the god Ashur), is that, before leaving, the Assyrians ravaged Urartu wherever they went, looting and burning towns, setting growing crops on fire, destroying gardens, opening and spoiling granaries, smashing down dams so that the waters of productive canals ran to waste in swamps, and leaving pasture lands as bare earth. They cut down trees – it was all one whether they were orchard trees, trees planted to set off a palace, or stretches of natural forest – and burnt them.

In the course of his return to Assyria, Sargon left his main army and led a column of a thousand cavalry over difficult routes to a city, Musasir, part of Urartu, deep in the mountains somewhere north-west of Rowanduz, which (trusting in its remoteness) had neglected to make formal submission to Sargon. Musasir was the main shrine of the Urartian national god, Haldia, where the king of Urartu was customarily crowned. The sacredness of Musasir and its royal associations had made it into a vast national treasure house, and Sargon catalogues the enormous booty he took away – precious metals, precious stones, furniture inlaid with gold and silver, gold and silver vessels of many kinds, ceremonial weapons of precious metals, bronze vessels from small pots to great vats, statues, and ornaments. Many of the terms for the objects we do not understand, and even the Assyrian scribes recording them found some of these Urartian art treasures strange, commenting 'their names are not easy to write'. Musasir was formally incorporated into Assyria, but was too remote to be held effectively after Sargon's departure.

Sargon's response to the Urartian problem was not only military. He also used diplomacy to gain allies; we have, for example, a letter giving details of negotiations for friendship with Mita of Mushki. Mita stood across the route to the west, which gave his state great wealth (he was the Midas of the golden touch of Greek tradition) and, doubtless for his commercial interests, maintained relations with both Urartu and north Syria. In north Syria, Carchemish had attempted to secure the active support of Mita for an anti-Assyrian coalition. It was to neutralize such threats to Assyrian interests that Sargon negotiated with Mita, pointing up his diplomatic overtures with demonstrations of military might in north Syria and beyond.

Sargon in Babylonia

With Urartu crippled, Sargon could now turn to the festering problem of Babylonia. His operations there, begun in 710, lasted until 707. Sargon, copying the earlier tactics of Tiglath-Pileser in moving south on the east side of the Tigris, gained control of the

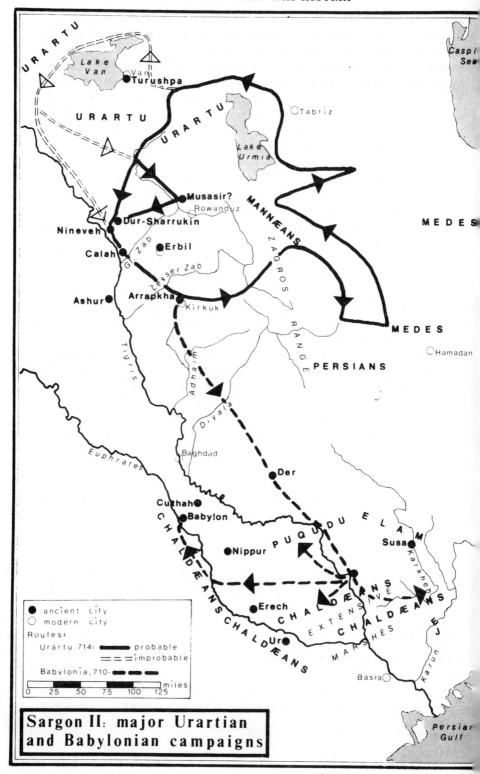

Sargon II: major Urartian and Babylonian campaigns

whole length of the river right down to the Karkheh, thereby driving a wedge between Merodach-baladan and potential Elamite allies. He then turned to Babylonia proper. Merodach-baladan claimed in inscriptions to have protected the interests of ancient Babylonian cities, but a sizeable part of the populations of those cities may have questioned this. We hear later of prisoners from the northern cities being released from Merodach-baladan's capital, of confiscated lands being restored, and of banditry against trading caravans having to be suppressed. There was thus a strong faction within the north Babylonian cities very ready for Assyrian intervention; and some of these cities, the capital amongst them, opened their gates and welcomed Sargon, who was formally recognized as legitimate ruler of Babylon by participation in sacred rites.

Meanwhile Merodach-baladan had escaped from Babylon, and after attempting a stand further south withdrew to his tribal area in the southern marshes. Besieged in his tribal capital, he bought off Sargon by a heavy payment in 707 and was left unmolested in control of his tribal territory. We shall meet him again.

The end was now near for Sargon – perhaps brought nearer by his crippling of Urartu. In the eighth century a new wave of very mobile Indo-Europeans – the Cimmerians, Gomer of the Bible – were thrusting into Anatolia from the north, down the east side of the Black Sea. Even before Sargon's major attack on Urartu these Cimmerians had effected serious devastation on Urartu's northern provinces. The further dislocation resulting from the ravaging of south Urartu by Sargon left Urartu unable to stem the invaders, and the Cimmerians erupted across the width of Anatolia. Archaeological evidence hints at a raid on Assyria itself; they certainly threatened Assyrian interests in north Syria. Sargon took his army against the Cimmerians in that area and, on one interpretation of obscure evidence, died in battle. Certainly he departed from the scene in 705, and at the same time the Cimmerians moved on into the interior of Asia Minor.

The building of Fort Sargon

Sargon was one of the Assyrian kings who moved to a new administrative capital; though he does not tell us why, we can make an informed guess. In the ancient world, the citizens of major cities, particularly capital cities, quickly drew special privileges to themselves. The king had to rely on his officers in the capital, rewarding them with exemptions from tax and corvée and with land grants, and in a feudal system such privileges could go well down the line. They tended to become hereditary, so that, adding in various officials of the temples, influential from their place in the state rituals, a powerful entrenched group would soon emerge, able to outface the king himself. Calah had been the administrative and military capital for nearly a century and a half, ample time for the rise there of a group able to resist the king; indeed, the ruler Sargon claimed as his father, Tiglath-Pileser III, had attained the throne from the position of governor of Calah. Sargon himself knew from personal experience the risk to the royal authority from the vested interests of the ancient cities, for his accession followed an insurrection against his predecessor by the people of Ashur – whose support he had to repay by confirmation of their traditional privileges. This, then, was one factor in his creating a new capital, Dur-Sharrukin ('Fort Sargon') some twelve miles north-east of Nineveh, today represented by the site of Khorsabad.

The second factor was strategic. The foothills of the Taurus begin less than thirty miles north of Nineveh. Beyond those hills was Urartu, the only power which now could threaten Assyria, and at any time the army of Urartu might (until Sargon destroyed the threat in 714) come snaking down from one of the passes on to the Nineveh plains. The site chosen for Dur-Sharrukin stands sentinel between Nineveh and the nearest pass emerging from the foothills; its tactical importance is confirmed by the fact that a site near Dur-Sharrukin was used as a main base by the Iraqi army at the time of the revolt of the Kurds in the same northern mountains around A.D. 1970.

Sennacherib

Sargon's successor, his son Sennacherib (704–681), came to the throne as an experienced administrator and soldier. He knew, none better, the problems on the northern frontier, for he had held command there, and his recognition of the new situation, in which Urartu was not only in no position to harm Assyrian interests but was positively needed as a bulwark in the north, led to rapprochement with Urartu.

Nineveh, world capital

Sennacherib's first work, and his most enduring, was another shift of capital. Sargon's new city, Dur-Sharrukin, placed to guard the main population centre Nineveh, continued in use as a fortress to that end, but it was Nineveh itself which, rebuilt and brought to unparalleled splendour, was now adopted as capital; such it remained in historical fact until the overthrow of the Assyrian empire, and in tradition for ever. Sennacherib threw a huge wall around the city, nearly eight miles long, with fifteen major gates. A classical author, Diodorus of Sicily, transmitted a tradition that the walls of Nineveh were of sufficient width for three chariots to drive on them abreast, and in the nineteenth century A.D. was laughed at for his tale; but the remains of the walls today provide ample space for two large saloon cars side by side. Within the walls, Sennacherib cut new streets, enlarged squares, diverted water-courses, built great stone flood-defences to protect his new palace, and around the palace laid out a great park 'like Mount Amanus, wherein were set all kinds of plants and fruit trees such as grow in the mountains and in Chaldaea'. Beyond these botanical gardens were orchards. Subsequently Senna-cherib laid out further extensions, with 'all the plants of the land of Syria, myrrh plants, which grew more luxuriantly than in their native habitat, and all kinds of mountain vines'. All this needed a great deal of water in the long hot summer of Nineveh. Although the Tigris then flowed at the foot of Nineveh, it lies too low in its banks to be conveniently usable during the summer for major irrigation; but there is another more manageable source of perennial water. A minor river, the Khosr, joins the Tigris at Nineveh and is much better placed for irrigation. But the Khosr has the disadvantage of an irregular flow, which reduces to a minimum when it is most needed. Sennacherib dealt with this by major engineering works, tapping several mountain streams up to thirty miles away and using their waters as feeders for the Khosr. The remains of some of these works can still be traced. One source of water for Nineveh, at a place generally known (wrongly) as Bavian, has inscriptions and reliefs on a cliff alongside and still makes a delightful picnic spot; the presence of the reliefs suggests that it was a spot Sennacherib himself enjoyed visiting to escape the summer heat of the Nineveh plain. Other remains of Sennacherib's engineering works include an aqueduct, over three hundred yards long, twenty-four yards wide, and containing half a million tons of rock, built to carry the water over the bed of a wadi. Sennacherib undertook corresponding engi-neering projects to improve the water supply of Erbil, the other great city of north Assyria; Calah's water supply had been taken care of when Ashur-nasir-pal first built it.

More Chaldaean trouble

The work on Nineveh occupied most of Sennacherib's reign. Mean-while there were political troubles in Babylonia. There was always a problem about Babylonia: should it be given the maximum independence, with its own sub-king subject to Assyrian overlordship, or should it be wholly annexed and directly ruled by the king of Assyria? There were pro-Babylonian and anti-Babylonian advisers at the Assyrian court, and at different times the Assyrian kings showed adherence to one party or the other. Sennacherib's father Sargon and his son Esarhaddon both favoured a gentle handling of Babylonia, with the greatest possible consideration for Babylonian nationalist sensibilities. Sennacherib may have had an initial inclination to follow his father's policy, for it was two years before he underwent the religious ceremony that made him formally king of Babylonia. But by this time factors had begun to operate which eventually led Sennacherib into the harshest possible action against Babylonia. By 703 the old enemy, Merodach-baladan, had organized the Chaldaeans and some Aramaean tribes, and won assurance of Elamite support; confidently, he raised Babylonia in rebellion. Confusion ensued. A Babylonian governor, perhaps a puppet of Sennacherib, occupied the throne for a month, only to be removed by Merodach-baladan. Sennacherib reacted vigorously, led his army south and besieged and took Cuthah, Merodach-baladan's main base. Merodach-baladan, more politician than soldier, fled southwards, leaving Sennacherib to enter Babylon. The Assyrian army was sent south to search (fruitlessly) for the rebel leader (see plate 3A) and to defortify and devastate the whole of the Aramaean and Chaldaean areas – virtually all southern Babylonia from Nippur to the Persian Gulf:

> In the course of my campaign, I besieged, conquered, and carried away the spoil of. . .a total of 33 strong walled towns of the Bit-Dakkuri tribe, together with 250 surrounding villages;. . .8 strong walled towns of the Bit-Sa'alli tribe, together with 120 surrounding villages;. . .39 strong walled towns of the Bit-Amukkanni tribe, together with 350 surrounding villages;. . .8 strong walled towns of the Bit-Yakin tribe, together with 100 surrounding villages; altogether 88 strong walled towns of Chaldaea, together with 820 surrounding villages. I let my troops eat up the grain and dates in their palm-groves, and their harvest in the plain. I tore down and demolished (their towns) and set light to them, and turned them into forgotten mounds.

Given this sharp lesson, Chaldaea was left under the administration of Assyrian officials, with a native Babylonian nobleman, Bel-ibni – brought up, so Sennacherib tells us, at the Assyrian court – installed as puppet king of Babylonia.

The siege of Jerusalem

Assyria now (701) faced rebellion elsewhere. Hezekiah of Judah, possibly subverted by Merodach-baladan, who is mentioned in the Bible (2 Kings 20: 12) as sending an embassy to him, had joined an insurrection of coastal cities, backed by Egypt. Sennacherib's army entered Palestine, dealt with the coastal cities, repelled the Egyptians, overran Judah, and put Hezekiah's capital, Jerusalem, under siege, as the Bible (2 Kings 18: 17ff.) and Sennacherib's inscriptions agree. Sennacherib's account of the affair has been quoted *ad nauseam* in books on Old Testament history, but for anyone who happens not to have met it, this is what he said:

> As to Hezekiah the Judaean, who did not submit to my yoke, I besieged and captured 46 of his strong walled towns with innumerable surrounding villages, by consolidating ramps to bring up battering rams (to the walls), by infantry attack, mines, breaches, and siege engines. . . .He himself I shut up inside Jerusalem, his royal city, like a caged bird.

Hezekiah paid tribute in token of submission, and Jerusalem was spared – miraculously, from the Bible's point of view; more soberly, because the return of the Assyrian army to Mesopotamia was demanded by a deteriorating situation in Babylonia where, with the withdrawal of the Assyrian army, Merodach-baladan had resumed his intrigues. Bel-ibni proved incapable of maintaining effective government, and in 700 was deposed and replaced by Ashur-nadin-shum, a younger son of Sennacherib. The Assyrian army made another punitive expedition into Chaldaean territory, and Merodach-baladan fled to Elam and is heard of no more. On his first appearance in history over thirty years before, he was already the respected chief of a major tribe, so that he was now at least in his fifties and possibly a good deal older; thus a natural death is likely. But there remained other anti-Assyrian factions and leaders in Babylonia, with Elam, now well-organized and attempting expansion, increasingly giving support.

War with Elam

The Chaldaeans had already shown themselves seriously disruptive to the interests of Assyria and the north Babylonian cities during the previous four decades. With Elamites supporting them and providing a sanctuary from Assyrian punitive action, they were likely to become uncontrollable. Sennacherib decided to deal with the problem by striking directly at Elam, and in 694 made an attack by sea across the Persian Gulf. This was a major operation in logistics. He had ships built in Nineveh, sailed down the Tigris by Phoenician sailors, transferred overland on rollers to a canal joining the Euphrates, and then sailed to the Gulf. There, Assyrian troops were embarked and transported to the Elamite coast where, despite opposition, they secured a bridgehead. From here they captured and looted a number of southern Elamite cities, though they came nowhere near the capital, Susa.

Elam responded with tactics which caught Sennacherib unprepared. Instead of defending in the south, Elam made a raid across the Tigris into north Babylonia. With this element of surprise, the Elamites both cut Assyrian communications and captured the son Sennacherib had installed as king of Babylonia, installing their own puppet in his place. It looks as though the Assyrian intelligence system was less effective in relation to Elam than it had earlier been against Urartu. But the invading Elamite force was no match in the field for the Assyrians, and withdrew after an engagement with Sennacherib's returning army.

To prevent a recurrence of the Elamite intervention, Sennacherib in late 693 mounted an attack on Elam through the province of Der, through which Elam's raid on north Babylonia had been made. Another claimant to the Babylonian throne then raised a rebellion, and sought alliance with the Elamites. In consequence, a considerable alliance of Elamites, Chaldaeans and their supporters faced Sennacherib's army in 691 on the Tigris, somewhere north of Babylon. Sennacherib claimed a victory; but a Babylonian chronicle says that Sennacherib was forced to retreat, leading one scholar who has discussed this question to stigmatize Sennacherib's account of the battle as 'a prodigious falsehood'. This may be going too far. The site of the action cannot have been significantly south of the Diyala, which had long been claimed as Assyria's south-eastern border, and the fact that the Elamite army, heading north, faced the Assyrian army there, meant that Elam was threatening an invasion of Assyria. The success of Sennacherib's army in that bloody battle was to maul the Elamite–Chaldaean coalition so severely that, though they stood on the border, they could not pass. From Sennacherib's point of view, with Assyrian territory under imminent threat, this was indeed a victory. Yet in the bloody engagement described by Sennacherib, with vicious hand-to-hand fighting, his units also must have suffered heavy losses, leaving them in no position to move effectively into Babylonia. The necessary return to base was, from the Babylonian point of view, a retreat.

The sack of Babylon

The Assyrian army had certainly not suffered a major reverse, for by summer 690 it was back in Babylonia, with Babylon in serious plight. A legal document, so far published only in translation, reads:

> The land was gripped by a siege, famine, hunger, want. . .Two qa of barley sold for one shekel of silver [about £1 for a pint measure, in modern terms]. The city gates were barred, and a person could not go out. . . .The corpses of men, with no one to bury them, filled the squares of Babylon.

Fifteen months later, Babylon fell to Sennacherib's army. The Babylonian who had recently held the throne briefly escaped from Babylon but was quickly caught and killed, his captor receiving from Sennacherib the dead usurper's weight in silver. As to Babylon itself, Sennacherib, with his attitude to that sacred centre of religion and culture changed by a decade and a half of opposition and the loss of his son, ruthlessly wrecked the city. He gave his troops general licence to loot; they robbed the temples, carried off the divine statues, razed houses, temples, city walls, and dug canals across it to destroy its very foundations.

For the remainder of Sennacherib's life, a further eight years, Babylonia officially had no king of its own, although *de facto* Sennacherib himself was king, and was so regarded in a Babylonian King List.

Sennacherib's sack of Babylon was quite understandable but not at all a good idea. We have had indications that there were pro-Assyrian and anti-Assyrian factions in Babylonia; in the same way, in Assyria there were those who held Babylonian culture in high regard as well as those who wished to see it destroyed. Sennacherib's action polarized these feelings within Assyria. There were factions even within the royal family, and Sennacherib died in Babylon in 681, murdered, according to the Bible (2 Kings 19: 37), by two of his sons, one of whom has now been identified as a certain Arad-Mulišši, whose name is corrupted in the biblical text into Adrammelech.

8

Zenith and Collapse

The Royal Succession

The son who succeeded Sennacherib was not one of the patricides but Esarhaddon (680–669). The circumstances of his succession illustrate several features of Assyrian society. He was the son whom Sennacherib had designated to succeed him, as he tells us in his inscriptions; this cannot have been a false claim, since the heir apparent lived in a special palace, so that the royal intentions for the succession would be known to all. Be it noted that succession was by nomination: the first-born did not automatically become king. But even the ruling monarch did not possess unfettered control over the succession. His nomination had to be ratified by decision of the gods (meaning, in practice, in view of the possibility of manipulating oracles, decision by the priesthood) and accepted on oath by the royal family and representatives of the people. Esarhaddon's inscription tells us the procedure:

> Although I was younger brother to my older brothers, yet at the command of Ashur, Sin, Shamash, Bel, Nabu, Ishtar of Nineveh and Ishtar of Erbil, my father who begot me truly promoted me in the assembly of my brothers, saying: 'This is the son of my succession'. When he enquired of Shamash and Adad [the oracle gods] by divination, they answered him a firm 'yes', saying 'He is your successor'. Giving proper respect to their solemn word, he brought together the people of Assyria small and great, my brothers, the seed of my father's house; and before Ashur, Sin, Shamash, Nabu, the gods of Assyria, the gods dwelling in heaven and earth, he made them swear their solemn word to protect my succession. In a favourable month, on a favourable day, according to their [the gods'] exalted command I joyfully entered the Palace of the Succession, the awe-inspiring place wherein is the essence of kingship.

Things did not work out quite as Sennacherib had planned. Esarhaddon had to fight for his succession.

When the murder of Sennacherib occurred, Esarhaddon was in

command of an army somewhere in the west. One might guess that the assassination was timed to ensure the absence of the crown prince. Esarhaddon must have kept his army on instant battle alert, for he was able to move off towards Assyria almost immediately, without pause for inspections or commissariat arrangements. His only delay was to apply to the principal gods of Assyria for an oracle, duly given –

> Go! Hold not back!
> We go at your side.
> We slay your foes.

– a message to make Esarhaddon's own army confident in his cause and to sow doubts among the troops of his rivals. The regicides' army met him in the region of the Upper Habur. There was a sharp engagement. The morale of the regicides' troops, involved in civil war against one whom they knew as the crown prince endorsed by the gods, was low, and in the middle of the battle the word spread 'This is our king!'. The regicides' troops went over to Esarhaddon, the representatives of the people of Assyria paid homage, and the throne was securely his.

Divine favour for Babylon

Esarhaddon manifestly belonged to the pro-Babylonian party within Assyria, and devoted considerable effort and resources to undoing the devastation his father had wrought in Babylon. There was the initial problem that under his father the gods were believed to have placed the city under curse for seventy years. This interdiction had to be undone. This kind of situation – the explaining away of a change in the divine plan – is one in which the theologians come into their own. It was explained that although earlier the gods had decreed for Babylon seventy years (in cuneiform 𒐋𒌋) of sterility, yet now the merciful Marduk, chief god of the city, had modified the curse by transposing the ciphers 𒐋𒌋 to read 𒌋𒐋, that is, eleven years, so terminating the ban on Babylon in 680, Esarhaddon's first year.

Cut through with water channels, Babylon had become a place of reed beds and thickets. Esarhaddon diverted the water and cut down the vegetation that had been taking the city over. Then he proceeded to rebuild the city walls and the great temple of Marduk, Esagila. He himself carried a basket on his head like a common labourer and moulded a brick. He resettled the citizens who had fled, and returned them their lands. He reinstated the citizens' privileges and tax exemptions. He re-endowed the cultic offerings of Esagila, and reinstalled the many classes of temple functionaries. Likewise in other cities of Babylonia, citizens had their old privileges restored.

This policy of favour towards Babylonia served Assyria's interests. Though the Chaldaean areas initially gave some further trouble, Esarhaddon, after meeting this firmly, was able to replace hostile chiefs by others from their tribes willing to accept Assyrian vassaldom.

The ascendant Medes

Further north in Iran, Esarhaddon paid increasing attention to the Medes, assisting their stability by giving some of their chiefs military assistance against rebel movements. The Medes, still basically tribal in organization though they had cities, were widespread in northern Iran. They were evidently very powerful, and to Esarhaddon would have appeared as useful potential allies against Elam and a second bulwark, alongside Urartu, against new peoples – two of whom we know as Cimmerians and Scythians (present in north Iran as well as in Anatolia) – pushing south out of Russia. Esarhaddon's recognition of the Medes' growing political importance is reflected in treaties with vassal Median princes, which contained an obligation upon them to support his arrangements for the royal succession after his death. Briefly, the arrangement was that two of his sons were nominated by Esarhaddon and approved by the gods as kings in succession to him, respectively of Assyria and of Babylonia. This was formalized at an assembly in Nineveh in 672, one of the two favoured sons, Ashurbanipal, being proclaimed crown prince of Assyria, and the other, Shamash-shum-ukin, crown prince of Babylonia. Provincial governors and vassals were put under oath to support the settlement, the terms of the obligation being:

> When Esarhaddon King of Assyria dies, you will seat Ashurbanipal the Crown Prince upon the royal throne; he will exercise the kingship and lordship of Assyria over you. You will protect him in country and in town; you will fight to the death for him. . . .Should Esarhaddon king of Assyria die whilst his sons are minors, you will help Ashurbanipal the Crown Prince to take the throne of Assyria and you will help to seat Shamash-shum-ukin, his coequal brother, the Crown Prince of Babylon, upon the throne of Babylon. . .

Doubtless Esarhaddon hoped to preclude a recurrence of the civil war that threatened his own accession. We shall see that in the long term his plan failed.

Pax Assyriaca in the west

In the north-west, Assyria had gradually been pushing its control beyond north Syria and Cilicia into Asia Minor, but this advance now received a check from the Cimmerians and Scythians (the Gomer and Ashkenaz of the Bible). With Cilicia unsettled by this development, Sidon, one of the Phoenician cities linked to Cilicia by common maritime interests, miscalculated Assyrian strength and rebelled; it was sacked and its territory made into an Assyrian province. But Assyria still preferred indirect rule where possible, for the king of the neighbouring Phoenician maritime area of Tyre, who had remained loyal to Assyria in the rising, was left in possession, with some of the outlying settlements of Sidon made over to his kingdom.

Apart from Sidon, Syria and Palestine gave no trouble to Assyria, and Esarhaddon was able to call on a large group of kings of the petty states of the area for materials for the rebuilding of his palace at Nineveh. The kings he lists include those of Tyre, Judah, Edom, Moab, Gaza, Askelon, Ekron, Byblos, Ammon, Ashdod, as well as some from a land 'Yadnana in the midst of the sea', which was probably Cyprus, now accepted as part of the Assyrian empire. The king of Judah was named as Manasseh, and it is interesting that the late biblical book of 2 Chronicles has a tradition in 33: 11–13 that Manasseh was taken away to Babylon by the 'commanders of the army of the king of Assyria' but afterwards allowed back. The Book of Chronicles was not composed until Babylon had superseded Nineveh as an imperial capital, which may explain the mention of Babylon in place of Nineveh, and the tradition may stem from Manasseh's having visited Assyria to comply with Esarhaddon's demands for his building operations.

East and south of the states of Transjordan – Ammon, Moab, Edom, firmly in Assyrian control – was the desert, with its Arab tribes. These tribes also had their importance for Assyria, in two respects particularly. The Arabs controlled the important trade in incense and spices from south Arabia, and it was the Arabs alone who could safely negotiate the Sinai desert between south Palestine and Egypt. Assyria had been in contact with desert Arabs at least since the reign of Tiglath-Pileser III, gradually extending influence into the desert. Esarhaddon continued this policy, increasing Assyrian control by intervening between rival contenders for tribal leadership to support the candidate willing to accept Assyrian suzerainty.

The invasion of Egypt

With Palestine and Transjordan firmly in Assyrian control, and with the desert Arabs under pro-Assyrian leaders, Esarhaddon now executed a major extension of the empire. There had long been trading contacts between Assyria and Egypt, and since the reign of Tiglath-Pileser III, when Assyria gained control of the Palestinian coast right down to Gaza, there had nominally been a frontier with Egypt, albeit with a considerable desert buffer before Egypt proper began. Esarhaddon's aim was to attempt to secure direct control of Egypt. One factor in this may have been the rise in Egypt of an aggressive new dynasty of southern origin, which was attempting to increase its influence among the coastal cities of Palestine, a policy illustrated by a revolt of Tyre, hitherto a loyal vassal of Esarhaddon.

The attack upon Egypt began in 675 and occupied several years of difficulties and set-backs. An inscription narrating the final and successful attack in 671 gives some idea of the problems. The king speaks of advancing to Rapihu, 'by the side of the wadi of Egypt [today, El Arish], where there is no river'; he therefore had to draw water for his troops from a well by ropes and chains. His transport had to be camels, made available by his allies, the kings of the Arabs. He found the going really nasty – fifteen days through sand dunes, two days through a region with (so he says) two-headed deadly snakes, and still more space to traverse – a good month and a half in all, if the figures have been correctly transmitted. He comments that the god Marduk came to his aid and kept his troops alive, a clear indication of times when he did not think it humanly possible that his army could win through. Once within Egypt proper, he routed the army of the Pharaoh Tarqa, and then besieged and took Memphis, the capital nearly twenty miles south of present-day Cairo. At this success, the princes of all of fragmented Lower Egypt hurried to acknowledge Esarhaddon's suzerainty. Assyrian officials were appointed in the native princedoms, and Esarhaddon proclaimed himself king of Lower and Upper Egypt and Ethiopia. But this was a hollow claim. No sooner had the main Assyrian army withdrawn from the country than Tarqa returned to re-take Memphis. Esarhaddon set out in 669 on a further Egyptian campaign, but died on the way.

Ashurbanipal

Esarhaddon's plans for the succession went into operation, with Ashurbanipal remaining in Nineveh and Shamash-shum-ukin in Babylon. But both kingdoms had their problems, and the tensions these produced eventually combined to bring about civil war.

Our knowledge of the reign of Ashurbanipal is patchy. Although he has left extensive inscriptions, the way in which his scribe arranged them – with a tendency to group together campaigns in a particular area even though they had occurred at different times – leaves confusion in the sequence of incidents. Different scholars might well reconstruct the course of events in rather different ways in detail.

Ashurbanipal's immediate problem was the uncompleted conquest of Egypt. In 667 he was able to send a strong Assyrian army there, and once again Memphis was taken. Some of the northern princes, led by Necho of Sais, had withdrawn allegiance from Assyria in favour of Tarqa, but the Assyrians were able to arrest the ringleaders. But in a country such as Egypt, the native princes were indispensable for efficient administration, and Necho was treated with clemency. Taken to Nineveh, he was loaded with gifts and favours and then, after swearing a fresh oath of vassaldom, allowed to return to Egypt. The Assyrian administrators in Egypt were instructed to give Necho any necessary military backing, and his son (who bore an Assyrian name) was appointed to a major administrative post.

The southern Egyptian dynasty continued its attempts to regain Lower Egypt, Tarqa's successor besieging the Assyrian garrison in Memphis in 664. An express courier brought the news to Nineveh. Ashurbanipal's army again entered Egypt in 663, driving the besiegers from Memphis and following them up as far south as the ancient capital Thebes, which was captured and looted, its treasures and its people being taken off to Assyria. The fate of Thebes, under its Hebrew name of No-Amon, is referred to in the Bible in Nahum 3: 8–10.

This marked the maximum extent of Assyrian expansion in the south-west; the same brief period saw its maximum influence in the north-west, in Asia Minor. Here a Cimmerian invasion drove some of the native rulers to seek Assyrian protection. One such ruler was Gyges of Lydia, in south Asia Minor, whose god, Ashurbanipal tells us, instructed him in a dream to apply to Ashurbanipal for military assistance against the Cimmerians. The sequel indicates that this was given, since Gyges was able to inflict a defeat upon the Cimmerians and afterwards sent some of the spoil, including two captive city-governors, to Nineveh (c. 663).

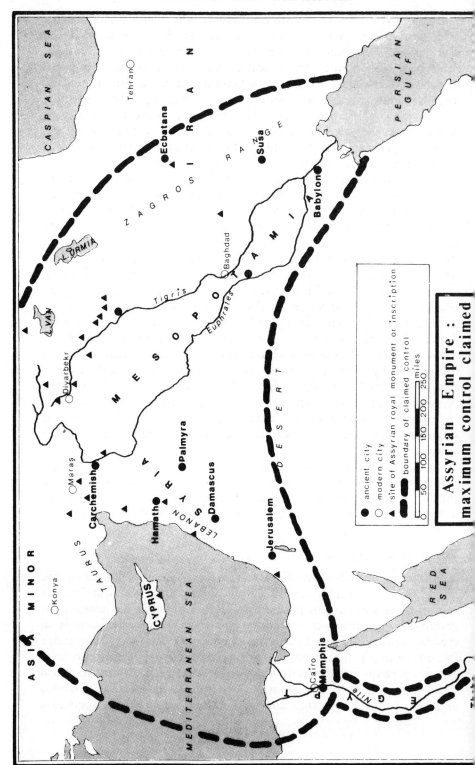

Assyrian Empire :
maximum control claimed

ancient city
modern city
site of Assyrian royal monument or inscription
boundary of claimed control

miles
0 50 100 150 200 250

But it was a brief honeymoon. Assyria was facing major trouble in Egypt. Nearly half a century before, an Assyrian general had warned the Jerusalem government, 'Never trust an Egyptian', though he put it more dramatically; 'Lo, thou trustest in the staff of this broken reed, on Egypt; whereon if a man lean, it will go into his hand, and pierce it: so is Pharaoh king of Egypt to all that trust in him' (2 Kings 18: 21). The Assyrians neglected their own warning. At the death of Necho, paramount prince of north Egypt, in 663, they appointed in his place his son Psammetichus, already a senior administrator for Assyria and ostensibly so pro-Assyrian that he was known to the Assyrians by an Assyrian name. Early in the 650s, Psammetichus began to assert his national independence by expelling the Assyrian garrisons that had been left in the cities of Egypt. This had repercussions elsewhere. Herodotus, the fifth-century Greek historian born in western Asia Minor, tells us that at the time of Psammetichus pirates from Asia Minor and Greece were landing in Egypt, but that Psammetichus won them over to his service. These so-called pirates may well have been subjects of Gyges of Lydia; Egypt and southern Asia Minor had common maritime trading interests, and initially both Psammetichus and Gyges were favoured vassals of Assyria. But as soon as Psammetichus initiated measures to rid Egypt of Assyrian influence, Gyges had to choose between Egypt and Assyria. He opted to assist Egypt. Ashurbanipal formally cursed the ungrateful Gyges, and let it be known that Assyrian support for him would no longer be forthcoming, thus clearing the Cimmerians for a fresh attack in about 652, when the kingdom of Gyges was invaded and overrun, and Gyges himself lost his life.

By 651 Psammetichus had cleared the Assyrians out of Egypt; with troubles mounting elsewhere, Assyria could no longer afford the considerable resources necessary to maintain its forces in Egypt, at the end of a long and difficult line of communication.

The elimination of Elam

The main problems were in the east, the immediate trouble-centre being Elam, the millennia-old kingdom in south-west Iran. In this region there were at this period two factors in particular making for instability: a number of ambitious members of the royal family in rivalry for control; and a surprising proneness among Elamite kings to sudden death (which points to congenital disease within the royal family, perhaps contributed to by the fact that Elamite kings married their sisters). Social and political instability harms trade relations and can spread across frontiers, and Ashurbanipal at the beginning of his reign worked for a stable Elam. He relates the measures he took to assist the king of Elam in time of national distress:

> When there was famine in Elam and a food shortage developed, I had corn sent to him to keep his people alive. I clasped his hand (to support him). People of his who had fled before the famine and taken up residence within Assyria until the rains came to his land and a harvest ensued, these people, who had been able to stay alive in my land, I sent back to him.

Yet despite Ashurbanipal's generous foreign aid, the Elamite king, Urtaki, afterwards responded to overtures from tribal leaders in Babylonia, and took advantage of Assyria's preoccupation with Egypt to launch an attack on Babylon in 665. Ashurbanipal had to send an army south to repel Urtaki; this contributed to souring relations between Ashurbanipal and his brother by making it all too clear that despite Shamash-shum-ukin's kingship of Babylonia the effective defence of that country resided with Ashurbanipal. Urtaki, like several other Elamite kings, died a sudden and unexpected death, whereupon a royal cousin, Teumman, seized the throne and sought to secure his position by attempting the murder of the sons of his two predecessors. These five princes and sixty other members of the Elamite royal family, accompanied by some of the Elamite nobility, then fled for protection to Ashurbanipal, who gave them asylum, despite Teumman's application for their extradition. It is an interesting indication of the international importance attached to protocol that Ashurbanipal felt it necessary to offer a reason for rejecting the extradition application.

We now run up against a problem of historical reconstruction. Ashurbanipal's inscriptions – not arranged strictly chronologically, as we have noted – would suggest that a campaign in which Teumman was killed followed quite shortly after the period when he was seeking to extradite his potential rivals. But the Elamite records indicate that Teumman reigned for about a decade, with steady expansion within Iran. That the Elamite records are the more to be trusted is shown by the bitterness with which Ashurbanipal speaks of Teumman, clearly the Elamite king whom he most hated. This reaction of Ashurbanipal must surely have had a substantial period, not just a few months, of friction with Teumman behind it.

Eventually, in high summer of 653, Ashurbanipal, then at Erbil, received news of the mobilization of Teumman's army against him. Ashurbanipal sought and obtained a favourable oracle from the goddess Ishtar of Erbil, the War Goddess. His army advanced into

Elam by the route through Der, whereupon Teumman retreated to his capital Susa and attempted to escape. But he had bad luck. Ashurbanipal described what happened: 'Teumman king of Elam. . .fled to save his life and hid in a wood. The crossbar of the chariot, his royal transport, broke, and it overturned on him. Teumman in desperation. . .said to his son "Raise the bow!" [presumably some component of the broken chariot under which he was trapped].' Teumman's son attempted to help him escape, but he was caught and beheaded. Teumman's head was taken to Ashurbanipal, who vented his hatred by slashing the dead face and spitting on it, and celebrated his victory by a ceremonial meal with his wife, shown in a bas relief, with Teumman's head prominently evident, hanging from a tree (see plate 2A).

There were still powerful tribal factions in Babylonia, and throughout all this period there had been constant anti-Assyrian intrigues between these people and Elamites, which was unsettling for the Babylonian administration under Shamash-shum-ukin. The consequent need for troops under Ashurbanipal's command to operate in Babylonia was also unfavourable to good relations between the two royal brothers and their administrations. However, friendly relations certainly persisted until 654 for, according to a chronicle, in 655 'the former bed of Bel came back from Ashur to Babylon', and in the following year the chariot of Bel was brought back, both of the objects being part of the loot taken away thirty-five years before when Sennacherib had sacked Babylon. But under two insecure puppets, whom Ashurbanipal made respectively king and sub-king in Elam, intrigue between various factions in Elam and in Babylonia intensified, and in 652 civil war broke out, with Shamash-shum-ukin, backed by an Elamite army, attacking the Assyrian garrison in Cuthah. Despite attempts by Shamash-shum-ukin to foment a general anti-Assyrian revolt in Babylonia, some citizens of the great cities certainly continued to support Assyria. The Assyrians defeated the Elamite army, cleared south Babylonia of organized Chaldaean forces supporting Shamash-shum-ukin, and then seized the initiative by putting Borsippa and Babylon, held by Shamash-shum-ukin, under siege. No support for Shamash-shum-ukin was forthcoming from Elam, where civil war had broken out between rival claimants to the throne. Shamash-shum-ukin, blockaded in Babylon, defended that city until famine compelled surrender in 648; so grim had conditions become at the last that the citizens 'ate the flesh of their sons and daughters for their starvation'. Shamash-shum-ukin died in a palace fire, possibly by suicide, although this is not explicitly stated.

Ashurbanipal was scrupulously careful that his dead brother and his wife should have proper burial in a tomb with all the due rites. But other rebel leaders were hunted down, and their bodies cut up and 'fed to the dogs, the swine, the wolves, the vultures, the birds of heaven and the fish of the deep'. For the rest of Ashurbanipal's long reign, Babylonia, still gravely stricken with tribal turbulence in the south, was ruled through an obscure sub-king named Kandalanu, little more than a front for direct Assyrian rule.

In Elam, Teumman had had some success in establishing stability, but after his ill-judged challenge to Assyria and his consequent death, civil strife between rival claimants to the succession quickly brought chaos. Ashurbanipal, whose protection had at various times been sought by most of the leading claimants to the Elamite throne, made several interventions in the succession. The matter was complicated by a social difference between Assyria and Elam. Whereas in Assyria the royal succession was basically from father to son, in Elam it was transmitted through the mother, so that one king's brothers might have a superior claim to the succession over his sons. Thus a legit-imate claimant to the throne on Elamite principles might appear a usurper to the Assyrians, whilst the man who was the obvious successor in Ashurbanipal's eyes might have uncles with a superior claim from the Elamite point of view.

No permanent stabilization was achieved by Ashurbanipal's inter-ventions. It was unlikely that it would be, since the ancient kingdom of Elam was suffering not only from its own internal dissensions but also from tensions produced by the thrust from the north of new peoples attempting settlement, the Persians. The situation in Elam was a continuing threat to Babylonia. Not only did Elamite disorder dislocate trade with regions to the east, but also a lawless Elam made an admirable base, away from Assyrian control, for Chaldaean tribes seeking independence in Babylonia.

This situation in Elam finally drove Ashurbanipal to take the drastic step of ravaging the whole country. This occupied two campaigns, probably to be dated just before the mid-640s. The Assyrian army marched through Elam, devastating its major cities, and capturing and looting the ancient capital, Susa. Ashurbanipal's troops paid no respect to the temples, which were desecrated, deities and cult objects being dragged off to Assyria. Even royal tombs were violated, so that the Elamite kings might suffer after death the Assyrian vengeance they had escaped in life. Ashurbanipal is explicit about his intentions in this: 'I pulled down and destroyed the tombs of their earlier and later kings, who had not revered the deities Ashur and Ishtar my lords,. . .and I exposed them to the sun. I took away their bones to Assyria, I put restlessness on their ghosts, I deprived them of food-offerings and libations of water.' Many senior administrators and the whole royal family were taken prisoner to Assyria, and Elamite army units were incorporated into the Assyrian forces. The Bible tells us that deportees from Elam, including Susa, were taken to north Palestine (Ezra 4: 9–10); the later Samaritans had Elamite blood in them. Many districts, stripped of their human and animal populations, taken spoil to Assyria, were left a wilderness: 'I left his fields empty of the voice of mankind, the tread of cattle and sheep, the merry shout of harvest-home; and in them I made wild asses couch, and gazelles, and all kinds of wild beasts.'

Ashurbanipal had moved a long way from his policy, at the beginning of his reign, of attempting to stabilize Elam by economic aid. His devastation of Elam was worse than brutal; it was bad statecraft. It was not only the wild animals Ashurbanipal mentions that were lurking to enter the wilderness he had left behind. Persian tribes, already pressing into the peripheral areas of the venerable kingdom of Elam, were poised to complete the occupation of that region. At this time the Persians were still vassals of the Medes, who under Assyrian pressure had been hammered into a major kingdom in north Iran. A century later they were to rule, from the base they had succeeded in establishing out of the wreck of Elam, the whole region – and more – which had been the Assyrian empire.

Ashurbanipal's historical inscriptions peter out just after his final solution of the Elamite problem. A dearth of royal inscriptions, when it is not an accident of archaeological discovery (and there has been digging aplenty of buildings associated with Ashurbanipal), is usually an indication of trouble for the ruler concerned. Ashurbanipal got the trouble he deserved. We only have his own inscriptions and reliefs to show what sort of a ruler, and what sort of man, he was; but judging by these we may conclude that he had become a tyrant, motivated more by thirst for personal revenge than by sound political considerations. One of the last incidents he records is his treatment of an Arab king. Arabs had assisted Shamash-shum-ukin in his rebellion in Babylon, and Ashurbanipal appointed a surviving prince, who had made submission, as king of the Arabs. Ultimately this king joined the Nabataeans, Arabs who controlled the trade routes up western Arabia, against Ashurbanipal. With Damascus as a base, Ashurbanipal penetrated into the desert, plundering the tribes wherever he went, and seizing all their water-holes, until the Arabs were forced to desert their king. Ashurbanipal caught him, and took him to Nineveh, where he humiliated him by tying him up with a collar to a kennel, as a watch-dog at a city gate.

Earlier Assyrian kings had been harsh, yes, and ruthless. Where there was rebellion, they crushed it; where opposition, they destroyed it. But only Ashurbanipal put vindictiveness on display; only he slashed the face of a dead enemy, desecrated tombs of the dead he had not been able to punish when living, spared the lives of captive kings that he might humiliate them better living than dead. It is not the historian's part to lay blame, but the historian must record; and malice as a driving force behind the later Ashurbanipal is a fact of history. His was the kind of conduct that gives warfare a bad name.

It was a defect of Ashurbanipal as a king that he had nothing in him of the great strategist, statesman, or soldier. He was as barren in political insight as he was rich in vindictiveness. It was his misfortune that he was called to be king when by inclination he was a scholastic. Yet we do owe him something. Earlier Assyrian kings had collected ancient texts and begun the creation of a library, but with Ashurbanipal this became a passion. He gives the impression of having been the sort of man who was never so happy as when curled up with a good clay tablet, although his motivation was probably more a matter of superstitious regard for ancient wisdom than love of literature for its own sake. Wherever he heard of ancient texts, he had them sent, or had copies of them made, for his library in Nineveh (see pages 279f.). And these texts, hidden in the earth until the mid-nineteenth century, and since their excavation hidden, at times almost as inaccessibly, in the British Museum, remain our major single source for knowledge of the ancient culture of Babylonia and Assyria.

The use of the word 'scholastic' above, rather than 'scholar', was deliberate. There is no indication that Ashurbanipal was interested in scholarship as such. What he was concerned with in the ancient texts was their theological or religious application; the proper prayers, the proper rituals, the meaning of omens, incantations to ward off this evil and to preclude against that – these were the kinds of things that were Ashurbanipal's concerns. The theological establishment with its vested interests in this area doubtless encouraged him, for he could always get the kind of oracle he needed in an emergency, as several passages in his inscriptions narrate in detail.

All we have to indicate what was happening in the final decade or more of Ashurbanipal's reign are a few economic documents, not very informative. There are, indeed, some religious texts associated with Ashurbanipal, speaking in terms of being encompassed with trouble, which have sometimes been taken as reflecting an adverse turn in Ashurbanipal's affairs. However, not only are these not necessarily from the end of Ashurbanipal's reign, but also they are probably formal compositions of the type we would call Penitential Psalms rather than expressions of any foreboding by Ashurbanipal personally of coming doom. Ashurbanipal was not a great statesman, and he was unlikely to have foreseen the cataclysm which was to engulf his empire.

The Downfall of the Empire

Within forty years of the rampage of Ashurbanipal's army through Elam, the Assyrian empire was at an end. Hard facts for the detailed sequence of events by which this came about are few. All we have are scattered clues – a reminiscence of an old lady, kings' names in the dating of economic documents, the fragmentary text of royal grants of land, allusions in a chronicle, a few inscribed bricks and bits of building inscriptions, and traditions preserved in Greek records centuries later.

The old lady referred to was the mother of Nabonidus, one of the kings of the Neo-Babylonian ('Chaldaean') dynasty which ruled Mesopotamia and the west after the downfall of Assyria. A monument erected at her death makes her say that she lived

from the twentieth year of Ashurbanipal, king of Assyria [her birth date, 649] to the forty-second year of Ashurbanipal, the third year of Ashur-etillu-ili his son, the twenty-first year of Nabopolassar, the forty-third year of Nebuchadrezzar, the second year of Amel-Marduk, the fourth year of Neriglissar, during ninety-five years.

until her son gained the throne, in 555. This fixes the date of Ashurbanipal's death at 627, one of the assured facts of the chronology of the final period of the Assyrian empire. The other relevant facts may be summarized as follows:

1   After the death of Shamash-shum-ukin, Babylonia was nominally under the government of a figurehead known as Kandalanu.
2   Ashurbanipal was succeeded by his son Ashur-etillu-ili, whose reign began several years before Ashurbanipal died.
3   There were widespread disturbances throughout the empire. Over in Palestine, the reforming activities of King Josiah of Judah in 629, which included throwing out cult objects with Assyrian associations (2 Kings 23: 12), probably included elements of anti-Assyrian feeling; while his attacks on neighbouring territory (2 Kings 23: 15–20) without Assyrian intervention reflect Assyria's problems of order at the time. Jere-

miah 1: 13–15, dated perhaps to 634, knows of northern tribal peoples on the move, a potential threat to Palestine. There were other revolts, including one by a general Sin-shum-lishir, who briefly claimed kingship.

4 Another son of Ashurbanipal, Sin-shar-ishkun, was accepted as king of Assyria for most of the period from his father's death until 612.

5 A Chaldaean prince Nabopolassar was proclaimed king of Babylon in 626, but did not immediately succeed in controlling all Babylonia.

6 Nineveh was taken in 612.

This provides the material for an elaborate chronological jigsaw puzzle, which – in view of the large number of pieces missing – scholarly ingenuity may assemble in various ways. The following reconstruction attempts to fit in data which are certain, without making assumptions beyond positive evidence.

There were disorders (as in Judah) towards the end of Ashurbanipal's life. Ashur-etillu-ili, either to relieve his ageing and troubled father or from personal ambition, took over the actual rule from about 630. At the death of Ashurbanipal in 627, disorder erupted into actual revolts. There was a power struggle, centred first on Babylonia, in which Kandalanu, sub-king of Babylonia, if not merely the *alter ego* of Ashurbanipal, was quickly removed, with Ashur-etillu-ili then attempting to hold Babylonia through a general loyal to him, Sin-shum-lishir, appointed as sub-king. In the same year, 627, another son of Ashurbanipal, Sin-shar-ishkun, possibly Ashur-etillu-ili's twin, obtained the support of major Assyrian garrisons in Babylon, and made a temporarily successful coup, taking Babylon and assuming the kingship. Thereupon, a Chaldaean prince, Nabopolassar, successor of Merodach-baladan in ambition and possibly in lineage (although of that we have no proof), who had already made himself king of the southern marshland tribal areas, moved north to oust Sin-shar-ishkun and assert his own claim to the kingship of Babylon. But there were still powerful Assyrian forces throughout Babylonia, and Sin-shar-ishkun continued to hold some Babylonian cities, notably Nippur and Erech, until 620 or even later.

We have no knowledge of what was happening to Ashur-etillu-ili or of his eventual fate, but he had no effective control in Babylonia after 627, and it is clear that by 623 certainly, and possibly as early as 626, Sin-shar-ishkun had established himself as king of Assyria in place of his brother. Meanwhile Nabopolassar, despite setbacks, was gradually extending his grip on all Babylonia. He was also taking measures to win himself allies abroad. Thus, immediately after his accession in Babylon he had sent back to Susa Elamite gods formerly looted by the Assyrians, a means of buying good will.

By 616 Nabopolassar was in a position to take the offensive against Assyria, although his initial moves may have been no more than attempts to adjust the borders – so frequently disputed between Babylonia and Assyria – in Babylonia's favour. Reported clashes indicate that Assyria was receiving support both from Egypt and from the Mannaeans from north-west Iran.

The following year Nabopolassar moved up the Tigris and reached the old capital, Ashur. But his advance was premature, and he was forced to retreat to Takrit, where he himself was put under siege. The Assyrians were clearly still able to take the offensive, but now had to withdraw, presumably because they had received intelligence of an imminent attack by the Medes, which took place later the same year in south-eastern Assyria. From there in 614, the Medes moved in to the heart of Assyria, taking both Tarbisu (modern Sherif Khan), a fortress about five miles north-west of Nineveh which controlled the capital's communications with the north and west, and also the ancient capital, Ashur. A chronicle mentions that Nabopolassar's army arrived soon after the capture of Ashur but took no part in it; this was possibly true, but is likely to have been emphasized to exonerate Nabopolassar from religious censure for the looting of that city, which was a venerable religious centre. Nabopolassar and the Medes, who had hitherto been acting independently, made a formal treaty of alliance at their meeting at Ashur.

Assyria still had allies. In 613 the tribal peoples along the Euphrates, who had in the past so often been troublesome to the Assyrians, now rebelled against Nabopolassar. This tribal rebellion was certainly in alliance with the Assyrians, since whilst Nabopolassar was besieging one of the rebel cities an Assyrian army arrived and forced him to withdraw to Babylonia. There is a problem here: how could the Assyrians deploy an army on the Euphrates, powerful enough to compel the retreat of Nabopolassar, when in the previous year they had been so hard-pressed in metropolitan Assyria that the Medes had taken cities at both ends of the country? Something must have been inhibiting the Medes. There are two possibilities. Either Assyria had made a truce with the Medes (a purely speculative suggestion, without independent evidence), or the Medes had had to withdraw to face some other threat. This threat could have been the Scythians, a people who had come into Anatolia and north-west Iran behind the Cimmerians, and had been in relationship, mainly friendly, with the Assyrians since the reign of Esarhaddon. Greek

tradition suggests that the Medes were at one time seriously threatened by the Scythians, and it could have been such a threat that
caused a temporary withdrawal of the Medes from Assyria in 613.

The Babylonian records of this time say nothing of Scythians but
do mention a people called Ummanmanda. This term probably
denoted tribal hordes from the north of which the Scythians were
part. Greek tradition speaks of Scythians eventually coming into
alliance with the Medes, and Nabopolassar must have been a party
to this, for in 612 he joined the Ummanmanda and the Medes in
besieging Nineveh. The city fell within three months, a surprisingly
brief period in view of the fact that the comparable city of Babylon
withstood the Assyrian army, masters of siegecraft, for well over a
year. Greek tradition and the Bible (Nahum 1: 8) join in reporting
that the capture of Nineveh, with its enormously powerful defences,
was made possible by flooding – probably not by the Tigris but by
the tributary known as the Khosr. The flooding of the Khosr, which
ran through the city, swept away a section of its defences and
admitted the besiegers. The city was sacked and looted, and Sin-
shar-ishkun died in the destruction.

The Assyrians were not yet finished. The survivors fled westwards
to Harran, where Ashur-uballit of the Assyrian royal family was
proclaimed king. Meanwhile the Medes and Ummanmanda had
withdrawn. Nabopolassar, now in competition with his former
allies for the inheritance of the Assyrian empire, hastened to consolidate his position in Assyria, occupying the region as far west as
Nisibin and mopping up pockets of resistance within Assyria itself.
This gave Ashur-uballit two years to reorganize at Harran, from
where he called for assistance from Egypt. In 610 the Ummanmanda
returned to Mesopotamia and attacked Harran, being quickly joined
by Nabopolassar, arriving to safeguard Babylonian interests. Ashur-
uballit withdrew to make contact with approaching Egyptian allies.
After an attempt to regain Harran, the combined Assyrian–Egyptian
forces made their base at Carchemish. At this point there was a
change of king of Egypt. The new Pharaoh, Necho II (610–595),
decided upon maximum support for Ashur-uballit and led the main
Egyptian army into Syria. It proved that Chaldaean diplomacy had
met with substantial success in Palestine. Not only did Necho have
to put down a rising in Gaza (Jeremiah 47: 1), but also Josiah of
Judah made an attempt, fatal for himself, to harry the Egyptian
forces at Megiddo in 608 (2 Kings 23: 29). Despite these hindrances,
Necho got his forces through to the main Assyrian-Egyptian base
at Carchemish. But now came disaster for Egypt. Up to this time
the Chaldaean forces had not been conspicuous for military prowess;
their major successes had depended earlier upon Assyrian civil strife

and later upon support from the Medes and Ummanmanda. But now they threw up a general of outstanding ability, Nebuchadrezzar, son of Nabopolassar. In 605 Nabopolassar handed over control of the Babylonian army to Nebuchadrezzar, who took his forces across the Euphrates to make a direct attack upon the powerful Egyptian army in Carchemish. Jeremiah records the events:

> The Lord God of hosts holds a sacrifice
> in the north country by the river Euphrates. . . .
> O virgin daughter of Egypt!. . .
> The nations have heard of your shame,
> and the earth is full of your cry;
> for warrior has stumbled against warrior;
> they have fallen both together.   (Jeremiah 46: 10–12)

Though the final lines indicate that both sides suffered heavy slaughter, it was the Egyptian army whose morale broke. Jeremiah depicts the panic flight of survivors back to Egypt:

> Their warriors are beaten down,
> and have fled in haste;
> they look not back –
> terror on every side! says the Lord.   (46:5)

We hear nothing further of Ashur-uballit or of any survivors from his forces. With the collapse of the Egyptian army, its final buttress, the Assyrian empire was at an end. The Egyptians routed, Syria and Palestine fell to Nebuchadrezzar. The same year he succeeded his father, a new king of a new empire, with the world capital no longer in Assyria but at Babylon.

121

Part Two

9

Assyrian Society and Customs

Assyrians: a Nation, not a Race

Any human group, to be recognizable as a coherent society, must have certain features which link its members to each other and set them apart from their neighbours. Our quest is to discover what it was that characterized the Assyrians and set them apart as a distinct people in the ancient world.

Care is needed with terminology. Just because we have a mental picture of a group which we call 'Assyrians', it does not follow that a member of that group would look at things in the same way and identify himself by the term 'Assyrian'. Indeed, we know that at some periods this would definitely not have been the case, since the term *Aššurayau*, of which the translation is 'Assyrian', meant something much more limited than what we understand by 'Assyrian'; in Middle Assyrian laws the term seems to have had some class sense, being applied only to lower-class people (see page 131).

Some peoples of the ancient Near East gave an explicit definition of what they thought was the basis of their unity and set them apart from their neighbours as unique. Views on such a matter could be strongly held without corresponding at all closely to historical fact. The biblical Israelites are a good example of a people with strongly-held beliefs of dubious historical basis. Their traditions held very firmly that two factors united them within themselves and set them apart from others: their tribes were, they said, all descendants of sons of one father (which was certainly untrue), and these tribes had all entered into an exclusive treaty with a particular god, Yahweh (which was very dubious). The Israelites felt a national consciousness based on the concept of common descent from one man, with separation from breeds excluded from their traditions, their nation, and the protection of their laws. But the Assyrians were free of this kind of racialism. No Assyrian god ever proclaimed that the seed of a particular individual were uniquely his. No Assyrian lawgiver ever legislated against foreign peoples: 'thou shalt not make marriages with them; thy daughter thou shalt not give unto his son, nor his daughter shalt thou take unto thy son' (Deuteronomy 7: 3).

124

The Israelites' beliefs were linked to the tribal background of Israel. But the people of Assyria, as we know them in historical times, were not basically tribal, and beliefs about descent from a common ancestor played no part in uniting Assyrians. Nor, so far as we know, was there any tradition of an actual treaty of Assyrians with their gods, even though the god Ashur played such a major part in Assyrian self-identity that we can properly call him the national god. The Assyrians never thought of themselves as self-sufficient or exclusive; from the beginning they accepted trade with other peoples as an essential element of life, and did not, like the Israelites, see any ill consequences as likely to arise from mixing with other peoples. Their later policy of deportation was linked to this, and we often find them stating that deported peoples were settled and treated as Assyrians.

The deportation policy of the Assyrian kings created a new and unique form of society – a mingling of national groups in which ethnic differences were not significant. People from different parts of the Near East were moved into Assyria and put to work as farmers, craftsmen, merchants or soldiers, and in due course became integrated into the hotchpotch that was Assyria. This was not wholly a matter of accident and expediency; there was an accepted theoretical basis for it, expressed in theological terms. The Assyrians credited their gods with claiming sway over all the known world. Tukulti-Ninurta I called himself 'the one whose name the god Ashur and the great gods faithfully called, the one to whom they gave the four quarters to administer and the one to whom they entrusted their dominion'. The great gods allotted the foreign lands to the kings of Assyria.

To return to what unified the Assyrians themselves, we note that one unifying feature was their language. They were conscious that, from their point of view, people in the mountains around 'talked funny'. Royal inscriptions sometimes comment on the languages spoken by other peoples, or mention that some objects of booty had names 'difficult to write down'. But this was not a sufficient mark of separation, as their southern neighbours in Babylonia spoke another dialect of the same language.

The most potent unifying force was religion. All the peoples of the ancient Near East believed in a multitude of gods, though accepting that in certain areas or social contexts a particular god or group of gods had a unique position. Ashur was such a god, believed to hold supremacy in a particular land, which was therefore called 'the land of Ashur' – hence the name Assyria. The claim was made that Ashur's sway extended over the civilized world and that it was the function of the king to assert and maintain Ashur's sovereignty.

125

At first sight it might seem that this was simply nationalism and imperialism in a particular form, with the abstract idea of nationalism personified as a god. But it is not so straightforward as that. It was based on a particular theology of Ashur, the view that the god had a plan for his land and that he was separate from his land and his people. Nationalism is unthinkable without a human group, but in ancient Near Eastern thought a god could exist independently of his people and even of his land; he could even reject and punish his people, a thing that the abstract conception of nationalism cannot do.

Assyria comprised a series of sub-units. The ordinary peasant was in some way linked to a particular piece of land, either by having recognized rights over it or by having to cultivate it. His piece of land belonged in a particular village. The village was in turn linked, either immediately or via a town, to a major city, such as Ashur, Nineveh, Erbil or Arrapkha. It was linked with the city by way of the taxes it had to pay, the periodic religious festivals in which it had the right and duty to share, the possibility of appealing to authorities in the city in the event of legal or administrative disputes, and above all by the fact that the city was the eventual destination of much of the products of the land and the centre of production or distribution of imported or manufactured goods which could not be produced in the village. The great cities themselves were linked together on the one hand by functioning under similar city administrations, and on the other by all being subject to some measure of direction from a common central administration under the king. And at this point the circle is completed, and we find that the king is a focus in common for all Assyrians – and moreover the king provides a link with the supernatural world, in that he is the human representative of the god Ashur.

Politically, Assyria was remarkably stable over many centuries. There were occasional intrigues in the top level of society to replace the current king by someone from another branch of the royal family, but there are no known instances of popular rebellion or attempts to change social institutions. The political stability was both a reflection of, and a consequence of, the stability and unfragmented nature of Assyrian society.

The Assyrians were mongrels, and knew it. To them ethnic purity was an irrelevance. From earliest times they had a very mixed ethnic history, and although antique antecedents may not have been in their consciousness by the late second and first millennia, they were well aware – for it is mentioned frequently in royal inscriptions – that peoples from outside Assyria were constantly being added to the mix and treated as themselves. In the period known as Middle

Assyrian (the second half of the second millennium), quite a few Assyrians, including some high officials, bore Hurrian names. The test in the first-millennium Assyrian empire was not the line a man came from but how he behaved to the greater community, his loyalty to the world empire ruled by the god Ashur. There is even the possibility that in one instance a defeated and deported Babylonian king was introduced into the top level of the Assyrian administration. The names of several senior Assyrian provincial governors show that they were of Aramaean or Phoenician or Israelite origin. A man did not even have to worship the Assyrian national god Ashur, for the pantheon ruled over by Ashur was flexible enough to accommodate gods who originated elsewhere; unlike the Israelite Yahweh, Ashur was sure enough of his supremacy not to have to be a Jealous God.

We have seen the different strands in the make-up of prehistoric Assyria – chief among them the cultural groups of Hassuna, Halaf and (marginally) Samarra. Later came influences from the south, the Ubaid just before history and the Sumerian at its dawn, both of them doubtless mirroring in ethnic strains the contribution so clearly manifest in cultural terms. Traces of these early strains (other than Sumerian) may remain in place names, some of which cannot be explained as either Sumerian or Semitic. Early in the Sumerian period – perhaps before – began the massive influx of Semitic-speaking peoples from the south-west, to be continually reinforced until Assyria as an empire existed no more. In the second millennium there came into the area a strong Hurrian influx, to leave permanent marks on Assyrian culture and, less visibly but no less surely, on ethnic make-up. This formed the framework.

Into this framework other ethnic elements were ceaselessly infused by the three principal channels of immigration, deportation and mixed marriages by such people as merchants, long resident abroad. The last was the channel of which we know least, and was the least significant.

Immigration could effect massive changes in the population make-up. We know that in the middle of the second millennium Hurrian immigrants from the north almost swamped the older population of some parts of Assyria, whilst Semitic Aramaeans from beyond the Euphrates effected major population changes at the end of the millennium. Settlers of these kind may well have remained separate enclaves for some generations, but in the long term they, too, fully entered the Assyrian mix: the area where the Assyrian empire found its final support and made a last stand was between Harran and Carchemish, an area which at one time had been strongly Hurrian and later predominantly Aramaean.

Other classes of immigrant included peoples displaced by disturbances in Asia Minor at around 1200. There was one such people called the Mushki, related to the later Phrygians, who after vigorous clashes with Assyria were allowed to settle and were counted as Assyrians (see page 59). On a more modest scale, but not negligible over a long period, was immigration into the Assyrian plains of single families from the mountains. Because of their individual insignificance we are unlikely to hear of actual instances of such settlement, but we can infer them from references to people called Nullu (a form of the term 'Lullu' used for the peoples of south Kurdistan) among the population mentioned in documents from near Kirkuk in the fifteenth century.

But in the end the biggest contributor to population change and population mix was the policy of deportation. In the modern world this is an emotive issue, and it is easy for the basic facts to become obscured in a welter of compassion. The whole matter has been very well discussed by B. Oded in *Mass Deportations and Deportees in the Neo-Assyrian Empire* (1979).

Deportation of conquered peoples was already practised by Assyrian kings of the thirteenth century, but it became a major feature of state policy from the ninth century, with the numbers deported totalling a quarter to half a million under several rulers. This served to produce a society within the Assyrian empire, and within Assyria itself, which was very mixed in both race and language. The Assyrian kings had no racialist background to their military exploits and expansion and deportations. They incorporated the troops of conquered or vassal states into the Assyrian army, and Ashur-nasir-pal even populated his new capital Calah with people from conquered territories. He is quite specific about this: 'Calah. . .I built anew. People conquered by my hand from the lands I ruled, from Suhu,. . .Laqe, Suqa at the crossing of the Euphrates, Zamua. . ., Bit-Adini, Hatti. . .I settled therein.' Since these peoples were not a single ethnic group, but represented a wide spread of nationalities, such deportations ensured in due course an entirely new mix. It was, in fact, the cities of Assyria which were the destinations of a majority of known deportations. Assyrian cities thus became cosmopolitan and polyglot, with the possibility that within them people of actual ancient Assyrian descent were a minority.

Since migrants moved in groups, and the Assyrians deliberately deported foreign peoples in groups which retained their ethnic unity, such groups did not immediately assimilate to the population amongst which they were placed. The Assyrian kings were conscious that a number of languages were spoken within some of their cities. While every attempt was made to induce resettled peoples to accept their position as members of the empire, there is no reason to suppose that this implied pressure to use a particular language or serve a particular god. Thus Sargon II speaks of his treatment of the mixture of peoples settled by him in his new capital Dur-Sharrukin (Fort Sargon):

> peoples of the four quarters, of strange tongues and different speech, dwelling in mountains and plains,. . .I took as spoil at the word of Ashur my lord. I made them of one purpose, I made them take up abode therein [i.e., inside Dur-Sharrukin]. I sent natives of Assyria, competent in everything, as overseers and supervisors, to instruct them in custom and to serve the gods and the king.

The culture of the new Assyrian empire was by no means purely Assyrian nor even purely Assyro-Babylonian; it was a hybrid culture. One of the main elements which first came in during the first millennium was due to the Aramaeans, nomads from the Syrian desert. Their language, Aramaic, had a considerable influence on Assyrian, which came to take in many loan words and turns of phrase from it. The much simpler Aramaic writing system, on potsherds, leather or papyrus, even began to be used alongside cuneiform writing on clay, which it was eventually (but not until after the fall of Assyria) to supersede entirely. Aramaic was, in fact, already an official language in Assyria in the reign of Tiglath-Pileser III (745–727), for on his monuments we see a scribe with writing materials appropriate for Aramaic alongside one who was evidently writing cuneiform, the two of them making duplicate records of war booty.

Aramaeans were not the only people likely to have had an effect on Assyrian culture in the New Assyrian period. Amongst scribes, we find Egyptians listed alongside Assyrians and Aramaeans, as people in receipt of rations, and thus officially attached to the court. These ration lists also mention other foreigners, whose profession is in many cases not stated but who are likely to have been military officers, merchants, foreign emissaries, or perhaps princely hostages held at the Assyrian court as a guarantee of the good conduct of the state from which they came. Amongst such foreign personnel at court were Israelites, Phoenicians, Medes and Mannaeans (from north-west Iran), and people from north Syria, Asia Minor and Anatolia.

A large number of languages would be represented at the court. Royal princes from vassal states were brought to the Assyrian court to be educated, to be moulded into pliable vassal rulers for the future, and to serve as hostages for the good behaviour of the reigning vassal. There were also administrators with foreign experience and knowledge of foreign languages, as well as formal interpreters. We have a glimpse of this in a text telling us how an ambassador arrived in Assyria from a remote country, usually assumed (though with no final proof) to be Lydia in Asia Minor. King Ashurbanipal is represented as speaking:

> He reached the border of my land.
> When the people of my land saw him, they said to him,
> 'Who are you, stranger,
> From whose country messenger never (before)
> Set foot on the road (hither)?'
> They brought him before me in Nineveh, my capital.
> But of the languages of east and west,
> over which Ashur had given me authority,
> there was no one who commanded his language.
> His language was strange,
> and they could not understand his speech.
> He brought with him from the border of his land. . .

What he brought is no longer extant, but presumably it was a letter written in Akkadian, to overcome the language barrier.

Social Classes

Our knowledge of Assyrian social stratification is patchy and uneven; for some periods we have information directly bearing upon aspects of social life, whilst for others we are limited to deducing what we can from allusions in texts of which the primary concern may be something quite different, so that the hints they give us are tantalizingly obscure.

As in any other culture, Assyrian society underwent changes in the course of time, and what is true of it at one period may not be so at another. One of the times about which we are best informed – despite many gaps in detail – is the Middle Assyrian period, towards the end of the second millennium. This is the consequence of a lucky accident, namely, the finding at Ashur of cuneiform tablets bearing the text of Middle Assyrian laws of special relevance to some aspects of society. In particular, there is one longish tablet (of fifty-nine clauses according to the modern division) solely concerned with matters related to women.

We learn from the laws that society comprised two distinct social estates: the free and the non-free, the Akkadian terms for the member of the two groups respectively being *a'ilu (amilu)* and *urdu (ardu)*, usually translated respectively 'free man' and 'slave'. A complication is introduced by the occurrence of a third term for a social group, *Aššurayau*, 'Assyrian'. It is clear from the laws that the *Aššurayau* was a free man, but since some laws make a difference between the treatment of the *Aššurayau* and of the *a'ilu*, he must have been a particular kind of free man, and the difference implied by the laws indicates that the *Aššurayau* was of lesser importance. That is, there were gradations of status amongst free men, and when it was desired to refer particularly to free men of lower status, the term *Aššurayau* was employed. (Some scholars have interpreted this differently, and seen a tripartite division of social orders – *a'ilu* being taken specifically as 'patrician' – but since *a'ilu* seems sometimes to subsume *Aššurayau*, this seems difficult to maintain.)

The situation had become significantly different by the time of the New Assyrian empire in the first millennium. The leading position amongst free men now lay with royal officials, who owed their position and authority to royal favour, not to hereditary status – even though it often happened that a man would be appointed to an office formerly held by his father. And at the bottom of the social scale, the distinction between free man and slave had become blurred, by the reducing to serfdom of whole communities of peasants who had lost their old rights over land.

The Agricultural Basis of Assyrian Life

Assyria was basically a land of farming villages and country towns, with a few, but only a few, major cities. Ashur, Nineveh and Erbil, and perhaps Arrapkha, and those alone, were always substantial cities; a fifth city, Calah, despite its heyday impressiveness reflected in the massive ruins at Nimrud, was of national importance for only two centuries in the first millennium. Amongst frequently-mentioned substantial towns of more local importance were Kalizi, Kurbail (unidentified), and Shibaniba; quite a number more of what we would call country towns are marked today by large mounds, some identified, some not. But there was nothing like the conglomeration of cities which existed, from Sumerian times onwards, in Babylonia to the south, along the Euphrates and Diyala. The difference was linked to climate. In Babylonia agriculture was impossible without irrigation, and this, with the major water-courses involved, required a large concentration of people within a unified social

131

structure. This factor was less crucial in Assyria, where rain-fed agriculture is possible almost everywhere. This does not imply that irrigation was not (and is not) practised in Assyria; it was (and is), but it is a useful auxiliary rather than an indispensable prerequisite of agriculture there.

Life in towns and cities is touched upon elsewhere. For the present we may consider the land. The question of land ownership in Assyria is complicated and still not fully understood; even where we have a fair understanding of the situation no statements can be made which are valid for all areas and all periods. Our evidence comes mainly from a Law Book of the late second millennium dealing, amongst other matters, with land tenure, and from many documents concerned with the sale of land.

It seems that originally in Assyria, before the state developed as a national entity, land was owned by extended families. There are still very clear relics of this system in the Middle Assyrian period, though by that time extended families had usually grouped together into a wider village community; this development in some respects limited the freedom of action of any particular extended family. Much of the land controlled by the village community was divided into sections known as 'lots'. There are indications that these lots were periodically re-allocated amongst the extended families and such individuals as had acquired rights in them by purchase.

How individuals from outside could acquire such rights is a complex matter. We know that in the Kirkuk area of Assyria, at about 1450 (the date of the so-called Nuzi documents), land was still not legally alienable outside the family. There were, however, ways of getting round this little problem of customary law. Although transfer of land was only possible within the family, sale to someone outside the family could be arranged by the fiction of the seller adopting the buyer and giving him the piece of land in question as his inheritance share. However, we have a practice here which was not strictly Assyrian in origin, since the predominant ethnic and cultural element around Kirkuk at about 1450 was Hurrian, from immigrants of the preceding two or three centuries. In Assyria generally by the Middle Assyrian period it was already possible for individuals to buy rights in land without any subterfuge; this practice of selling ancestral land was to be considerably extended by the Neo-Assyrian period in the first millennium.

Probably, with most transfers of land in early times, the hereditary holder of land rights originally had no intention of selling. But the rights could be mortgaged as security for a loan and all too often such a transaction could become the prelude to the original owner losing his rights. A loan might be needed to tide the family over from seedtime to harvest, and a poor harvest would render the debtor unable to pay. Foreclosure would result. Thus it happened in the Middle Assyrian period that money lenders, who had presumably originally acquired wealth as merchants, were prominent among those buying up land rights. A person who bought land could in principle choose his plot, subject to not infringing rights of the community as a whole or of particular extended families. Originally the purchase of a plot of land resulted in the buyer becoming a member of the village community and taking over not only the privileges which went with rights over land but also the community duties which such rights involved. In such a situation the land was not lost to the community; rather, the land remained part of the community land, and the community acquired a new member. But gradually certain economically powerful people or families succeeded in building up compact estates out of plots that had once been community land, and these ceased to be available for periodic re-distribution. In consequence, the extended family or individual concerned now enjoyed not merely rights over land but in effect owned it.

What happened to the families who, through debt and foreclosure, lost their rights over land? Since rights in the community were linked to rights in land, such persons certainly lost status. A debtor might pledge not only his land and house but also sons and daughters for a loan, and if he failed to repay, not only could he lose his property but also the pledged members of his family could be made slaves and sold. There were other possibilities. Membership of the community brought not only the right to a share in the community land but also certain obligations for community service, such as road-making, irrigation work or military service. Privileges and obligations now became separated, the privileges being grasped by the rich, and the obligations being imposed upon the poor. As differentiation into landowners and dispossessed increasingly developed, it came about that the landowners treated the dispossessed, not quite as slaves, but as dependants to perform the community service which was originally the responsibility of those who held the land. These dependants could also, of course, continue to work on the land over which they themselves, or their ancestors, had formerly held rights.

Whilst during the Middle Assyrian period it was money lenders who were most commonly involved in buying out the old peasant landholders, during the Neo-Assyrian period the most prominent people in this respect were officials in the royal administration. Although by this time most of the land had already been lost to the original peasant holders, the process was not wholly complete, and in the early eighth century there still remained some land in the hands of small landowners, since we find it being sold to high officials building up estates. A corresponding situation in Judah is castigated in Isaiah 5: 8: 'Woe to those who join house to house, who add field to field.' It has been suggested that in some cases officials involved in land purchase were acting in an official capacity in creating royal estates, but this is difficult to prove.

Poor Peasants, Serfs and Slaves

By the eighth century, the peasants who actually worked the land were no longer fully free citizens; they were accepted as belonging with the land they cultivated and could be sold or transferred with it. Thus a typical royal charter gives a favoured official tax exemptions in respect of 'the fields, orchards and people which he had acquired and made as his own estate'. But may we properly speak of these depressed peasants as slaves?

We need to consider what slavery implied, and what part it played, in Assyrian life. Slavery existed, but slavery as an institution was not of major economic importance. This remark could be challenged, and it is therefore important to be clear what we mean by 'slavery' in the present context. These comments relate to individual slaves, not to prisoners of war, nor to national groups deported en masse, nor to whole agricultural communities which stood in a position of dependance to some major landowner. The individual slave was a person without rights, owned by another person, and able to be bought and sold. Prisoners of war and deportees, on the other hand, while they could be moved from their original home and required to undertake certain duties for the state, remained technically free. This is put beyond doubt by the records of negotiations between Assyrian officials and people undergoing siege (as at Babylon or Jerusalem). There the besieged were frankly told they might be deported, but nothing was said about their being enslaved. Descendants of resettled deported persons could become indistinguishable, except in their tell-tale foreign names, from native free Assyrians. The greater part of the agricultural work was performed not by slaves but by free men; these could be either free Assyrians or deported communities of free men. The depressed Assyrian peasants were in the same situation as deported foreign free men; though they could be sold with their land they could not be sold as individuals away from it, and in that respect were not slaves, even though on occasions the term was applied to them.

The term translated 'slave' (*ardu* or *urdu*) was not in itself one implying stigma; rather it indicated an inferior status relative to someone of recognized authority. High officials writing to the king would regularly designate themselves 'your *urdu*', but this was no more than a conventional politeness, implying 'your humble servant', and certainly not indicating slave status as we understand it. Even the king could speak of himself as a 'slave' in relation to the gods. However, these were special usages, not directly relevant to real slavery in which all rights over one person are owned by someone else. This situation is widely attested in legal documents, where one person is formally described as the slave of someone else. But paradoxically, even in such contexts there are instances in which persons described as slaves possessed property, including sometimes other slaves, and this property could be inherited by their descendants.

Slavery stirs such deep emotions in modern times that it is hard to look at it dispassionately in the context of the ancient world. But in the ancient Near East it was a neutral fact of life, like 'jobs' in the Western economic situation today which dictate our activities and limit most people's free use of their time for most of their lives. Just as economic pressures may today force a worthy citizen into a job he dislikes or into unemployment, so in ancient Assyria corresponding factors could combine to reduce a corresponding person to slavery for debt. An Assyrian slave might well dislike some of the consequences the status of slave brought him, just as a free man or the king might dislike some of the consequences (taxes in one case, certain taboos in the other) which his status brought him. But there is no reason to suppose that anyone – slaves themselves or others – challenged slavery as a social concept, any more than most people in the modern Western world challenge 'jobs' as a concept, even if they find their own particular job – or lack of one – irksome.

Prisoners of war were not, in the strict sense, slaves. Kings sometimes made this clear by specifically saying of them 'I made them like the people of Assyria'. Their status, when settled on the land, was similar to that of poor native Assyrians; that is, if the land was sold they were sold with it, but they were not normally liable to be sold separately from the land. We see a corresponding situation with soldiers of foreign origin. Assyrian kings sometimes say that they took contingents of young men of a conquered people into their forces, but the word for 'slaves' is not used to denote the status of such persons. On the contrary, it is clear that such military units within the Assyrian forces were under no disability of status relative to native Assyrians.

Slaves in the fullest sense were people who had been sold for debt, or who were the children of such people. By the nature of their circumstances they would originally own no property, though it seems that there was the possibility of their acquiring property, since, as already noted, we have texts mentioning the property of persons described in legal documents as slaves. Moreover, such persons had no protection against either ill-treatment or being sold abroad. The Middle Assyrian Law Book is quite explicit about this:

> If an Assyrian man, or an Assyrian woman who lives in a man's house as pledge for his value, has been taken in discharge of the full value of the debt, the creditor may beat him, pull out his hair, crush and pierce his ears.

> An Assyrian man or an Assyrian woman who has been taken at full price for debt may be sold into a foreign country.

Thus at one end of the scale were citizens with full rights and at the other a class who were fully slaves, who had no rights, normally owned no property, and who could be sold at the will of their master. Between these extremes were people who were in some respects under the jurisdiction of a master, but yet retained some rights. This intermediate group would include the poor native peasantry, and also the deportees who had been settled on land in Assyria. Their status was in some respects tantamount to slavery in so far as they were not free to leave the estate to which they were attached. On the other hand, they did retain some rights, since communities and families could not be split up and moved at the whim of the landowner. They could also acquire, retain and bequeath property, on a regular basis.

The number of native Assyrians sold as serfs with land was relatively small, in some cases averaging less than one to ten acres. It is estimated that today in Iraq one person can cultivate, by extensive rather than intensive cultivation and without mechanization, about seven or eight acres or more (R. McC. Adams, *Land behind Baghdad*, 1965, 14). Thus there is no need to suppose that there was any considerable agricultural labour force beyond the persons actually listed in land sales as attached to the land sold. We do know that some holders of estates owned substantial numbers of slaves, but most of these are likely to have been employed in the household. There could, however, have been an additional agricultural labour force available on some estates in the form of war captives, who were taken in very large numbers and distributed amongst royal lands, temple lands, the major cities and royal officials.

Mention was made above of officials building up estates. Royal officials might own some land by inheritance or purchase, and they could also receive grants of land from the king, which served to give them an income in recognition of the duties they performed. In the case of a high-ranking official, the land grant from the king could run into several thousand acres. The land they owned personally could also be substantial: we know that some royal officials, not of the highest rank, owned as much as a thousand acres.

Peasant families

We are fortunate in possessing some fairly detailed evidence about the composition of Assyrian peasant families, provided by a group of first-millennium documents sometimes called (not very accurately) an Assyrian Census List. These documents give details of the cultivators associated with certain estates in the district of Harran, naming the people concerned and summarizing their families. The following example is typical:

> Adad-duri, farmer,
> Nashuh-dilini his adolescent son,
> 1 woman; total 3.
> 30 units of land, 15 cultivated thereof;
> 1 orchard,
> 1 cow.
> Total of the estate Arrizu
> in the administrative district of Harran.

The exact purpose of these documents remains open to discussion, but in one aspect they were evidently a kind of land register, held at the state capital, possibly for use in connection with taxation. For our present purpose their interest is in the details given of the personnel. These show that the Assyrian villager was usually (but not invariably) monogamous, and the statistics give an average of 1.43 children per family. As it stands, this would indicate families too small even to maintain the population. However, the real average number of children must have been rather larger. There would in some cases be married daughters who had left the nuclear family to live with their husbands. There might also be married sons who had left to set up households of their own, or other adult sons who had left for military or other state service. Some of the sons still at home are described as adolescents and some of the girls as 'of marriageable age'. Although this strictly does not require the people concerned to have been more than thirteen or fourteen, it may not be unreasonable to assume that the average age at which girls married or sons left home was a little later, say, around sixteen.

We may also assume that an Assyrian woman had about twenty-four years (say, from sixteen to forty) during which she was bearing children. If child-bearing was fairly evenly spread across this period, by the time the woman was forty, one-third of her children would have been over sixteen, with the possibility of having left home. If she survived to the age of fifty-six, all of them could have left home. The average of 1.43 children per family mentioned above therefore need not represent more than perhaps a half of the average total of surviving children. Thus surviving children could have amounted to between two and three per family, sufficient to maintain a stable population.

Childbirth and Infant Mortality

It should be remembered that the children who survived to adulthood may only have been a small proportion of those born. Infant mortality was a great scourge of ancient Mesopotamia, as we know especially from magical texts intended to protect against the demons who so viciously attacked mankind on the threshold of life. Texts speak of crying 'over the small child who died prematurely' or 'the Daughter of Anu [a female demon] who torments babies', or express the chilling belief that 'the Daughter of Anu keeps going after women about to give birth'. The royal family no less than commoners felt the cold hand of infant mortality, and the name of one of the best-known kings, Sennacherib – Sin-ahhe-eriba, meaning 'the god Sin has replaced the brothers' – gives testimony to earlier infant princes who had gone to the grave.

Pre-natal care was largely a matter of magic, involving amulets, rituals and incantations. We find, for example, mention of 'stones worn round the waist of a woman who does not give birth easily'. We also possess a text dealing with the treatment of a woman ill during pregnancy. First, a number of drugs of vegetable origin were compounded over a fire and then mixed with oil and beer. Some woollen material was soaked in this and then put in the woman's vagina as a pessary. This had to be done twice daily. Anointing and bandaging are also mentioned as complementary procedures. In case these did not work, the services of magic were called in, the woman making a visit to a mortuary. The text then gives an incantation to help the unfortunate woman, part of which reads:

The woman having a difficult delivery . . . is in great difficulty. The baby is held fast. . . . She who is creating a child is shrouded in the dust of death. Her eyes fail, she cannot see; her lips are

138

sealed, she cannot open them. . . . She wears no veil, she has no shame. [The woman is now represented as speaking] 'Stand by me, . . . O merciful Marduk! Now am I surrounded with trouble. Reach out to me! Bring forth that sealed-up one, creature of the gods, as a human creature; let him come forth! Let him see the light!'

There follows the recitation of a myth about Maid-of-the-Moon-god, the name of the consort of the Moon-god in the form of a cow, who was having a difficult delivery until the two daughters of Anu came down from heaven to anoint her with oil and 'waters of labour pangs'. The incantation concludes: 'Just as Maid-of-the-Moon-god gave birth easily, so may the maid having a difficult delivery give birth.'

Certain drugs might also be used to assist in childbirth, for example, the bark of a certain tree, which the woman in labour had to chew. The woman might also be massaged all over her stomach with an ointment compounded of various substances, or have a kind of rolling-pin of magic wood rolled over her. Midwives might be in attendance at a birth, and presumably gave some commonsense practical assistance, within the limits imposed by the magico-religious mumbo-jumbo. Death in childbirth was an ever-present peril; there are many references to this, and the threat the dreaded demoness Lamashtu (*alias* Daughter of Anu) posed to mother and infant was expressed by saying that 'she touches the bellies of women in labour'. Another name of Lamashtu was 'the one who kindles fires', a reference to the high fever occurring with fatal cases of puerperal septicaemia.

Even when a baby had come safely into the world, it might still be at risk if the mother failed to lactate. The well-to-do might compensate for this by using a wet-nurse, but for a baby of the poor it spelt death. A text speaks bluntly of the breast drying up so that the baby will not live.

Long before there was any nuclear fall-out to blame for deformed births, babies were born with various abnormalities; we know this in particular because such births were thought to have significance as omens, and were duly reported. We find, for example, references to a child born with one foot, or Siamese twins, or a hermaphrodite. As a normal but very exceptional birth, we find quadruplets reported.

A newly-born baby would be placed in a basket as a cot. As he grew bigger, his mother or nurse would wear a baby sling to carry him around. It may be added that in Assyria, as predominantly in the Near East both ancient and modern, it was the birth of boys that really counted as a blessing; infant exposure, which we mention elsewhere, probably befell daughters more frequently than sons.

Marriage

Marriage in Assyria was predominantly monogamous, though this general statement has to be qualified for different periods and different social strata. Moreover, so far as men were concerned, monogamy was not a synonym for monotony; it related to legal status rather than sexual limitation, and there was usually nothing, other than his wealth and stamina, to prevent a man from having a secondary wife or concubines in addition to the lady who enjoyed full status and legal rights as wife. But there were exceptions even to this, and as early as the Old Assyrian period (beginning of the second millennium) we meet a form of marriage contract in which a man is debarred from taking a second wife, although he is explicitly conceded the right to use prostitutes. A marriage contract sometimes specifically laid down that if the wife did not bear children the husband might take a slave-girl for that purpose, the children so born counting as the wife's.

The family was patriarchal, in both legal and social aspects. Descent and inheritance were tied to the father's side, and the senior male of the family wielded the authority. The extent of patriarchal authority was such that a husband could in certain circumstances execute his wife, whilst a father-in-law could dispose of a widowed daughter-in-law in marriage. This was in accordance with the principle that a woman was under the control of the male head of the family, and on marriage left the jurisdiction of her father for that of her father-in-law.

Marriage, to be legally recognized, entailed certain requirements. For a normal marriage, written documents had to be drawn up; marriage by elevating a concubine to the status of wife (see below) required her to be formally invested with a veil; and marriage with a widow became recognized by cohabitation for two years.

Relationships between husband and wife could be as varied as in the modern world. At the one extreme we hear of love and accord to old age; at the other of quarrels between husband and wife – sometimes so severe that the wife walked out.

As was stated above, a man might promote a concubine to the rank of wife. The Middle Assyrian laws set out in detail how this is to be done: 'If a man will veil his concubine, he shall have five or six of his neighbours seated, and shall veil her in their presence and shall declare thus: "She is my wife". She is then his wife.'

The reference to veiling is to be seen in the context of the law preceding this one, which lays down in some detail which classes of women must be veiled and which must not. Veiling was the more honourable situation, and at one extreme married women had to be veiled in public, whilst at the other, veiling was strictly forbidden to prostitutes; if it were discovered that a prostitute was going about veiled, she was subject to severe penalties, including fifty strokes of the rod and having pitch poured over her head.

The normal form of marriage was for a woman to leave the family of her birth and enter her husband's home. However, some scholars have thought that in the Middle Assyrian period there was another possibility, since the Assyrian laws make provision for a situation in which the wife remained in her father's house. The relevant law says: 'If a woman lives in her father's house, and her husband continually visits her. . .', and then goes on to legislate for rights over the property which the husband has settled on the woman. It is clear from other laws that although the wife remained in her father's home, this might be only temporary, and that the ultimate authority over the woman herself, and over the property which went with her, lay with the family into which she had married and not with her own father.

Some people have supposed that the situation here, in which the wife remained in her father's house, was related to infant marriage; infant marriage undoubtedly occurred, since the Assyrian laws specifically provided for the marriage of boys from the age of ten. One could suppose that in infant marriage the juvenile wife might continue to reside with her father until she was old enough for consummation, when she would go to her husband's home. But even if this did sometimes happen, there is nothing to suggest that infant marriage of a girl was the only case this law covered.

The simplest explanation is that the law rested on the distinction between two different stages in the process of marriage. In Assyria, as in some other societies, the legal formalities of marriage (the drawing up of contracts) could be separated by a period of time from the physical consummation. The law about the husband visiting his wife at her father's house would then simply refer to a situation in which, after the contracts had been drawn up in the usual way, there may have been some delay in the woman moving to her husband's home, with the marriage eventually being consummated in the woman's original home. Infant marriage might be one special case of this. Nothing in the situation would prevent the wife at some subsequent time removing to her husband's home in the usual way.

There were various gifts and payments linked to marriage. At the time of the marriage jewellery was handed over to the bride, though

it did not become her absolute property, but remained in the ownership of her husband and on his death passed to his heirs; if he lacked
heirs, however, his wife retained it. So long as there were sons, the
wife was not her husband's heir. The husband might also set aside
a portion of property to provide for the wife in the event of her
being left a widow, though legally this remained a part of his estate
as long as he lived. Another sum of money passed from the
husband's family to the bride's father, but had to be returned if the
bride died without male issue. Some lawyers and anthropologists
object to this being called a bride-price, but in effect that is what it
was. The bride herself might bring property into the marriage, as
a kind of dowry. We find, for example, a seventh-century marriage
contract which sets out the dowry with which a high female palace
official equipped her daughter. It included jewellery, clothes, beds
and chairs and various pots and pans and food vessels. The dowry
remained in the ownership of the wife and eventually went to her
children, not to her husband's heirs, who might be his brothers; but
although ownership remained vested in the wife, she seems not to
have had the right to dispose of it whilst her husband was alive.

It will be clear that the Assyrian family was basically man-orien-
tated, women being essentially under the authority of their men-
folk. According to the Middle Assyrian laws, the husband had the
right to inflict corporal punishment, even mutilation, upon his wife.
But the prescribing of such barbarisms in the laws probably represented not a norm but a statement of the limits beyond which the
husband must not go; he was at least prevented from killing his wife,
save for proved adultery. A man's rights over his wife apparently
extended to selling her, though this cannot have been common, as
we have only one document concerning such a transaction.

There seem to have been some customary ceremonies which took
place between the time of the marriage contract and the consummation. Two of the laws allude to the husband pouring oil on the head
of his bride, and although we have no further details, such a
ceremony clearly belongs with the religious practice of anointing,
very common in the ancient Near East and frequently mentioned in
the Bible. As the same two laws have reference to the bringing (by
the bridegroom) of dishes of food for a banquet, evidently there
was also a wedding feast.

The sexual code was very strict in respect to wives, and a married
man might put his adulterous wife to death, unless she successfully
claimed that she had been raped. Widows had more freedom and one
law envisaged a widow cohabiting with a man without a marriage
contract; if this situation continued for two years the widow form-

ally became a wife with legal protection, notwithstanding the lack of marriage contract.

A man might divorce his wife. At some places and periods this might involve his cutting off the hem of the lady's garment before official witnesses. In Babylonia there is mention of divorce money, but in Assyria the man was not required to give his ex-wife compensation, though she retained the gifts which he had brought her at the time of the marriage. The woman had no comparable rights of divorce at will and, indeed, in some places and times in ancient Mesopotamia, if she ventured to express such a wish she could be put out of her husband's house naked and penniless. But matters were not always and everywhere so unevenly loaded against the wife, and in the Nuzi area of Assyria (near Kirkuk) in the fifteenth century we find a woman, adopted as a daughter and married to a slave, saying: 'Take me away from Mannuya [her husband] and give me to Arteya as wife!' In general in Assyria, if a woman's husband went off and left her without either direct support or sons to support her, after five years she might take another husband, and in normal circumstances her first husband could not reclaim her if he subsequently returned. There were, however, exceptions to this. If the first husband had been absent for reasons beyond his control, such as capture by a brigand, he might reclaim his wife even after five years, subject to providing the second husband with a woman in lieu. And if his reason for absence was that he was abroad on royal service, the wife did not acquire the right to remarriage even after five years.

One wonders how a woman left without provision for five years managed. She might have gone back to her father's home, or to the home of one of her husband's brothers, though the law says nothing about this. What it does say, however, is quite revealing: 'If, before five years, [the woman] has gone to live with a man and has borne children, her husband, when he comes, because she has not waited in accordance with the marriage contract, but has got married, shall take her and her progeny.' The law gives the impression that, although the woman had acted irregularly, the situation was accepted without the imposition of a specific penalty upon her – possibly in recognition that in some circumstances a woman had either to take another husband or starve. It is interesting that the children born during the woman's illicit union, though illegitimate, were regarded as valuable property and could be claimed by the first husband. It is also interesting that the Assyrians did not set a premium on virginity, so absurdly overvalued in Judaism, Islam and Christianity.

Sexual Life

We know a certain amount about the sexual side of life in ancient Mesopotamia, though only a small part of our evidence is specifically linked to Assyria rather than to Babylonia.

Sexual intercourse is depicted on a number of cylinder seals and terracotta plaques, which show that several different positions were practised; in addition to the face-to-face position regarded as normal in modern Western society (though not in some other parts of the world), there is frequent representation of intercourse with the man entering the woman from behind. Some Assyriologists speak of this position as anal intercourse and others interpret it as homosexuality. But in at least some instances the person at the receiving end is a woman, and the position is perfectly compatible with vaginal intercourse from behind. On the other hand, we do know that some ancient Mesopotamian men engaged in anal intercourse with their wives. We learn this, as we do much else about life in Babylonia and Assyria, from a collection of omens, one of which refers to a situation in which a man 'keeps saying to his wife: "Bring your backside".' Whether between a man and wife this was used as a form of contraception, or just because they fancied a change, we are left to guess. But elsewhere there is explicit reference to a high priestess having anal intercourse in order to prevent pregnancy.

Another position mentioned envisages a man lying on his back with a woman on top. This, rather than transvestism, may be the allusion in a text which speaks of an Amorite saying: 'You be the man, let me be the woman.' Transvestism was, however, certainly known in Babylonia and presumably in Assyria. Sometimes people had intercourse standing up. There are references to sex play, with a man encouraging the woman to grasp his penis, and the woman asking a man to caress her vulva. Kissing and the caressing of breasts are mentioned in texts, and the latter is depicted. We also find mention of a woman masturbating whilst exchanging glances with a man. Both men and women sometimes lubricated their sexual organs with oil to assist penetration.

Contraception was certainly sometimes practised, for we find texts which refer, for example, to 'the naditu-women [a class of temple personnel] who by skilful ways keep their wombs intact'; we do not know what 'skilful ways' were meant in this case. In other instances, however, we have specific information that pessaries were placed in the vagina for this purpose. Charms and herbs might also be employed.

When naditu-women and other classes of temple personnel engaged in sexual promiscuity, their attempts at contraception were not always successful, for we have mention of children born to them. If unwanted babies were born (not only to temple women), they might be thrown out to die in the street or be eaten by dogs. But such callousness occurred alongside goodheartedness, and we find mention of a person snatching a child from a dog's mouth in such a case.

Homosexuality amongst men is well attested in Mesopotamia from the third millennium onwards, though some of the plaques and seals which have been interpreted as showing this may rather be instances of intercourse (vaginal, not anal) with a woman from the rear. There are texts which refer to homosexual relations, including sodomy, between men and men or men and boys, and in Babylonia there seems to have been no condemnation of this. But in Assyria in the Middle Assyrian period such behaviour was in some circumstances severely dealt with. It is possible that in this respect there was an actual difference of attitude between Babylonia and Assyria. The Assyrian laws lay down that a man who committed sodomy upon another should first have sodomy performed on him and then be castrated. It is not clear whether this covered sodomy in all discovered cases or whether the reference was only to homosexual rape; in view of the ancient principle of making the punishment fit the crime and the fact that the offender was himself subjected to homosexual rape, the latter seems more likely.

Eunuchs were quite common, but a man who achieved this by castration as a punishment was exceptional; the usual practice was to castrate boys. A particular function of eunuchs was to serve at court, and many of them became high officials – an administrative practice which continued in the Turkish and Persian empires up to the nineteenth century A.D. But not all Assyrian courtiers were eunuchs, a point emphasized by the listing together as courtiers of ša-ziqni, literally 'having a beard', that is non-eunuchs, and ša-reši, 'eunuchs'. There was also, in Assyria as elsewhere, a small proportion of males who failed to develop normally and became natural eunuchs; this was probably the source of many male prostitutes.

The Mesopotamians recognized that sex had a religious component. There were religious prostitutes – male, female and neuter – associated with some temples, with sexual practices which in Babylonia included homosexuality. References to temple sexual activity are less common for Assyria than for Babylonia, but there are sufficient to show that it did occur in Assyria. Although male prostitutes were often eunuchs, this was apparently not always the case. Mesopotamian women seem to have been markedly normal, for there is only a single known allusion to lesbianism. This contrasts with the multitude of references to wives taking lovers which, since it could be fatal for all concerned, must have had powerful attractions. If the aggrieved husband caught the lovers at it he had the right – after due accusation and proof – to kill them both, or to cut off his wife's nose and have the lover castrated. Both had to be treated correspondingly, and letting the wife go unpunished meant letting the lover off also. The husband might also be at risk if his wife took a lover, for we find a reference to a woman urging her lover to murder her husband so that she could marry her paramour.

Incest is sometimes mentioned, for example, a man with his sister, his niece, his daughter, his mother-in-law, or his mother after his father's death. It may be unfair to attribute this last to Assyrians, for our evidence for this piece of nastiness is actually from Babylonia, from the laws of Hammurabi in the early second millennium. It was considered a heinous offence, for which the penalty was the burning of both mother and son.

As in other periods and places, people fell madly in love, and ate their hearts out if rejected. We find references to severe depression from this cause. Sometimes a man or woman would pray to a deity, or resort to a magic spell to win the affection of the loved one. Some magic rituals were guaranteed, such as one of which it is claimed that, if the man performs it, 'this woman will speak to you whenever you meet her. She will be powerless to resist and you can make love to her'. If lovers' quarrels occurred, the disconsolate lady might have resort to charms and spells. Thus of a lady in such a sad case we find the recipe 'with this charm she will not sleep alone; she will be loved'.

Men had other problems in this area, amongst them greying hair, impotence and premature ejaculation. Greying hair could be treated both with a lotion and with an incantation. A whole series of rituals, and various medical preparations including ointments and aphrodisiacs, existed to counter impotence. But whilst premature ejaculation is referred to, no mention of treatment has been found; presumably this was accepted as something that time and practice would cure.

Education

Our knowledge of education in ancient Mesopotamia is patchy. We are best informed about the education of scribes, for the obvious reason that it was scribes who composed the texts, and it was their own kind of education that would interest them. Even in this, all our detailed evidence comes from Babylonia in the early second millennium, and the situation in Assyria at a later period might have been very different.

Our most detailed information for education in first millennium Assyria relates to the royal family. Ashurbanipal in the seventh century narrates how he 'studied the wisdom of Nabu, explored the entire scribal art, the knowledge of all the experts; learned shooting with the bow, and riding horses and chariots and taking the reins'. Elsewhere he elaborates on his literacy: 'I have read complicated texts of which the Sumerian version is obscure and the Akkadian version is difficult to get clear. I research into the cuneiform writing on stones from before the Flood.' But this was almost certainly not typical. Literacy in cuneiform writing was largely limited to scribes and administrators, though from the late eighth century the Aramaic language was making big advances in Assyria, and the alphabetic writing system associated with it – much simpler than cuneiform – was coming into wider use. For the training of scribes there were schools; we find, for example, a group called 'the scribes of Kalizi' (a town in eastern Assyria) referring to their pupils learning the scribal craft. But we have no evidence for the existence of schools for other areas of education.

The hereditary system was deeply ingrained in Assyrian society and normally at most levels a son would learn his father's trade or profession by watching and helping from as soon as he could walk, and would in due course carry it on after him. Apprenticeship to a craftsman was also possible and we have the texts of apprenticeship contracts laying down the obligations upon the two sides.

King and Court

'*L'État c'est moi*' could with full justification have been put into the mouth of any New Assyrian king. Every aspect of state life – international, political, military, religious – was linked to the king. In theory the king's power was absolute, though in practice it was held within tight bounds by the operation of taboos with which his exalted position surrounded the king.

Compared with the Assyrian kings, the Israelite and Judaean rulers of David's line were newcomers and upstarts. A long line of kings, over ninety of them, whose names are preserved to us in an unbroken though sometimes shadowy chain, had ruled in Assyria for well over a thousand years before ever David founded his dynasty. As noted earlier, although we, like the later Assyrians themselves, regard the earlier rulers as kings, down to the fourteenth century the Assyrian ruler – with the one exception of Shamshi-

Adad I – did not call himself by the title we translate 'king'; instead he would use a term meaning 'vicegerent of the god Ashur', reflecting his status as the god's representative on earth. The Assyrian ruler was not quite divine, but he was effectively the shadow of god. We find an official writing to the king saying so in so many words: 'The father of the king my lord was the image of Bel, and the king my lord is the image of Bel also.' The kings could even be called 'the divine sun of the people'. We might call these rulers priest-kings, for within the city of Ashur they were heirs to both sacerdotal functions and secular power. As the city-state of Ashur extended its area of control to become what we think of as Assyria, the authority of the ruler of Ashur extended with it over the other cities of ancient foundation – Arrapkha and Erbil and Nineveh, and their territories. But to the end, even when the capital had moved elsewhere, the kings of Assyria retained a special religious link with the city Ashur.

The king lived in a building called in Akkadian *ekallu*, meaning literally 'big house'. As the king's residence, the term is customarily translated 'palace', but the same word is used of administrative buildings away from the capital, when it is appropriately rendered 'Government House'. The royal palace was in fact more than the king's residence; it was also the state's main centre of government. As such, it housed not only the king's domestic quarters and provisions for state entertaining, with cooks, bakers and brewers, but also a vast staff of state officers, civil administrators and military officers, as well as foreign ambassadors, and princes from vassal states kept at court both as hostages and to be educated in Assyrian ways. Other persons within the royal palace would include scribes for various languages and writing systems, tax officials, interpreters, physicians, musicians, and people within the area of religion and magic, such as various classes of priests and diviners. There was also, of course, a royal treasury, with appropriate staff. The provisioning of all the personnel concerned was a heavy charge, acquitted from the stream of supplies sent in by provincial officials. At one period there were also lions attached to the court, receiving regular rations of sheep.

Within the royal court there were – or could be – several sub-courts, such as that of the queen mother or the crown prince, with their own staffs, though at some periods the crown prince had a palace of his own, called the Succession House. The provincial governor might also have a palace in the capital, separate from the royal palace.

The king was not readily accessible to all the people at court, since as a semi-divine being he was subject to many taboos. Norm-

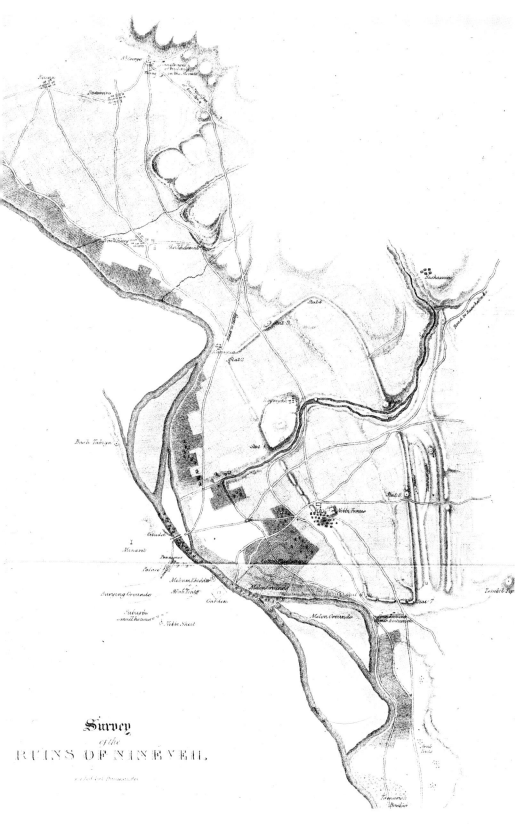

17   C. J. Rich's plan of Nineveh (C. J. Rich, *Narrative of a Residence in Koordistan and on the Site of Ancient Nineveh*, 1836)

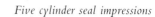
Five cylinder seal impressions

18A   A god and a winged bull hunting a dragon
(Staatliche Museen zu Berlin)

18B   Suckling goat beside tree
(Staatliche Museen zu Berlin)

18C   Stag amongst trees
(Pierpont Morgan Library)

18D   Lion-man in combat
(Staatliche Museen zu Berlin)

18E   The Assyrian king
'Sacred Tree' scene
(British Museum)

19A Vulture carrying off entrails of those killed in battle (British Museum, photo H. W. F. Saggs)

19B Lion colossus (Mansell Collection)

20A A woman's face in ivory – the so-called 'Mona Lisa of the Well' (Hirmer Fotoarchiv, Munich)

20B Carved ivory showing a Nubian bringing a monkey and an antelope as tribute (The Metropolitan Museum of Art)

21A Drawing from a late eighth-century bas relief of officers' tents in camp (A. H. Layard, *The Monuments of Nineveh*, London, 1849–53)

21B Watering and grooming horses, on a bas relief (British Museum, photo H. W. F. Saggs)

22A Artist's reconstruction on façade of temple at Khorsabad (Oriental Institute, University of Chicago)

22B Seventh-century bas relief with a three-stage representation of a lion being released and killed (Mansell Collection)

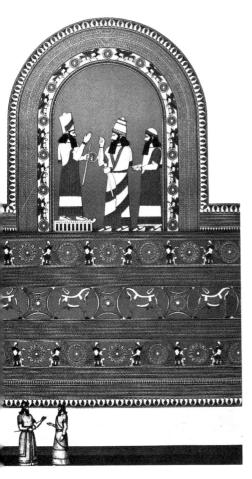

23A Restored wall painting of King Sargon, from the throne room at Khorsabad (G. Loud, *Korsabad*, Volume II, Chicago, 1938)

23B Carved ivory plaque embellished with gold and precious stones. Recovered from a well at Nimrud (ancient Calah), it depicts a lioness killing a Negro (British Museum, photo H. W. F. Saggs)

24A Prisoners in Assyrian camp (Brit Museum, photo H. W. F. Saggs)

24B Deportation in comfort – transport provided for women and children (British Museum, photo H. W. F. Saggs)

24C Soldiers drawing carts, from a bas relief (c. 700) (British Museum, photo H. W. F. Saggs)

ally only one official – the superintendent of the palace – had permanent direct access to him. Even the crown prince might only come into his presence when the astrological omens were favourable. Yet there were occasions when other courtiers could have interviews with him, for a correspondent mentions to the king the practice of a courtier accepting a present from a suppliant who wished him to speak to the king on his behalf. An outsider admitted to a royal interview was blindfolded. The likelihood is that the king would be formally approachable when the omens were good, but kept in seclusion when they were unfavourable – a situation which would have put considerable influence in the hands of the experts who interpreted the omens.

There were occasions when all the high officials of state appeared before the king to pay their respects. This could be a costly business for the persons concerned, for substantial presents were expected. The possible scale of presents from high officials to royalty is given by the pound of gold which one governor sent to the crown prince; in the values of the 1980s A.D., this would be worth over £3000.

Mention has already been made of taboos to which the king might be subject, either to satisfy the requirements of religious ritual or as a safeguard against a day or event of ill omen. Some of these could involve indignity or discomfort. Thus on different occasions we find the Assyrian king having to fast several days until the new moon appeared, abstain from cooked food, wear the clothes of a nanny, remain indoors, wear a special white robe for several days, or sit for a week in a reed hut being treated as if he were ill. Omens could bring about the suspension of all state business; for instance, treaties, which had to be ratified by an oath to the gods, might only be concluded on certain days, because taking an oath on a day of ill-omen might have dire consequences. The most curious taboo was one by which, at the appearance of certain particularly grave omens, the king had to abdicate temporarily, handing the throne over to a substitute; the substitute married a bride and reigned for a hundred days, standing ready to bear the evil threatened for the king and so save the state from disaster. At the end of the hundred days, the substitute king and his wife were executed and buried with great ceremony and the real king resumed office in safety.

One New Assyrian king in particular, Esarhaddon, was markedly hag-ridden by superstition about omens, and it must have been child's play for the experts in these matters to manipulate him. We find him, for example, worried about the portent of a mongoose which had run under his chariot. He knew an omen about a mongoose running between a man's legs; did this still apply if the man was in a chariot at the time? (It did.) Another time he was

149

worried about an earthquake – not the event itself but the evil it foretold. The diviner reassured him: 'He who caused the earthquake has also made the counter-ritual to cancel the evil it portends.' Esarhaddon also expressed worries, and had to be comforted, about eclipses. Another time he had apparently been trying to work out for himself from the appropriate textbook what a certain birth-omen foretold. The expert discouraged such amateur meddling. That textbook, he said, was very difficult, and no one who had not made a minute study of it could possibly understand it. He would explain it in person when he came to the king (which is, incidentally, evidence for the diviners having easy access to the king).

The household quarters of the king were of course quite separate from the part of the palace concerned with state administration. His major problem here was keeping his womenfolk in order, and we have the text of a series of edicts (from between the fourteenth and eleventh centuries) dealing with this. This must have been quite an embarrassment, for, in addition to any wives or concubines which the king might have taken from personal choice, he would have a large number of other ladies arriving at his court, either sent from foreign princes seeking dynastic alliance, or brought as part of the booty from conquered cities. Life could become tedious and tense for a brood of women shut up together, in competition for one very busy man, and the edicts have reference to the king's wives and other women fighting and cursing between themselves. They could be a bitchy lot. This may have been entertaining to members of the palace staff, but if such a person listened to women quarrelling – or singing, which then as now in the Near East probably sounded remarkably similar – he risked a severe beating and having one of his ears cut off. Between the women themselves, discipline was harsh. A palace lady had the right to give her maid thirty strokes of the rod for a first offence, and it was grimly envisaged that this might be done so viciously that she killed the girl, though if that happened the lady herself was liable to punishment.

There were rigorous rules about encounters of courtiers with palace women. If a palace woman called to a courtier whilst she was undressed and he glanced at her whilst answering, he was severely beaten; this looks as if some of the women were so bored that they titillated themselves by teasing the courtiers. In no circumstances might a courtier approach to within seven paces of a woman to speak with her, and an illicit meeting, if discovered, meant death for both. If an official had to go into the interior of the palace, all the women had to be hustled away from the area outside the harem quarters.

There was the usual oriental taboo upon menstruating women,

and one edict reads: 'When the time of offerings arrives [a particular religious occasion], an unapproachable woman [implying a menstruating woman] may not enter the king's presence.' The specifying of the particular occasion is interesting, since it suggests that at other times she might.

10

The Domestic Scene

The objects with which people surround themselves are often as revealing about their attitudes as a study of their institutions. Thus, an examination of the dress and household equipment of the Assyrians may well help us understand what manner of people they were.

Clothing

Our object here is to concentrate as far as possible on the evidence which is particularly applicable to Assyria, mainly in the later period (first millennium). There are two main kinds of evidence. Firstly, there are texts, which provide us with many words relating to clothing, including a detailed list in an ancient lexical composition, a kind of forerunner of *Roget's Thesaurus*. Unfortunately, this does not take us as far as we might hope. In many cases we have no clear idea of what items the words applied to, or what the garments looked like. This is where we seek for help from our second main source of evidence: actual representations of clothing. These are to be found on many art objects, such as sculptures, bas reliefs, plaques, carved ivories and cylinder seals.

Did everyone wear clothes? So far as we know, from the third millennium onwards, normally the only people who sometimes went naked were certain priests, in rituals that called for cultic nudity. Occasionally, also, war prisoners would be naked when making submission. A bas relief shows people in the nude amongst those towing a heavily-laden boat, but in this case they may have stripped off because at times they had to wade in the water. The possibility of whole groups of population being naked is suggested by a passage in which King Esarhaddon says he provided the naked with clothing. But this was in Babylonia, when Esarhaddon was attempting to undo the devastation his father Sennacherib had wrought there, and so the situation, with large numbers of penniless refugees, was exceptional; it is even possible that Esarhaddon was exaggerating the extent of penury to emphasize his own bounty. One text mentions the possibility of people being so destitute that they might wear garments made of papyrus, the ancient equivalent of paper.

We may consider first the typical clothing of a woman. The basic item was a garment round her hips to cover her genitals. We know that it must have passed between the legs and then been tied, from the fact that a text mentions a prostitute having to untie hers to make herself available. It must have been similar to the old-fashioned type of baby's nappy, though fastened with a knot rather than a safety pin. There are some hints that a woman might also have worn a garment over her breasts, but the evidence is not sufficient for us to speak more definitely on this. We do meet representations of maid-servants with bare breasts, but this may have been an artistic convention and does not necessarily prove a prevalence of topless slave girls.

Whatever the situation may have been with the slave girls, an Assyrian lady would not have been seen in public without substantial top clothing, although in the privacy of her own home she was probably very lightly clad. This certainly seems to have been the case with palace ladies in the late second millennium, since the royal harem edicts of that period decree that a palace lady must get permission to send for garments to wear for going out. It is likely that the specified garments, making a lady properly dressed, were those in which ladies are represented in art, so that indoor garb must have been skimpier. Representations show that a lady, when seen in public, customarily wore a loose gown from shoulder to ankle, half-sleeved, and held by a girdle (see plate 1A). Beneath the bottom of the dress three or four anklets showed on each leg. Her long hair (sometimes helped out by false hair, as the texts reveal) would be elaborately braided in several plaits. Mention in the royal harem edicts of shoes as an addition for going out proves that indoors a lady would go barefoot.

Prostitutes, not unexpectedly, tarted themselves up in a special way to attract attention. We hear of them wearing a particular type of leather jacket, and one type of temple prostitute was distinguished by curly hair. Modesty was not encouraged in prostitutes; they were forbidden by law to veil themselves, which respectable married women always did out of doors.

The basic form of male dress was clothing which covered the man from neck to knees, with short sleeves and held by a belt at the waist, but there were variations upon this. From the way the clothing hangs, it must in many cases have been a single garment, a sort of smock. However, in other representations the part below the belt, and that only, has a full-length vertical fringe, showing that it must have been wound round the body, and suggesting that

153

it was a separate item of apparel rather like a kilt. The upper part of this basic form of dress could be modified in various ways: in some instances we see straps running down diagonally from each shoulder and crossing on the chest: in others it has been developed into a form of chain-mail for archers.

The common soldier and the ordinary man wore this knee-length garb by itself, but people of higher status, such as officials and military officers, added a cloak over it. This was certainly a matter of status, for the royal harem edicts laid down that if a courtier were guilty of neglect of duty he would be stripped of his cloak. A cloak was commonly of wool, sometimes of linen, in a colour range which included blue, red, purple and white. Distinct from the cloak was another over-garment, which, since it usually had no armholes and was put on over the neck, must have been rather like a poncho, or the ecclesiastical chasuble.

The dress of the king, and also that of high officials, could be very elaborate, so much so that it is sometimes difficult to decide exactly what the king is wearing when we see him represented on bas reliefs. When he is shown dressed for ceremonial occasions, we can see several layers of cloth, though whether or not more than one garment was involved is disputable. The part visible to us could have been a single length of fringed cloth wound round the king like a sari; it was richly decorated with jewelled rosettes and sometimes embroidered with religious motifs. In situations in which more freedom of movement was necessary, as in war or the hunt, the king might wear a simpler form of dress, based ultimately on the tunic of the common soldier, but with the added dignity of its being of ankle length. It looked rather like a nightshirt, or what in Iraq today is known as a *dishdashah*.

The most common material for clothing was wool, although linen had been known from an early period and was often used for better-quality garments. Cotton did not become available until Sennacherib introduced it into Assyria in about 700, from which time it was used for the making of cloth. Other materials sometimes used, of which instances have already been noted, included leather and papyrus.

Footwear

To judge by bas reliefs, Assyrians often went barefoot, even in war. When they did use footwear, the commonest form was the sandal, of a type with a wedge heel and secured by thongs passing over the top of the foot and round the big toe (plate 5A). But more elaborate footwear is sometimes shown (plate 5B). One form was a shoe covering the whole foot, with the part over the arch made of a different material from the rest of the shoe; it looks as if it was cloth stitched into leather. Boots are quite often shown, particularly worn by hunters and men on campaign. These were usually calf-length, worn over long stockings. Here also two different materials were used, the front of the leg of the boot apparently being of cloth, with the remainder of leather. There was also a leather reinforcement at the heel. Some foreigners wore a type of shoe with toe caps curling upwards, like a form of slipper still found in Turkey. From the area around Kirkuk in about 1400, we hear of leggings made of some sort of cloth, though it is not clear whether these were parts of boots or separate items. Information about ladies' footwear is less abundant, though we do find references to particular types of shoe worn by ladies, and amongst other evidence we possess a representation of Ashurbanipal's queen wearing a kind of slipper, covering the front half of the foot, of the type currently known as 'mules'.

Jewellery

Both men and women in Assyria wore jewellery, though not of identical type. Mention has already been made of the wearing of anklets by women, a custom continuing amongst peasant women in Iraq to the present day. At some periods in Mesopotamia women of the highest class wore a breast-plate of precious metals and jewels, but there seems to be no evidence for this in the late period in Assyria. Some jewellery of Assyrian women, consisting of pendants of chalcedony on a gold chain, have been found in graves. Men might also wear such pendants, as we know from an agate bearing the inscription 'neck-stone belonging to Tukulti-Ninurta'. This was the second king of that name, who reigned from 890 to 884; his greater predecessor Tukulti-Ninurta I (1244–1208) is depicted on a relief wearing earrings. A man might also wear a stone amulet hung from his neck, either in the form of a demon's head to keep away evil or inscribed with a charm. Cylinder seals – often of semi-precious stone – were frequently worn in the same way. It was usual for Assyrian men of rank, and sometimes women also, to wear bracelets on the wrists. These bracelets often carried a circular rosette, making them look curiously like wrist-watches (see plate 12A).

Earrings were a common item of adornment of both men and women, basically having the form of a crescent of gold or silver with pendants of various shapes soldered to them. The reader who

THE MIGHT THAT WAS ASSYRIA

wants more comprehensive details of these will find them well set out in K. R. Maxwell-Hyslop, *Western Asiatic Jewellery c. 3000–612 B.C.* (1971), pp. 235–46.

Hair and Headgear

Those Assyrians who had it in them to do so, wore very full beards and heavy moustaches; men represented without face hair were probably either very young or eunuchs. The hair was worn long but very carefully coiffured, with the ears left exposed. Both beards and head hair are commonly shown waved, and curled at the ends; as it is unlikely that the hair of all Assyrian men was both wavy and curly naturally, many must have had the services of hairdressers. Some officials with a function in religious cult, whom we might loosely call priests, received a tonsure as a mark of their admission to office, as did physicians.

We have many representations of Assyrians wearing headgear, but a large proportion of these are gods, royalty, soldiers or religious personnel, who are certainly in some cases wearing archaic or professional head-dress associated with status or ceremonial. These may no more represent general wear at the time than do today the busby of the guardsman, the biretta of a Roman Catholic priest, or a don's mortar-board. The only form of Assyrian head-dress sufficiently widely represented for us to conclude that it was an item of everyday wear was basically a headband. There were various forms of it, which the art experts distinguish and give special names to, but for practical purposes they were all headbands, though they could be decorated or plain, and with or without streamers. Either men or women might wear such a headband by itself to keep their hair tidy; or it might be fixed over a turban which, in the case of the king and high officials, could be of a very elaborate type.

Household Furnishings

That our knowledge of Assyrian household equipment is patchy is no fault of the scribes of ancient Mesopotamia. The educated class had a passion for bringing system into their world, and in aid of this they drew up long lists of almost anything, from lists of gods to terms relating to sheep. Contents of houses were no exception, and cuneiform texts give compendious catalogues of items of household equipment. Unfortunately in many cases these terms remain no more than words to us. Sometimes, however, additional textual

156

details, or discoveries of artifacts, allow us to fit the name to an actual item of equipment or piece of furniture. But even with identifiable objects from ancient Mesopotamia, not all can be assumed to have been in use in Assyria; in what follows we are concerned only with what can be proved, or reasonably inferred, for Assyrian houses and palaces in the second and first millennia.

The variety of furniture used by mankind is limited by certain common needs. Basically people need, if possible, some means of insulating them from the dampness, coldness and hardness of the ground whilst they sleep, and some surface from which to eat their food. The former requirement gives rise to the use of mats and blankets, developing into beds; the latter involves either trays directly on the ground, or trays on legs, which we know as tables. With trays, the eaters sit on the ground, perhaps with cushions for comfort, but tables – favoured by the ancient Mesopotamians – require the addition of stools, benches or chairs. All the basic furniture items – stools, benches, chairs, tables, beds – were found in ancient Assyria. But this does not mean that everyone in ancient Assyria used them; the more elaborate pieces were limited to the better-off, and the ordinary man might well go through life with no furnishings beyond a few reed mats, which had to serve for sitting, eating, sleeping and, at his final end, for burial.

Stools, tables and chairs

The basic stool was of reeds on a wooden frame, though from the upper reaches of Assyrian society we hear of stools of much more elaborate structure: these might be made of choice hardwoods decorated with inlays of ivory or gold. Stools might be used either as seats, or to support the feet of a person sitting on a chair.

Benches, most commonly of mud-brick or baked brick, though sometimes of wood, and usually fixed along walls, are attested archaeologically from early periods in both temples and dwelling houses. Specific evidence for them in later Assyria seems to be lacking; a word found in a New Assyrian context which one scholar takes as meaning a bench for sleeping on probably denoted something quite different.

There is, however, abundant Assyrian evidence for chairs. These might have their frames of various hardwoods, and were sometimes decorated with inlays of copper, bronze, silver, gold or carved ivory. The seat could be covered with leather, palm fibre or rushes, and might be padded with felt. Sometimes the chairs were provided with loose linen covers. Various elaborations were possible upon the simple chair. For example, it could be developed into an armchair, which in an extreme case would become a royal throne; we see Sennacherib sitting on such an armchair at the siege of Lachish (see plate 4b). Chairs might also be provided with poles and used as sedan chairs – a development which strictly speaking disqualifies them for inclusion within household equipment. We hear of Sennacherib using such a chair.

There is no difficulty in finding examples of tables from Assyria; both actual tables and models of them have been found in excavations, and we also see them represented on reliefs. Normally they were made of wood, though metal decoration could be added, and exceptionally a table might be cast in bronze. In first-millennium Assyria the predominant type seems to have been a fairly small square table on four ornamented legs, which might terminate in feet of ox-hoof design. Evidence for the use of tablecloths comes in such passages as one which mentions 'a linen cloth on the gold table of the god Shamash', though this particular example is from Babylonia, not Assyria. Even table-napkins were used, though not in the manner usual with us. Rather, they were held by a servant and offered to the diner to wipe his hands when he washed them after the meal; a relic of this ancient Near Eastern usage persists in the way an Anglican High Church server offers the priest a cloth to wipe his fingers at the ablutions during the Eucharist.

Beds

Not everyone possessed a bed; the poor would sleep on straw or a reed mat. Where there were beds they normally consisted of a wooden frame supporting a base, usually also of wood, though there were other possibilities. Alternative materials included rope, interwoven reeds, or a criss-cross of metal strips. Some (but not all) beds were provided with wooden sides, making them in effect shallow wooden boxes. They were supported on legs which could be of ornamental form, often – just as with tables – a foot carved to the shape of a claw or ox-hoof. As with chairs and tables, beds for kings and gods might be highly decorated with gold, silver or carved ivory.

The bed was, of course, simply a support for a yielding mattress; the mattresses used in ancient Mesopotamia might be stuffed with wool, goats' hair or palm fibre. Bed-covers were of linen or wool, and, depending on the meaning of a doubtful Akkadian word, pillows may possibly be mentioned. Bedside mats certainly were used.

The mention of bedside mats raises the general question of floor-coverings. We do know that at least in palaces there must have been carpets, since some floors at doorways actually have limestone slabs carved to simulate carpeting, which would seem to have complemented actual carpeting over parts of the floor less subject to heavy wear (see plate 1B).

Artificial lighting

One of the comforts we take for granted in civilized existence is the provision of some form of artificial lighting for the hours of darkness; this had been available to the dwellers of the land that was later Assyria since prehistoric times. The ancient lamps were in the form of a container holding linseed oil with a wick made from a reed or some other plant, or from wool. In earliest times shells were used as the container and these were subsequently imitated in clay or metal. At palace ceremonies light was sometimes provided by blazing torches, made of bundles of reeds dipped in oil, held aloft by servants.

Toilet requisites

The Assyrians used mirrors of gold, silver or bronze, the metal being burnished to a highly-reflecting surface. This may have been achieved by polishing with a particular kind of leather, comparable to chamois, since a text mentions 'dušu-leather for a mirror'; but there is the alternative possibility that the passage is only speaking of a leather pouch used as a container for the mirror.

Assyrians are commonly represented with long but very well-kempt hair, and it is not surprising to find that they had combs; these were skilfully sawn from wood or ivory. Razors are mentioned, but we have no specific details about them, although, to judge by the very neat appearance of moustaches and beards represented in art, they must have been efficient.

Women used cosmetics, both for the eyes and for the complexion. There is no doubt that, at least at the beginning of the second millennium, eye-shadow was felt to be sexy; this is clear from a myth. The Sumerian goddess Inanna (the later Ishtar, goddess of love), was preparing to descend into the underworld, and the Sumerian text states that as the final stage of her preparing herself, she put on her eyes the ointment called 'May he come, may he come!' Whether the connection between eye make-up and sexual come-hither was still as consciously recognized in first-millennium Assyria, we do not know. Eye cosmetics, which were mainly of antimony paste, were applied with a carved ivory pin. Evidence for the use of rouge is slight but certain, provided by a synonym list where a Sumerian term meaning literally 'gold paste' is explained in Akkadian as 'red pigment of the face'.

Cutlery

Household equipment also included spoons and knives. The spoons were usually of wood or metal, occasionally of ivory, though some of the earliest spoons known from ancient Mesopotamia were of bitumen, which gives the respectability of antiquity to using plastic material for household equipment. Knives had blades of either bronze or iron or (a survival from the Neolithic period) of flint. Metal cutting implements were honed on small flat whetstones about the size of a finger; the writer found that some of these, discovered at Tell el-Rimah west of Mosul, were the most efficient means he had come across for sharpening a penknife.

Storage Equipment

An Assyrian household, like any other, needed containers for its utensils and provisions, and these might range from small cases of wood or leather for holding mirrors, instruments, daggers or shoes, to large wooden chests. Two particular types of wooden containers, perhaps what we would call crates, are specified as being for vegetables. Another versatile material for storage purposes was reeds, which, if waterproofed with bitumen, could take the form either of containers for keeping linen garments dry, or of vessels capable of holding liquids. Another available material was ivory, although because of its costliness its use was normally limited to the carved lids of small decorative boxes.

Containers for food and liquids included copper or wooden bowls, earthenware jugs or pots, and earthenware or metal drinking flasks. Some particularly attractive pottery goblets, of very delicate ware, datable to the seventh century, were found in a palace at Nimrud (ancient Calah). Glass was also used, especially for bottles. Wine was stored in special jars of several gallons' capacity; a number of these, each marked with its volume, were found at Nimrud.

Water Supply

The availability of water originally determined the siting of settlements. Assyria is well-watered; it has the great river Tigris with its major tributaries the two Zab rivers, and a large number of lesser streams which eventually feed into these. There are also many wadis or brooks, some of them perennial, and some major springs feeding perennial ponds, like one at a village named Tell Abu Mariah in the Jazirah, west of Mosul. Some Assyrian kings added to the water supply around their capitals by major feats of engineering to bring water by aqueducts and canals from the mountains. Where there is no surface supply immediately available, water can often be obtained by digging a well; several Assyrian wells were found and cleared at Nimrud, and the writer had the experience of descending one to a depth of ninety feet or so, to check the Assyrian brickwork. Every third course of bricks had a royal inscription, a justifiable piece of pride on the part of the royal well-maker, whose work had withstood the earth's pressure for approaching three thousand years. From this well, water had been raised by sturdy pots of about half-gallon capacity, fastened by their necks to a rope forming an endless chain, and turned by a winch at the well-head so that the pots successively dipped into the well.

For transporting water home from its source, pails were available, sometimes of wood, otherwise of copper or bronze. General Near Eastern custom suggests that this was the task of the women, though there seems to be no specific evidence on this.

Weights and Measures

Buying and selling certain commodities demanded some means of weighing; this would also be necessary in order to measure correct quantities for certain technical processes, perhaps including cooking. For such purposes balances were used, some small enough to weigh a fraction of a shekel (amounting to little more than a gram), others large enough to weigh a man. We learn the latter from reports that one Assyrian king had a captured enemy put on the scales, so that his weight in silver might be paid to his captor. The weights used were of stone or bronze, often attractively carved or cast into the form of a duck or lion (see plate 7A).

For measuring by volume, the largest measure was the *emar* (*imer*), literally 'donkey-load', divided into ten *sutu*, and that in turn into 10 *qu*. The *qu* was just over three pints or just under two litres. This makes the *emar* almost exactly five bushels. We know the values of the Assyrian volume measures precisely, from the fact that some of their storage jars were marked with their capacity.

11

Agriculture, Animal Husbandry and Trade

The Assyrian way of life was from first to last based on the two activities of farming (agriculture and animal husbandry) and trade.

Agriculture

Assyrian kings, even those with the most formidable military reputations, fully recognized the importance of farming. More than one of them speaks of development in agriculture and animal resources as one of his major achievements. Thus Tiglath-Pileser I (1115–1077) tells us:

> I had ploughs put into operation throughout the whole land of Assyria, whereby I heaped up more piles of grain than my ancestors. I established herds of horses, cattle and donkeys from the booty which by the help of my Lord Ashur I had taken from the lands over which I had won dominion.

Nearly four centuries later, Sargon II (722–705) was praised, or rather praised himself in the third person, because

> he set his mind to. . .open up fallow land, and plant orchards; he set himself to gain a crop on steep rocky slopes which formerly had never produced vegetation; he set his heart on putting furrows into waste land which under former kings had known no plough, to have people sing for joy.

The social and economic consequences of Sargon's policy were recognized and set out. It was 'to save all mankind from hunger and want;. . .that oil, the comfort of mankind for soothing the muscles, should not be too dear within my land; that linseed could be bought in the market as cheaply as barley'.

It has earlier been pointed out that irrigation was not indispensable for agriculture in Assyria. But irrigation, where available, was a

food the cereals were either crushed for use as groats or ground to make flour for bread. Barley was also used for making beer.

Amongst other crops identified by Hans Helbaek from their carbonized remains, one to which some controversy attaches is linseed, the source of the oil called by that name and of the fibre flax. Without question, this was grown in ancient Mesopotamia well before the first millennium. The controversial point which arises is that there was also cultivated an oil-producing plant called in Akkadian *shamashshammu* (which in origin just means 'oil-plant'). When one knows that Akkadian -*sh*- becomes Arabic -*s*-, it is clear that as a word this is the origin of the name 'sesame'. But did it mean the actual plant sesame? Professor Helbaek said 'no'; he thought it originally denoted the oil-plant linseed, of which he had found abundant remains, and not sesame, of which he found none. According to him sesame was only introduced to Mesopotamia from India in the first millennium A.D., when it displaced linseed as the main oil-plant and took over its former name. But the assumption about the late date of introduction of sesame is not beyond question, and some scholars continue to argue that it was used in ancient Mesopotamia, including Assyria.

Other food plants of which remains have been found include lentils, chick-peas and cucumbers. Orchards are often mentioned in texts and sometimes shown on bas reliefs, and amongst fruits both known from such sources and identified botanically from their remains are grapes, figs, olives and pomegranates. Dates were also a common food in Assyria, though date-palms do not produce well there and their main source is likely to have been importation from Babylonia.

We have various other sources of information about things cultivated in Assyria. For example, there is the menu for the inaugural banquet which Ashur-nasir-pal II (883–859) gave at the completion of his new capital, Calah, listing a large number of foodstuffs, many of vegetable origin. Unfortunately the identification of a majority of the items is conjectural, but we can confidently recognize onions, garlic, shallots, turnips and the spice cumin.

Some of the Assyrian kings deliberately established parks in which they grew plants and trees native to other lands, but in many cases the new introduction may not have made much impact on Assyrian agriculture generally. One instance, already touched upon, in which a new introduction certainly came to have economic importance, was cotton. Sennacherib mentions this as one of the plants set in his park around Nineveh, under the description 'wool-bearing trees', and is quite explicit about its use: 'they plucked the wool-bearing trees and wove it into cloth'.

Animal Husbandry

Of equal importance with the crops were the herds of animals. The national significance of animal breeding was sufficiently recognized for it to be the subject of omens reported to the king. Thus we find forecasts of the type, 'When a halo encircles the moon, and Pegasus. . .stands therein, the cattle of the land will do well', with others in the opposite sense: 'When Jupiter approaches the constellation Hyades [literally, 'Jaw of the Bull'], (this means either) the favourable circumstances of the land will disappear, (or) alternatively, the procreation of cattle and sheep will not prosper.'

Cattle had a dual importance; they were valuable not only as a source of food but also as draft animals, oxen commonly being used for pulling ploughs and carts, as well as for threshing. As now, bulls not needed for breeding were usually castrated, though some had to be left entire because certain religious rituals required the sacrifice of an uncastrated bull. Beef was an accepted item of diet, though not common except among the rich, and a hundred pickled oxen (probably in the form of joints, as it would be difficult to pickle a whole ox quickly enough to preserve it from decomposition) were included in Ashur-nasir-pal's banquet. One important aspect of the cow was of course its milk yield, and we have a representation of a milking scene from a very early period (though not from Assyria). In addition to use in its original form, cows' milk might be used as something called sweet milk (perhaps yoghurt), cream, ghee (a form of boiled butter with excellent keeping properties) and probably cheese, although the only cheese with a specified origin in Assyrian texts is from sheep's milk. The cattle were run in herds in enclosures and housed in sheds. There must have been quite frequent re-invigoration of the stock of domestic cattle, for texts refer to wild bulls entering the enclosures and pasturing with the cows: those bulls were not there just for the grazing.

Sheep were very common, in various breeds. We know the names of some of the breeds from inscriptions, but mostly we have no means of knowing what their characteristics were, though one breed called 'wiry-haired sheep' explains itself. Another named breed giving us no problem in identification was the fat-tailed sheep, still common in Iraq today. Specific regional breeds are named, such as Amorite, Akkadian and Hana sheep (the last named from a place on the Middle Euphrates), though we cannot be certain these were found in Assyria. We do, however, know that one breed very common in Assyria was that known as Habha, from its place of origin in the northern mountains. This has muddled some scholars in their study of ancient geography, when they have assumed that

166

every place from which a Habha sheep is mentioned must be in the area called Habha.

Sheep were important for their meat, their milk (used in all the forms mentioned for cows' milk and referred to more frequently) and their wool. Down to about 1400 sheep were, in at least some parts of Assyria, normally plucked, not shorn; that is, the wool was pulled or combed out at the time of moult. Shearing, already known much earlier, became the usual practice later, possibly accompanying a genetic change in the sheep which made the wool less easy to pull out; the main shearing season was at the onset of summer, in May.

All the domesticated animal species could be used for offerings for the gods, but the sheep played an additional role in the magico-religious sphere. One of the commonest ways of obtaining an omen was to present a question to the god, and then kill a sheep and examine its liver. Any abnormalities in the liver were interpreted by an expert diviner to give the god's answer. This became less important in Assyria with the increasing prestige of astrology for the same purpose.

Goats, often herded with sheep, seem to have been relatively less numerous. They were already being shorn when sheep were still being plucked. Today goats' hair is a very important fibre for making tents and rugs, and presumably was already so in antiquity, though specific evidence for this is lacking. We do, however, know for certain that goats' hair was used as a filling for beds.

Goats' milk was used in the same ways as sheep's milk, and goat meat was eaten, as it is today in Iraq. Goatskins were very useful: they made very serviceable water containers and, suitably tied, could be inflated to make floats. Single floats of this kind could be used by swimmers, a practice shown on Assyrian bas reliefs (see plate 11A) and still in evidence amongst boys on the Tigris at Mosul as late as the 1970s A.D. Groups of inflated goatskins were used to give buoyancy to the type of raft called a *kelek*, used for transport on the Zab and Tigris rivers from Assyrian times until the 1950s A.D. (see plate 10A).

The flocks of sheep and goats were in the charge of shepherds, whose job was to protect them as they grazed around the villages or further out in the open country. The shepherds, assisted by savage sheepdogs, not uncommonly had to cope with attacks on the flocks by wolves or lions. For their own protection and comfort they built huts. The flocks might belong to private persons, temples or the king, and some could be very numerous. In Babylonia, the temples might own such huge flocks that citizens, whose own grazing rights would thereby be affected, sometimes complained. Thus we find a report to the king of Assyria, at the time when he ruled Babylonia, that the citizens of Borsippa (a city near Babylon with a temple of the god Nabu) were complaining: 'The cattle and sheep of Nabu cover the face of the land.' The Assyrian temples were more firmly held in check by the king, and were not in a position to abuse citizens' rights.

Whilst most sheep in Assyria were in large flocks, some poorer individuals must have had one or two for domestic use – to give milk for cheese-making and so on. Mention of 'sheep of the roof' presumably indicated that a house owner might keep a sheep or two on the flat roof of his house.

The flocks (and herds of cattle) could diminish much more rapidly than they had increased, for we hear of epidemic animal diseases bringing heavy mortality. Parasitic maggots, possibly of warble flies, could also attack sheep, cattle and horses.

The pig was a well-known animal of ancient Mesopotamia, serving as a scavenger amongst the garbage of cities. In early times there were large herds of them and their meat and lard were accepted items of food. But a taboo on pig-meat – retained to this day in Judaism and Islam – gradually developed, for in the later period the pig is described as 'taboo of all the gods'. But this was not till after 1400, at which time we still find lard in use in parts of Assyria.

Donkeys, horses and mules

The donkey (which was quite a different species from the wild ass native to Mesopotamia) was another animal of economic importance, mainly as a pack beast, and in Assyria at the beginning of the second millennium donkey caravans were used for trade with central Anatolia. The donkey gave its name to the largest volume measure (in Akkadian the *emar* or *imer*, in Hebrew the cognate homer, meaning a donkey load) and also to a unit of area (the same words), which represented the amount of land which could be sown with a donkey-load of grain. In early times the donkey was also a riding animal, and although it began to be superseded by the horse in the second millennium, riding donkeys were still included in the royal communications system in first-millennium Assyria; they are much safer than horses in rocky terrain where a slip might spell disaster. As far as we know, donkeys were not normally used as human food, but (like almost any other dead animal) a dead donkey could be used as dog meat.

The horse, introduced into Mesopotamia from the north or northeast in the third millennium, was, as it has always remained, a prestigious animal, although occasionally, on grounds associated with religious conservatism, the donkey or mule was considered more appropriate for ceremonial purposes. The horse became extremely important in Assyria in the first millennium, mainly for military purposes, both for chariots and for cavalry. Constant streams of horses were imported, mainly from the north and north-east, deriving from tribute or plunder. There was an area particularly famous for horse-breeding just south of Lake Urmia in north-west Iran, and Assyria and its major northern neighbour, the kingdom of Urartu, consequently competed for control of this area. King Sargon II says admiringly:

> As to the people who live in that area in the land of Urartu,. . .their like does not exist for skill with cavalry horses. The foals,. . .which are reared for the royal contingents and caught yearly, until they are taken to the land of Subi (for training) and it is seen what they are capable of, will never have had anyone straddling their backs, will not have been taught advancing, wheeling, retreating or battle drill.

Two breeds of horse are commonly referred to, the Kusian and the Mesian, originating from different parts of the lands to the north or east, and different colours of horses are also mentioned. White horses were donated (apparently as living animals for ceremonial purposes rather than as sacrificial offerings) to certain gods. Despite the many references to import of horses, they must also have been bred in Assyria, for we have many mentions of mares and foals. It was only stallions that were used for military purposes by the Assyrians, and one Assyrian king speaks with contempt of a defeated enemy king escaping on a mare.

Provisioning of horses for military purposes was of course of great importance. King Sargon refers to burning the stores of hay which an enemy king north of Assyria had laid in for his horses. When Sennacherib went down to the Persian Gulf to make an attack by sea against Elam (south-west Iran), he carried grain and straw by ship for his horses; the horses themselves probably went by land as far as the Gulf, but must have been shipped across.

As already stated, the horse was first known from further north, and it was from the north or east that the Assyrians obtained most of their horses to the very end. It is therefore not surprising that the Assyrians owed their horse expertise to peoples from these areas. We have already seen the compliment Sargon paid to certain peoples in north-west Iran in this connection, and further proof that the north was the centre of horse expertise is given by a second-millennium Hittite text dealing with the training of chariot horses. This must have been known in Assyria, for we have the text (much damaged) of a Middle Assyrian manual on the same subject, which obviously owes some of its material to the Hittite source. We find from this that horses were treated with the same care that they still normally receive today. Part of the instruction reads: 'You shall unharness (the horses), let them have a roll, give them fodder, keep them warm, and rub them down'. Horses might fall victim to epidemic disease, just as cattle and sheep did, and we find mention of this.

The mule, a sterile cross between a donkey and a horse, was another common animal in ancient Mesopotamia, including Assyria. A humorous Babylonian saying reflects the fact that the mule might inherit the qualities of either donkey or horse: 'When the rutting horse mounts the she-donkey, as he rides her he whispers in her ear: "the foal you will bear, let it be a courser like me, don't make it a pack-beast like a donkey".' Despite the stallion's paternal ambitions, mules in Assyria were probably used as much for draft and pack purposes as for mounts.

Birds

Wild ducks and geese were netted by the fowler, and domesticated varieties in various breeds, such as the Aramaean goose, were reared for food, being fattened on barley, sometimes in the form of dough. As now, goose fat was used medicinally. In Babylonia in the first millennium there were fowl yards for ducks, sometimes attached to temples, and it is likely that the same was true of Assyria.

Pigeons – almost invariably graced by the more poetic designation 'doves' in modern assyriological literature – were also bred and eaten. The Babylonian Flood story, taken over into the Bible in the guise of Noah's Ark, refers to the pigeon coming back when released, so that the ancient Mesopotamians were certainly aware of its homing instincts; there is, however, no evidence of the use of carrier pigeons.

Trade

The second factor in Assyrian prosperity was trade, with both internal and international facets.

Internal trade

In our own economy we take for granted a distribution system based on money, serving both as a standard of value and also as a means of exchange, enabling the individual easily to dispose of what he produces and to obtain what he needs. Still further flexibility is achieved by a system of credit based on banks.

A money economy, in the strict sense, was not available to ancient Assyria. Despite an enigmatic reference by Sennacherib in 694 to casting bronze colossi 'like the casting of half shekels' (which probably only meant that his craftsmen could handle large amounts of bronze as expertly as though no more than half a shekel of metal was involved), coined money never played a part in the Assyrian distribution system; it first came into use in Asia Minor, not earlier than the very end of the Assyrian empire. On the other hand, there was available in Assyria a rudimentary precursor of a money economy. Metals were frequently used as a means of exchange, not indeed as stamped coins but as pieces weighed out. At different times gold, silver, tin, copper and bronze were all employed for this purpose, though the commonest in the New Assyrian period was silver. Assyrian practice sometimes went beyond the use of silver simply as a medium of exchange to the concept of using it as a standard of value; thus there are cases where a debt or obligation is quoted in terms of an amount of silver but actually paid by some other means, for example, with a quantity of barley. As a convenient shorthand term, not to be understood as setting up any economic theory, we may call this a quasi-money economy.

An economy using metals as the medium of exchange was by no means the only distribution system present in first-millennium Assyria. Very large amounts of land were owned by the state, in the person of the king, and there were many people, from high officials down to serfs and slaves, who were totally dependent upon the state (alias the king) for their livelihood. This permitted a direct-allocation system of distribution. The products of state lands would go either to the capital, or to granaries and storehouses in major provincial cities. That which went to the capital would be used to maintain the court and the temples, and some of it would be parcelled out as rations to various officials and workers. The grain stored in the provincial cities would in part be distributed correspondingly, and some of it would form a strategic stockpile for the use of the army when campaigning in or from that area. This was a direct-distribution system, totally outside the quasi-money economy. These state grain supplies could also – still outside a quasi-money economy – enter international trade; we hear, for example, of famine relief being sent from Assyria to Elam in a time of emergency.

The products of land other than that owned directly by the state tended to generate a mixed form of distribution. Many officials had allocations of land from the state, some high officials owning very large estates. Such estates would normally pay a proportion of their crops to the state as taxes, although the lands of some favoured officials received tax exemptions. A share of the crop of an estate would go by direct distribution to the families attached to the land, analogously to the way in which direct dependants of the king received their income. The remainder, after the deduction of any tax liabilities, would be at the disposal of the estate owner. The same would be true of any surpluses of the constantly diminishing number of peasant landowners.

These surpluses would then be available to enter the quasi-money economy. Sometimes there was direct contact between the two parallel economies. Thus we find a contract empowering two persons to buy grain with silver they have been given; the grain is to be bought in one province for delivery by river transport in another. It would appear that the quasi-money economy made it possible to use a grain surplus in one province to alleviate a shortage in another; and by transactions of this kind goods could move from the direct-allocation economy to the quasi-money economy.

With a society too complex for direct barter to be possible on a large scale, and not sufficiently centralized for a direct-allocation economy to be totally applicable, a quasi-money system was essential. There were in the cities substantial numbers of people who were neither officials entitled to state rations nor workers directly involved in food production. One thinks of such people as potters, weavers, metal-workers, seal-engravers; that individuals in these categories might be in royal employment does not affect the fact that as classes they were independent. There were also poor free men who owned no land but were not attached to any estate which would give them a right to a share in the crops. Such people lived by serving as workmen in various capacities, such as assisting at the harvest, undertaking building operations, and so on. Whilst such workmen could be, and sometimes were, in part paid in basic rations of food and drink, in the long term their other needs could only be met by payments in some form which could be utilized as a medium of exchange. That this actually happened is shown by the existence of memoranda referring to the payment of silver or copper to workmen. The following is an example of a contract for building work, in which a group of men, engaged for a project expected to take a month, were paid both rations and a weight of copper:

> [List of personal names.]
> Total: 6 workers.
> 2 talents of copper,

> 3.6 homers of bread (and) beer
> for the month they do the work.
> [A line of uncertain meaning.]
> They shall fasten the beams,
> They shall put on the roof,
> They shall put the 'box' in place.
> If the brickwork
> is not complete,
> they shall carry on and finish
> their work after the month.

(The 'box' mentioned may refer to the wooden cowling of a ventilation shaft on the roof.) The amounts of food stated work out, per man per day, at about six pounds of bread and six pints of beer if there were 3.6 homers of each of those commodities, or half those quantities if the 3.6 homers was the total of bread and beer. Clearly the men received adequate basic rations and the copper represented wages which they could eventually use as quasi-money for satisfying their other needs. At current copper prices, the two talents specified would work out to about £20 sterling per man for the month, though because of the enormous differences between the subsistence economy in ancient Mesopotamia and the consumption-orientated economy in modern Western society this is not a very meaningful figure for evaluating ancient wages in terms of purchase power.

We do not know in any detail how the workman would use his small quantity of copper or silver to obtain other goods. However, there were plenty of merchants, and whilst some of these were concerned with trade on a large scale, such as the transaction already mentioned to bring grain from one province to another, there are indications that there were some who operated on a sufficiently small scale to be the equivalent of shopkeepers or pedlars. There were certainly people who sold on a small scale to individuals, for we find mention of 'a merchant's leather bag for weights'. There is also a text which mentions the possibility of dishonest practices by such people as retail merchants, speaking of the kind of person 'who, as he holds the balance, indulges in cheating, by substituting weights'. As to the possibility of pedlars, we find mention of a 'firewood man' and (though from Babylonia, not Assyria) a 'salt man', and both could be instances of house-to-house small traders.

Assyria also knew credit procedures to facilitate trade. Both temples and private persons might advance silver for business purposes. The 'money' would be repaid in due course in the form of commodities. The lender of the silver would expect to benefit by a favourable price for the commodities at the time of repayment, or by the payment of interest, or both. Most commonly the commodity concerned was grain, but the following is an example of a transaction for delivery of wine:

> 2½ homers [about 100 gallons] of wine
> belonging to Mannu-ki-Nineveh
> is a liability upon Partama.
> He shall deliver the wine in Nineveh
> in the month of May.
> If he has not delivered by then,
> he shall pay silver according to the price in Nineveh.
> Month of January, 25th day.

Wine was produced in the mountain areas to the north and north-west, and delivering a hundred gallons of it in Nineveh in early summer was obviously a major trading operation. The man to whom the silver was advanced would hope to make his profit by buying cheaply in the winter in the production area. The lender was protected, in the case of default of delivery, by having the right to compensation for the hundred gallons of wine at the price ruling in Nineveh in May, well into the hot season, when the price of wine and other drinks would be likely to rise, particularly if adverse circumstances further north had made supplies scarce.

At some times and places in ancient Mesopotamia attempts were made to control prices by government decree; this was not the case in the New Assyrian empire. Contracts quite frequently specify – as in the one just quoted – that payment is according to the price in a particular place at a particular time. This shows clear recognition of the fact that prices in Assyria were determined by economic forces, not by official decree. We also find letters in which prices for various commodities in various areas are reported to – not promulgated by – the king; obviously, these were market-play prices, not controlled prices. The inscriptions of kings themselves comment on the effect of various economic forces on prices. King Sargon II, speaking of his policy of improving agriculture in his land, commented on the result of this in bringing down the price of oil and linseed; the passage is quoted on page 162. The same king commented on the effect of a glut of war booty upon prices in Assyria. After listing the mineral wealth he had brought back from his campaigns, he says: 'property, too much to enumerate, such as my forefathers had not received, I heaped up in my capital Fort Sargon. In the land of Assyria people could pay a price in silver as though it were copper.'

Ashurbanipal (668–627), after taking huge quantities of camels as booty and distributing them widely, commented on the effect of this over-supply on the price: 'within my land camels were sold in the market at one shekel or half a shekel of silver.' In terms of silver value in the 1980s A.D., this was a price of about £2 – cheap for a second-hand camel.

It may be added that the importance of trade to the state was fully recognized, for trade is coupled with the harvest as of importance in astrological omens, which were confined to matters of consequence to the state. Typical extracts from such omens are:

When the moon appears at a time not expected for it, business activity will be reduced.

When a planet rises heliacally in the month Elul [September], business activity will be high, there will be abundance of grain.

An omen of the same class, though actually meteorological rather than astrological, reads:

When there is a fog in the land, the harvest will be abundant, trade will be firm.

These references to reduction or increases in business activity show a rudimentary recognition of the existence of trade cycles (boom–slump–boom), and the linking of these movements with astrological phenomena indicates that these movements were felt to have no rational basis.

International trade

Assyria's international trade had its roots far back in prehistoric times. Because of its position along the Tigris and athwart the routes from the Mediterranean to the Zagros and from the Taurus to Babylonia, the region we know as Assyria was always important. Because of their geographical position, the people of Assyria were particularly well placed to serve as middlemen.

But there was another factor which encouraged international, or at least inter-community, trade in the ancient Near East: uncertainty in the food supply. It is self-evident that if a community is wholly self-contained economically, without any trading links with its neighbours, it will be extremely vulnerable to crop failure, and there are but few areas where crop failure is unthinkable. Where the grain crop depends upon irrigation, an inadequate rise of the river or too severe flooding may equally end in dearth, as may a dry year in

175

areas dependent upon rainfall. A promising crop anywhere may suddenly be destroyed by either locusts or blight. The only safe-guards against such disasters are the long-term storing of the surpluses of good years, or the obtaining of grain from more favour-ably circumstanced communities who currently have surpluses. The transfer of grain from the haves to the have-nots could only be by war or by trade, and a community which was in the fortunate position of having surpluses would, from the pressure of its hungry neighbours, be as likely to be forced into one or the other as a starving community which had to fight, trade or die.

Trade and war were closely linked in Assyria, from first till last. The early farmers on the plains of Assyria must often have suffered by raids on their crops and stores by peoples from the surrounding hills or the desert, and when they became a major state they them-selves used sometimes trade and sometimes war to obtain the goods they desired from other parts of the Near East. The earliest Assyrian international trade which is known in some detail, is the trade between the city of Ashur and Cappadocia (central eastern Turkey) at the beginning of the second millennium. This has already been discussed in Chapter 2.

We also know something about the role of Assyria in international trade later in the second millennium; the negotiation of king Ashur-uballit I (1365–1330) with his Egyptian counterpart to establish trade in the form of an exchange of presents has already been discussed above (see pages 42f.). Long-distance trade was by caravans. Here one of the main problems was security, a factor which contributed to the link between international trade and military activities. In the correspondence between Ashur-uballit and the Egyptian king, the latter had evidently complained about the delaying of his messen-gers. Ashur-uballit told the Egyptian king that this was the fault of nomads along the middle Euphrates and that he had now taken steps to deal with these bandits. In the same period a Babylonian king complained to his Egyptian counterpart about poor security in Palestine, an area then under nominal Egyptian control: 'Canaan is a land of yours, and its kings are servants of yours. I have been robbed in your land. Arrest the people concerned,. . .otherwise they will come again and kill my caravans and even your own messen-gers.' Elsewhere we repeatedly hear of the killing or kidnapping of merchants, emphasizing the need for the state to ensure security if trade was to flourish.

In general, there was tight state control of international trade in the late second millennium. Thus, a text from a Hittite king just after 1300 gives us the conditions under which merchants from Anatolia were permitted to trade inside Ugarit, a vassal city-state in north Syria. There had obviously been local complaints that the merchants were attempting to acquire rights to the disadvantage of the natives; the Hittite overlord therefore decreed that the merchants could only operate in Ugarit during the summer, not during the winter, and that they were not to be permitted to acquire rights of residence or to buy houses or land there. From later in the same century we find tin being imported into Assyria from Anatolia by a private merchant, but we have no information upon the conditions under which he or his agents operated abroad.

When we come to look at Assyrian trade in the first millennium we encounter a difficulty: was there anything in the international field to which the term 'trade' can properly be applied? Beyond question, considerable quantities of goods came into Assyria from abroad, but the overwhelming proportion of this about which we have information came as spoils of war or tribute. It would be possible to say that this was a form of trade, paid for by invisible exports in the form of good communications, security of routes, and freedom from external attack. Although this kind of statement is likely to vex anti-imperialists, this was certainly the way in which some vassal rulers thought of it. We have a clear example of this in the Bible, in the relations of Ahaz of Judah with Tiglath-Pileser III. Ahaz was threatened by a coalition of Israel and Syria, and appealed to Tiglath-Pileser: 'Come up and rescue me from the hand of the king of Syria and from the hand of the king of Israel, who are attacking me' (2 Kings 16:7). Tiglath-Pileser did so, and Ahaz sent a present to the king of Assyria. Clearly, in this case the tribute paid by Ahaz was for services received. Another king, up in north Syria, left an inscription saying how much his father and he had prospered for their loyalty to Tiglath-Pileser III, which included payment of tribute; he specifically mentions the economic benefits to his country.

Whether or not we choose to include the delivery of tribute as an aspect of international trade, international trade of an indisputable kind continued in the Assyrian empire. One letter establishing this comes from an official in Tyre. The people there carried out lumbering in the Lebanon forests, bringing the timber down to the city, where the Assyrians taxed it. After trouble about the tax, the Assyrian administrator had imposed an embargo on selling the timber to Egypt; evidently the Tyrians might now sell it only to Assyria. A real trading link must have been envisaged, as the Assyrian official had threatened that if there were any more trouble about the tax the Tyrians would not be allowed to fell the timber; this would have been an absurd threat if the Assyrians had been receiving the timber as tribute without payment. Although in this instance the Assyrian authorities forbade the Tyrians to trade in timber with Egypt, Sargon II specifically stated that he encouraged trade between Egyptians and Assyrians.

Elsewhere we find a record of delivery of lead, apparently brought from the region we now call Kurdistan, in the Zagros foothills; there is no indication that this was a tribute payment. A document about a consignment of 730 horses explicitly says that they came from the merchants; this is particularly significant evidence for real international trade, since the main importance of horses in Assyria was for military purposes, and horses in those numbers can only have been destined for government use. The merchants may well have been acting as agents of the state, but the fact that merchants were involved shows that this was real trade, not delivery of tribute.

Mention of certain commodities which originated outside the area controlled by Assyria is further evidence of international trade; even if in their final stage they reached Assyria as tribute, they can only have left their country of production by an exchange-trade mechanism. One such commodity is tusks of ivory, which we find arriving in Assyria at the end of the eighth century, after Syrian elephants had been rendered extinct and before Assyria controlled Egypt, the only country from which they could have come. Another such was lapis lazuli, much used for beautifying temples and palaces. The only source of this was Afghanistan, east of Iran, which was never under Assyrian control. It was only at the end of the eighth century that the Assyrians began to play a major role east of the Zagros. From that time they might have obtained all their lapis lazuli by way of tribute from tribes in west Iran, who had themselves obtained it by trade from further east. We do indeed find mention of some coming in as tribute from Iranian tribes, but not with such regularity as to make it likely that this ever became the main source of lapis lazuli for Assyria; the rest may well have reached Assyria by undocumented trade.

Certainly trading caravans were still moving internationally during the New Assyrian empire at its heyday, and with the approval of the Assyrian king, for King Sargon actually refers to the action he had to take against Aramaean tribesmen who kept raiding the caravans of the citizens of Babylon.

However, although we have the foregoing indications, and a few others like them, of international trade in relation to the New Assyrian empire, the documentation is extremely scanty. There are two ways in which this might be explained. One possibility is that Assyria indeed had very little international trade other than in the form of receipt of tribute, if that is to be considered as a form of trade. But it is also possible that international trade was in fact extensive, but operated with a mechanism which has left no records. We know that the language Aramaic, in an alphabetical form of writing which was much simpler than cuneiform Akkadian, was coming into increasing use in the final century and a quarter of the Assyrian empire. This was written, not like cuneiform on virtually indestructible clay tablets, but in ink on potsherds, papyrus or parchment. Potsherds would have some chance of surviving, and a few examples of such Aramaic documents (not concerned with international trade) have been found; but in the climate of Assyria, inscribed papyrus and parchment are most unlikely to survive over millennia, so that any international trade documented on these materials would have left no trace.

12

Mastery over the Environment: The Assyrians and Natural Resources

The heading originally planned for this chapter – 'Science and Technology' – was rejected as misleading. Although the Assyrians certainly knew some facts which, with us, would come under the general heading of scientific knowledge, and used processes which we might consider to fall into the sphere of technology, they lacked the organization of their knowledge which would justify the use of the term 'science'; and although the term 'technology' could more easily be justified, it does sound a little pretentious when applied to such a skill as, for example, making mud-bricks. One could, of course, play with words and say that since 'science' by etymology means 'knowledge', and the Assyrians had knowledge, they therefore had science. But, as commonly used today, the word 'science' does not mean just 'knowledge'. It means a systematized body of knowledge, ever expanding by experimental research which confirms or disproves hypotheses; and in this sense there was no science in Assyria, or indeed anywhere in ancient Mesopotamia, with the possible exception of the time of the turn from the fourth to the third millennium. In that early period, when the alert Sumerian mind was devising both the material and the spiritual foundations of all ancient Mesopotamian society, there were rapid changes which implied that readiness to experiment with materials and ideas which is at the basis of science. But the early Sumerian achievement was so overwhelming, and gained such enormous prestige, that Sumerian knowledge quickly came to be regarded as something fixed and final. After the third millennium, with very few exceptions, whatever might be done in any sphere of life was only respectable if it was felt to be in conformity with what had been done in the past. But the environment is not static. For example, an old source of timber may become completely deforested, or a settlement may have to be abandoned because of the salination of its land through irrigation over a long period. This kind of development made some degree of change inevitable in the course of time. But in ancient Mesopotamia, such changes as occurred were strictly circumscribed by tradition; the new had to be in conformity with the old. From the typical point of view of the ancient Mesopotamian, knowledge was static and final; it had been given by the gods at the beginning. Knowledge was not something growing organically, which could be developed by a spirit of enquiry. This view is stated explicitly by Berossus, a third-century Babylonian priest, part of whose writings (to explain the Babylonian way of life to his Greek contemporaries) have come down to us in Greek. Berossus describes how Oannes, a divine being in the form of a fish-man, appeared from the sea in primeval times and gave the people of southern Mesopotamia all knowledge: 'He gave them an insight into letters and branches of learning, and arts of every kind. He taught them to construct cities, to found temples, to bring in laws, and to measure land. . . .From that time nothing material has been added by way of improvement to his instructions.'

In the second millennium the Babylonian scribes made great endeavours to systematize (but not to extend) their knowledge. They collected and collated all available texts relating to all available subjects, and drew up approved versions of such texts as myths, incantations, hymns, prayers, omens, medical prescriptions, astronomical observations, and lexical material. The lexical material could be about almost anything – inventories of household furniture, catalogues of terms applying to sheep, lists of gods, plants, minerals, trees, professions, grammatical forms, stars. But producing the approved form – or, as Assyriologists say, the canonical form – of the text series was regarded as the end in itself. The scribes never went on from their lists of plants, animals or minerals towards a systematic study to give the beginnings of the sciences of botany, zoology or geology.

The mass of texts, produced in second-millennium Babylonia from third-millennium Sumerian roots, was taken over into first-millennium Assyria. Some of the texts were found at Ashur, the greatest mass of them at Nineveh, in a library which various Assyrian kings, mainly Ashurbanipal (668–627), had collected. Thus, almost anything we may say about Assyrian learning on the basis of such literary texts really relates to what Assyria had directly and consciously borrowed from Babylonia. However, there are some elements of Assyrian culture, known to us either from archaeological finds or from statements in inscriptions specifically of Assyrian and not Babylonian origin, which we may attribute to Assyria itself. And it has to be said – although we do not propose to allow the Assyrians credit for organized science and shall be chary in using the term 'technology' – that there were occasional instances in Assyria of recognition that knowledge could be extended, processes could be improved, and innovations – consciously accepted as such, and not dressed up as age-old divine wisdom – could be made.

One of the paradoxes of the people of south Mesopotamia, where civilization began, was that they carried through their great achievement in an environment which was wholly lacking in most of the major natural resources – stone, good timber, and metal ores. The Assyrians, in north Mesopotamia, were distinctly more fortunately placed. They had stone close at hand: there were stone-bearing hills (containing limestone or marble) within sight of every one of the successive capitals. This stone was obtained by open-cast quarrying; one Assyrian quarrying operation has left very obvious scars in a rock-face near Eski Mosul, north-west of Nineveh. Stone was a raw material not only for temples and palaces, but also for other structures. Thus, quarried in great blocks five feet square by two and a half feet, in the early ninth century it was used at Calah for a quay wall (see plate 7B); even larger blocks, weighing up to twenty tons, were carved into bull or lion colossi (see plate 19B). Stone supply was one of the points at which we know of a conscious innovation, since in the reign of Sennacherib (704–681) teams of surveyors were sent out to search for new sources of specific kinds of the rarer and more ornamental types of stone.

Good timber, another building material important in ancient Mesopotamia, was fairly easily obtained by the Assyrians. In early times, hills quite near to the capitals would have carried substantial trees (the occasional one still remains where some favourable circumstance has protected it). As these became exhausted, Assyrian control was reaching out, so that the extensive forests of the Zagros and Taurus became available, the conquered populations being used to fell them and transport them to Assyria. Here again there was a conscious innovation under Sennacherib, who sent out surveyors into the mountains in deliberate quest of new sources of large timber.

But despite the use of stone and timber, the most commonly employed building material was just clay or mud. Predominantly this was used as sun-dried mud-brick, though frequently as burnt brick, and sometimes, for special purposes – such as the ornamentation of a palace or temple – as burnt brick glazed in black, red, blue or silver. In some temple or palace buildings, damp-courses were provided or waterproofing treatment was applied, and for these purposes bitumen was used. Limestone blocks forming the ninth-century quay at Calah were found to be set in bitumen, and Sennacherib nearly two centuries later refers to the same practice. Another common use of this material was for caulking boats. Bitumen was available from pits within Assyria itself; there is, for example, one such pit (really a seepage from the edge of an oil-field) within an easy walk of the centre of Nimrud. This material was applied in two forms, either as crude bitumen just as it came from the pit, or as 'dry' bitumen, which was a mastic produced by adding powdered limestone; the latter form served excellently for pavements.

A raw material lacking from the whole of Mesopotamia, Assyria as well as Babylonia, was metal ores. Alongside gold and silver (too soft to be of other than decorative use and too rare to be widely employed), the metals known in the ancient world were lead (also too soft for most purposes, though useful for watertight containers or tubing), and iron, copper and tin, the last two being alloyed to produce bronze.

Copper, and its alloy bronze, had been in use in the Near East from the fourth millennium, with iron beginning to come into general use from the late second millennium. Copper and iron ores are found, and were known to the ancients, in the Taurus and Zagros mountains and in Anatolia, and it was in and around these regions that metal production began and developed. What is not yet clear is how the metal producers of the Taurus and Anatolia became involved in the production of bronze, which requires an admixture of tin. At least down to the second millennium the bronze-makers of Anatolia did not know of any tin ores in the region of the Taurus and Anatolia, and they therefore had to import tin through Assyria from somewhere else, assumed (without any positive proof) to be Iran, known as a source of tin from early times.

In this situation, the Assyrians from the beginning of the second millennium (and perhaps even earlier, see page 28) were involved in the metal trade. This did not, however, make them pioneers in metal technology, in which to the end they remained technically inferior to the peoples in the mountains to the north of them. By the mere facts of geography the Assyrians always had to import their metals from abroad, and whenever possible did so in the form of refined metals rather than as ores requiring smelting. The Assyrians did, however, have some acquaintance with mining for ores – necessarily outside Assyria proper, where there are none – since Esarhaddon (680–669) specifically stated that the source of some of the gold he used was 'the product of the underworld, ore of its mountains, not (old material) reworked for the purpose.'

Throughout the second millennium, copper and bronze were practically the only metals available to Assyria; they had to serve for all purposes, from weapons and tools to shoes for horses. Iron of meteoric origin had indeed been known in Mesopotamia from the third millennium, and even – though to an extremely limited extent – used; but not until the second millennium was it produced by smelting from ores. The centre for this development was Asia

Minor, but even there iron remained a product with a high scarcity value until late in the second millennium. Its main early use was for weapons, and there is the possibility that the Hittite king attempted to exercise a strategic control over its export. This view is based on a letter written by a mid-thirteenth-century Hittite ruler to another king, possibly Shalmaneser I of Assyria. The Hittite ruler apologized for his tardiness in delivering iron which had been requested; his excuse was one still familiar in export circles – production difficulties. Was his excuse genuine, or did it conceal an attempted trade embargo? There are certainly ancient parallels for attempts at strategic control, the best-known being the biblical account of how the Philistines in the eleventh century denied metal technology to the Israelites 'lest the Hebrews make themselves swords or spears' (1 Samuel 13: 19). But whether the delay in the spread of iron production was due to a Hittite attempt at retaining a monopoly, or to production difficulties, the metal was certainly beginning to be available to Assyrian kings in small quantities from the thirteenth century, when we find an iron dagger mentioned. In the twelfth century we find mention at court of a blacksmith, to whom two sheep were given at the order of one of the kings; the blacksmith had a good Mesopotamian name, indicating that not only iron but also the knowledge of the working of iron had been exported from Asia Minor to Assyria. It may have been this court blacksmith or his son who made the iron arrowheads which Tiglath-Pileser I (1115–1077), a generation later, boasted of using with devastating effect against wild bulls. But it was not until the early ninth century that iron became sufficiently available to equip sizeable numbers of troops with iron daggers. From the same century onwards iron was used for making scale armour (worn not only by soldiers but also by war-horses), for helmets, and for axes for clearing tracks for the army.

It should not, however, be supposed that as soon as iron became available it automatically supplanted copper and bronze for all uses where it had a potential technical advantage. It did not. One factor in this may have been that the quality of the iron was, as we shall see, not easily controlled. Poor iron can be inferior for some purposes to good bronze or copper. Thus although iron axes were used for road-making under Ashur-nasir-pal II (883–859), his son Shalmaneser III in the same century, and Sargon II in the late eighth century, both refer to the use of bronze and copper implements for road-clearing on campaign.

By the eighth century, iron was being used for a wide variety of tools and utensils. In booty lists we find mention of such things as braziers and lamps of iron, whilst actual specimens have been found of chains, hoes, chisels, saws, knives, ploughshares and hammers, all of iron. A considerable store of iron objects, booty brought back by Sargon II, amounting to about one hundred and sixty tons of iron, was excavated at Khorsabad, the site of Sargon's capital Dur-Sharrukin. An analysis has been carried out of some of the iron objects found at Khorsabad. Results were not consistent: a hoe and an adze were found to be of relatively soft wrought iron, whilst an iron bar, although not homogeneous in composition, in some parts contained enough carbon to make it hard steel. The expert who carried out these analyses does not appear to have been very impressed by the technical skill of the ancient blacksmiths (who may not have been Assyrians in these instances, since the objects were booty) in controlling the quality of the metal in its gradation from pure soft wrought iron to hard carburized steel.

The bronze smiths, with a much longer tradition behind them as well as less difficult technical problems, seem to have managed rather better. As early as the pioneer excavations in Assyria in the middle of the nineteenth century A.D., it was noticed that the Assyrians (or whoever made their bronze for them) had recognized the different properties of bronze alloys of different composition. Whereas bowls, dishes and rings were made of a bronze comprising one part of tin to ten of copper, the bronze for bells contained tin in the proportion of one to six. The Assyrians were capable of quite fine work in bronze, for they were able to make tubing of small enough diameter to insert into the penis for medical treatment (see pages 229, 231).

There were certainly contemporaries of the Assyrians who were much more skilled as workers in bronze. To the north of Assyria, in the mountains which later became Armenia, was the kingdom of Urartu. Much Urartian bronze work has been excavated, and both artistically and technically it is superior to Assyrian work. The Assyrians would probably have agreed with this judgement, for when the opportunity presented itself, as in Sargon II's conquest of Urartu in his campaign of 714, they took vast quantities of Urartian bronze as booty, not simply as metal but as fabricated objects. Sargon lists the objects taken – in iron and silver as well as in bronze – running into hundreds of thousands, the item most heavily represented being bronze daggers, of which there were over 305,000. Many of the objects taken we are unable to translate, a difficulty Sargon himself to some extent shared, when he included in his list '120 bronze objects, craftsmanship of their land, the names of which are not easy to write'.

185

Chemical Technology

Little is known about chemical technology in ancient Mesopotamia; our information is limited to what we can deduce from remains of equipment found in excavations, a few texts specifically dealing with such matters, and random allusions elsewhere.

It need hardly be pointed out that food preparation in ancient Mesopotamia, as elsewhere, involved aspects of chemical technology; these included heat processes, chemical processes using added chemical substances (as in preserving meat by pickling), and such microbiological processes as the use of enzymes, bacteria and fungi in the making of beer, wine, yoghurt and cheese.

Apart from food preparation, the main chemical processes known from ancient Mesopotamia (including Assyria) were glass-making, perfume-making, dyeing, tanning, the preparation of alkalis and soap, metallurgical processes involving reduction in furnaces, and possibly distillation. It is only for glass-making and the preparation of perfumes that we have any operational texts directly linked with Assyria.

The suggestion that the people of ancient Mesopotamia were capable of employing distillation processes is based on deduction from the finding of a type of pottery vessel with a peculiar double rim, the inner lip of which is sometimes pierced with a hole and sometimes not. With a lid above and heat applied beneath, the form of pot without drainage holes in the inner lip could have served as a distillation apparatus, whilst the form equipped with drainage holes in the inner lip could have been an extraction apparatus, comparable with a coffee percolator. However, whilst this seems plausible, we have no positive evidence that pots of these types were ever actually used as distillation or extraction equipment.

The making of fire is another aspect of ancient chemical technology about which we are in ignorance. From the first millennium there are several references to the use of sulphur in producing flame; there is, for example, the instruction in a number of rituals, 'You shall light a torch from fire of sulphur', but we are given no indication of how the sulphur was ignited. From first-millennium Assyria, double-convex lenses of ground rock-crystal have been found, and these could have been used to concentrate the sun's rays to produce ignition; there is, however, absolutely no evidence that they actually were so used.

The most extensive collection of known cuneiform texts concerned with chemical technology are a few dozen pieces about the making of coloured glass, most of them from the library of Ashurbanipal at Nineveh. It should be pointed out that these texts are not in themselves proof that the precise processes they describe were utilized in Assyria in the seventh century; the texts clearly had a long literary history behind them and in their final form they may reflect procedures of several centuries before, possibly in Babylonia rather than Assyria. However, glass-making certainly was carried out in Assyria in the first millennium, as we know from the finding at Assyrian sites of actual glass vessels and other objects such as glass beads.

The technological instructions are placed in a magico-religious framework, with the usual mumbo-jumbo. The technologist had to discover (presumably by means of omens) a favourable month and day; only then might he set up his kiln. He then had to install some images called *kubu*; the other meaning of this word is 'stillborn child', so possibly the images represented ghosts of stillborn infants. Libations and sacrifices had to be offered to these images, and no ritually unclean person might come near. Clearly, the incorporation of these magico-religious preparations reflected a feeling on the part of the glass-makers that their technological control was insufficient by itself to guarantee success.

The technical instructions then follow. Basically they involved weighing out prescribed ingredients, grinding and mixing them, and then firing them in a kiln under specified conditions until the mass became molten and homogeneous, with repetition as necessary. The interim product was then cooled, ground, combined with other ingredients (providing the required colour), and then re-fired. It is instructive that one of the texts prescribes that in the final stage the kiln door is to be left open until the molten glass glows red, when the door is to be closed; clearly, the Mesopotamian technologists recognized that different results were produced by oxidizing and reducing conditions.

We have referred to texts concerning perfume-making. All but one of these come from the city of Ashur in the twelfth century. Basically the process they described was to steep and simmer aromatic plants in water for several days, then absorb the aromatic substances in added oil, which was subsequently skimmed off. An attempt has been made to interpret some of the doubtful technical terms in the texts as referring to a distillation process, but this is very questionable.

Town Planning

Deliberate attempt at control of the environment, marked by the creation of towns, is another aspect of man's growing mastery over nature. But at the same time, the form of ancient towns could reflect nature's shaping of man, since they had their origin in geography. The sites of ancient towns, and to a large extent their ground plans and their materials, were determined by natural features – by the presence of a river, a hill, fertile soil, perhaps proximity to sources of stone or wood for building. Within these parameters the original cities grew up as interlocking collections of neighbourhoods – for example, the temple area, the coppersmiths' bazaar, the potters' bazaar, residential houses – without any conscious overall planning. But later, when there was a national authority with the power to override sectional considerations in the interest of the state as a whole, some degree of town planning became a possibility if national interests demanded the rebuilding of a city. Yet even in such cases there were constraints upon what could be done; the most obvious arose from religious conservatism, which demanded that, wherever there had been a temple, there should evermore be a temple on precisely the same site. But within such limitations, a considerable amount of replanning and rebuilding was effected in the first millennium at both the best-known capitals of ancient Mesopotamia: Babylon and Nineveh. The scope for complete rebuilding was greater at Babylon, since this was sacked and razed to the ground by Sennacherib; but the details of that rebuilding are a matter for Babylonian rather than Assyrian history. Nineveh, the final Assyrian capital, does however very much concern us. This was to a considerable extent expanded and rebuilt by Sennacherib.

One of the quests of some ancient historians is for 'firsts', and on this basis we might call Sennacherib the first town-planner. A typical technocrat, he displayed the leading characteristics, good and bad, popularly associated with technocrats. He had a sincere desire to do what was best for his state, his city and his people; and he was convinced that he knew what was best for them. And he was not averse to giving the facts a little twist to suit his own purposes.

This last point comes out at the beginning of Sennacherib's account of the work he carried out on Nineveh. Although a city of first importance since the third millennium, and already ousting the old capital Ashur in political and commercial importance for several centuries before Sennacherib, it had never before actually been the capital of a united Assyria. Despite this, Sennacherib designates Nineveh as the place 'where from ancient times the kings who preceded me, my forefathers, had exercised the kingship before me and directed the subjects of the god Enlil'. There is nothing actually false in this statement; Sennacherib's predecessors had indeed reigned *at* Nineveh as the statement says; but they had not reigned *from* Nineveh, as the clause 'directed the subjects of the god Enlil' leads the reader to suppose. Probably political infighting underlay this claim, and indeed the whole question of shifting the capital. With an empire extending to north, east and west, Ashur in the far south of Assyria was strategically less adequate as capital than a city further to the north. But there was also a second factor. Because Ashur was a venerable religious centre, its citizens had acquired and retained considerable privileges in such matters as exemptions from taxation and corvée (forced labour) duties. Several earlier kings had felt the constraint of this. Tukulti-Ninurta I had built himself a new royal city across the Tigris from Ashur; Ashur-nasir-pal had created an entirely new capital at Calah out of an earlier minor town; Shalman-eser V had lost his throne because of the antagonism of Ashur; and his supplanter Sargon II, Sennacherib's father, had needed to concede all the claims of the people of Ashur in order to obtain their support in his bid for the throne, though to escape from their clutches he built himself a new royal base north-east of Nineveh, at the site he named Dur-Sharrukin (today the mound Khorsabad).

Sennacherib extended himself in his account of what he did in the way of rebuilding Nineveh. But there was nothing unusual in an Assyrian king describing building operations. Assyrian royal inscriptions had actually grown out of building inscriptions; in building inscriptions in early times (and until very late in Babylonia), the king introduced himself by his titles, added a brief note of some current state event to identify the date, and then described his pious works of building. Assyrian kings produced their royal historical inscriptions by expanding the reference to a current state event into a detailed narrative of the royal campaigns, but the building inscription always remained as the final section of the text, albeit often amounting to no more than the account of minor repairs to a temple or other public building. This meant that a traditional literary form was ready at hand when Sennacherib wanted to describe what he did for Nineveh, and he took full advantage of it. The following account of what he actually claims to have done puts together a number of different accounts of his work at the city, and represents an overall account of Sennacherib's achievements in that respect, not a blow-by-blow account of the order in which he said he had done the work.

It must be said at once that there is much that Sennacherib does not tell us that we would gladly know. We should very much like to know how the ordinary people lived, how their houses were built and grouped, how they lay in relation to food markets and temples; but this we can only discover from excavation. Sennacherib's only stated concern for such matters was that private houses should not encroach on the royal road.

189

Sennacherib's principal interest was in his own house, the royal palace. There had long been a royal palace at Nineveh, but now that Nineveh was the imperial capital, that palace was too small, covering a mere half acre or so. Sennacherib set himself to create a more worthy palace and a more worthy capital. There was no shortage of resources: his wars had given him plenty of serf labour; teams of geologists had been into the mountains looking for new sources of semi-precious stone and good building stone; and Sennacherib had at his disposal fine timber from mountains ranging from the Lebanon and Amanus in the west to the Zagros in the east. Another valuable building material was the giant reeds (up to twenty-five feet high) from the vast marshes of south Iraq, which, he says, he had 'dragged' up to Assyria; he does not explain further how they were dragged, but his statement may mean that they were towed up the rivers in barges.

The workforce came from all over the empire, from the marshes of south Babylonia, from north-west Iran, from Asia Minor, from the coast of Palestine. This mixing of many different ethnic and cultural groups must have contributed to the gradual unification of the Near East. The numbers actually used for the works at Nineveh are not stated, but Sennacherib had hundreds of thousands at his disposal.

Nineveh is situated where a tributary called the Khosr joins the Tigris. One arm of the Khosr, known as the Tebiltu, had run alongside the old palace, and in time of flood had not only eroded the platform on which the palace stood, but had run into the inner city, damaging a building of particular sanctity, called the *gigunu*, and exposing the ancient graves it contained. Sennacherib dealt with the problem by altering the course of the stream, and filling its old bed with limestone blocks from the mountains, set in bitumen. Above this was a fill of reeds, presumably thoroughly compressed against the risk of subsidence. Further protection against flooding was provided by a retaining wall reinforced with limestone slabs. On top of all this a terrace was raised to a height of 170 courses of bricks (elsewhere Sennacherib says 180 or 190) above the base of the foundations. On this the new palace was to stand.

In many respects the new palace was a fairly standard building of its type, comprising basically rooms round a series of courtyards, some of the rooms being domestic quarters or administrative offices and others long chambers constituting state rooms. We know this, not from any description by Sennacherib, but from modern excavation. There was, however, one architectural innovation, which Sennacherib regarded as sufficiently important to mention. This was the placing at the front of the palace of a columned portico constituting a replica of a Syrian type of building, an innovation which demonstrated Sennacherib's willingness to adopt foreign ideas.

The other aspects of the palace which Sennacherib considered it worth recording in some detail were the size – exceeding two and half acres – and the decoration. The basic material for giving splendour to the building was ornamental and scented woods. The king says that the gods had shown him where giant cedar trees grew in the mountains, and he had cedars and trees of other fine woods brought from the Zagros and Amanus and used for beams, pillars and doors. Oddly, he must then have lost most of the beauty of the woods by decorating over them. He tells us that he made great double doors of scented woods, and then had them clad in silver and copper. The roofing beams were also decorated in some way. Sennacherib tells us that he 'made them bright as day', which presumably meant either that he had them painted a light colour or that he overlaid them with glittering metal; the latter interpretation is the more probable, since in the following lines the king says that he fixed knobbed nails of silver and copper around the chambers concerned. Use was also made of carved ivory for panelling. The exterior walls were embellished with coloured glazed bricks on cornices and copings. As already mentioned, Sennacherib must have sent prospectors out to seek new sources of minerals, for he tells us that alabaster, so scarce in the days of his forefathers that it was 'too costly even for the pommel of a sword', was discovered in a certain mountain, so that he could now have statues sculpted from it. New sources of other stones were also found, including a vast supply of white limestone, from which massive bull-colossi were carved, to be floated down the Tigris to Nineveh on rafts at the flood season. Other colossi were cast on the spot from bronze, by a new process of hollow casting on a framework devised by Sennacherib himself. The palace was provided with a water supply from wells equipped with a pulley on a cross-beam and buckets rising from the well on an endless bronze chain.

Heating and sanitation are aspects of the technology of building about which Sennacherib does not deign to inform us, but actual excavation of his palace and others in part supplies the gap. It can be bitingly cold in winter in Nineveh, and Sennacherib must have had some way of keeping himself comfortable. Excavation has revealed in his palace, and in others, structures which may bear on this, in the form of parallel grooved stone rails set in the floor, like tram-lines. It has been plausibly suggested that these were intended for a large brazier on wheels which could be moved along the room to where the warmth was required.

The use of braziers in the palace would (if the inmates were to escape carbon-monoxide poisoning) require some form of ventilation. Archaeology can provide no clue to this, since any such installation would have been in the upper parts of the walls, which have invariably disappeared. However, texts do speak of something in a palace called literally a 'breeze door', which was presumably some sort of ventilation grille which could be opened and closed.

For the Assyrian, cleanliness was very close to godliness, and there were many occasions when washing had to be undertaken for ritual purposes, quite apart from the needs of hygiene or personal comfort. This was particularly the case with the king, and Sennacherib's throne-room had a bathroom leading off, a common feature of palaces. Typically a bathroom had a floor of burnt brick, water-proofed with bitumen, which also protected the lower parts of the walls. In a depressed part of the floor would be one or two drainage holes with stone plugs. There is nothing in Sennacherib's palace which can be positively identified as a lavatory, though there are a number of drainage holes which could have been surmounted by a seat. Possibly, however, a seat may have been unnecessary, if Assyrians squatted to excrete, as Iraqi Arabs still do unless they have succumbed to recent European influence.

In addition to the main palace, Sennacherib restored and enlarged a second major administrative building which we might describe as a barracks, though it mainly housed not troops but war horses, military vehicles (chariots and wagons) and war equipment in general. A large parade ground was incorporated for the training of the cavalry and chariotry horses, as well as of other animals used on campaign, such as mules and camels.

The approach to the new palace was taken care of. Sennacherib had the existing streets broadened to create a 'royal road' over ninety feet wide, comprising a raised road of white limestone slabs, marked by steles along both sides, bearing a warning that, if anyone rebuilt his house with its foundations encroaching on the royal road, he would be impaled on a stake on top of his house.

Sennacherib did not fail to give his palace a suitable setting. Alongside it he created what he called 'a great park, like Mount Amanus, in which there were all kinds of scented plants and fruit trees, the produce of the mountains and Chaldaea', and also, as he specifically mentioned, 'wool-bearing trees', that is, cotton. It is no easy task to get trees established in the region of Nineveh, where there is considerable heat and no rain from May until October; the Tigris could not conveniently be used for large-scale irrigation in the time of Sennacherib because it lay too low in relation to the land around Nineveh. Sennacherib dealt with the problem by cutting a system of canals to bring water to his city from mountain streams and springs up to thirty miles away, from at least three directions. The part of the system about which we have most information from Sennacherib's inscriptions, and which was probably the most important part of the system as a whole, channelled the mountain waters by means of canals and aqueducts into the Khosr tributary, where dams and weirs were built to permit control of the level as the Khosr approached Nineveh. Many parts of this considerable engineering project are still visible, and at low water Assyrian embankment works can still be seen along parts of the Khosr. To feed the mountain streams into the Khosr there was at one place, where a valley had to be crossed, an aqueduct three hundred yards long composed of some two million stone blocks weighing a quarter of a ton each, built on a bed of rough boulders. The top of the aqueduct was twenty-four yards wide, graded for an even fall, with buttresses to strengthen its sides.

One may ask whether this ambitious scheme was economically profitable in terms of raised agricultural production in the immediate neighbourhood of Nineveh. Probably it was not, but that clearly was not the object of the exercise. What Sennacherib was attempting to do – and all credit to him – was to improve the quality of life for himself and the people of Nineveh by making a city pleasant to live in. The excess water from the canal system, after serving the park, rather than being allowed to run to waste into the Tigris was fed into an area which was deliberately allowed to become a swamp, with encouragement to appropriate flora and fauna – cane brakes, water-birds, wild pigs. The citizens of Nineveh were encouraged to play their own part in making the city agreeable and fruitful, for land upstream of the city was divided into plots of the order of an acre or so and granted to citizens of Nineveh for planting orchards.

The area of the city was much increased. It had formerly been about 180 acres; now Sennacherib built a great inner wall to enclose a city area of about one thousand acres. The wall was said to be forty bricks thick and 180 courses high, which in view of the dimensions of Assyrian bricks at the time would mean that the wall was more than forty feet thick and forty-five feet high. Within the wall were fifteen gates. Beyond, and forming a great arc round the city meeting the Tigris to north and south, was a great outer wall. North and south of the city were further parks, and it is likely that the cultivated land of the city spread out from five to ten miles beyond.

Private houses

We know a good deal less about the private houses of Assyria than about the palaces. This is almost inevitable. Assyrian kings tell us a great deal about their palaces in their inscriptions, but had no interest in describing private houses. Further, the remains of palaces, which are normally in the major mounds of an archaeological site, are much more easily identified than the remains of private houses. It also has to be recognized that palaces are much more likely than private houses to contain museum-worthy objects, so that it has generally been the case up to quite recent times that, given the choice, most archaeologists in Assyria would have chosen to excavate a palace area rather than remains of private houses. Finally, whereas palaces had considerable parts of stone, many private houses were predominantly or even totally of mud-brick, so that even when the remains of private houses could be identified and excavated, there could well be serious technical problems in extracting meaningful information about the form of the house.

We do nevertheless possess some textual information about private houses. This comes mainly from documents relating to the sale of houses, which sometimes give a basic inventory of what the house comprised. Thus one such text records the sale of 'a built house together with its beams and its door, its courtyard building, its bathroom, its servants' quarter of the main building, an upper storey, a store room, a lean-to, a tomb'. Another text of the first millennium describes a house in Nineveh as 'a built house with its beams and its doors, a dining room, a bedroom, a bathroom, a *guršu* room [whatever that may have been], a store room, an upper storey with four doors'.

In addition to what such texts tell us, we know something about private houses and their contents from actual structures excavated at the two capitals of Ashur and Calah, and at a provincial town Shibaniba (today the mound Tepe Gawra) about twelve miles northeast of Nineveh.

At Calah a block of six adjoining houses against the town wall was excavated. Walls were of mud-brick, covered by mud plaster, and beaten mud was the material for most of the floors, although some passages and courtyards were paved with burnt brick or with pebbles. The largest of the houses had about a dozen ground floor rooms, and occupied, not as the excavator erroneously stated, about three thousand square metres, but rather less than 250 square metres or about one-sixteenth of an acre. However, even this was still about twice the ground area of a substantial modern four-bedroomed detached house. The thickness of some of the partition walls, and the presence of stairs, indicates that the house had an upper storey. In estimating the actual living accommodation, it should be noticed, though, that part of the area comprised courtyards. Entrance was through an outer courtyard, and there was an inner cobbled courtyard with storage rooms leading off on one side and the main reception room on the other. Behind the storage rooms was the family burial vault, since frequently the Assyrian dead were buried under the floor of their houses. One small room contained a conical bread oven of terracotta. A largish room off the outer courtyard revealed the skeleton of the house's watch-dog. Another room contained a collection of storage pots, bowls and jars, which still contained analysable traces of wheat, barley, millet, linseed and oil. Agricultural equipment found in the house included a sickle and bill-hook, and an iron axe. Another indication of the type of household equipment present in an Assyrian house was a decorated bone spoon. No objects of precious metal were found, but the house had been looted and burned, and it would have been stripped of any precious metals at that time.

Some Assyrian private houses had lavatories provided with drains, mostly channels in burnt brick, though in the late second millennium there were drainage systems of terracotta piping. The internal doors of houses swung on pivots turning in holes in burnt bricks. Some walls had niches as cupboards, and valuable objects might be hidden in spaces in the floor.

Animal Power and Land Transport

Another important stage in ancient man's mastery over nature was his use of animal power. In Mesopotamia generally, this seems to have begun not later than the fourth millennium, with oxen pulling sledges. It was in Mesopotamia that the wheel was invented, late in the fourth millennium, the sledges thereby becoming primitive wagons or carts. Developments from these formed part of Assyria's transport system, with wagons (technically improved by spoked instead of solid wheels) still drawn predominantly by oxen, less often mules, until the end of the empire, and highly mobile horse-drawn war chariots used from the time of the Middle Assyrian empire. An improved form of light chariot or trap (two-wheeled carriage), used if not invented by New Assyrian kings, was provided with a canopy for protection from the sun.

A second early use of the ox, marking another stage in man's control of his environment, was for drawing the plough, and a third application of ox-power was in threshing, the animal dragging a kind of sledge studded with flints over the heads of corn spread out on the threshing floor.

Other animal power available comprised the ass, the horse, the hybrid mule, and to a limited extent the camel. It was the ass which served as the principal pack animal, a caravan of them enabling the transport of large quantities of goods over long distances and difficult terrain, their range limited only by the availability of water. Obviously the ass could also be used as a riding beast, but it was less comfortable than the mule and slow compared with the horse. But as late as the first millennium even the donkey was by no means universally available, and we find even such an official as a royal astrologer having to request the king: 'Let me be sent a donkey to ease my feet.'

The domestication of the horse and its introduction into Mesopotamia by the end of the third millennium made a considerable impact upon human life. Used for chariotry, first by the Mittannians and then by the Assyrians, it provided a mobile platform for shooting arrows, which in suitable terrain could dominate the battlefield. Used for cavalry, as it was by the Assyrians in the first millennium, the manoeuvrability and speed of the horse gave an overwhelming tactical advantage in battle, and contributed much to the success of Assyrian arms throughout the Near East.

But the riding horse was not used only for war. It permitted rapid communications. This was a point at which the Assyrians made a positive advance. As the Assyrian empire made its greatest expansion from the eighth century, it became necessary, in order to control and administer this major power structure, to ensure regular and punctual communication between outlying administrators and the capital. The Assyrians made the horse part of this system. Chains of posting stages were set up across the empire, with relays of horses (or occasionally, in mountain territory unsuitable for horses, mules or donkeys). Along these routes mounted messengers could now make rapid transit, so that, with the exception of Egypt, which involved the crossing of the Sinai desert, there was no part of the empire which could not send a message to the capital and receive an answer within about a week.

This implied the maintenance of highways. There is no evidence of paved roads away from the capitals, but there were certainly main routes which were kept clear and recognized as highways. As early as the thirteenth century, Tukulti-Ninurta I, telling of the events of the beginning of his reign in 1244, says of a campaign in the mountainous Tur Abdin region (south of Diyarbekr in eastern Turkey): 'I cut into their mountains with copper picks and widened their unopened paths.' At around 1100 we have Tiglath-Pileser I telling us that, in the same difficult terrain: 'I hacked a troublesome mountain and difficult tracks with copper picks, and made the road good for the passage of my chariots and troops.' Subsequent kings tell of similar road works. With such attention to lines of communication in the mountains, it would have been surprising had the main high-ways not been well maintained in the plains. And indeed they clearly were. Although not paved, the highways were sufficiently well defined and permanent to be named as boundaries for fields in documents of land sale; sometimes in such cases the road would be specifically called either just 'the royal highway', or more explicitly 'the royal highway to such-and-such a place', or 'the highway which goes from. . .to. . .', with the names given of the towns at each end of that section. Without question these were recognized permanent highways, maintained by the state to provide an efficient communi-cation system.

In times of war the highways would be used by the royal chari-otry; in peacetime they made it possible for wagons to carry over long distances loads too cumbersome to be committed to ass caravan. Special wagon roads are sometimes mentioned. As to the actual wagons, it would seem that native Assyrian technology did not always keep abreast with that of some other countries; Ashur-banipal specifically mentions that for one of his major building projects bricks were brought in from all over his land in Elamite wagons which he had taken as spoil, the implication being that they were either larger or stronger (or both) than the native Assyrian article. Loads too heavy for wagons, such as stone colossi which might weigh up to twenty tons, could still be moved; they were dragged along on rollers, with the assistance of long poles as levers. We see this demonstrated on a bas relief (see plate 6B).

Water Transport

Ashur, Calah, and Nineveh, the three most important of the succes-sive capitals of Assyria, all lay alongside the Tigris, which therefore constituted an important potential means of transport from one end to the other of the central part of the Assyrian kingdom. Evidence that this resource was exploited is provided by a great quay wall excavated at Calah (see plate 7B), close to the ziggurat and some of the palace buildings. Its line has been traced for some 240 yards. It was built up in great stone blocks rising some thirty-three feet above bedrock, and set twenty-one feet deep into the river-bank. Sennacherib built a similar quay alongside Nineveh, as we know from the fact of one of the fifteen gates of his city being named 'the Quay Gate'. Sennacherib also describes using river transport for bringing very heavy cargoes – in this case limestone colossi – to Nineveh. The quays were a source of national revenue, since we know that harbour dues were charged for their use.

Several quite different types of vessel were used on the rivers of Assyria. The most ingenious, if in some respects the most primitive, was a large raft called a *kalakku*, a word which survives in the modern Arabic term for the same craft, *kelek*. Craft of this type were still to be seen on the Tigris up to the 1950s A.D. (see plate 10A), since when their use has been discouraged as non-progressive. The method of construction of *keleks* was described by H. A. Layard (see pages 299ff.), who used such craft in the 1840s:

> The skins of full-grown sheep and goats are used. They are taken off with as few incisions as possible, and then dried and prepared. The air is forced in by the lungs through an aperture which is afterwards tied up with string. A square framework, formed of poplar beams, branches of trees, and reeds, having been constructed of the size of the intended raft, the inflated skins are tied to it by osier and other twigs, the whole being firmly bound together. The raft is then moved to the water and launched. Care is taken to place the skins with their mouths upwards, that, in case any should burst or require filling, they can be easily opened by the raftmen. Upon the framework of wood are piled bales of goods, and property belonging to merchants and travellers.

By the nature of its construction a *kelek* could be as big as the load required. The raftmen's task in navigation was simply to bring the *kelek* into the main current, and to avoid any rapids that might be encountered; subject to this, the craft would then float downstream at the speed of the Tigris. It would obviously be out of the question to take such a raft back upstream by water, so that in the latest period of their use, and presumably also in Assyrian times, the practice was to dismantle the *kelek* when it reached its destination and either to sell off its materials on the spot or send them back by road.

A second type of water craft, still to be found on the rivers of Iraq within the last two decades, was a round flat-bottomed coracle. The modern Iraqi Arabic name is *guffa* or *quffa*, representing the original Akkadian *quppu*; *quppu* meant 'basket', which is basically what this craft was – a very large and sturdy reed basket, water-proofed with bitumen. Although very stable, it was not convenient to propel upstream for any considerable distance, and so was more useful for local transport, including ferry work, than for long-distance traffic.

The third type of boat was of conventional shape, with a prow and stern. As to method of propulsion, there seems to be no proof of the use of sails; all representations of boats relating to Assyria show them being rowed or paddled. In the matter of water transport, as in some other things, the Assyrians recognized that other nations might have superior technical expertise. Therefore when Sennacherib decided upon a seaborne campaign against Elam across the Persian Gulf, he used north Syrian shipbuilders to build his fleet at Nineveh, entrusting the vessels to Phoenician sailors to sail to the south (see page 102). These ships were presumably of the same kind as Phoenician war-galleys, shown on an Assyrian bas relief as having seventeen oars on each side (see plate 11B).

Already in the second millennium the Tigris was so busy with cargo boats plying to the capital Ashur that collisions occurred. This was sufficiently a problem that the Assyrian laws of the twelfth century needed to legislate on questions of responsibility if such an accident resulted in the sinking of a cargo.

Boats plied not only on the main rivers but also on the canals, presumably to bring produce to the capital from distant estates. We have an account of a ninth-century governor widening a canal so that it could take boats up to twenty-five cubits (nearly forty feet); this measurement, giving an idea of the size of boats used, denoted the length, not the breadth.

Apart from their function in carrying goods along the canals and rivers, boats also acted as a link in the overland communication system, in two ways. Firstly, they were used as ferry vessels, ferries being maintained at a number of riverine towns, under the control of governors. Secondly, they were employed as bridges; this was achieved by lashing a number of vessels together across the river, a system still in use at Baghdad up to 1957 A.D. In ancient Assyria both these uses of boats were of sufficient national importance for matters affecting them to be reported to the king.

13

The Supernatural World

For most of us, our first impression of ancient Near Eastern religion comes from the Bible. We therefore need to be aware that what is said there on the subject is prejudiced; the Israelite prophets, those fearsome men of God, were capable of deliberately misleading – with the best of intentions, be it understood. A case in point is the picture of the Mesopotamians' view of their gods which we get from the prophet we usually call Deutero-Isaiah (responsible for Chapters 40 to 55 of the Book of Isaiah):

> *Those who lavish gold from the purse,*
> *and weigh out silver in the scales,*
> *hire a goldsmith, and he makes it into a god;*
> *then they fall down and worship.*
> *They lift it upon their shoulders, they carry it,*
> *they set it in its place, and it stands there;*
> *it cannot move from its place.* (Isaiah 46: 6–7)

Here there are two implications about Mesopotamian religion. One is that the Mesopotamians thought of the god as being no more than his image, and the other is that worshippers made such gods just as it took their fancy. Both implications are false.

Images of the gods there certainly were, but they were recognized as being images and not the ultimate divine reality. Certainly the gods could be approached through the image, but so could the Israelites' Yahweh be approached through the Ark. The divine image of an ancient Mesopotamian was no more the essence of his god than the Ark was the essence of Yahweh, or than a crucifix, to the Catholic who reveres it, is Christ. To the ancient Babylonian or Assyrian, a divine image was a point at which contact could be made with the god, a point where the divine presence could be focused; it was not the totality of the god himself. The ancient theologians were quite explicit about this. One text says of Marduk, supreme god of Babylon though worshipped also in Assyria, 'The underworld is your washbasin, the highest heaven your censer bowl'. A god of such cosmic vastness could not be confined within an image. Moreover, far from the great gods being identified with their images, they were often represented and revered not as an image at all but as a symbol. Thus we see on one sculpture a worshipper kneeling before an altar on which is a sword (plate 9B), and in judicial documents of the early second millennium we find mention of an oath being taken 'before the dagger of the god Ashur'.

Polytheism

An aspect of Mesopotamian religion which might with more justification have been held up to ridicule by the Israelite prophets was its polytheism. Inscriptions of Assyrian kings listed long series of deities, such as 'Ashur the great lord, father of the gods, Anu, Enlil and Ea, Sin, Shamash and Adad, Marduk, Nabu, Nergal, Ishtar, the Seven, the great gods who stand at the side of the king', but such lists constituted only a small fraction of the total pantheon recognized by ancient theologians. What Jeremiah said of Judah was an understatement for Mesopotamia: 'As many as your cities are your gods' (Jeremiah 2: 28). In ancient Mesopotamia, not only did every city originally have its own god, but in addition many aspects both of the physical world and of human society had their divine patrons. There were, for example, deities of brewing and building. Thus the modern scholar who goes to the ancient Mesopotamian texts finds that they list literally thousands of deities in the pantheon. But this huge list was not a reflection of general religious belief nor indeed the belief of any individual, but rather the artificial creation of ancient scholars bringing together the personnel of a number of different local pantheons and trying to put them into some sort of order. Outside scholarly circles no one, either in Babylonia or Assyria, ever saw the universe as operated by this huge organized official pantheon.

Without any doubt, the ordinary Assyrian saw himself surrounded by a great variety of supernatural forces, but his picture of the supernatural world was by no means the official pantheon of the scholars. The ordinary man, though aware that there was a pantheon, was probably acquainted with the details of it no better than the ordinary Christian is with the canon of saints; and the gods (as distinct from demonic forces) with whom the average Assyrian was in practice concerned were very few. Foremost was the national god Ashur; Ashur could never be forgotten, as he was involved in everything done by the king and would be honoured at every state occasion. But the ordinary Assyrian would probably not be aware that theologically Ashur had absorbed many features both of the old Sumerian god Enlil, one of the supreme triad, and of Marduk, god of Babylon. Alongside Ashur was the goddess Ishtar, never far from mind, because of her association on the one hand with sexual activities and on the other with war. Ishtar manifested herself in various forms – as Ishtar of Nineveh, Ishtar of Erbil, and Ishtar of Bit-Kitmuri, for example – and some Assyrians certainly thought of these as distinct deities. They may well, indeed, have been justified in so thinking, since the various forms of Ishtar may have developed by the imposing on different local mother-goddesses of the attributes of Ishtar. Then there were gods of natural phenomena, the Sun-god Shamash (also god of Justice), the Moon-god Sin, and the Weather-god Adad, each of them too intimately concerned with everyday life to be ignored. Ea, god of Wisdom, might also be in the forefront of general religious consciousness, though perhaps not so much for his association with wisdom as for his importance in magical operations and in water-cults. Nergal, god of the underworld and of death, necessarily claimed a gruesome interest; whilst Ninurta, a god of war and hunting, had an obvious place in Assyrian life. At those periods and social contexts in which prominence was given to the Babylonian connection, the two Babylonian gods Marduk and Nabu might also find special significance in Assyria. But apart from these, whilst virtually any of the thousands of deities in the official pantheon might in some circumstances find mention in Assyrian texts, there is little evidence of other members of the pantheon being much in the popular consciousness. However, the last statement needs a reservation; quite a few other god names occur as elements in personal names, and this might imply the widespread worship of those deities, for which other evidence is lacking.

The official pantheon came about not so much to serve the needs of worship as to give expression to the compulsion felt by the intellectuals of ancient Babylonia and Assyria to bring order into all aspects of life. In accordance with this the theologians sought to arrange all the gods of diverse origin into an organized pantheon, with defined interrelationships and precedence. But alternative local traditions were too strong, and the ordinary Assyrian was probably as hard put to it to appreciate the complexities of the formal pantheon as the ordinary Christian is to define the relationship between God the Father, God the Son and God the Holy Ghost. Precedence amongst Assyrian deities, and questions of their inter-relationship, clearly remained a problem until nearly the end of the empire. Thus we find Sennacherib having to establish by divination the proper precedence of a number of gods for processional purposes, and there is another text reflecting doubt whether a goddess Sherua was the wife of Ashur (whose wife was otherwise often known as Ninlil, originally the name of the wife of the Sumerian god Enlil) or his daughter.

The great gods mentioned, whilst regarded as being concerned with the life of Assyria (and Babylonia) as a whole, might at the same time be thought of as having a particular link with certain cities. Thus Nergal, who as god of the underworld controlled the terrors of death, was, with his consort Las, described in Babylonia as 'dwelling in the city Cuthah' and in Assyria as 'dwelling in Tarbisu' (just up-river from Nineveh). Ashur, the Assyrian national god, was of course specially associated with the city of the same name; and, as already noted, Ishtar, in different forms, had a particular association with Nineveh and Erbil. Sin, the Moon-god, had his Babylonian home in Ur, and in greater Assyria was specially linked with his temple in Harran.

Basically, the gods were thought of as beings in human form. However, behind this there were older beliefs, which still show traces in some representations and texts. Thus, Ashur-nasir-pal II carried a bird-headed sickle which represented the god Ninurta, the Assyrian god of war and hunting. A myth, originally from third-millennium Sumer but still popular in Assyria in the first millennium, told how this god overcame a divine being in bird-form called Anzu and took his powers; this was a way (by a procedure common in myths) of reflecting that an earlier form of Ninurta was that divine being in bird-form. Similarly, the fact that we sometimes find the god Ashur represented as seated on a lion may suggest that at an earlier stage the supernatural powers he incorporated were thought of in the form of a lion.

Incipient Monotheism

Even with the limited pantheon of ordinary usage, there was a strong tendency to reduce it further. This trend was probably influenced as much by political development as by religious speculation. In Assyria, the citizen saw himself in a society where all the authorities to whom he was subordinate were in the last resort representatives of a single power-source, the king. It was a reasonable analogy that in the divine world all the gods were in the last resort manifestations of a single god who embraced all the divine powers. We find this explicitly stated in a number of texts, such as the following, addressed to the god Ninurta:

> *Your eyes, O Lord, are Enlil and Ninlil;*
> *Your two lips are Anu and Antu;*

Your head is Adad, who made heaven and earth. . . . ,
Your brow is Shala, his beloved spouse, who
    rejoices the heart;
Your neck is Marduk. . . .

(As a side-issue, it may be pointed out that this quotation illustrates another aspect of the flux present inside the pantheon, despite the attempts of the theologians to produce a single consistent view. Here it is Adad who 'made heaven and earth', but several other gods are given the same title, and quite a number are credited with creation in mythology). Another text states: 'Jupiter is the star of the god Sin [normally the moon], and the god Sin is Ashur', and then goes on to say that certain other stars, elsewhere related to other gods, are also Ashur.

Does the recognition of other gods as aspects of one God represent monotheism? The answer depends very much upon how one defines monotheism. Christians call themselves monotheists, but there are Muslims who deny that Christianity is monotheistic, on the ground that Christians accept in God the three Persons of the Father, Son and Holy Ghost, and that three Persons implies three gods. If by monotheism one means a belief that ultimately all divinity is one, then some Assyrians were certainly monotheistic. Contrariwise, to anyone who takes the view that to accept that the divine can appear in several distinct forms precludes monotheism, no Assyrians were monotheistic.

The Temples

The great gods were everywhere, and we have such statements about the gods as this: 'He wears the heavens on his head like a turban; he is shod with the underworld as with sandals.' But just as in Judaism, Christianity and Islam, the particular place associated with encounter with God is the synagogue, church or mosque, so in ancient Assyria it was particularly the temple where the gods were to be approached.

The temples were as old as the cities themselves; at the first settlement the original settlers would have provided a dwelling, originally often quite small, for the god who incorporated their group identity. The god would come to have his family and house-hold staff just like a human ruler, represented by subsidiary deities with chapels or shrines attached to the building of the main deity. As the settlement prospered and grew into a city, the temple grew with it, becoming, in some instances from a very early period, a building of considerable size, wealth and splendour. As the city came into relationship with other communities, this would be mirrored in the relationships of the city god, and there might be chapels, or even separate temples, added for deities brought into such a relationship.

One would expect the cult of the gods to be especially associated with temples, and so indeed it was, although it was not restricted to it and the royal palace could also be concerned with cultic matters. As it happens, we have a great many more texts from Babylonian temples than from Assyrian, and know correspondingly more about them. In view of this, we have to avoid the temptation of arbitrarily filling in gaps in our information about Assyrian temples from what we know from Babylonia, since there were certainly big differences. In Babylonia, the temples were in some cases owners of estates on a vast scale; for example, at some periods the temple of Eanna in the southern city of Erech was able to operate an economy parallel to, and to some extent independent of, that of the state. This was not true of Assyria in the first millennium. There the royal administration had such a firm grip on the whole of the economic and administrative life of the country that there were cases in which a temple did not even own the land immediately surrounding it. Even where an Assyrian temple did own land, the extent of its domains was not likely to be sufficient to give it a major economic function. This does not mean that an Assyrian temple could not be wealthy; a major temple, with a cultic function and prestige which brought it into direct contact with the king, might well find means from time to time to present a divine decision requiring a grant of land or a gift or the renovation of some temple building. Offerings from worshippers might also be considerable. We find one temple functionary reporting to an Assyrian king that he had made twelve minas of gold received from offerings into ornaments for the god's wife – around £40,000 worth in terms of gold price of the early 1980s A.D. This was, however, almost certainly the great temple in Babylon.

We turn to the cultic aspect of Assyrian temples. Because temples were primarily the earthly homes of the gods, we should expect some evidence there of the divine presence. Customarily the gods were represented by statues, which might be of either wood or stone overlaid with gold, or images cast in copper or precious metals; normally each statue would stand on a pedestal or dais. But, as already pointed out, representations of Assyrian deities were not exclusively in human form, and although we have no specific knowledge of any image of an Assyrian deity in animal form, there were certainly instances in which the god was represented by a divine symbol, such as a dagger, rather than by a statue.

The statues in Assyrian temples were not exclusively of deities. From the temple of the Moon-god in Harran, we hear of two big royal statues being set up, one on the right and one on the left of the statue of the god, with smaller statues of the royal princes in front. This did not imply the divinity of the king. Rather, the purpose of this was to bring the king some magical benefit by the permanent association of his image with the Moon-god. The religious official who had recommended this arrangement explained: 'As the Moon-god, lord of the corona, unceasingly rises and sets month by month, he will send to the king my lord favourable signs for long days, stability of reign and accession of power.'

The god's house

The basic human needs are shelter, food and clothing; and it was a reasonable assumption, from the ancient Mesopotamian point of view, that a god in human form shared these needs.

The first need of a deity was a temple as his (or her) house. The earliest Assyrian examples, in the third millennium, were of modest dimensions, but they later became splendid, the equal of royal palaces. A temple had one important difference from a palace: it included a solid stepped tower (which in Assyria was square) called a ziggurat (other spellings are possible), with up to seven stages. A representation on a cylinder seal (plate 2B) gives us an idea of how they looked. Several ziggurats still stand in Iraq as massive landmarks, the most striking example in Assyria being that at Nimrud, a spectacular man-made hill (plate 9A), although it no longer clearly shows its original stepped formation. For known ziggurats from Assyria the original base dimensions range from just under eighty feet square to just over two hundred feet square (from twenty-four metres square to sixty-two metres square). At Khorsabad there were remains of four stages with a continuous six-foot-wide ramp of burnt brick round the outside protected by a crenellated parapet. The vertical faces of the four stages were stuccoed and painted successively white, black, red and blue, which must have had a religious symbolism which escapes us. There could have been three more stages, but we have no proof that there were.

There has been much discussion as to what these ziggurats were for. They were certainly not (as sometimes suggested) astronomical observatories. Nor did they serve as tombs, like the pyramids. The building of ziggurats may originally have had something to do with the widespread idea in the ancient Near East that gods lived in mountains – a ziggurat being a credible substitute for a mountain in the plains of Mesopotamia. It is doubtful if the Assyrians (or

Babylonians) of the first millennium had much more knowledge than we have of what ideas lay behind the development of this architectural feature in the third millennium.

It was necessary not only to provide a deity with a temple as his house, but also to clothe him and feed him. The ritual clothing of the images of deities was an important part of the cult at all times in ancient Mesopotamia; and we know in general that this applied as much to Assyria as to Babylonia. In Assyrian art there are representations of processions showing the gods clothed, but we have no texts to give us details of how and when the clothing was put on. We have actual lists of divine garments and jewellery for Babylonia, and there it seems that the ceremonial dressing of the gods was something which was undertaken only for special processions or festivals, not every day. We know that in Assyrian temples the deities were fed daily, for we find mention of 'providing food in the temple of Nineveh' and of 'the morning and evening meals (for the gods) at Nineveh'. Once again, information is fuller for Babylonia, from where we have texts giving details not only of the ceremonial involved in serving the gods their food, but even the menus. They were provided with two main and two lighter meals each day, with food which included beer and milk, barley bread and emmer bread, mutton, beef, ducks and other poultry, ostrich eggs and duck eggs, and dates and figs. Oddly, despite the quantities the gods theoretically ate in the cult, no provision seems to have been made for their needing to excrete. This seems to have been a human function they managed without, since mythology also is silent about it, although deities mythically participated in most other human activities, such as eating, drinking, making love, losing their tempers, sulking, weeping and sleeping.

Outside the daily care of the god's image, there were a large number of other ceremonies; some of these took place monthly, some on particular days of the year, some others only on special occasions, such as the enthronement of a new king. At any time the temple might be called upon for special rituals to avert the evil of an ill omen. Some of the ceremonies involved the image of the deity, splendidly arrayed, leaving the temple to go in procession and to return. In many cases we know of ceremonies only from passing allusions, and details are scanty or wholly lacking. We may, for example, find a single line in a text which refers to 'when the king makes a sheep sacrifice before the stars'; from this we can deduce that something of sufficient national importance to involve the king was going on at night, possibly in the temple courtyard or on the temple or palace roof, but as to what it was all about, we know nothing.

Some of the rituals were of great complexity, involving the images of large numbers of gods. Thus we find one text which speaks of fifteen deities standing to the left of the god Ashur and fifteen to his right; clearly this was some very magnificent ceremony. What the gods were doing in this particular ritual we do not know, but it seems to have been some sort of divine conclave, for they were provided with a meal – wholly vegetable on this occasion, comprising linseed, nuts, grapes, pomegranates, figs, bread, wine and beer.

Most of the temple rituals comprised various permutations upon such elements as processions of gods, sacrifices of animals, feasting or offerings of food and drink, recitation of incantations or prayers, singing of lamentations, washing ceremonies, music on kettledrums, and (less predictably) dramatic representations of mythological events. Elements of the last kind might include ritual fights, races, or going to bed with amorous intent, a ritual which modern scholars shyly refer to as the Sacred Marriage. Ceremonies with music – particularly on kettledrums – were quite common for various gods, and a list enumerates thirteen of these divine concerts at Ashur between September and April. An ancient text (though not from Assyria) explicitly tells us that the purpose of drums was to summon the gods.

One feast of which we hear a good deal was called the Akitu; although this is often translated 'New Year Feast', we do not really know what this term meant originally. The translation is used because at Babylon in the first millennium this is what it had become, held in the opening days of the first month of the year, Nisan (approximately April). At Babylon it included the recital of the whole of a myth of creation – the representation of a ritual combat between the city god and the primeval monster Tiamat (both woman and dragon), a Sacred Marriage, ceremonies designed to ensure the well-being of the city for the coming year, and the enthronement anew of the earthly king. But it is not legitimate to assume that we have to see the Akitu festival in Assyria as reproducing that of Babylon in all details. In Assyria the Akitu ceremonies did not even necessarily take place at the beginning of the year in the month Nisan (April); we find references to such ceremonies, for example, in either Ab (August) or Elul (September) at a place near Erbil, and in Addar (March) at an unidentified place. The occurrence of the festival in Addar is already evidenced in the early second millennium.

However, from the city of Ashur there is also evidence for an Akitu ceremony in Nisan, with strong indications that much of what happened paralleled the Akitu ritual in Babylon. This, however, may represent not age-old Assyrian custom but the fairly recent influence of Babylon. On the second of Nisan the god Ashur, after receiving a meat breakfast, left his temple in a chariot drawn by white horses leading a procession of gods to a building called the Akitu House. This was a temple built by Sennacherib outside the city. Sennacherib clearly regarded the open country as the only proper place for the Akitu House, since in rebuilding this temple he chidingly refers to the fact that the custom had developed of holding the 'festival of the banquet of Ashur, king of the gods' within the city instead of in the open country. But this serves to prove that, despite Sennacherib's strong views, there was an alternative Assyrian tradition about the matter, and Sennacherib's certainty about what was right may well have been influenced by Babylonian practice.

What Ashur did when he reached the Akitu House we are not directly told. We can, however, infer that, in addition to presiding at the banquet mentioned by Sennacherib, he re-enacted the primordial cosmic fight with the monster Tiamat. Our reason for thinking this is that Sennacherib describes the gate of the Akitu House as decorated with a representation of 'the image of Ashur, who is going into battle into the midst of Tiamat, as he raises his bow, riding in a chariot, girt with the Deluge-weapon'. But here again, one wonders how far these details were ancient in Assyria and how far they had been quite recently borrowed from Babylonia.

Assyrian religion was basically a state religion, and the state depended on the king; it is therefore not surprising to find that it was on the king that many of the temple rituals centred. This remained true even of temples in cities far from the capital, where the king could not be present in person at the great festivals; in such cases a ritual garment of the king would be sent to the temple to play the part that ideally the king should have played himself. Other members of the royal family, including women, could also be involved in temple rituals. Thus we find mention of either the daughter or the sister of the king being required, in one ceremony, to summon by name the consort of the supreme Assyrian god Ashur as she was presented with an offering of cooked meat.

Temple and other religious personnel

The major temple of a major city, though it lacked the huge estates that a corresponding temple in Babylonia enjoyed, was still a large and complex corporation; it correspondingly required administrators as well as cultic personnel.

In the case of the main temple of the old religious capital Ashur, administration fell to an official, who was not a cultic person, known as the *abarakku* ('Steward') of the house of the god Ashur. In some other Assyrian temples the chief administrator was known as 'Man over the household', and in yet others he was the *shangu*, who was also the main cultic functionary, so that the title is often translated 'priest'. It is possible that the same man sometimes bore both the titles 'Man over the household' and *shangu*, used alternatively according to whether his administrative or his cultic function was paramount at the time. There was often also a deputy *shangu*. The *shangu* of a major temple was a man of considerable importance, often in direct contact with the king both in person on ritual occasions and by correspondence about events in the city or state. He could also be of considerable wealth, owning large estates, in addition to the emoluments he received as a share in the temple's income.

These officials were appointed by the king, though usually the king's freedom of choice in such appointments was circumscribed by two factors. One was the general acceptance of the hereditary principle. Thus we find a report being made to the king that the 'Man over the household' of a certain temple had died; it was suggested to the king that he should appoint as replacement either the dead man's son, or his nephew, or his cousin once removed, who was currently deputy *shangu*; appointments in that temple were clearly kept within a close circle. The other limitation upon the king's freedom of choice was that his nomination of a *shangu* (and some other officials) had to be approved by the gods at a divination ceremony. The professional diviners controlled the procedure for obtaining a divine decision, and clearly this situation gave them the opportunity of vetoing any unwelcome nomination.

The shangu

The *shangu*, assisted where necessary by his deputy, looked after the temple's financial affairs. He controlled the receipt of offerings, administered the temple treasury, and (except in the special case of the main temple at Ashur, where there was an *abarakku* (steward) for the purpose) held responsibility for its property generally. The safeguarding of temple property had its problems, for instances of embezzlement by members of a temple's staff were not rare, and on occasions we find temple administrators complaining to the king that a provincial governor had taken treasure from the temple. It was also the *shangu* and his deputy who had the overall responsibility for the ritual of the temple, and often played the leading part in it, although other cultic personnel might also be involved. The Assyrian king himself, as nominal head of the state ritual, included *shangu* amongst his titles.

There were many classes of religious personnel other than the *shangu*, some specifically linked to temples, others not; whether or not we call such personnel 'priests' depends upon our subjective view of what the term 'priest' means. In what follows, the term 'priest' is for convenience sometimes used hyphenated to some qualifying term, but despite this the view taken here is that (with one possible exception) these other religious personnel were not priests in the same way that the *shangu* was, inasmuch as it was only the *shangu* who came into constant direct contact with the god by having overall charge of the running and ritual of his house, the temple.

In fact, the distinction between priest and non-priest was not a primary concern of Assyrian culture. There was, however, a clear-cut distinction between persons who were members of the temple personnel and those who were not. The general term for a member of the temple personnel was *erib biti*, literally 'one who enters the House', a simple recognition of the fact that such personnel regularly had the run of the temple and other people did not. This term could include craftsmen as well as cultic personnel, and sometimes royal officials. Such persons had a right to a share in the temple offerings.

The *kalu*

The second class of cultic functionary regularly on the staff of a temple was known as the *kalu*, conventionally translated 'lamentation-priest', although he performed other cultic activities than lamenting. Except for the leading part in the principal ceremonies taken by the *shangu* or his deputy, the majority of the temple rituals were actually performed by, or with the assistance of, *kalus*. We find them doing such things as setting up kettledrums in the temple courtyard for a noisy ritual at the time of an eclipse of the moon, or performing nocturnal rites in connection with astrological portents. With an *ashipu* (see below, pages 212ff.) as an assistant, the *kalu* might have to carry out purification rites for a temple, involving ritual cleansing, fumigation with incense, and libations. We also find a *kalu* being dispatched by Sennacherib, accompanied by an *ashipu*, to perform the necessary rites at the opening of a canal.

But the main function of the *kalu* was his chanting – hence the conventional translation of his title. The god had his earthly home in the temple, and it was necessary to keep him well-disposed, with the lines of communication kept open to enable the god's compassion or intervention to be invoked. This was the job of the *kalu*, who in the rituals addressed to the god his chants, which typically took the form of laments, prayers, and the type of religious song we should call a psalm. He seems usually to have had an instrumental accompaniment, either a drum or a harp. Musicians of lower status (see below) could assist in the actual chanting and playing, under his direction.

The *kalu* could be a man of substance. Since he had to read and sing difficult rituals, he necessarily belonged to the class of the literate minority, and we find *kalu*s acting as scribes. In Babylonia (but we cannot be sure that this also applied to Assyria), a well-connected *kalu* could collect temple appointments, being *kalu* in one temple and *shangu* in another. But the *kalu* was not necessarily of high status, and we find a case of a *kalu* being set free 'for the god Bel' as a religious act. Whether he had previously been a slave or a prisoner is not clear, but indisputably he had been under a cloud socially.

Temple and royal musicians

Music played an important part in both temple and state rituals, and in addition to the chanting provided by the *kalu*, there was a class of persons devoted to this, providing vocal and instrumental music. The term for a person of this class was *naru*, feminine *nartu*. Musicians were often mentioned alongside *kalu*s in temple rituals, but were of lower status. The responsibility for arranging the songs of the rituals lay with the *kalu*s; the duties of the *naru*s were to sing the songs properly and to play instruments. Musicians – woman as well as men – were often mentioned in large numbers in connection with palaces; Assyrian kings tended to collect them, and on conquering other countries they sometimes brought back groups of such people as part of their booty. Musicians also accompanied the Assyrian king on campaign.

The ashipu

What we call Assyrian religion was very complex, containing a hotch-potch of attitudes of different origins and operating at different levels. The temple and state cults, based on belief in anthropomorphic deities, were not the whole of Assyrian religion. In this sector, the underlying belief was of the existence of gods with human attitudes and super-human powers, who had an interest in humans and who could be approached by humans. Such divine beings, if suitably and reverently approached, could be persuaded into using their powers to benefit their worshippers. Readers brought up in the Christian or Jewish traditions may think this a statement of the obvious. In fact, by no means all Assyrian religious attitudes were deistic. There were other attitudes to the supernatural with different origins and different associated practices; some of these went back to prehistoric times, before ever there was an Assyrian state or an Assyrian king, and in some instances even before the idea of anthropomorphic gods had been clearly formulated. This area involved what in modern terms we would call magic rather than religion. Much of what happened in this area was concerned with combating evil influences, sometimes completely amorphous, sometimes partly personified into the form of demons. But in Assyria there was no clear-cut distinction between magic and religion, and in consequence some functionaries, whose activities were specifically magical and not religious as we would understand it, had found a place in the temple rituals and state ceremonies.

The most prominent cultic functionary in this area was the expert in magical incantations known as the *ashipu* (alternatively *mashmashu*), usually translated as 'exorcist', although 'magician' or 'witch-doctor' would be equally accurate and more revealing of his actual function in Assyrian society. *Ashipu*s were thought of as wielding enormous magical power, so much so that in religious texts, particular gods are sometimes described as '*ashipu* of the gods'; the idea behind this is clearly that the power of an *ashipu* was so great that it surpassed even divine power, so that the gods themselves might be glad to avail themselves of it. Thus the *ashipu* had considerable prestige.

*Ashipu*s were not in the nature of their office temple officials, though some *ashipu*s could be appointed to the staff of temples to perform their specialized functions as required, as for example in the recitation of incantations, or to expel evil demons from the presence of the king. Most *ashipu*s probably worked outside the temple. Some were in the service of the king; there were certainly some on the palace staff, and we find an *ashipu* as one of the two cult functionaries involved in ceremonies at the opening of an aqueduct built by Sennacherib.

Other *ashipu*s sent regular reports to the king on matters concerning the well-being of the king, his family and the state, and rituals necessary to safeguard against perils. The king took the ritual instructions of an *ashipu* very seriously, and it appears that the king might be so terrified that he overdid things. We have a letter from an *ashipu* to the king indicating a case of this. We do not know what preceded, but what the *ashipu* says, *inter alia*, is:

Why, for this second day, does the (dining-)table not come in for the king my lord? Whoever is in the dark for the Sun-god, the king of the gods, is in the dark for a whole day and night, and again, for two days. But the king, the lord of the lands, is the image of the Sun-god. He must be in the dark only half a day.

213

It seems that something had happened in connection with the sun – presumably a solar eclipse – for which the ritual requirement was to be in the dark (some scholars suggest that the verb is to be taken here in the sense 'to mourn', although that is not its usual sense) for two days. The king had been observing that rigorous requirement, but the *ashipu* now came up with the argument that, because the king was himself a human manifestation of the Sun-god, his period of remaining in the dark (or, perhaps, being in mourning) might be limited to half a day.

Why did the *ashipu* only come up with this suggestion after the king had apparently already exceeded the half-day? The *ashipu*'s argument as to why the king could get away with only half a day's penance is specious; if, as the *ashipu* indicates, there was a rule of two days' penance for the particular event of ill omen, it must have been primarily the king – representing the state of Assyria – who had to undertake this. There is a break in the *ashipu*'s letter but, where it resumes, it gives a clue to the reason for the *ashipu* making an excuse for the king to break his fast. The text (somewhat damaged) seems to say:

> Eating of titbits and drinking of wine will soon dispel the illness from the king. (This) good advice should be considered: irritability from not eating or drinking upsets the mind and brings on illness. May the king listen to his servant about this.

Clearly the enforced fasting and shutting away of the king has been found to upset him, and the *ashipu* had to find a formula by which to limit the damage to the royal person, without casting any question on the authority of preceding ritual demands.

Not only the king, but also other members of the royal family, and probably also senior state administrators, might have *ashipu*s on their permanent staff. Thus we find mention of 'the chief *ashipu* of the house of the Crown Prince', indicating that the crown prince had a whole contingent of *ashipu*s at his disposal if evil threatened him. Many *ashipu*s, however, earned their living by the fees they earned for attending ordinary people troubled by evil or demonic influences – the presence of which was manifested by illness or a series of random adversities of the kind we might call bad luck. The following is a text illustrating the way in which an *ashipu* might operate. The text reads:

> For the substitution of a man for Eresh-kigal [goddess of the underworld].
>   At sunset the sick man shall make an unmated she-goat kid lie with him in bed.

At the end of the night, you shall get up at dawn. You shall make a prostration towards the other side (of the bed). The sick man shall take the kid into his crutch. [In the case of a man and woman, the terms used would definitely imply that the man had sexual intercourse with the woman. In the case of the goat, we may give the man – sick as he was – the benefit of the doubt, and accept that possibly he only had to take up a position suggesting intercourse, inoperative but sufficient to deceive the infernal powers.]

You shall then make the sick man and the kid lie on the ground. You shall touch the throat of the sick man with a tamarisk dagger [tamarisk was a magical wood]. You shall cut the throat of the kid with a copper dagger.

You shall wash out the entrails of the deceased with water, you shall anoint her with oil, you shall fill her entrails with spices. You shall attire her in clothing. You shall put shoes on her. You shall daub her eyes with kohl. You shall pour sweet oil over her head. You shall take the turban off the head of the sick man and fix it on her head. You shall treat her properly like a dead man.

The sick man shall get up and go out through the door. The *ashipu* shall recite three times the incantation 'That one, the god's touch has touched him'. . . .

The *ashipu* shall give a cry for so-and-so the sick man: 'He has gone to his fate', he shall say. He shall institute mourning. Three times you shall make funerary offerings for Eresh-kigal. You shall place a dish of barley porridge while still hot. You shall praise and honour (the dead). You shall pour out libations of water, beer, roast corn, milk, honey, butter and oil. You shall make a funerary offering for the ghost of your family. You shall make a funerary offering for the kid. You shall recite before Eresh-kigal the incantation 'The *sheshgallu* [an archaic synonym for *ashipu*] is his brother'.

You shall treat the kid properly as if it were alive, and then bury it. : . .

The wording of the ritual instructions seems to indicate that at least two officiants were involved, the *ashipu* mentioned by title, and another person addressed as 'you'. This other officiant could have been the *baru*-'priest' (see below), who was also concerned with sick people. On the other hand, texts of this kind had a long history of development, and the alternating use of 'you' and 'he' could be the consequence of piecemeal additions. Thus it is quite possible that all the instructions were directed to the *ashipu*.

Beyond question, the operations involved in the quoted ritual were straightforward matters of magic. The sick man is identified with the goat kid as intimately as possible, and the life of the kid then substituted for his life by magical means. What is done is assumed to have its effect by the mere fact of its being done; religion, in the sense of an approach to the gods to secure their benevolent intervention in the man's fate, is nowhere mentioned. Although the name of Eresh-kigal, goddess of the underworld, does occur, there is not the slightest indication of any approach to her as a deity having a relationship with humans and able to be approached, appeased or supplicated. The introduction of the name Eresh-kigal seems to be no more than the slightest nod in the direction of anthropomorphic religion, used as a term subsuming the nameless and faceless forces of evil and death which have to be deceived by magical means. We actually know of an occasion when the foregoing ritual was performed. It was on behalf of the Crown Prince, who had had a fever, a malady which the *ashipu* attributed to some sin (probably a breach of ritual) of the king himself.

Another example of the kind of magical activity in which an *ashipu* might be involved is given by the following extract from a letter written by a chief *ashipu* to the king:

About the rites for the incantation entitled 'Verily you are evil', about which the king my lord sent me a message; they are performed for expelling the evil *alu*-demon and the Falling Sickness [generally taken as epilepsy].

When something has touched him [the afflicted person], the *ashipu* shall get up and hang a mouse and a twig of camel thorn on the lintel of the door. The *ashipu* shall dress in red clothing, and put on a red mask. He shall hold a raven in his right hand, a falcon in his left hand. . . . He shall recite the incantation 'Verily you are evil'.

When he has finished, he and a second *ashipu* shall do a circuit of the bed of the sick man, with a censer and a torch by their sides. He shall recite the incantation 'Hultuppu-demon, be off!' as far as the door. He shall put a spell on the door.

Until (the evil) is expelled, he shall do this morning and evening.

It is clear from the typical texts quoted that the term 'witch-doctor' would be more appropriate for the *ashipu* than the designation 'priest'. His dress as well as his rituals served to convince the superstitious of his efficacy in expelling evil influences. The garment for his official activities was red – which in many cultures serves to drive off demons – and for some of his ceremonies he was given a sinister grotesqueness by the mask he wore. Mythological texts mention various hybrid creatures, such as fish-men and scorpion-men, with magical qualities, and on some Assyrian monuments and other objects we see men portrayed wearing masks which make them appear as fish-men, lion-men, and the like (see plate 6A). These representations are obviously concerned with magical ceremonies, and the men wearing these masks can hardly have been anyone other than *ashipu*s in action.

Diviners; the baru

Man has in most societies sought means to see into the future, and the people of ancient Mesopotamia were no exception. Many divination techniques were devised to foretell what was to come, and some of these, traceable to third-millennium Sumer and probably having their origins even earlier in prehistoric times, still flourished in first-millennium Assyria. The importance in Assyrian culture of means of foretelling the future is demonstrated by the contents of the library various Assyrian kings, mainly Ashurbanipal, built up at Nineveh. Excavated last century, it has been found to contain up to twelve hundred different ancient literary works, of which over three hundred are concerned with divination.

From the point of view of the people of ancient Mesopotamia generally, the form of divination with the highest prestige was that associated with a functionary called *baru*, although towards the end of the New Assyrian empire this was being overtaken by astrology. The *baru* had in early times been associated with various techniques, but predominantly his divination was by examining the organs of a sacrificed animal. The details of his procedure (known as extispicy) differed from period to period and place to place, but basically what happened in first-millennium Assyria was as follows. A question was written on a clay tablet and set before the god. A sheep was then sacrificed and its organs examined. An interpretation of the god's decision was then arrived at on the supposition that the god would have put his answer on the organs of the animal in the form of particular configurations, sizes, colours, spots and other abnormalities. The diviners had keys, in the form of clay models of organs (predominantly the liver), indicating which features were positive and which negative. Positive and negative features would be totted up, and a favourable or unfavourable answer to the question put to the god would be given according to which was in the majority.

We have the actual texts of some of the questions on which

Assyrian kings sought answers through the techniques of the *baru*. The following is part of one such:

> O Shamash, great lord, in the matter about which I enquire,
>   answer me a firm assurance,
> From this day, the third of this month of Ayyar [May], until
>   the eleventh of the month of Ab [August] of this year,
> For these hundred days and nights, the period under
>   consideration for this extispicy,
> Will the troops of either the Cimmerians, or the Medes, or the
>   Mannaeans, or any enemy whatever,
> Strive and plot (against me)?

The *baru* had to set the scene for his divination by certain preparations of a magical nature, such as chewing cedarwood, burning incense, and whispering spells into the ear of the sacrificial animal. Clearly, under the surface of a procedure which appeared to appeal directly to an anthropomorphic god for an answer, there lay something more primitive and non-deistic, a belief in non-personal supernatural powers which could be controlled by magical means.

Like the *kalu* and the *ashipu*, the *baru* needed to use cuneiform texts in his professional activities, and he therefore necessarily belonged to the literate minority, with all the advantages that gave both of status and of access to the state and temple administrations. The *baru* certainly belonged to the upper stratum of society, and we know, for example, of *baru*s who were sons of *shangu*s. A cuneiform text explicitly lays down that no one could be a *baru* unless he was without physical defect and of free descent. The *baru* was not necessarily either a temple official or a royal official, although the nature of his office might often result in his coming into the service of the temple or of the king. For important occasions *baru*s often operated in groups, and several Assyrian kings refer to a number of *baru* diviners taking part in an extispicy, sometimes divided into four teams.

We have a substantial collection of letters written to the Assyrian king by a man who was a chief *baru*. He was in the royal service, with responsibility for organizing other *baru*s, and as his emolument held a grant of land from the king. The chief *baru* just mentioned would have operated from an office in the royal palace, but not every *baru* working on behalf of the king would have performed his duties exclusively in a palace or temple. For example, we know that there were *baru*s on service with the royal army, ready to perform the rituals and give decisions by divination when required. Other *baru*s put their services at the disposal of private persons, particularly for such purposes as discovering the prognosis of an illness, when the *baru* might work alongside the *ashipu*.

Other types of diviner

We have considered the *baru* first, as being the most highly regarded class of diviner. But there were several others. For instance, a list of professions mentions two classes called *sha'ilu* and *mahhu* alongside the *ashipu* and *baru*.

Of the *sha'ilu* we know very little in detail from first-millennium Assyria, probably because he (or she, since women could so serve) had become restricted to the lower strata of society, so that they would not be mentioned in surviving cuneiform texts, which mainly reflect the interests of the upper literate class. By the late Assyrian period the *sha'ilu* – and particularly the female of the species, the *sha'iltu* – were specially associated with the interpretation of dreams and with necromancy, so that in lack of more detailed evidence we may assume that a *sha'iltu* had something in common with the witch of Endor mentioned in the Bible (I Samuel 28: 7–14).

We know rather more about the *mahhu*. By etymology the word means 'frenzied person', and the person so described was someone who went into an ecstatic state and gave a message supposedly from the god; there were female as well as male versions of this, who could be either temple personnel or private persons. Several other terms were in use in Assyria to denote persons of this kind. Their prophetic messages were much on the lines of those mentioned in the Old Testament as given by 'false' prophets (as in 1 Kings 22: 10–12): mainly prophecies of approval and encouragement for the king. Assyrian kings took them seriously, so much so that in a treaty with a vassal, Esarhaddon (680–669) bound the vassal not to conceal words coming from this type of person. The *mahhu* could take part in a temple procession, presumably in the manner of a dervish.

There were other types of diviner active in first-millennium Assyria. Thus, we hear of the 'observer of birds', an official person in the service of the king, who had to report to the king omens drawn from the movement of birds. One Assyrian document contains a list of names, the various sections being summarized as

17 *ashipu*s
5 *baru*s
9 physicians
6 *kalu*s

219

3 observers of birds
3 *harṭibi*.

Now *harṭibi* was not a native Assyrian word; it was Egyptian,
denoting interpreters of dreams, and the three names so designated
were all Egyptian, not Assyrian. It is thus clear that Assyrian kings
must actually have brought in specialist Egyptian dream-interpreters
from Egypt, to add to their equipment for foretelling the future.

Astrology

The most prominent means of divination for state purposes towards
the end of the New Assyrian empire was astrology. There were a
number of highly qualified experts regularly making reports to the
king, stating their observations of the configurations of the moon
and planets, and the portent of what they had observed. It must be
pointed out that astrology in Assyria differed significantly from
what goes by that name today. Present-day astrological nonsense is
supposed to tell something about the fate of individuals, with
mumbo-jumbo based on the relative position of heavenly bodies at
the time the individuals were born. Assyrian astrology, though no
less mumbo-jumbo, related only to affairs of state, not to individuals
(except the royal family, and then only in a context in which the
king embodied the state), and the predictions were arrived at by
applying traditional interpretations to current events in the heavens,
such as eclipses, rings round the moon, or positions of planets.
Thunder and earthquakes could also come into this category. The
nature of Assyrian astrology can be best understood by looking at
a few examples, all in the form of reports to the king.

> When the moon is seen on the thirtieth day, (the meaning is
> either) frost, (or) there will be the sound of the enemy.
> When at the observation of the moon it is high, the enemy will
> take the land by force.
> When the moon at its observation becomes visible earlier than
> expected, the month will bring trouble.

Here is one of the more detailed reports:

> Tonight a halo surrounded the moon, and Jupiter and the constel-
> lation Scorpio were inside it.
> When a halo surrounds the moon and Jupiter (SAG.ME.NÍG)
> stands inside it, the king of Akkad will be shut in (by siege).

When a halo surrounds the moon and Jupiter (Nibiru) stands inside it, there will be epidemic mortality of herds and wild animals.

(The star of the god Marduk at its (first) observation is ŠUL.PA.È; when it has risen for one[?] double hour it is SAG.ME.NÍG; when it stands in the middle of the sky it is Nibiru).

When a halo surrounds the moon and Scorpio stands within it, (this means either) priestesses will have intercourse[?] with men, (or) ditto, lions will ravage and block the roads of the land.

These (omen formulae) come from the Series 'When a halo surrounds the moon and Jupiter (ŠUL.PA.È) stands inside it, the king of the westland will exercise power and destroy the land of his enemy.' This is of ill portent.

The foregoing may require some explanation. The basic phenomena observed are clear: there had been a ring round the moon enclosing particular heavenly bodies. The astrologer had then looked up the meaning of these portents in the 'Series' (that is, textbook) to which he refers at the end; like most ancient cuneiform texts, it was named after its first line. He explains that astrologically the same planet, Jupiter, is designated by different terms according to its altitude, and hedges by giving the interpretations appropriate to two different positions. The earlier scholars who had compiled the textbook had also done some hedging, by offering alternative interpretations in relation to the constellation Scorpio. There was thus quite a choice of prognostications, none favourable, and the astrologer therefore concluded that the phenomena he had seen meant something bad for the state.

Some reports were much briefer and clearer. Thus: 'When a halo surrounds the moon and Regulus stands inside it, in that year women will bear male children.' In this instance (and the first one quoted above), the phenomena mentioned were what the astrologer had witnessed, and he simply gave the meaning for economy of words.

Finally, we may quote a small section from a long astrological report, for the sake of the social comment it contains: 'When the moon reaches the sun and goes side by side with it, (that is) horn embraces horn, there will be upright behaviour in the land, son will speak truth with his father.' It was obviously assumed that the standard situation was otherwise.

Some of the astrological reports contain weather lore, perhaps based originally on observation, such as: 'When it thunders in the month Ayyar [approximately May], wheat and vegetables will not do well', or: 'When it thunders in the month Shabat [approximately February], there will be a plague of locusts. When it thunders in the month Shabat, it will hail.' In this last report, the astrologer is quoting two different omens he has found in his collection of texts relating to the month Shabat. The forecast relating hail to thunder in February is the result of observation: thunder in February is often followed by hail. The forecast is more likely than not to be correct because there is a causal connection: the combination of a thunderstorm and February temperatures does in Iraq favour precipitation in the form of hail. The forecast about the plague of locusts also probably derived from someone having noticed that on some occasion thunder in February had been followed by a plague of locusts. In this case, however, there is no causal connection between the two events, and the forecast is made on the basis of the Latin tag *post hoc, ergo propter hoc*, which is to say, This followed That, therefore This resulted from That.

However, most of the forecasts were on a basis different from this, a kind of symbolism. One can see how this works from the passage above which reads, 'When a halo surrounds the moon and Jupiter stands inside it, the king of Akkad will be shut in'. Jupiter was the planet of the god Marduk, Marduk was the god of Babylon, and Babylon was the capital city of Babylonia, known in astrological parlance as Akkad. The Akkadian word which we translate 'halo' can also be used for an enclosure for cattle. Thus for the planet Jupiter to be seen inside the moon's halo suggested the idea of the chief power in Babylon being inside an enclosure, which would be the situation if the king of Babylonia were under siege. Similarly, in the omen which reads 'When the moon reaches the sun and goes side by side with it, . . . son will speak truth with his father', the fact of the sun and moon going side by side offers an easy symbolism for fathers and sons living in accord.

Eclipses have always caused alarm to primitive – and sometimes not-so-primitive – peoples, and accordingly in Assyria eclipses were predominantly of evil omen. None the less, it was possible for an astrologer to devise an interpretation of an eclipse to spare the king anxiety. Thus we find the following:

An eclipse was due, but it was not visible in Ashur. That eclipse by-passed Ashur, the city wherein the king dwells. There were clouds everywhere, so that we do not know whether the eclipse took place or did not take place. Let the king my lord send messages to Ashur and to cities everywhere – to Babylon, to Nippur, to Erech and to Borsippa; perhaps they observed it within those cities. Let the king hear the regular reports. . . . The great gods, who are in the city wherein the king my lord dwells, shaded the sky over and did not show the eclipse. Thus the king may assuredly know that this eclipse was not against the king my lord or his land. Let the king be happy.

Thus the astrologer neatly establishes that whether the eclipse happened or not, the implication was favourable for the king. (In passing, we may also notice the oddity that at the time in question the astrologers knew enough about the movement of the moon to predict lunar eclipses – which are generally at six-monthly intervals – but yet, through superstitious conservatism, still regarded eclipses as having ominous significance.) There were, in fact, two aspects of these astrological reports. One was to give the king warning of forthcoming events of importance for the state; the other was to give an opportunity for the performance of rituals to avert any evil happenings of which these reports gave warning. This latter aspect was taken care of by the king's staff of *ashipus*.

It may have been noticed that, although we are still in the chapter on religion, it is many pages since any significant mention was made of the gods. This is a fair reflection of the place of the gods in the Assyrian attitude to life. We began our discussion of Assyrian religion by talking about the nature of the great gods, but this approach is a concession to our own way of thinking about religion in society. To the ordinary Assyrian the great gods were not the part of the supernatural world by which he felt most immediately affected; although he accepted that control of the world he lived in ultimately lay with the great gods, his immediate personal contact with those divine beings might be very slight. But that does not mean that the ordinary Assyrian would disregard the supernatural world. Far from it. The supernatural world was all around him, and touched his life at all points. Thus, if he suffered illness, it was demons, or even an impersonal evil, attacking him; if he lost a child, he saw a malevolent supernatural power at work; but he did not see a decision of the great gods. There was no resigned faith in the divine purpose which would allow the Assyrian to say in the face of the latter calamity: 'The Lord gave and the Lord hath taken away. Blessed be the name of the Lord.' The great gods came into the matter only as powers who might, if suitably supplicated or conjured, circumvent the evil of the malevolent forces.

The Assyrian saw the world around him as full of forces affecting him. So of course do we, but whereas we see a river flood or storm as a physical force, or certain illnesses as an infection of cells with a virus, the Assyrian saw all these phenomena as involving wills. There must, the Assyrian thought, be some intelligence that willed floods, storms or diseases. In the case of major forces affecting the whole world and having some intelligible function in the scheme of things, such as storms or the motion of the sun, it seemed clear to the Assyrian that the wills activating these forces must be rational. These supposed wills became personified as gods, with all the good and bad qualities of humans on a vaster scale. But some things that happened were irrational and arbitrary. All too frequently newborn babies languished and died, or their mothers were smitten with an evil-smelling discharge accompanying fever and delirium and culminating in a painful death. The great gods could indeed kill, but they killed with a purpose. These so-common deaths of babies and women in childbirth were senseless, and could only be the doing of an irrational malevolent demon. The culprit was in fact identified as a female demon called Lamashtu, with no function in the world order other than to attack such helpless and unoffending victims.

Lamashtu, though the best known, was by no means the only demon. The world was full of these nasty beings. Almost any misfortune or annoyance or bizarre occurrence of an apparently arbitrary nature which befell a man might be the work of a demon. But it would not be correct to say that demons were personified disasters; far from being personified, some of them were explicitly said to be sexless, nameless and formless, and so lacking in specific characteristics that they were, as one text puts it, 'not even recognizable by the wise gods'. Demons were not personified disasters; they were no more than the malevolent will which activated the disaster.

It was this attitude to life which was the background to the magical activities of the *ashipu*; the enormous influence of this class of magician both on the royal court and on the ordinary Assyrian was because the *ashipu* by his rituals had the key to fending off the evil influences of these supernatural forces which enclosed the Assyrian – king and commoner alike – on all sides.

To give a balance, there was a corresponding belief in good spirits, which might dwell in and protect a building, or accompany and guard a person. We find the statement that for the man who does as he should, 'the gods will give him a *shedu*' – a kind of guardian angel looking after him. In Babylonia the term used for the protecting spirit was *ilu* or *ishtaru*. As these are the ordinary words for 'god' and 'goddess', it is often said that everyone had his personal god or goddess; but, with the possible exception of the king, these so-called personal gods or goddesses were not named members of the pantheon, and 'personal protecting spirit' would give a more accurate reflection of the underlying concept.

Witches and Wizards

The *ashipu* used his magic to protect humans from the supernatural forces of evil that surrounded him. But there were people who might use corresponding techniques to direct these forces against humans. These malevolent beings were the wizards and witches, who could bewitch a person, send evil spirits against him, separate him from good spirits, and bring upon him any kind of misfortune or disaster. We have a long series of texts giving the counter-magic against such witchcraft. Curiously, one scholar, who has failed to appreciate the part played in many societies by a belief in witchcraft, has attempted to argue that Assyrian belief in witchcraft was associated with psychosis, and on the basis of this makes the remarkable claim that the texts of counter-magic against witchcraft were 'one of the main textbooks of Babylonian psychiatry'. The fact is that a few of the conditions troubling the people of ancient Mesopotamia, thought by them to be due to witchcraft, would by us be regarded as suitable cases for psychiatry. But everyone in ancient Mesopotamia believed in the possibility of witchcraft, and the attribution of disasters, misfortunes or illnesses to witchcraft was a cultural trait, not a matter of psychosis. Babylonians no more had a science of psychiatry than a science of nuclear physics.

14

Assyrian Medicine

Assyrian medicine is placed in a chapter by itself out of deference to modern classification. The Assyrians themselves linked the physician (*asu*) very closely with the functionary whose title (*ashipu*) we translate as 'magician' or 'witch-doctor'. The linkage was quite explicit; as we shall see, the two functionaries worked closely together, and a text already quoted (page 219) lists physicians with *ashipu*s, *kalu*s ('lamentation-priests') and various kinds of diviners.

There are indications that in Assyria the *asu* was inferior in professional standing to the *ashipu*. A letter from an *ashipu* to the king shows that the king had consulted the *ashipu* before allowing the crown prince to drink some concoction prescribed for him (presumably by a physician). The *ashipu* advised that drinking the medicine was quite in order, but proposed that as a precautionary measure a slave should drink some of it before the crown prince did so. This brings out the superior status of the *ashipu* in two ways. Firstly, the need to obtain the approval of the witch-doctor before medicine could be taken clearly shows that the expertise of the *ashipu* had priority. Secondly, whereas a lack of confidence was reflected by the king's query about treatment by medicaments, there is no indication of the king's seeking a second opinion when some magical procedure was decreed as necessary by an *ashipu*.

Scholars have made attempts to define the dividing line between the activities of the *ashipu* and of the *asu*, but with no conclusive results. This is probably because there actually was no clear-cut demarcation between them; their functions overlapped, and in some circumstances the two might work in collaboration. For example, there is an Assyrian letter in which an official excused himself to the king for not coming to the city Ashur, on the grounds that he was ill. He concluded with a suggestion about treating his illness: 'Let the king appoint an *ashipu* and an *asu* at my disposal; let them perform their functions together.'

The Assyrian View of Disease

The people of ancient Mesopotamia (both Babylonia and Assyria) regarded disease as of supernatural origin. We have many statements of this. Symptoms were noted, and then related to the particular supernatural intervention. Thus, to quote a few random but typical examples:

> If (the patient) keeps crying out 'My skull! My skull!', it is the hand of the god [so-and-so].

> If his head is dizzy and his calves are cold, it is the hand of the god [so-and-so].

> If his head keeps affecting him and fever keeps attacking him, it is the hand of the goddess Ishtar.

> If his temple affects him and he keeps crying out 'My belly! My belly!', it is the hand of a ghost. A second possibility: it is Ishtar; he will die. (If it is) the hand of a ghost, he will linger on and then die.

> If his speech is changed and fever keeps attacking him, it is the hand of the god Ninurta.

> If blood flows from his penis, it is the hand of the god Shamash. Prognosis: (to) the Land of No Return [the underworld].

> If his penis and his testicles are inflamed, the hand of the goddess Dilbat has reached him in his bed. [I.e., the goddess Dilbat has masturbated the patient.]

All the examples quoted are from a text series directed not to the physician (*asu*) but to the witch-doctor (*ashipu*); it bears the title, from its first line, 'When an *ashipu* goes to the house of a sick man'. This text series proceeds, in the manner illustrated, right through a host of possible symptoms. There are somewhat corresponding texts bearing on the functions of the *asu*, with lists of symptoms followed by the prescribed treatment (medical substances and manner of application) in place of the reference to supernatural causation. This difference might suggest a complete contrast between the *ashipu*'s view of disease (superstitious), and the *asu*'s (rational), but the matter is not so simple. Both witch-doctor and physician recognized that diseases had physical symptoms which could be treated, and sometimes cured, by medical procedures and by the use of medical materials; but at the same time the *asu* as well as the *ashipu* accepted that there was often a demonic or supernatural element in the causation, which required treatment by magical means. We certainly cannot pin down a difference between the two professions by saying glibly that the *ashipu* operated with magic and incantations, and the *asu* with drugs and bandages. Certainly the use of drugs and bandages predominated with the physician, but he also might employ incantations, using them alongside what we would accept as rational methods of treatment. Thus, we find an *asu* very reasonably prescribing a tampon as a treatment for nosebleed – but at the same time directing that an incantation should be recited. A patient is suffering from flatulence; we find that the *asu* makes him drink a certain medicine to give relief, but accompanies this with an incantation. An *asu*, treating the king, prescribes bandages fastened in a certain way – but at the same time he provides an amulet to hang round the king's neck. A chief physician (*rab asi*), writing to the king, discusses the efficacy of the particular drugs he uses: 'The drugs which I have sent to the king are of two kinds. They are different from one another. . . . Perhaps the king my lord will say: "What are they good for?" They are good for dispelling witchcraft, and they are good for a woman in childbirth.' Obviously, medical materials were thought to be capable of acting against malevolent supernatural powers. Indeed, it was sometimes specifically claimed that the drugs of the *asu* could be used against demonic influences against which the methods of the *ashipu* had failed: 'If the activity of the hand of a ghost is persistent, so that the *ashipu* is unable to remove it, in order to remove it you [i.e., the *asu*] shall mix together (eight drugs). . . .'

There was no necessary conflict in the ancient mind between knowledge that a certain substance alleviated certain symptoms, and belief in supernatural causation of those symptoms. For example, if it was believed that certain fever symptoms were caused by demonic possession, and it was known that administration of a certain substance gave relief, the two could easily be reconciled on the view that the drug was good for expelling that particular demon.

The *asu*'s use of medicaments should not therefore be taken as evidence in itself of a rational attitude to disease. There is plenty of reason for concluding that the operation of the medical materials was regarded as magical (that is, acting upon the demons which caused the symptoms) rather than directly therapeutic. This is put beyond any doubt when we find medical substances sometimes being placed in a container round a patient's neck; there could hardly be clearer indication than this that in at least some cases drugs were thought to operate by magical means.

The nature of the medicaments themselves leads to a similar conclusion. Let it be said at once that some substances used would certainly have alleviated some symptoms, if not cured the disease. In this category are oils, wine, salt, alum, and certain plants and plant products. However, some other medicaments were used of which the actual benefit was very questionable, with the name giving an obvious indication of thinking on magical lines. There was, for example, something called 'she-donkey's vulva'. This was a sea shell, doubtless getting its curious name from its shape and size. *Inter alia*, it could be used for treating troubles of the penis, either ground up and blown into the penis through a tube, or drunk in beer. For the purpose in question this can have been of no significant practical benefit, but one can easily see how magic-dominated thinking would suggest that a type of shell with that name should have some effect on the penis.

One might have expected that the specialization of the *asu* in the use of medicaments would eventually give birth to the rudiments of the science of pharmacology; but the prevailing intellectual climate left little possibility for experiment and advance in that direction. Even disregarding the magical elements which sometimes came into the activities of the *asu*, it was not (at least in the late Assyrian period) the skill or knowledge of the physician personally which was thought to effect a cure; we have texts of prescriptions used by the *asu*, but their principal value was thought to derive from their ancient divine authority. This is clear from a colophon (i.e., summary of bibliographical details) appended by Ashurbanipal to some of the medical texts added to his library in the seventh century. One such colophon describes the texts as 'healing-prescriptions (for everything) from top to toe, a collection outside the recognized group, containing expert learning, whatever pertains to the function of the great physician-gods, Ninurta and Gula'.

Ashurbanipal adds: 'I deposited them within my palace for reference and for my repeated reciting of them.' This suggests that, from the point of view of Ashurbanipal, it was the ancient divinely-inspired wisdom on the texts themselves that was efficacious. This is in line with the ancient attitude. The medical texts (like a majority of all texts in Ashurbanipal's library) had been committed to writing in the second millennium and constantly re-copied, independently of the state of current medical practices. The texts had the authority of ancient tradition, which could actively oppose any attempt at experiment or innovation.

The Physician in Practice

We turn, then, to what we know of the actual activities and procedures of the physician. The texts indicate that the *asu*, in examining a sick person (and the same applies to the *ashipu*) went thoroughly through his symptoms. He noted, for example, which parts of the body were hot or cold, skin colour, colour of the urine, blood in the urine, pains, paralysis or abnormality of movement, state of the veins, and discharges of pus, as well as his mental state. He then proceeded to his treatment, which involved either medications or bandages or both. The use of bandages was a characteristic feature of the treatment provided by the *asu*. This was not quite as straightforward as it sounds, for once again magico-religious ideas could come into the matter. It was not only sores and wounds that were treated with bandages; bandages might also be applied in the case of diseases to which a supernatural origin was attributed, such as 'hand of a ghost'. In such treatment the bandages would hold specified drugs against particular parts of the body, and since there was no local tissue damage to be healed, the purpose would seem to have been to drive the disease out of the body magically by the close contact of drugs effective against the demon causing it. The magico-religious element is also shown by the incantations which were sometimes prescribed for use with the bandages. There were also right and wrong ways of applying bandages – again with reference not to practical considerations but to magico-religious ideas. One official rebukes the king for having permitted, when taken ill on campaign in enemy territory, the use of a foreign technique in using bandages, 'which is not fitting for the land of Assyria'. The writer adds, 'Let us maintain the norms which the gods themselves gave to the king my lord' – that is to say, the Assyrian way of applying bandages was divinely ordained, and experiments with alternative methods must be considered impious.

We have so far referred only to the physician's activities in connection with disease. His work could, however, extend beyond this into surgery, though at a very elementary level. The eighteenth-century Code of Hammurabi (which of course is Babylonian, not Assyrian) has several references to the *asu* in a surgical context, making it clear that he might make incisions in a person's body (presumably referring to lancing) or set broken bones. The Assyrian laws, towards the end of the second millennium, refer to an *asu* treating a testicle damaged in a fight – without much assurance of success, apparently, as the law goes on to make provision for what was to happen to the person who committed the injury, should the other testicle become infected. We also know that at the same period in Assyria there were physicians attached to the court, whose duties included the inspecting of male palace personnel to ensure that they were properly castrated – a necessary qualification for the privilege of being allowed near the ladies. We assume, but are not specifically told, that any necessary castrations were performed by the physicians.

Medicinal Materials

The substances used by the physician were of varied origin. Many herbs or plant extracts were employed; these were the commonest ingredients of medicines, so much so that the word for 'herb' came to mean 'medicine'. The scholar R. C. Thompson, in his *Dictionary of Assyrian Botany* (1949), made a valiant attempt at identifying all plants mentioned, comparing names used in later Near Eastern languages and taking into account which plants might have the required effect upon the stated symptoms, but a great deal of doubt about identifications still remains. The kind of problem we face in identification is that we find mention, for example, of a plant of which the name means literally 'hound's tongue', which was used for coughs and jaundice; but we have no means of knowing whether or not this was the plant called Hound's Tongue in England. Some plants, to judge by their names, were thought of as cure-alls; one such, bearing the name 'It heals a thousand (diseases)', was a purgative, the prescription for its use reading: 'The patient shall drink it in beer and he will have a bowel movement.'

Other medical substances were of animal origin, blood being an obvious example. Creatures such as lizards and scorpions are less obviously appropriate but were still included; and some minerals were used, such as salt and alum. The physician kept his materials in a wooden chest or leather bag. When required for use, they were prepared by such processes as grinding or boiling and then incorporated into a suitable carrier, such as beer if the medicine was to be swallowed, or oil or fat if it was to be applied as ointment. Bathing a particular affected part with a lotion was another form of treatment. Medications could also be introduced into the body by such means as suppositories and enemas. Another possibility was for the physician to blow the necessary medical substances into an orifice; thus we find prescriptions in which the physician had to blow the medication prescribed through a specified kind of reed into a man's nostrils or ear, or through a bronze or lead tube up his penis.

The efficacy of the substances used medicinally must have varied considerably, though it is still not possible to say very much on this, as many of the substances named in the ancient texts have not been identified beyond doubt. Sulphur, mixed with cedar oil, was used for an itching head, and this, depending upon the cause of the itch, could well have been very effective. Other treatments, such as making a patient drink milk in which a lizard had been boiled, seem to have been more magical than rational; there is a close parallel to this in an English folk prescription, still used as treatment for whooping cough within living memory, of snails boiled in milk. Patients were sometimes suspicious about medicaments; thus, we find the king insisting that a certain drug which had been prescribed for the crown prince to drink should first be tried out on slaves.

A physician's house-call

We have one literary text which tells us something about the way the physician actually plied his profession, which we do not learn from the medical texts. The story, set in the second millennium (not in Assyria but in Babylonia), is known as 'the Poor Man of Nippur', the Poor Man in question being one who had been wronged and therefore set out to get his own back on his oppressor. He had been done down by the mayor, and so planned to beat him up three times; to this end he engaged in various tricks. The one relevant to us was when he disguised himself as a physician to gain admission to the mayor's house. He had his head shaved – showing that at that period the physician wore a tonsure. He then went along with a jar of water and a brazier of burning charcoal, which must have been regular equipment for the physician of the time, doubtless to help him in compounding his drugs. The Poor Man introduced himself to the doorkeeper as a competent *asu*, and was admitted to examine the wounds the mayor had received from his previous beating. He performed a thorough examination leading the mayor to comment on his expertise. The Poor Man then got the mayor alone with him by stating that his treatment was only effective in the dark, whereupon they went into a dark room; here the Poor Man extinguished the light from his brazier by pouring water over it, and once again gave the mayor a good thrashing. But the point relevant to us about the latter part of the story is that it was accepted that a physician might demand darkness for his treatment; this – since darkness had no practical relevance – once again emphasizes the magico-religious component of medical treatment.

15

Assyrian Art

In studying ancient peoples, it is often difficult to avoid imposing our own framework of ideas upon them. This risk is not least when we come to talk about Assyrian art, with a tendency to lump together everything which is visually pleasing or of interest. However, even from our modern point-of-view there is a generally accepted division between fine arts (such as painting and sculpture) and useful or applied arts (such as architecture), so that even on modern criteria some limitation of range should be imposed. This comment is made because some otherwise excellent books on Mesopotamian art include in their scope everything from the ground plans of temples and palaces, through furniture, jewellery and cylinder seals, to sculptures, wall paintings and reliefs. There is, however, no reason to suppose that ancient peoples placed all these in the one conceptual category 'Art', and indeed there does not appear to be an Akkadian word for 'Art' which would cover all these genres. On the other hand, it must be accepted that, although architectural ground plans should certainly be excluded, for the rest there is some justification for the art historian studying many of these diverse types of material together, inasmuch as the same motif may recur on objects as different as, say, a cylinder seal, and a bas relief (see plates 18E and 15A).

Several authorities have produced excellent works on Mesopotamian art, with separate sections on the Assyrian material; particularly to be commended are H. Frankfort, *The Art and Architecture of the Ancient Orient* (1956) and A. Moortgat, *The Art of Ancient Mesopotamia* (1969). No claim is made here for expertise in art history, and this chapter attempts no more than to give a factual account of some of the main types of material which we may (within our modern categories) include within Assyrian art.

Bas Reliefs

The most striking, and deservedly the best known, objects of Assyrian art are the bas reliefs from the walls of palaces in Nimrud

233

(Calah), Kuyunjik (Nineveh) and Khorsabad (Dur-Sharrukin). The best examples of all these are in the British Museum.

These bas reliefs, as an extensively used medium, began under Ashur-nasir-pal (883–859). In origin they represented the combining of two earlier art-forms. One was the use of pictorial friezes in low relief on the type of tapering square stone pillar which we call an obelisk; the earliest of these was from the eleventh century. This earliest example had a single scene, showing vanquished enemies before the king, with the symbols of Assyrian deities above; on another obelisk later in that century this single scene had expanded into a series, giving the beginnings of narrative relief.

The other genre in the ancestry of the first-millennium Assyrian wall bas reliefs was wall painting. The lower parts of the walls of Ashur-nasir-pal's palace at Calah were lined with slabs of alabaster, which were then carved with reliefs; we know they were carved in position, since some are left blank. These reliefs show an evident link with earlier wall painting; one distinguished authority on Meso-potamian art describes these early alabaster reliefs of Ashur-nasir-pal as 'actually wall painting transformed into stone', the link being emphasized by the fact that, as remaining traces of pigment prove, paint was applied to the reliefs (see page 309). There is the possibility that the upper parts of the walls, which have not survived, were adorned with wall painting complementing the alabaster reliefs. Ashur-nasir-pal's reliefs comprised two quite different types of subject matter. One type showed ritual, ceremonial or mythological scenes centred on the king; the other displayed scenes of hunting or war.

The ritual scenes are, at first sight, simply a static balanced design with figures. A typical example is illustrated (plate 15A). In the centre is a curious symmetrical non-naturalistic object obviously representing a conventionalized leafy tree. On each side of the tree stand the same two figures facing the tree, differing on the two sides only in some small variations in the disposition of the arms and in the fact that one pair are viewed from their right side and the other from their left. Above the tree is a symbol constituted by the wings and tail of a hovering hawk, enclosing a disk in which is the upper part of a being, indicated by his head-dress as divine.

This ritual scene is, in the proper sense of the word, sacramental. The Anglican Catechism defines a sacrament as 'an outward and visible sign of an inward and spiritual grace', and this is precisely the significance of this relief. It tells the viewer that the king of Assyria is filled with divine power. The central stylized tree is the Sacred Tree. This is a religious symbol very ancient in Mesopota-mian art, found in Sumer from the beginning of the third millennium. It represents life and plant fertility; it is the link between living things and the life-force evident in vegetation. Its link with the divine is emphasized by the winged-disk figure above it, with outspread wings and tail. This is a complex symbol. Assyriologists, whose orderly minds prefer their data to be neatly catalogued, have argued whether this symbol represented (a) the national god Ashur, or (b) the Sun-god, indicated by the disk. In fact, the symbol probably suggested both, and more. In early Sumerian times, the outspread wings and tail of the hawk were associated with a divine power known as Imdugud ('Mighty Wind'), which evolved into a divine bird-being Anzu (the word 'god' is deliberately avoided here), who robbed the supreme god Enlil ('Lord Wind') of the insignia which gave him his powers. Anzu was eventually overcome by Enlil's son, the god Ninurta, who took over the powers of Anzu; this was a mythological way of expressing that Ninurta was the anthropomorphic representation of forces which in an earlier stage of religious development had been the non-anthropomorphic Anzu and Imdugud. Thus Ninurta, who eventually crystallized as god of hunting and war, in fact incorporated all the forces of nature – the storm and animal life. Thus, implicit in the hawk-wings in the relief are not only the national god Ashur and the sun-disk, but also the powers in nature represented by Ninurta.

We return to the figures in human form. The nearer figure on each side of the Sacred Tree is in fact King Ashur-nasir-pal himself. In both representations of him he holds his right hand with three fingers closed, the forefinger pointing, and the thumb projecting under the forefinger; this is a conventional gesture in which a king shows reverence before the divine. The relative positions of the winged disk, the Sacred Tree, and the two representations of the king, link the king intimately with both religious symbols, thereby uniting him with the forces of fertility in both plant and animal life. The sacramental aspect is emphasized by the two winged creatures, identified as divine beings by the triple horns on their heads, who stand one behind each representation of the king, holding a bucket and a cone (another symbol of fertility), with which they asperge the king. The whole scene makes a statement: the king of Assyria is raised to the plane of the divine, where he incorporates all the powers of nature, making them available to bring fertility and prosperity to the land he rules. The statement is one of assurance and well-being for Assyria.

The bas reliefs of Ashur-nasir-pal of the other type are on quite a different plane. There is nothing of the mythological in them, and they are not static; they are direct and narrative. They depict action, telling of the activities of the Assyrian army and of the Assyrian king. We see scenes of siege and scenes of the battlefield; we see prisoners brought before the king; we see the king valiant in the lion hunt. But all this narrative, so different in immediate impact, adds up to the statement as before – the assurance that under the leadership of the king in all his majesty, Assyria will always conquer and prosper.

The bas reliefs introduced by Ashur-nasir-pal were continued by his successors, with some developments in style, to the end of the Assyrian empire. But another art form introduced by this monarch has not yet been found after the reign of his son. The form in question is worked on bronze and is technically known as *repoussé*. The technique used in *repoussé* work is to produce a raised design on a sheet of metal by hammering from the back. In the Assyrian examples, the result is strips of bronze bearing scenes comparable with those on the narrative type of bas reliefs. Examples from both Ashur-nasir-pal himself and his son Shalmaneser III were found at the small site of Balawat (ancient Imgur-Bel), where these kings had a country residence, twelve miles north-east of their capital Calah. The strips of embossed bronze had been fixed as cladding on great wooden doors giving access to a temple. Those of Ashur-nasir-pal, not discovered until 1956, are not only badly damaged but also currently (1983) inaccessible in Baghdad, but those of Shalmaneser, found in 1877, are well displayed in the British Museum. The bands of bronze on Shalmaneser's gates are about eight feet long, eleven inches high and one-sixteenth of an inch thick; each band is divided into two registers five inches high, and it is on these that Shalmaneser's craftsmen produced a remarkable series of narrative scenes. They are accompanied by short inscriptions engraved above the figures, describing the events. The art experts tend rather to sniff at this work – one says 'there is little beauty in this mass of detail', whilst another sums it up as 'only factual prose' – but they are full of interest and well worth a detailed examination. We see horses, urged on by their grooms, struggling to drag chariots over steep mountains; lines of naked prisoners with their hands bound behind them and their necks yoked (see plate 13A); the dragging off of booty from conquered cities; the delivery as tribute of what the artists make to appear as an endless line of goats, horses, cattle, and two-humped camels; one dreadful scene in which prisoners have had their hands and feet cut off; the king himself, standing majestically under a ceremonial sunshade with his bodyguard behind, receiving tribute; again the king, seated on his throne on a hillock, directing siege operations, undertaken by a powerful body of archers operating behind battering rams; and a culminating series of scenes showing the king undertaking an expedition to the source of the

Tigris, deep in Anatolia, far to the north. Here, to mark his furthest boundary, he had sacrificial ceremonies performed, and an image of himself cut in the rock face – all faithfully recorded on these bronze strips five inches high (see plates 12B and 13B). It is not of the interest of these scenes, but of their composition, that the art experts complain; but from the point-of-view of Shalmaneser it was the subject matter only which was of concern. Once again, through all this *repoussé* work, the whole was a narrative designed to glorify the exploits of the Assyrian king and to record the achievements of the Assyrian state in bringing into submission all peoples, as the national god Ashur decreed.

Although *repoussé* work is not known after the reign of Shalmaneser III, wall painting continues to be represented; probably, in view of its fragile nature relative to bas reliefs in stone, there was a good deal more of it than we actually know from extant examples. In all extant remains the colours used are typically blue, red, white and black. From the middle of the eighth century (with scholarly dispute about the exact date and reign), there are examples of wall paintings from an Assyrian palace at Til Barsip on the Euphrates in Syria. Whole walls were (as remaining traces prove) covered with scenes glorifying the king, showing lines of officials and conquered enemies being brought before him as he sits on his throne in splendid state. But there are also examples of compositions in the ritual-mythological sphere comparable with those of Ashur-nasir-pal discussed earlier.

From near the end of the eighth century there comes a good example of an Assyrian wall painting from the throne room of Sargon II in his newly-built capital, Dur-Sharrukin (see plate 23A). This again is a scene in the ritual-mythological sphere. Along the wall are several bands of friezes of a decorative nature, built up symmetrically from a combination of a number of religious motifs. Above these friezes towers the single main panel, framed by the topmost friezes rising up into an arch. Inside the panel Sargon, with an attendant behind him, stands upright before the god, his hand in the pointing position of reverence previously described. But the composition of the figures is so arranged that it is Sargon, and not the god, who appears central. The whole of the composition of the wall decoration draws attention to the prominence of Sargon; once again, the composition has a propaganda function, expressing the might and near-divinity of the king of Assyria.

We return to the bas reliefs. These show development in the eighth century, and reach their highest point under Ashurbanipal (668–627) in the seventh. In the narrative bas reliefs of Ashur-nasir-pal, scenery is at best sparse, more often totally lacking, leaving the incident depicted in a vacuum, unconnected with any particular setting. By the eighth century this has changed. Scenery is now introduced more extensively, so that the events shown give more the impression of occurring in a real place. There also develops a greater freedom in the use of the space on the stone slabs. Earlier the relief on any slab was virtually treated as complete in itself; now scenes are allowed to run over from one slab to the next, emphasizing the sense of movement. Vertical space also comes to be used more freely. It has to be said that even in the narrative reliefs of Ashur-nasir-pal it was not the case that all figures were placed on the same base line, yet the base line was certainly very marked as the point of reference of most of the figures. But in some of the latest reliefs the figures are distributed throughout the whole field in apparent independence of the base line. A particularly good example is Ashurbanipal's depiction of the defeat of the Elamites (plate 16A). In this scene of battle in the open country, the mêlée of pursuing and pursued, of victorious and smitten, and the dead and mutilated bodies scattered over the whole face of the relief give a vivid impression of the carnage of the battlefield.

Some of the most striking reliefs are the hunting scenes from the period of Ashurbanipal. Although the art experts can point out the repeated use of recurring themes, showing that the carvings were not wholly spontaneous but used accepted conventions, what strikes the ordinary viewer is the marked degree of realism; one feels compassion at the sight of the fleeing wild ass-mare turning its head to look back at its foal about to be seized by hounds (plate 15B) and pity is evoked by the dying lion shot through with arrows (plate 14A).

Some of the bas reliefs show difference of scale and others contain elements of composition representing nearer and more distant objects. This has engendered much discussion as to whether or not the Assyrians ever attempted to represent perspective and whether one can properly speak in relation to the reliefs of foreground and background: there seems to be no consensus amongst the experts.

The narrative in the reliefs is not photographic, and the intention of the relief is often to describe a developing situation spread over a period of time. There are some reliefs in which the same group of warriors may recur in different situations, showing development of the action. A good but simple example of this principle of composition is shown in a lion-shooting scene (plate 22B). A lion is released from a cage, is rendered furious by a dart shot into its shoulder, and then runs and springs at the king and receives the *coup de grâce* from his spear. In the relief there seem to be three lions; in fact, what is intended in one lion, shown in three successive stages, just as if photographed on a camera with a triple exposure. The result, once one recognizes the convention, is to enhance the sense of movement.

Sculpture in the Round

There was also Assyrian sculpture in the round, of life-sized stone statues. The books on Mesopotamian art spend little time on this, quite rightly. Compared with the bas reliefs, it is insipid stuff. The main works are representations of gods and kings. Typically, the figures stand stiffly at attention, the only concession to the line of the body being some slight regular curves in the robe which completely covers the body. The best examples, however, like the statue of Ashur-nasir-pal (plate 14B), are not without dignity, majestic though static. There are a few Assyrian statuettes in the round, made of material other than stone (bronze, amber), about which the art experts exhibit a cautious enthusiasm in respect of their pleasing material and workmanship.

Worth further comment under this heading are the colossal winged lions and bulls which served as guards to palace entrances, their supernatural powers marked both by their wings and by the triple horns on their heads, a mark of divinity. The whole effect is one of power, which was doubtless the intention. Properly speaking, these are not examples of sculpture in the round, since they are not wholly detached from the blocks of stone out of which they are carved. Since they stood in pairs close up to the two sides of a gateway, they were not meant to be seen from all sides. In fact, they are works in high relief, designed to be viewed from two aspects only, the front and the side. In consequence, they have the curious feature of being provided with five legs – four visible from the side, and two from the front, the outer front leg being included in both views (plate 19B).

Carved Ivories

Another genre well represented from first-millennium Assyria is carved ivories. By this term we commonly understand – because of their preponderance – flat strips of ivory, either incised or carved in shallow relief; it can, however, be applied to several other techniques which occur. Great masses of carved ivories have been found from various sites, and a considerable amount of the material is still unpublished. Although from Assyria, not all of it may properly be referred to as 'Assyrian Art'. The Assyrian kings made full use of the human resources of their empire, and used skilled craftsmen no less than unskilled labour. It is clear that a substantial proportion of the carved ivories from Assyria were of Syrian or Phoenician workmanship, and they contain elements which are not properly Assyrian. Quite a number of them, indeed, bear motifs which are clearly Egyptian in origin, a consequence of the close cultural links always prevailing by sea in ancient times between Egypt and Byblos on the Phoenician (Lebanese) coast.

Although ivory objects have come from a number of Assyrian sites, the greatest number of them, and the most striking, have come from Nimrud. Pre-eminent among finds from Nimrud is a concave mask more than six inches by five overall, representing a woman's face in natural relief, carved from a single piece of ivory (plate 20A). Unconcealed tool-marks on the back show that it was intended to be placed where only the front was seen, perhaps on a piece of furniture or a wall; it could not have been part of a statue. A second object of the same class (though solid at the back instead of concave) is even larger (seven and a half inches by five and a half) but less accomplished in workmanship, leading some art experts to conclude that it was of earlier origin; it is certainly less attractive aesthetically to modern taste. Stratigraphy gives no help as to their relative dates, since both were found in the same well, into which they must have been thrown – after stripping of the gold ornamentation they probably once bore – when Calah was sacked.

From the same well came also a piece of ivory carved almost completely in the round, to form the head of a roaring lion, of maximum diameter nearly three inches, with some fine realistic detail. Two further striking objects found in the well were a pair of ivory plaques carved in relief. They are near duplicates, showing a lion holding a negroid man to the ground by the throat. Forming a background to the main figures is a formalized floral lacery, covered (like some details of the main figures) with gold leaf, with a pattern of blossoms picked out in alternate red carnelians and blue lapis lazuli (plate 23B).

An ivory relief very attractive to modern taste – and also, judging by the number of extant examples of it, to ancient – was a group representing a cow suckling its calf (plate 3B). The ivory carvers were very skilled in their depiction of animals, and some other remarkable ivories in the round include a group showing foreigners bringing animals as tribute, such as one of a Nubian with a monkey on his shoulder, an antelope by his side, and a leopard skin over his right arm (plate 20B).

There are many other ivories in relief, and some in the round, which would merit description or illustration if space permitted; there were also variant techniques, such as the carving of a strip of ivory in shallow relief on both sides, caryatid figures (female figures used as supporting columns), open-work plaques (work in which the background was removed, leaving the figures standing free inside their frame), and *cloisonné* technique (partitioning of the relief with decorative inlays). But the great mass of carved ivories consists of small panels not in relief but with the motifs or scenes incised. These mainly constituted part of the decoration of furniture, although they sometimes had an individual existence in the form of such things as combs, spoons or spatulas. Almost any motif or scene found on the stone bas reliefs or wall paintings may appear on these – processions, animals (naturalistic, supernatural or heraldic), war or hunting scenes, religious motifs, geometrical patterns, scenery.

Cylinder Seals

We should not leave Assyrian art without some mention of cylinder seals. A cylinder seal was a cylinder, usually of some kind of stone ranging from common limestone to precious lapis lazuli, and typically of any length from under an inch to the size of a thumb, bearing an engraved design sometimes accompanied by the name and title of the owner. These had been in use from earliest Sumerian times, rolled over a lump of clay pressed round the fastening over goods as a check upon theft, or on a legal document as authentication of a contracting party or witness. In the later period the seal always had a hole drilled through its length so that it could be worn on a cord.

The artistic importance of cylinder seals lies in the designs they bear, sometimes of interest and aesthetic appeal in themselves, but in the main of concern to art historians for the relevance of their motifs and style to the development of Assyrian art. We have information on these both from actual seals discovered in excavations (or sometimes dug up illegally by natives, since they are very portable and highly saleable), and also from the impressions rolled on clay tablets in antiquity.

There are a large number of seal impressions of the Middle Assyrian period (mainly fourteenth-century) on clay tablets from Ashur, as well as a substantial number of actual seals. The fourteenth century was, it will be remembered, a time when Assyria was just beginning to emerge from vassaldom to Mittanni, and when Babylonia to the south still retained something of its past greatness. Middle Assyrian seals contain examples showing influences of motifs and styles from both these areas, but a characteristic Assyrian style is developing, with motifs which link up with elements found in the later full flowering of Assyrian art in the wall bas reliefs, already discussed. Amongst such motifs we find pairs of winged animals symmetrically disposed, often facing each other one on each side of a stylized Sacred Tree; the winged disk; a hero in combat; scenes of hunting in a chariot. Some of these scenes appear to be in the mythological sphere (see plate 18D), suggesting that related representations in the later bas reliefs had their ultimate origin in the secularizing of what were originally mythological themes. But along with the apparently mythological scenes, the Middle Assyrian seals include examples of scenes with animals in a naturalistic setting, such as a suckling goat beside a tree (plate 18B), or stags amongst trees (plate 18C). This interest of the seal-cutters in wild animals and landscape may be seen as ancestral to the vivid scenes with animals found later on the wall bas reliefs.

The cylinder seals of the New Assyrian period, in the first millennium, have a wide range of designs, developing out of Middle Assyrian beginnings. They include ritual scenes, particularly a number of variations of the Sacred Tree scene (see plate 18E), also found on the bas reliefs. But above all, hunting and combat scenes abound, where remaining traces of mythological elements (winged animals, dragons; see plate 18A) show their origin in much earlier Mesopotamian art, but at the same time by their vivid action point the way to the splendid animal bas reliefs of Ashurbanipal.

16

The Assyrian Army

For the final century or so of the Assyrian empire there were few people in the Near East who were not in some way or other touched by that empire. The areas in which daily life was (for better or worse) affected were mainly matters of the economy and administration, but the point at which the ordinary man came into immediate contact with Assyria was often the Assyrian army. This is also the point at which the modern Western reader, if acquainted with the Bible, is likely first to encounter the Assyrians, since the Second Book of Kings devotes two chapters (18 and 19) to the Assyrian siege of Jerusalem (with a parallel account in Isaiah 36 and 37), and bits of several other chapters to Assyrian attacks on the northern kingdom of Israel.

Assyria was capable of deploying forces running into hundreds of thousands of men, but Assyrian military activities were not always represented by campaigns on that scale. There could be operations by quite small contingents, or garrisons holding key points, only a few dozen strong. But whatever the size of the force, its efficient use depended upon the twin factors of organization and discipline.

The Assyrian grand army was not simply a horde of bloodthirsty peasants become infantry, backed by a furious cavalry out for loot. It was in fact a complex well-organized force, integrating specialist units of many types. At its core was a standing army. This was necessitated by several types of duty which had to be performed on a permanent basis. First was the personal security of the king, which called for a permanent bodyguard. Also, there were permanent garrisons at various key points of the empire, which required manning on a long-term basis; only professional soldiers could provide this. That at least some of the garrisons in this latter category were directly responsible to the king, and not to provincial governors, is made clear by the reports which were sent to the king by commanders of such units.

One particular unit of the standing army about which we frequently hear was a group of tribal origin called the Itu'a. Ethnically they were not Assyrians; they were from an Aramaean tribe from the very south of Assyria, somewhere near the city Ashur, who had at one time been very troublesome to the Assyrian authorities. But they were brought to heel, and when we hear of them in the royal correspondence from the late eighth century onwards, they had become a distinguished unit who could be called upon for special duties. We find them, for example, being brought in to restore order in the Lebanon region when the people of Sidon had rioted over taxation and killed a tax inspector. The case of the Itu'a illustrates that the Assyrian army did not comprise only Assyrians. As emphasized elsewhere, the Assyrians had no racial prejudice, and they conscripted subject peoples into their forces on equal terms with native Assyrians. Each ethnic group retained its identity for fighting purposes, constituting, according to the numbers involved, a regiment or smaller unit, retaining both the type of weapon and form of dress associated with the region of origin. Thus we find depicted on the bas reliefs such groups as bowmen, slingsmen, swordsmen, pike-bearers, light infantry, and heavy infantry, often distinguished by their footwear, clothes and headgear as well as by their weapons. But these battle-fighters also needed technical support, and both the friezes and the texts inform us of specialist technical units. Accompanying the army were chariots for the battle-field, and wagons for transporting necessary equipment, which would include not only the obvious items of rations and tents but also such specialist pieces of equipment as siege engines and rams; when the track became difficult for the passage of the wagons and chariots, roads had to be cut. This was the task of a pioneer corps, equipped with bronze, copper or iron axes and picks. Sometimes the forces would come to a river which could not be forded; this would necessitate the construction of either rafts or bridges, in the making of which the pioneer corps would again come into their own. The rafts would be of the *kelek* type (see page 198); the bridges were most commonly boat bridges, that is, bridges formed by lashing a number of boats together across the stream, with planks on top to make a footway or even a road for chariots. Then, when the Assyrian army eventually reached a defiant city which was to be put under siege, the pioneers were needed again for building ramps and for mining operations (see page 260). Other specialist personnel in lesser numbers included scribes for recording booty and other details of the campaign. There were at least two categories of such scribes – those writing in cuneiform on clay tablets and those who used alphabetic Aramaic on parchment or on papyrus imported from Egypt. There were also interpreters and intelligence officers (see pages 256f.).

The Assyrian army also had what, transposing into modern terms, we might very loosely – perhaps too loosely – call its chaplains' department, if one may be permitted such a parallel on the basis of religious personnel who were concerned only with cultic matters and certainly had no concept of caring for the souls of the troops. The personnel in question were cultic functionaries who accompanied the army, and *inter alia* engaged not only in offering sacrifices, but also in obtaining and interpreting omens when necessary. It seems clear that by their manipulation of omens, some of these functionaries played an important part in maintaining morale; we know of several crises in which diviners with the army gave most convenient omens, which served to steady the morale of the forces at a difficult moment. Thus when, at the assassination of his father Sennacherib, Esarhaddon moved against the army of the regicides, a message from the gods was reported in favour of Esarhaddon, heartening his own forces and bringing about desertions amongst those of the regicides. Ashurbanipal also reports a very useful omen from a diviner at the time of his campaign against his rebellious brother, the king of Babylonia: 'On the pedestal (of the statue) of the Moon-god was written: "Upon those who plot against Ashurbanipal and commit hostility, I will bestow an evil death. Through the flashing iron dagger, through outbreak of fire, through hunger and plague, I will bring their lives to an end".'

On another occasion, the army encountered a river in flood and took alarm. The cultic functionaries at once received a divine communication of reassurance:

The troops saw the river Idide, a raging torrent. They were afraid of the crossing. The goddess Ishtar who dwells in Erbil showed a vision to my troops in the night time. Thus she told them: 'I myself shall go in front of Ashurbanipal, the king whom my hands created'. My troops were reassured by that vision and crossed the Idide safely.

Presumably amongst the cultic functionaries with the army were some who performed funerary rites for those who died on active service, although no positive evidence for this seems to be available. Possibly it was taboo to make overt reference to personnel directly related to Assyrian deaths in war, and indeed when a casualty list is given in an official inscription, the numbers of dead stated are unrealistically small.

Antecedents of Assyrian Militarism

Assyria had not always been a state geared for war. At the beginning of the second millennium the main importance of the state based on the city Ashur had been as a centre of merchants, with trading colonies in other regions, some as far away as central Anatolia. Indeed, the mercantile component, although it became over-shadowed by militarism, was never wholly lost as a significant element in Assyrian life; at the very time of Assyria's final collapse and extinction at the end of the seventh century, a yapping Israelite prophet snarled: 'You increased your merchants more than the stars of the heavens' (Nahum 3: 16).

None the less, by the seventh century trade had long been over-shadowed in Assyria by war, and it is always of war that the royal annals speak, never of trade. The change began after the Mittannian domination of Assyria in the fifteenth century (see page 40). The Assyrians had to fight to recover their independence and, with their independence regained, having no easily defensible natural boundaries giving security to the corn and pasture lands which formed the nuclear Assyrian kingdom, could only protect them-selves from the danger of a repetition of their former vassaldom by expansion into the areas from which a threat might come. The threat of a recurring occupation by Mittanni was overcome by occupying what remained of Mittanni. But even with Mittanni neutralized, there were, in the Tur Abdin mountains to the north-west and much closer in due north and north-east, fierce hill peoples ever ready to raid the Assyrian plains. To hold them at bay, Assyria needed to take the initiative by patrolling campaigns through the fringes of the mountain areas. But this gave only a precarious peace to those fringes, likely to be broken as soon as the Assyrian force had withdrawn. This necessitated attempts at a more secure hold of these fringe areas, either by making them client states or by introducing direct Assyrian administration. But even if one area were brought into a situation of stability with Assyria, just beyond it the old threat to security would recur, making it necessary for Assyria to go ever further in quest of stability. This factor in expansion was reinforced by economic considerations. The mountains were a source of the large timber needed for building work in Assyrian cities, and the communities living in the mountain valleys could be conscripted to bring out that timber. Some groups of the mountain valley folk also produced metals and bred horses, and both of these were booty much prized by the Assyrians.

Economic advantage and the quest for security were, then, certainly two factors in the growth of Assyrian military expansion after the fifteenth century. It has also been suggested that there was an ideological factor: that is, it was the will of the god Ashur that the king should expand his domains. The epithets applied to Ashur seem to be an aspect of this: he is the one 'who overthrows all the disobedient', 'who scatters the wicked', 'who acts against him who does not fear his word', the one 'from whose net the evil-doer cannot flee' – all of these phrases being in the context of offence against the god Ashur by opposition to the military might of Assyria. One distinguished scholar even goes so far as to speak in connection with Assyrian imperial expansion of 'a kind of theology of holy war', based on a claim by the god Ashur to rule over all mankind.

Theological ideology appears to put Assyrian imperial expansion on an altogether higher plane than mere political and economic advantage. But the ideology cannot be divorced from the practical considerations. There is no evidence that at the beginning of the second millennium the god Ashur claimed universal rule; this idea only begins with Assyria's expansion. It seems that the theology did not prompt an expansionist policy but rather evolved to reflect and give religious expression to that policy as it developed. The 'theology of holy war' was not a driving force independent in itself, but an explanation in terms of myth of what was actually happening under the stimulus of economic and political forces. None the less, once it had developed, it did serve to maintain the momentum of the Assyrian imperial drive, represented as something which was not a mere human response to immediate circumstances but an activity decreed on the divine plane.

The Assyrian kings often refer to their divine mission. Tiglath-Pileser I in about 1100, addressing the gods and speaking of himself in the third person, says: 'You have bestowed on him his lordly destiny for power, and decreed that his high-priestly seed should for ever stand in the temple (of the national god Ashur).' More than four hundred years later, Esarhaddon claimed: '(The gods) commissioned me against any land that sinned against the god Ashur', and added: 'Ashur, father of the gods, empowered me to depopulate and to repopulate, to make broad the boundary of the land of Assyria'. King Sargon exemplifies in his annals the belief that Assyria had a mission to govern. In most cases he does not introduce the account of his campaign by saying where he went, but rather by giving his justification for going. Thus:

In my fifth year of reign, Pisiri of Carchemish sinned against the oath of the great gods, and kept sending to Mita king of the land Muski messages about hostilities against Assyria. I raised my hand to my lord Ashur; and so I took him away together with his family, as prisoners.

Or again, as he speaks of the action he took against the Chaldaean

Marduk-apal-iddina (biblical Merodach-baladan), the usurping king of Babylon, he shows that his action is in conformity with the divine will:

For twelve years he had exercised rule and control over Babylon, city of the Lord, contrary to the will of the gods. Marduk, the great Lord, who hated the evil deeds of the Chaldaean, . . . to take away his royal sceptre and throne was established on his lips. Me, Sargon, the humble king, out of all princes he truly called me and raised my head on high. To distance the Chaldaean, the evil enemy, he made great my weapons.

Psychological Warfare

It was consistent with the Assyrian sense of a divine mission that they should seek to impress a consciousness of this upon other peoples. To maintain a stability across the Near East based upon Assyrian power, it was necessary that other peoples should be persuaded that it was vain to attempt to oppose Assyria. This could be done on the one hand by a demonstration of overwhelming might, and on the other by propaganda. The two were by no means separate and unrelated. Demonstrations of Assyrian power, including the punishment of those who had offended against Assyria, were not infrequently consciously directed to the effect they would have, not merely upon those who suffered directly, but also upon those who heard of it at a distance. There are frequent references in the Assyrian annals to the king pouring out upon the enemy what we may approximately translate as 'awesome fear'. Several different Akkadian terms are used for this, but all of them have a particular nuance: they refer to the kind of awe-filled terror which comes from encounter with something on the divine plane. Thus, the Assyrian king, in perpetrating actions – sometimes including atrocities – which put the enemy into a panic, thought of himself as, in the most literal sense, putting 'the fear of God' into those who might have it in mind to oppose Assyria. This represented a conscious use by the Assyrians of terrorism not for sadistic purposes, but for psychological warfare. Sennacherib actually refers to the fact that he had gone to the trouble of making a cautionary demonstration against Elam, but that the untimely death of the Elamite king less than three months later put on the throne a younger brother who was not bright enough to draw the appropriate conclusion from this reminder of Assyrian military might. From Sennacherib's point of view, it was unexpected and unreasonable to have further Elamite interference in the affairs of Babylonia (a major Assyrian sphere of influence) after the Assyrian demonstration of force; Sennacherib's attitude is emphasized by the fact that the young Elamite king's lack of intelligence is explicitly referred to three times within less than thirty lines of text.

The more normal and expected consequence of Assyrian policy is shown in an incident in which Ashurbanipal devastated a district of the Mannaean land (in north-west Iran) and poured out 'awesome terror', as a result of which the anti-Assyrian Mannaean ruler was assassinated by his own subjects and replaced by his pro-Assyrian son. King Sargon even states explicitly that his victories had a propaganda aspect to them. After his defeat of the forces of the kingdom of Urartu and their allies in his major campaign of 714, he says 'the remainder of the people, who had fled to save their lives, I let go free to glorify the victory of my lord Ashur.' Some of these poor wretches died from exposure in the mountains, but others struggled home, where their terrifying account of the devastating striking power of the Assyrian forces struck their hearers dumb. Sargon records: 'Their leaders, men who understood battle and who had fled before my weapons, approached them covered with the venom of death, and recounted to them the glory of Ashur . . . so that they became like dead men.'

The same principle of psychological warfare, to minimize the need for actual military action, may even be seen in the Bible at the siege of Jerusalem. The Assyrian general insisted on making a proclamation in Hebrew, so that the whole of the citizenry might hear it, and then emphasized *inter alia* that no country had been able to oppose Assyria with success: 'Has any of the gods of the nations ever delivered his land out of the hand of the king of Assyria?' (2 Kings 18: 33).

The psychological aspect of Assyrian warfare is also brought out by the manner in which bas reliefs with war scenes were used. In Ashur-nasir-pal's palace at Calah, scenes of war predominated in the bas reliefs only in the hall which probably served as an audience chamber; it is a reasonable conclusion that this predominance of war scenes was to reinforce in the minds of visiting rulers and ambassadors their consciousness of Assyrian military might. In other rooms of the palace the scenes were mostly of religious or ceremonial topics.

Some of the atrocities perpetrated by the Assyrians also had a propaganda aspect; they were not simply acts of retribution, nor were they mere sadism. There is a good example of this with Sargon II. On the other side of the Zagros from Assyria, in north-west Iran just south of Lake Urmia, were the Mannaeans, who were in the uncomfortable position of being a buffer between Assyria and its major northern rival Urartu in Armenia. In 716 the king of the Mannaeans was pro-Assyrian. The king of Urartu, however, induced two Mannaean governors to rebellion against the pro-Assyrian king, whom they murdered. Sargon took action. He says: 'I raised my hand to Ashur that he might avenge the land of the Mannaeans and return it to the boundary of Assyria.' He caught one of the rebel governors and flayed off his skin, putting it on show to the Mannaeans. This was not a mere cruel punishment. The propaganda intention – of emphasizing the folly of anti-Assyrian activities and rebelling against a pro-Assyrian king – is unmistakable. The Mannaeans quickly took the point. Ullusunu, the murdered king's brother and successor, had initially allied himself with Urartu. He now saw the folly of his ways, and, says Sargon: 'Ullusunu the Mannaean together with the whole of his country assembled as one and grasped my feet. I had mercy on them. I forgave Ullusunu his sin and set him on his royal throne, and received tribute from him.' It is clear that Sargon was not simply concerned to inflict retribution upon anyone who at any time opposed Assyria. The Assyrian army was an instrument of statecraft, and it was a matter for satisfaction if a show of force could render a hostile ruler into a reliable vassal.

Where captured opponents were subjected to harsh treament, as was the rebel governor mentioned above, this was not a matter of vindictive torture, but was manifestly directed to making a public example and giving a warning by demonstrating what happened to those who actively opposed Assyria. Another good example of this principle is given in a statement by Ashurbanipal. He mentions in a letter that on the occasion of a rebellion in Babylonia, his grandfather Sennacherib had given the weight in silver for the body of the ringleader; he himself, he said, would pay the weight in gold for the body – alive or dead – of a rebel leader active against him. The fact that the offer held equally for delivery of the man dead shows clearly that it was the publicity of showing the fate of the rebel, and not any sadistic delight in inflicting tortures upon him, which was the concern of the Assyrian king.

The Army on Campaign

According to King Sargon, there was a proper campaign season. He describes it as 'the month of the mighty one, Ninurta, the firstborn son of Enlil, mightiest of the gods, which the Lord of Wisdom, Ninshiku, had written down in a tablet of former times for the mustering of the army, for making the camp complete'. The month in question was Dumuzi (Tammuz; that is, approximately July), which, since the campaign would most commonly involve going into the mountains, showed good sense on the part of the Lord of Wisdom, since the temperature on the Assyrian plains rises at that time to up to 120° Fahrenheit. It was also within the period most convenient for mustering the national levies, since the harvest would have been completed by the end of May or beginning of June, making a large pool of peasants available for military service.

This formalization of the campaign season was, however, an innovation on the part of Sargon, which even he did not maintain consistently, since one of his campaigns began in May – though that was possibly forced upon him by a rebellion he had to deal with. But certainly during the ninth century we find campaigns commencing in any of the months April, May, June, August, October and November, with a preference on the part of the great warrior-king Ashur-nasir-pal for May or June. Winter campaigns were undesirable, and unusual. One factor in this was that agricultural activities in Assyria begin in October or November, so that serious problems would arise if the peasant levies were still with the army then; operations which could be undertaken by the standing army alone were not of course affected by this consideration. But a second factor was weather, which would normally rule out any military operations in the mountains in winter. However, we do occasionally hear in royal inscriptions of campaigns being continued into Tebet or Shabat (January or February), though accompanying comments on adverse weather indicate that this was considered abnormal.

Bases and logistics

A standing army needs permanent bases. Such were provided in the successive capitals, from several of which we hear of a building complex called *ekal masharti*, which literally means 'palace of the place for marshalling forces', in effect, 'barracks'. These were buildings with large courtyards for army purposes. But with the ever-growing military commitments of Assyria, these barracks quickly became too small for their purpose. Several kings are explicit about this. Thus, Esarhaddon (680–669) tells us that the *ekal masharti* in Nineveh 'which the kings who preceded me, my forefathers, had made to provide proper arrangements for the camp, to look after the steeds, the mules, the chariots, the battle equipment and enemy booty . . . that place had become too small for horse training and chariot exercises'. Other texts indicate that weapons and military provisions generally were stored in the *ekal masharti*, so that it constituted an arsenal as well as a barracks. It had its own staff of scribes, constituting the equivalent of a quartermaster's department.

A permanent barracks in the capital could come to fulfil other functions than serving as a base for royal campaigns; the presence of a strong trained military force immediately to hand would greatly strengthen the king against threats of rebellion – except for a coup led by the army commander. There may be a direct connection between the facts that it was Shalmaneser III (858–824) who founded the first *ekal masharti* at Calah, and that, although towards the end of his reign a major revolt broke out in which all the principal cities except Calah were implicated (see page 72), with Calah firmly in his control he and his legitimate successor were victorious.

It was not only the successive capitals along the Tigris which served as bases for military operations; we hear, for example, of Assyrian armies operating from Erbil, and from a city called Kalizi, south-west of Erbil and about thirty miles east of Calah. Bases were also established in conquered territory outside Assyria; often old strongholds of the native inhabitants were re-fortified and used for this purpose, under a new Assyrian name. They would then be stocked with provisions for men and horses. Sargon, for example, in the record of his campaign against Urartu in 714, tells us of one powerful fortress he took in north-west Iran, strategically placed to command two hostile districts: 'I reinforced the fortifications of that stronghold, and brought up into it corn, oil, wine and battle equipment.'

When the army was on the march away from its bases, inside Assyrian territory it was the responsibility of the local governor to make provisions available; correspondingly, in the territory of vassals this duty fell upon the native ruler. When operating outside Assyrian-controlled territory, the army would feed itself as far as it could by looting provisions, and this consideration must often have dictated the choice of route inside enemy lands; failing that source of foodstuffs, corn and straw were carried by the army and were available as ration issues for men and horses. One of the immediate benefits of capturing a city was that, as Assyrian kings sometimes record, the granaries were thrown open so that the troops could eat their fill without rationing. Problems of water supplies could arise away from inhabited areas; if they failed – as they easily could in many parts of the Near East – this could be very serious for discipline. Sargon mentions a near mutiny consequent upon campaign fatigue joined with water shortage (see page 94). Esarhaddon had water problems in his attack upon Egypt, and was only able to take his army safely across the Sinai desert because Arab tribes friendly to Assyria fetched water for his troops in skins, on camels.

On the march

When necessity demanded, the Assyrians could put into the field armies of well over a hundred thousand. Shalmaneser III specifically mentions crossing the Euphrates westwards with an army of 120,000 men in 845. Other statements of numbers tie in with this kind of figure. Numerically the greater part of the grand Assyrian army was composed of levies raised under provincial governors, and we find mention of the troops of one particular governor amounting to 1500 cavalry and 20,000 archers; as there were over a score of provinces, in a general call-up across the empire a muster running into hundreds of thousands would easily have been possible. This is consistent with a statement of enemy casualties in one major engagement – Sennacherib's battle with Elam at Halule in 691 (see pages 102, 258). Sennacherib claimed the Elamite losses were 150,000; this could have been an exaggeration for propaganda, but to have been credible the number stated cannot have exceeded the possible size of an Elamite army, with presumably comparable numbers on the Assyrian side. The carnage that ensued when forces of this order met in battle is vividly suggested in scenes on bas reliefs, such as one showing a vulture carrying off the entrails of the slain (see plate 19A).

There is no reason to think that the whole of the potential Assyrian army was called out every year. Some campaigns (which were sometimes completed within a month) may have been conducted with much smaller forces, sometimes perhaps with the standing army only, particularly when campaigns cut across the agricultural season. Sargon specifically tells us that in the latter part of his campaign against Urartu in 714, he sent most of his army back to Assyria and himself undertook an action over difficult mountain terrain with no more than one chariot and a thousand cavalry.

The order of march would obviously depend upon tactical considerations, such as the risk of ambush or the need for speed. There were several campaigns recorded in which a king explicitly says that he moved off without making the usual provision for a review of the troops or for the transport columns which normally brought up the rear. In the time of Sargon II the usual order of march when there were no special considerations would be as follows. First went the standards of the gods, accompanied by religious functionaries, and then came the king, probably in a chariot, accompanied by the chariotry and cavalry and surrounded by his bodyguards. Near the king would also be a crack infantry unit, whom he described as 'the battle troops who go at my side'. The king often took an active part in the fighting (indeed, Sargon probably died in battle), and the indications are that these crack infantry were under his direct command, constituting both a further bodyguard and a spearhead for an attack. Behind came the main body of the Assyrian levies, and finally the transport columns bringing up the rear. Occasional details of military itineraries allow us to calculate that the Assyrian army progressed by up to thirty miles a day; this would have been very easy going for the cavalry except over the worst terrain, but must have tested the transport.

Once in the field, at least the regular units which formed the nucleus of the Assyrian forces must have been kept in a permanent state of readiness for action. This is clear from what Esarhaddon says of events at the time of the assassination of his father Sennacherib in 681. Esarhaddon was then commanding an army in the west; he tells us that, upon hearing the news, after receiving a favourable oracle from the gods:

> I did not delay a single day; I did not wait for (the full muster of) my troops, I did not trouble about my rear units, I paid no heed to reviewing horses, harness and battle equipment, and I did not heap up provisions for the way. I did not fear the snow and frost of the month Shabat [February] and the hardship of winter.

On the contrary, he set off at once against the regicides (see page 105). This could only have been possible if amongst the troops under his command there were battle contingents in a state of preparedness to move into action at a moment's notice.

Assyrian campaigns were not all fighting. At least some Assyrians, and certainly some of the kings, obtained a good deal of pleasure out of these military expeditions into the hills, quite apart from considerations of engagement in battle. The mountains east and north of Assyria are scenically and (in summer) climatically very pleasant, and some kings recorded their reactions to this. Sargon was evidently much awed by the scenery of the Zagros; his poetic comments on this have already been quoted (see page 93). Sargon's son Sennacherib was less poetic but still found pleasure in going adventuring in the mountains. Of a scramble up a steep mountain in pursuit of some hostile mountaineers, he records, in his bald prose:

> I led the way like a fierce wild bull with my picked bodyguards and merciless battle troops. I traversed wadis, torrents, ravines, and dangerous slopes in my sedan chair. Where it was too hard going for my sedan chair, I took to my feet and went on in pursuit to the high peaks, like a gazelle. When my knees grew

tired, I sat down on a mountain rock and quaffed cold water from my water-skin to quench my thirst.

Communications

Mobility was, of course, a vital element in successful warfare. Much of the Near East outside the Mesopotamian plains offers obstacles to advance – rugged mountains, rocky terrain, or extensive desert – whilst on the plains there are the Euphrates, the Tigris, and their various tributaries, to give a check to the movemen.s of armies.

The army had wheeled transport, not only chariots, but also carts (sometimes mule-drawn, sometimes pulled by oxen or even by soldiers) for supplies and equipment (see plate 24c). Mention has already been made of the use of sappers to cut roads where the terrain would otherwise have made the progress of chariots and wagons impossible. In some places even this was not practicable, but this did not stop the Assyrian advance; the army either left the wheeled transport behind for later collection, or, where they knew that the road improved further on, manhandled the vehicles over the obstacles.

Rivers might check, but did not halt, the Assyrian army. Where fording was not practicable, the army had boats or rafts available, brought along with the army overland for this purpose. Ashur-nasir-pal speaks of building boats in a certain city (which doubtless contained appropriate materials and equipment) as he approached the Euphrates, and a few lines further on he amplifies this: 'By means of the boats that I had made – boats made of skins, that had moved along the road with me – I crossed the Euphrates at the town Haridi.' The 'boats made of skins' must have been the type of rafts we know as *keleks* (see page 198). This was no innovation on the part of Ashur-nasir-pal, since as early as around 1100 Tiglath-Pileser I had used the same means to get at troublesome Aramaeans on the far side of the middle Euphrates.

In the early seventh century Sennacherib made a more ambitious military use of boats. This was in the course of his war against Elam (south-west Iran) (see page 102). Accepting that the ordinary Assyrian river-craft were inadequate for his plans, he brought Syrian shipbuilders in to build him ships at Nineveh, 'of the workmanship of their land', he says, presumably meaning 'of the type used on the Mediterranean' (see plates 10B and 11B). These were then sailed (by Phoenician sailors) down the Tigris almost to where Baghdad now stands. From there (since the lower Tigris is difficult to navigate) they were manhandled to a canal leading to the Euphrates, and so down to the Persian Gulf, where they were used to embark troops and horses for a seaborne attack.

The king did not always accompany the army on its campaigns, but he was continuously kept informed of operations. We know this from numerous despatches in which officers in the field reported the activities either of the army as a whole or of various contingents. The king in turn sent instructions to the field commanders, including in some instances directions about negotiations with foreign states in the region. This well-maintained contact between the capital and forces operating beyond the Assyrian borders was made possible by the efficient communications system (see pages 196f.).

Assyrian communications also included a military intelligence system. The most extensive information about this comes from the north-eastern frontier where, in the late eighth century, Assyria was facing the kingdom of Urartu, in Armenia. Letters from Assyrian officers on this front give many indications of the use of spies to obtain information about Urartian positions and intentions. Thus we find officers sending reports to the king about Urartian troop movements, with details of numbers, route and destination. One letter reports that five named Urartian governors have mustered their troops in a certain city – obviously preparing for a campaign. There is then a significant addition: 'Regarding that about which the king my lord sent me a message, saying, "Send out *dayalu-men*", I have so sent twice. Some have come back and reported these items of information; some have not yet come out (from enemy territory).' The context leaves us in no doubt that *dayalu-men* were scouts sent out to obtain information. In order to obtain such details as the names of enemy governors, these agents must have made contacts with natives inside enemy territory, either by taking and interrogating prisoners or by paying spies; specific instances of both methods are known.

We have a letter mentioning the taking of prisoners for interrogation about enemy positions, though in this particular instance it was Babylonian rebels who had been attempting to do this to find out about Assyrian troop concentrations. After the Babylonian patrol had taken ten prisoners they themselves were captured in a counter-attack – and it was in the course of the Assyrian interrogation of the officer of the rebel unit that their objective was discovered and the tables turned. We learn all this from the Assyrian officer's report to Ashurbanipal.

Reports to the Assyrian kings indicate that military intelligence was concerned not only with enemy troop movements and disposi-tions, but also with any matter which might affect enemy morale. This has a bearing upon some details of the biblical account of the siege of Jerusalem under Sennacherib. The Bible describes, *inter alia*, how the Assyrian general, the Rabshakeh, made an attack upon the morale of the defenders. One of the several prongs to his argument was a challenge to their reliance on the help of their god Yahweh. The argument used to undermine their confidence was that it was that very Yahweh 'whose high places and altars Hezekiah has removed, saying to Judah and to Jerusalem, "You shall worship before this altar in Jerusalem" ' (2 Kings 18: 22). This was a reference to reforms King Hezekiah had initiated, directed to eliminating the old local cult places all over Palestine and centralizing the cult in Jerusalem. Some biblical scholars have argued that the Assyrian general could not really have said this, because he could not have known about these reforms – if indeed they ever took place. But why not? Certainly at least part of the record of the Rabshakeh's harangue must have come directly from someone who heard it; this is put beyond doubt by a revealing parallel in a cuneiform letter, written to the Assyrian king by a general besieging Babylon only three decades before the siege of Jerusalem. The general at Babylon tells the king that he had addressed the populace to urge their surrender – just as the Rabshakeh did later at Jerusalem – and informs the king of the arguments he used. Those arguments are so remarkably parallel to some of those attributed to the Rabshakeh at Jerusalem that the biblical record must be a genuine representation of the kind of approach Assyrian generals made at that time. No later Jewish writer could possibly have invented fictitious arguments to run so close to the actual arguments of the earlier general outside Babylon. With part of the Rabshakeh's speech authenticated, there is no good reason to question the authenticity of that part touching upon Hezekiah's reforms. There must have been considerable discontent throughout Judah at the wanton abolition of local forms of the worship of Yahweh which had great antiquity and considerable sanctity from their association with the patriarchs and with the prophet Samuel. The Assyrian Rabshakeh must have obtained intelligence of this widespread religious discontent, and cleverly made use of it.

This biblical incident brings out another feature of Assyrian military intelligence: the Assyrian forces contained persons who could speak Hebrew fluently, to the alarm of the Jerusalem authorities (2 Kings 18: 26). Equally, the fact that Assyrian commanders never seem to have had any problems of communication with Urartian or other prisoners indicates that an Assyrian general would always have had on his staff interpreters appropriate to his area of operations. Many languages were understood at the Assyrian court, as the text quoted on page 130 indicates.

Military tactics

The Assyrian forces were versatile in their tactics; according to circumstances, they might engage in guerilla warfare in the mountains, in set battles in open ground, or in the static siege of a city. We have Assyrian accounts of all these types of engagement. The bloodiest was likely to be the set battle between two armies in open country. Sennacherib describes one such, when his forces held an invading Elamite army on the Tigris in 691:

> Like the advance of locust swarms in spring, they came on together against me to do battle, the dust of their feet covering the face of the wide sky like a louring storm in harsh cold weather. They placed themselves in battle order against me at Halule on the bank of the Tigris. They blocked my access to drinking water and prepared for battle.

(Sennacherib then prayed to the gods for victory, put on his armour, got into his battle chariot and swung into action.)

> At the command of the god Ashur, the great Lord, I rushed upon the enemy like the approach of a hurricane . . . I put them to rout and turned them back. I transfixed the troops of the enemy with javelins and arrows. Humban-undasha, the commander-in-chief of the king of Elam, together with his nobles. . . . I cut their throats like sheep. . . . My prancing steeds, trained to harness, plunged into their welling blood as into a river; the wheels of my battle chariot were bespattered with blood and filth. I filled the plain with the corpses of their warriors like herbage. . . .
> (There were) chariots with their horses, whose riders had been slain as they came into the fierce battle, so that they were loose by themselves; (those horses) kept going back and forth all over the place to a distance of two double-hours [up to ten miles]. . . .
> As to the sheikhs of the Chaldaeans, panic from my onslaught overwhelmed them like a demon. They abandoned their tents and fled for their lives, crushing the corpses of their troops as they went. . . . (In their terror) they passed scalding urine and voided their excrement into their chariots.

Sennacherib claimed that the rout of the enemy was so complete that they lost 150,000 men; even if arbitrarily scaled down by a factor of as much as ten, on the assumption of gross exaggeration, this would still leave enormous casualties for an engagement of a few hours.

The battle of which Sennacherib speaks was clearly one in which both chariotry and infantry were heavily engaged. His father Sargon records an action won by cavalry. It was in the mountains of north-west Iran. Rusa, the king of Urartu, with his principal ally, had retreated into the mountains to draw Sargon on until (as Sargon concedes) his communications were stretched to the point at which the morale of his forces was affected and he had difficulty in maintaining tactical control over his army as a whole. Rusa then, as Sargon says, 'sent a messenger (to challenge me) to approach and join battle'.

Sargon gave praise to his god Ashur. He had good cause. The great German military tactician Clausewitz pointed out in his book *On War*:

> how unfavourable mountain ground is to the defensive in a decisive battle. . . . From the powerful resistance which small bodies of troops may offer in a mountainous country, common opinion becomes impressed with an idea that all mountain defence is extremely strong. . . . Very far from seeing a refuge for the defensive in a mountainous country, when a defensive battle is sought, we should rather advise a General in such a case to avoid such a field by every possible means.

Unlike Rusa, Sargon recognized the tactical situation. He seized the advantage that had been thrown to him. Disregarding the problems with his main troops, he led his personal guard of cavalry, under the command of an officer mentioned by name, against the centre of the ambush; he himself was in a light chariot, probably for reasons of protocol. Sargon's cavalry charge broke the enemy line, captured the Urartian headquarters, and reached the camp of Rusa himself, where they immobilized Rusa's chariotry by shooting the horses. The Urartian king abandoned his chariot and fled ignominiously on horseback – on a mare, to the derision of the Assyrians, with whom status demanded the riding of a stallion. There was heavy slaughter amongst the Urartian army, and the remainder fled in disorder over the mountains.

The punitive activities of the Assyrian army in hostile territory were not limited to military engagements. One of the most regrettable acts of Assyrian warfare, other than destruction of life, was the felling of trees. This was often resorted to as a punitive measure, with date orchards, vineyards, or groves of forest trees planted around palaces being wantonly destroyed. There were also occasions not a few when the Assyrian army deliberately devasted whole areas. Of one settlement, for example, Sargon records, in a formula which monotonously recurs with small variations:

> Aniashtania, a herding centre . . . together with seventeen villages around it, I demolished and levelled with the ground. I set fire to the long beams of their roofs. I burnt up their harvest and their hay. I opened up their heaped-up granaries and let the troops eat corn unrationed. I turned the livestock of my camp into its pastures like swarming locusts; they stripped off the grass on which (the city) relied, and devastated its meadowlands.

Elsewhere, Sargon describes his destruction of a canal system that had brought prosperity to a particular area.

The other main form of Assyrian warfare was siege, and this was highly organized. The first essential was efficient transport, needed to bring up the heavy siege engines, such as wheeled and armoured battering rams, shown on many bas reliefs. Ramps (mainly of packed earth and stones, with a wooden framework) were built to enable these machines to be trundled up to operate against the higher and less thick parts of the defending walls. Sappers would mine tunnels to bring about the collapse of sections of walls, infantry would scale ladders and surmount the walls at any weakly defended spots, and a hail of arrows and slingstones would come at the defenders from archers and slingsmen. Another weapon used was fire. One method which may sometimes have been tried in ancient Mesopotamia, judging by a reference in a cuneiform text to 'a fire of reeds that splits a fortification', was to crack the stones of a wall with the heat of a fierce fire, but this can only have been effective against very slight walls, and we have no evidence that the Assyrians ever used this procedure. What they did do with fire was to attempt – often with success, as we see from bas reliefs – to put the besieged city to the flames. One means of achieving this was to use arrows carrying flaming brands. Defenders might also throw fire on to the machines of the besiegers (see page 309). Crude petroleum (of which of course there are many seepages all over the Near East from its vast oil fields) was also used for military purposes, in the particular case we know of, by defenders attempting to destroy the ramps of the Assyrian besiegers. In this instance it misfired – literally. King Esarhaddon describes what happened:

> Whilst I was going about victoriously in this district, (there was) a ramp which I had had packed down against . . . the city Uppume. In the still of the night they sprayed petroleum on that ramp and set light to it. At the command of Marduk, king of the

gods, the north wind – the pleasant breeze of the Lord of the gods – blew, and turned the flaring tongue of the Fire-god back on to Uppume. It did not catch the ramp, but it burnt (the city's) wall and turned it to ashes.

Whilst the siege was in operation, the Assyrian army would set up a fortified camp outside the city, well-defended so that troops off duty could relax. We see on the bas reliefs scenes showing the tents of officers, equipped with furniture (plate 21A); we see meals being prepared; we see the watering and grooming of horses (plate 21B). Another scene (plate 24A) has been interpreted as troops out of their fighting kit relaxing in a party with female camp-followers, but it is more probable that the group consisted of prisoners under guard.

Whilst the siege operations proceeded, a ring of Assyrian guards around the besieged city cut the defenders off from supplies; the almost inevitable result was that if the city were too strong to be taken by assault, it would eventually fall from famine. One of the horrors of ancient siege warfare was cannibalism, not infrequently referred to in the cuneiform documents and, indeed, mentioned in similar circumstances in the Bible. Ashurbanipal grimly describes the consequences of his siege of Babylon: 'Famine seized them. For their hunger they ate the flesh of their sons and daughters, they gnawed leather straps.'

Treatment of prisoners

Once an enemy city had been taken, the treatment of the inhabitants varied with circumstances. Here there comes in the question of atrocities, which demands some discussion, as the Assyrians have been given a particularly bad name on this account. This has already been touched upon (see pages 248ff.), but will stand elaboration.

When one hears what Ashur-nasir-pal himself records of his exploits, there is no room for doubt that the Assyrians could be guilty of atrocities. He writes of the sequel to one engagement:

3000 of their combat troops I felled with weapons. . . . Many of the captives taken from them I burned in a fire. Many I took alive; from some (of these) I cut off their hands to the wrist, from others I cut off their noses, ears and fingers[?]; I put out the eyes of many of the soldiers. . . . I burnt their young men and women to death.

At the taking of another city he writes:

I fixed up a pile (of corpses) in front of (the city's) gate. I flayed the nobles, as many as had rebelled, and spread their skins out on the piles. . . . I flayed many within my land and spread their skins out on the walls.

This does not make pleasant reading. Yet these horrors need to be seen in the whole perspective of ancient war.

Most Assyrian kings from Ashur-nasir-pal onwards undoubtedly pursued an expansionist policy. But the savage treatment of the kind represented by the foregoing extracts was not meted out indiscriminately. A clear policy distinction was made between cities or territories which were newly being taken into the Assyrian orbit, and those already in the Assyrian orbit which had engaged in armed rebellion. It was only in cases of the latter sort – and then only in the most flagrant of these – that such barbarous retribution was meted out to the conquered inhabitants. The two incidents quoted were both cases in which major insurrections against Assyria had taken place; one involved a rebellion by Assyrian settlers who had attempted to capture a main Assyrian military base and store city; the other related to a revolt in a directly ruled Assyrian city, in which the Assyrian governor had been murdered and an Aramaean had been brought in as a usurping king from the major Aramaean state hostile to Assyria. Elsewhere in Ashur-nasir-pal's annals, where the military action recounted was a matter only of conquest and not of putting down a rebellion, there is no mention of mass atrocities; the reference in such cases is only to the taking of prisoners, with no indication of executions or mutilations.

Anyone who has been brainwashed into believing that the Assyrians were uniquely sadistic should take a hard look at our own culture, as reflected in the following extract (quoted in the *Financial Times*) from a children's TV programme in 1978: 'No one shall take his life but me. I shall flay the skin from his living body and wear it about me like a cloak.' Such atrocities as there were in Assyria were not sadism but deliberate punitive measures authorized – indeed, ordered – by the central Assyrian government in the person of the king. There is no proven case of any atrocities committed by individual Assyrian soldiers as matters of mere sadism. It is true that there are some scenes on bas reliefs which do show the mutilation or barbarous killing (as by skinning) of prisoners, but the indications are that these represent what was done to ringleaders by order of the king, not random acts of barbarity by private soldiers. Indeed, there are indications that the king insisted on very strict discipline in the matter of treatment of prisoners-of-war, and one royal letter to an Assyrian administrator dealing with provisions for such prisoners actually warns the official: 'You shall not be negligent. If you are, you shall die.'

The most usual fate of prisoners taken at the conquest of newly conquered or rebellious territory was deportation. The indication just quoted, of concern for the welfare of deportees, is typical, although the basis of this was probably practical rather than humanitarian; the prisoners were now part of the available resources of the Assyrian empire, and the Assyrian authorities wished them to arrive at their destination in good health, and to settle there usefully. Careful administrative measures were taken to this end. We hear not only of detailed arrangements for feeding the deportees on their way, but even for such matters as providing footwear for captives on the march, and in one case assistance with marriages. We also see from the bas reliefs that carts were sometimes available for the transport of women and children (see plate 24B), or they might ride on donkeys or horseback. There is no indication that families were broken up; rather, both the cuneiform and the biblical evidence indicate that whole families and communities were deported as a group.

The objective of deportation was not so much punitive as to benefit the Assyrian empire both economically and in terms of security. Some deportees were settled in cities, where they formed a useful pool of labour for major building projects, as well as providing a source of skilled craftsmen. Others went to under-populated rural areas, to extend the region of cultivation and to increase agricultural production and consequent economic prosperity. Still others went to repopulate some region of the empire which had been depopulated by an earlier deportation after rebellion; a well-known biblical instance is Samaria in Palestine, which had become so underpopulated in parts that lions were a problem – with God blamed as usual (2 Kings 17: 24–8).

It seems that generally, under the Assyrians, deportees did settle down into their new homes. It is noteworthy that the Israelites taken by the Assyrians from Samaria to the Habur (Habor) district of north-west Mesopotamia and to north-west Iran ('the cities of the Medes') (2 Kings 17: 6) appear to have assimilated completely, since we hear no more of them. This contrasts with the Judaeans of Jerusalem, later deported by the Babylonian King Nebuchadrezzar to Babylonia, who retained their sense of separateness sufficiently for a significant number of them subsequently to return to Jerusalem. The difference may be related to the fact that, with only occasional exceptions, the Assyrians deliberately chose to deport populations to an environment which was similar to that from which they came; the Assyrian Rabshakeh, in his speech urging the besieged people of Jerusalem to surrender, made a particular point of this principle, telling them that he would take them away to a land like their own land (2 Kings 18: 32).

Assyrian Motivation, Drive and Achievements

The Assyrians left such a forceful impression upon world history that, more than two and a half millennia after their final disappearance, they can still evoke emotional judgements, mainly directed against their imperialism and their (often over-stated) atrocities.

How did their contemporaries see them? The greatest of the Israelite prophets, Isaiah, who lived at the peak of Assyrian power, made a judgement upon them; but the condemnation he proclaimed was neither for brutality nor for imperialism. Indeed, as regards Assyria's imperialism, he explicitly accepted this as playing a part in the divine purpose:

> Ah, Assyria, the rod of my anger,
>   the staff of my fury!
> Against a godless nation I send him,
>   and against the people of my wrath I command him,
> To take spoil and seize plunder,
>   and to tread them down like the mire of the streets. (Isaiah 10: 5–6)

For Isaiah, Assyria's offence was something different from mere imperialism; it was arrogance, failure to accept the source and fountain of imperial power: 'Yahweh . . . will punish the arrogant boasting of the king of Assyria and his haughty pride. For he says: 'By the strength of my hand I have done it, and by my wisdom, for I have understanding.' (Isaiah 10: 12–13). 'Arrogant boasting' in this passage is a good rendering of a Hebrew phrase, literally 'fruit of greatness of heart', which implies treating one's greatness as coming from within. What Isaiah was condemning was Assyria's self-confidence, which for the Israelite prophets was not a desirable quality; reliance should be upon God alone.

Self-confidence was certainly a mark of Assyrian kings in the first millennium. Though most immediately evident in the royal annals, where the kings freely boast both of their personal qualities and of their national achievements, it is also to be seen at many other points. It is very apparent in the many war scenes on the bas reliefs. Nowhere is there any hint of questioning as to what the Assyrians are doing, or why or how they are doing it. And there is virtually no reference to Assyrian successes being totally dependent upon divine support. It is true that sometimes the figure in the winged disk (representing the god Ashur or other divine powers; see page 235) is shown up in the sky above the king, but there is nothing in this to suggest any faltering in the trust of the Assyrians in their own powers. In fact, in such scenes there is no indication at all that the king has any awareness of the god up above him; rather, it is the god who is showing awareness of the king, for almost invariably his activities (aiming the bow, or such) exactly reproduce the action in which the king is engaged. The Assyrians knew that they were right, and so they took it for granted that the supreme divine power was up there supporting Assyrian interests.

There are reliefs with ritual scenes, from which the conclusion is no different. In these the king is shown as being brought directly into relationship with divine powers; but yet there is no abasement of the king before the divine. For example, in the representation of Ashur-nasir-pal before the Sacred Tree (plate 15A), far from showing any abject recognition of the distance between mere human Assyrians and the divine, the king is himself raised to the level of the divine by the sacred forces which the two supernatural beings are directing upon him and by his investment with the power of the Sacred Tree. Even where the king is shown actually standing before a god, the self-confidence is still there. In the wall-painting representing King Sargon before the god Ashur (plate 23A), it is the king, not the god, who is central. The picture is saying, not that it is the king's duty to show abasement before the god, but that it is the god's function to strengthen and support the king.

This kind of attitude – confidence of Assyrians in their own human powers – was linked to a weakening of the dominance of traditional religion-based attitudes going back to the third millennium. The old attitudes held that the gods had established the world order in the beginning once and for all, and this imposed a heavy weight of conservatism, which acted as a severe restraint upon the possibility of any kind of change or progress. The Assyrians never overtly repudiated this, but in Assyria in the first millennium we begin to get clear indications of a different world view. According to the old ideas, the world was static, or at most cyclic; that is, if things changed at all, they changed only within a recurring framework. The new view of the world was that the gods had a plan in history, and that Assyria was the principal agent in that plan. The main element in the supposed plan was indeed religio-political, being the continuously expanding dominance of Assyria under the national god Ashur, but the very fact of a belief in development inside history implied the possibility of innovation and change generally. The forms of life were no longer completely bounded by the age-old ways.

The A ssyrians began to accept new ideas accordingly. Thus, as we have seen, Assyrian kings were able consciously to adopt new architectur al styles from abroad; they deliberately sought new sources of timber and stone; they encouraged the devising of new processes in metal working; they brought into use new materials, as, for exam ple, cotton; they used foreign craftsmen, such as ivory carvers and s hipbuilders, to introduce new skills to Assyria; under royal patronage artists experimented with new art forms, inventing and further developing the bas relief as a vehicle of narrative art. Assyrian kings even introduced foreign board games: we know this from several game boards, marked out with large and small holes or rosettes, from the reign of Esarhaddon (680–669). The game certainly came originally from Egypt, for it is attested there centuries before it is found in Assyria. Esarhaddon was the first Assyrian conqueror of Egypt, and it seems likely that he saw the game when there and took a fancy to it; the direct Egyptian link is put beyond question by the fact that the boards found in Assyria are all made of an Egyptian stone. Tiglath-Pileser I says that when abroad he took rare fruits that did not exist in his country and introduced them into the orchards of Assyria. Sennacherib brought in the cotton plant. A provincial governor introduced bee-keeping from foreign parts and proudly recorded the fact (see page 83). All these instances of innovation show an Assyrian willingness to look at the world around them with an open mind, to adopt new ideas, and to accept consciously that it was possible to improve upon the old framework of ideas and practices which had come down from the third millennium.

All the examples just given relate to the making of innovations from which Assyria directly benefited. But the interest of the Assyrians in the world around them went beyond this. As their geographical horizons widened, so did their intellectual, and they found interest in the different ways of life of some of the peoples they encountered. We find one correspondent (probably a Babylonian ethnically, but in Assyrian service and reflecting an Assyrian outlook) informing the king of some tribes he had come across who lived on 'flour made from the *murrutu*-plant and *sungirtu* seeds, which wild asses eat'. Of one mountain tribe who had sent tribute, Ashurnasir-pal commented that the men did their hair like women. Esarhaddon was struck by the very different way of life of the Phoenicians, whom he described as 'kings who inhabit the sea, whose fortification walls are the sea, the waves their outer wall, who ride a ship as though a chariot, and in place of horses oarsmen are harnessed'. We have already seen the admiration with which King Sargon spoke of the horse-training expertise of certain people beyond the Zagros (see page 169).

The Assyrians also showed a keen interest in nature, both scenery and wild life. Their sensitivity to scenery we have already mentioned (see page 254). As to wild life, although Assyrian kings certainly destroyed a great deal of it, some of them were in a sense conservators, setting up in their capitals zoos, or what might in some cases perhaps more appropriately be called safari parks. We have referred to Tiglath-Pileser I in this connection (see page 63), and Ashur-nasir-pal tells us in the ninth century, 'I caught animals alive. I collected in my city Calah herds of wild oxen, elephants, lions, ostriches, male and female monkeys, wild asses, gazelles, deer, bears, panthers. . . . all the beasts of plain and mountain, and displayed them to all the people of my land.' In this instance there is no proof that the animals were released into a safari park rather than kept in cages, and as a few lines earlier Ashur-nasir-pal refers to putting captured lion-cubs in cages, probably the other animals were similarly treated. However, the later King Sennacherib (704–681) certainly set up a safari park around Nineveh, where, as he put it, 'the cane-brakes developed rapidly; the birds of heaven . . . built their nests; the wild pigs and beasts of the forest brought forth young in abundance'.

The interest of the Assyrians in the world around them, and their willingness to accept new ideas, points to an intellectual vigour which paralleled, and perhaps fed, their military vigour and their administrative innovation. Much which they did under these stimuli had important consequences for the subsequent development of the Near East. New resources, of ores, timber and stones, were opened up. Technology spread. Some devices of government of considerable importance for the later Near East began under the Assyrians – for example, a system of imperial roads, with a rapid postal system to provide communication between provincial governors and the king. It could also be argued that the very survival of the values transmitted to the whole world from Sumerian civilization owed much to Assyrian military power. From the time of the Aramaeans and Mushki in the reign of Tiglath-Pileser I to the Scythians at the very end of the empire, there was frequently the threat of new barbaric immigrants into Mesopotamia; the Assyrians did not in all cases keep such people out, but where they did not, the close contacts resulting from the Assyrian military reaction did much to bring the immigrants' way of life into line with Mesopotamian custom. We see this particularly with the Medes and Persians who, first encountered as wild nomads in the ninth century, proved such apt pupils of their erstwhile Assyrian overlords that, a century after the fall of Assyria, a Persian empire ruled Mesopotamia and the rest of the Near East with no major break from the preceding system.

But perhaps one of the most important contributions of the Assyrians to world history came as a consequence of one of the things most objectionable to modern thought – their policy of deportation of conquered populations. The number of people affected by Assyrian deportations was enormous; it has been estimated that in the final three centuries of the Assyrian empire it amounted to between four and five million. The long-term significance of this was its effect upon racial mixing. Geographical considerations – mountains, rivers, desert – combined with historical factors to divide the Near East into many separate areas, which tended to develop in isolation; one sees an excellent example of this in Palestine, where in a very small area Philistines, Israelites, Judaeans, Moabites, Ammonites, Edomites and various tribal peoples all for a long time remained distinct. It was the Assyrian policy of deportation which was one of the most potent forces in beginning the breakdown of this isolation. The Israelites were a case in point. When taken away to Media and the Habur area, they eventually disappeared in terms of national identity; in fact, they were still there but had been assimilated. In some of the capital cities of Assyria itself, ethnic Assyrians were a minority, because peoples of language and ethnic origin other than Assyrian had been settled there and treated as equal citizens despite their antecedents. With this process of forcible though benevolent resettlement going on over the whole area of Assyrian rule for three centuries, there must have been a considerable increase in ethnic mixing and a corresponding weakening of residual racial exclusiveness (except where this was deliberately preserved by religious means, as in Judah). This was not a rapid process and its results were not seen immediately, but it prepared the way for a growing cultural unification of the whole area. And this affected the whole subsequent history of the Near East. It provided a substratum of homogeneity which made possible the hellenization of much of the Near East after Alexander. Hellenization, in turn, was an important factor in the rapid spread of Christianity across the region, and, half a millennium later, of the spread of Islam.

17
Assyrian Writing and Literature

Without its written documents, our knowledge of Assyria would be only a fraction of what it is. The physical remains of a civilization – its art, its tools, its furniture, its burial practices – can tell us much about an ancient people, but they cannot speak to us in the direct manner of the texts.

Writing was invented in south Mesopotamia shortly before 3000, the earliest extant form consisting of pictograms drawn with a reed on a piece of damp clay pressed to a flattened bun shape between the palms of the hands. In course of time the shape of the clay became standardized as a rectangular slab with flat or rounded edges and flat or slightly convex sides. It might be as small as a matchbox or as large as a quarto book, though typically it was about the size of a bar of soap. Early in the third millennium the form of the signs underwent a change when the scribes took to making them by impressing with a reed stylus of triangular cross-section instead of by drawing; this produced signs composed of straight wedge-shaped (cuneiform) strokes, which in most cases no longer showed their pictographic origin. Moreover, for reasons connected with the way

Object depicted	Sumer c. 3000	Sumer c. 2900	Sumer c. 2500	Babylonia 2nd. mill.	Assyria 1st. mill.
date-palm					
reed					
fish					
head					

Development of Cuneiform Signs

269

the scribe held the clay and the stylus, the direction of drawing of the signs was turned backwards through ninety degrees, so putting all the signs on their backs, which further obscured the link with the original pictograms.

In the form which cuneiform writing finally took, the script ran horizontally across the tablet, most commonly (though not always) parallel to the short axis, always from left to right. Smaller tablets were inscribed in a single column, larger ones in two or more. When the scribe reached the bottom of the first (obverse) face, he turned the tablet on its horizontal, not its vertical, axis; that is, he did not turn it as we turn the page of a book. In consequence, the writing on the obverse of a tablet is always upside down relative to that on its reverse.

The original pictograms were written to represent words in the Sumerian language. As Sumerian had a large proportion of monosyllabic words, this permitted a development by which a particular sign might represent not simply the sense of a word, but the sound which that word had. It was as if, for example, one drew a picture of a bee followed by a picture of a leaf, and used this to write the word 'belief'. One value of this development was that it became possible to use the system for writing languages other than Sumerian. From the middle of the third millennium it was so used for the Semitic language Akkadian; Assyrian was one main dialect of this language, the other being Babylonian. Some of the Sumerian signs which indicated whole words continued to be used in the same manner in Akkadian; for example, the sign for 'king', pronounced *lugal* in Sumerian, was used with the same meaning in Akkadian, though there it was pronounced *šarru*. But many of the signs became used as syllables. Because of this development, an Akkadian text is characteristically a mixture of signs of which some denote whole words and others denote syllables; the proportion of each varies with the type of text and the period.

Clay tablets, though the commonest vehicle for cuneiform writing, were not the only one. Cuneiform could be written on clay made into other shapes, such as cylinders, prisms, cones, figurines, or even (as a key to omens) models of animal organs. Another development was the use of writing boards made of slabs of wood coated with wax, into which the signs were impressed. Cuneiform could also be chiselled on to stone or metal, or be stamped into bricks. Sometimes it was painted on a surface, even occasionally as an addition to a tablet otherwise inscribed in the normal way.

The original purpose for which the Sumerians invented writing was to keep records of receipts and issues of goods in the communal store houses. But its use quickly developed into much wider applications. By the second millennium documents in Babylonia written in cuneiform included myths and epics, Wisdom literature (i.e., texts like the biblical Proverbs), laws, astronomical observations, mathematical problems, historical records, court decisions, date lists (i.e., sequences of years, each given a name derived from some event in it), agricultural instructions, business contracts, administrative documents, texts used in the cult, texts used for magical purposes, series of omens, school exercises of trainee scribes, international treaties, dictionaries (which Assyriologists call 'synonym lists'), studies in Sumerian grammar, and letters in thousands – to private persons, to kings, and even to gods.

Assyria shared in the legacy from the Sumerians, and most classes of texts found in Assyria, and almost all literary compositions, were borrowed from Babylonia. But there were exceptions, two of which are of considerable importance for our knowledge of Assyrian history.

Assyrian Royal Inscriptions

The most notable literary form which developed in Assyria was the Assyrian royal inscription. From the time of the Sumerians in south Mesopotamia in the third millennium, kings had written votive inscriptions, that is, inscriptions recording the dedication of something given to the god or done for the god. Such inscriptions could take various forms, simple or complex, but the essential elements were the identification of the king, the gift or pious work, and the occasion of the dedication. Development in course of time eventually produced the following framework:

(a) the king's name, titles, and special relationship with the gods,
(b) mention of events fixing the point in time,
(c) an account of the pious work, usually a building operation.

The element designated (b) provided a means by which the king could refer to others things he had undertaken on behalf of the deity. In Assyria, as the idea developed that the god Ashur claimed world-wide dominion (see page 247), an account of the king's campaigns on behalf of the god became eminently appropriate at this point. And so, from about 1300, the Assyrian kings (though not those of Babylonia) began to develop this section into a description of what they had been doing in the military sphere. Once this practice had become accepted, it opened considerable possibilities for the king's

271

self-glorification. This eventually developed into a form in which the king, speaking in the first person, gave an account of everything military that he had done in his reign to date. The details might be arranged in different ways, either region by region or year by year. The arrangement year by year, which we may properly call annals, first occurred in Assyria in the reign of Tiglath-Pileser I (1115–1077); it has been suggested that this type of arrangement owed something to the Hittites, but there is no evidence to support this, other than the fact that the Hittites had had texts in annalistic form at an earlier period. Although we think of texts of this kind as historical, formally they were still dedication inscriptions and always ended with an appropriate account of a pious work, most commonly the rebuilding of a temple or palace.

Interesting though they may prove to us, most of these royal Assyrian inscriptions were not intended in the first instance for human eyes at all. Many of them were written on cylinders or prisms and buried in the foundation of the building whose restoration they describe. For the time being, only the gods could see them. It was, however, recognized that no building was permanent and that later pious kings would need to dig down to the foundations once again, when they would find and read the inscription. There is a regular formula at the end of many royal Assyrian inscriptions, covering this circumstance:

> In later days, whoever it is among the kings my sons whose name the god Ashur proclaims for the shepherding of the land and people, when that palace grows old and falls to ruins, may he restore its ruins, may he look on the inscription written in my name, may he anoint it with oil, may he pour out a libation [over it], may he return it to its place; then Ashur will hear his prayer.

Not all royal inscriptions were hidden in the earth. Some were inscribed on bas reliefs along the walls of palaces, others carved into the colossal stone bulls and lions which stood guardian at gateways, and some were engraved on royal monuments set up on distant borders to commemorate Assyrians triumphs there. Some of the inscriptions in these categories were no long building inscriptions in form. They had broken away from the original framework to become texts limited to glorifying the exploits of the king. This development may have occurred as a result of the monuments themselves, or some activity of the king which they described, being felt to be pious works in honour of the gods, equivalent to the restoration of a temple or the like. We see the possibility of this interpretation very clearly in inscriptions engraved on some of the lion and bull colossi set up by Ashur-nasir-pal. The major part of these texts comprises self-glorification by the king about an expedition to the Mediterranean. But just before the end the king suddenly switches from military matters to claim that the gods Ninurta and Nergal had entrusted the wild beasts to him and commanded him to hunt them. Immediately afterwards the text concludes with a tally of the elephants, wild bulls and lions that the king had slain. This seems to represent an implicit dedication to the gods of the slaughter of the wild beasts.

We might suppose that with an inscribed monument set up in a public place, the primary purpose was that it should be read by humans at large. But even with a monument at the centre of a busy Assyrian city, that would not have been possible, since the literate were a small minority. With monuments erected on distant northern or eastern borders, where (except possibly for a few officers amongst scattered Assyrian garrisons) the population would be ignorant of the Akkadian language in which the inscriptions were written, the likelihood of readers would be even less; had the text been intended to remind conquered populations of Assyrian might, the Assyrian king could have written them bilingually in Urartian and Akkadian (as an Urartian king actually did in one case). As to the inscriptions on bas reliefs inside Assyrian palaces, these would only ever have been seen by a small number of palace staff, visiting officials, and foreign dignitaries.

Limu Lists

There was a second type of text of some historical importance which developed within Assyria. This was what is known as *limu* lists. The term *limu* (sometimes translated 'eponym') was applied to the official who presided over state cultic functions at the city Ashur. The king and the highest officers of state served as *limu* in turn, each for one year, the king in his first full regnal year and the others in an order originally determined by lot, later by seniority. The year was officially known by the name of the *limu* who served in it, so that lists of *limu*s gave the sequence of years.

There are several forms of the *limu* lists; some contain only the names of the officials, whilst others give the names plus the provinces of which the officials were governors (or comparable data) plus a brief mention of a campaign or some other event. A short extract from one form of the list for the years just before and after the accession of Tiglath-Pileser III will give some idea of the type of contents:

273

In the *limu* of Nergal-nasir	of Nisibin:	revolt in Calah.
In the *limu* of Nabu-bel-usur	of Arrapkha:	on the 13th of Ayyar [May] Tiglath-Pileser came to the throne. In Tishri [October] he went to Between-the-Rivers [north-west Mesopotamia].
In the *limu* of Bel-dan	of Calah:	to Namri.
In the *limu* of Tiglath-Pileser	King of Assyria:	in Arpad, he defeated Urartu.
In the *limu* of Nabu-danninanni	the Turtan:	to Arpad.

The extant pieces of the *limu* lists overlap, and this enables a restoration of the entries for 264 consecutive years. By good fortune one of the entries notes the following event:

In the month Siwan [June] the sun underwent eclipse.

Now, as we know approximately the year to which this must refer, astronomers can calculate precisely in which year an eclipse visible in Assyria took place in June. It proves to be 763 B.C. Thus, with this one year exactly fixed, all the 264 years of the sequence are dated, making Assyrian chronology throughout this period very precise. The notes of events in each year, though brief, give a valuable historical framework across most of this span of two and a half centuries – not quite all, since for part of the period the *limu* list is preserved only in the form limited to the officials' names.

Astrological Reports

A third class of text particularly associated with Assyria was one not directly relevant to history. These texts were the astrological reports, of which examples have already been given (see pages 220ff.). Astrology was by no means unknown in Babylonia, but it was only in first-millennium Assyria that astrological reports of this kind were systematically developed to provide omens bearing upon the welfare of the state.

Oracles

Another type of text found in first-millennium Assyria also gave messages bearing on the welfare of the state, but by quite a different technique. It is not uniquely Assyrian, since there are examples of it in other parts of the ancient Near East, not least in the Bible; but in Mesopotamia in the first millennium it is known only from Assyria, and even there it was not common. The texts in question are oracles given by inspired persons, usually women, who claimed them as messages for the king from a deity. The following is an example of a typical oracle:

> You shall not fear, O Esarhaddon. It is I, the Lord, who speak with you. I watch over your innermost heart, like your mother who gave you being. Sixty great gods are stationed with me to guard you. The god Sin is at your right hand, the god Shamash at your left. Sixty great gods are stationed round you, girt with the hurricane. Put not your trust in man; cast your eyes on me, gaze on me. I am Ishtar of Erbil. Ashur has granted you well-being. When you were small I carried you. Have no fear; revere me.

Letters

Most other classes of writings found in Assyria are either directly borrowed from Babylonia (which is the case with almost all texts which may be regarded as literature in the narrower sense), or examples originating in Assyria of types of texts well known from Babylonia.

The most important examples of the latter category, at least in terms of the information they give us, are letters. There are some of these from the Old Assyrian period (beginning of the second millennium) amongst the documents from Cappadocia (see pages 28f.). There are also a few private letters from several sites from the Middle Assyrian period (end of the second millennium). And from the first millennium there are collections of letters from Qal'ah Shergat (ancient Ashur), Tell Halaf (ancient Gozan), Nimrud (ancient Calah), and Kuyunjik (ancient Nineveh). The greatest number, of the order of two thousand, are from Kuyunjik, with about two hundred from Nimrud. The date of the two big collections is in the eighth and seventh centuries, with the others a little earlier. Although these collections do contain some private letters, they are predominantly state correspondence. Most are written to the king, a few by him. In the case of letters in the latter category, the tablets we possess must have been copies retained for filing, since the originals would have left the capital for the correspondents to whom they were addressed in the provinces. The letters written to the king fall broadly into two categories. One category comprises letters from the king's experts in magic and divination. These learned men interpreted various omens for the king and told him when he might or might not do certain things, since he was very much a prisoner of superstition. One or two examples may give some idea of the type of contents:

> To the king my lord, your servant Ishtar-shum-eresh. May it be well with the king my lord. May Nabu and Marduk bless the king my lord.
> Concerning the chapel of the god Nashuh, about which the king my lord sent me a message saying: 'Look up a day of good omen and write and send how they should set it up'; the month Siwan [June] is favourable and the seventeenth day is favourable. However, that month is ended and gone, so when will they be able to do it?
> Elul [September] is a good month; that is the month for it. Let them do it, let them set it up, within that period.

A good example of a letter about omens relates to the appointment of a 'substitute king' (see page 149). When omens threatened the king, he had to withdraw, temporarily taking (we do not know why) the title 'Farmer', whilst a substitute nominally reigned in his stead. The first half of the letter reads:

> To the Farmer my lord, your servant Nabu-zer-lisher. May it be well with my lord. May Nabu and Marduk bless my lord for many years.
> I have written down the portents, as many as there were, whether of the sky or of the earth or of monstrous births, and have had them recited one after the other in front of the Sun-god. I had them cook and eat birds prepared with wine, washed with water and anointed with oil. The Substitute King thereby took upon himself the portents of the land of Akkad.

The second broad category of Assyrian state letters are those to the king from administrative officials, principally provincial gover-nors and garrison commanders. These may touch upon virtually anything, though predominantly they cover matters of provincial administration generally, military intelligence reports or details of military actions, movements of prisoners of war, the collection of horses for the army, and disputes between officials.

Economic Documents

There are many Assyrian examples of such texts, which were widespread throughout Mesopotamia at all periods. The heading is a very loose term covering several distinct categories, but there are two justifications for using it. One is that the most important single publication of New Assyrian texts in these categories treated them all together. The other is that economic tablets in several different categories were stored together by the Assyrians themselves, as part of one person's business affairs. Types of text under this broad heading include amongst others the following: royal grants of land, sale documents (of land, houses, slaves), marriage settlements, adoption agreements, division of inheritance, loan contracts (for barley, silver, bronze), receipts, contracts for work to be done (harvesting, house building), court decisions, and wage chits. At some periods, contract documents might be protected from fraudulent alteration by enclosure in clay envelopes. The envelope would be inscribed with the terms of the contract, or a summary of them, and in the event of dispute might be broken to reveal the original tablet.

Laws

The best-known collection of laws from ancient Mesopotamia is that of the eighteenth-century Babylonian king Hammurabi, but there are other collections from Babylonia, and we also have examples from Assyria. Two groups of Middle Assyrian Laws were discovered at Ashur, one mainly concerned with land tenure and the other with women (see pages 132, 140ff.). Unlike the laws of Hammurabi, these were not drawn up in the form of decisions given by the king, but clearly were compilations by jurists (presumably acting under the instructions of the king) of traditional legal practice in particular areas. It is significant that no traces of these laws have been found in the great Kuyunjik library of texts from the seventh century (see pages 278ff.). This could be a matter of accident, but in view of the considerable amount of the library which is extant, if only in fragments, this is unlikely. The implication is that, whatever the purpose for which the Middle Assyrian laws were compiled, it was not to serve as a written corpus of national law, permanently used as the basis for legal decisions. Nor can these laws have been a regular part of the curriculum of study of scribes, or we should surely have found later examples of them, copied (like many other texts) as students' exercises.

Texts Directly Borrowed from Babylonia

The categories so far mentioned either developed in Assyria or were composed in Assyria upon Babylonian models. But outside these, the majority of texts found in Assyria were direct borrowings from Babylonia. The most striking illustration of this is the very large collection of texts from a royal library in Nineveh, which were discovered when Kuyunjik was excavated last century (see pages 312ff.) and brought to the British Museum. Strictly speaking, there was more than one library, since in some colophons (see pages 280ff.) there is mention of the text being placed in the palace, and in others it is said to belong to the library of the temple of Nabu. However, because all were controlled by the same king, and all are now present together in the same collection in the British Museum, it is often convenient to treat them as a single library. Assyriologists have been well served in the matter of this collection. The main part of it was catalogued by a German scholar, Carl Bezold, in five volumes of *Catalogue of the Cuneiform Tablets in the Kouyunjik Collection of the British Museum* (1889–99), to which a *Supplement* by L. W. King was added in 1914. A large number of tiny fragments are still uncatalogued. The total entries in the Kuyunjik catalogue amount to over 25,000, but since many of these are broken pieces and not whole tablets, the number of tablets from which these fragments come reduces to about 5000. In many cases, several tablets duplicate the same text, so that the number of distinct texts represented may be estimated at between 1000 and 1200.

Smaller libraries of cuneiform texts have been found at other Assyrian sites, notably Ashur and Calah, and also at the site Sultan-tepe (ancient Huzirina) near Harran in south-east Turkey. Many of the Ashur texts, which are in Berlin, have been published, and have proved to be of high importance for our knowledge of the cult in Assyria, though they bear upon many other aspects of Assyrian life as well; it is from Ashur that the Middle Assyrian laws come. The collection from Calah comprises the library of the temple of the god Nabu – whose temple usually possessed a library, as he was the scribal god – but with some small exceptions these have not yet been published. The Sultantepe texts, published in two volumes, contain much important literary material.

Not all the tablets and fragments listed in the British Museum Kuyunjik catalogue come from a library in Nineveh, or indeed from Nineveh at all. The methods of nineteenth-century excavation did not include careful registration of the exact spot at which each cuneiform tablet was found, and in a site covering a hundred acres and containing several palaces, it is not necessary to assume that all tablets found came from the same part of the same building. In fact, we know from the contents of tablets that some of those catalogued in the Kuyunjik collection actually came from some site other than Kuyunjik; there, are for example, several dated by kings of Babylonia a century after the final destruction of Nineveh. But even within the vast majority which certainly came from Kuyunjik, there are some which manifestly were not from Ashurbanipal's library. All the state letters, for example, are likely to have been in a state archive distinct from the library. And certainly the royal library cannot have been the home of those economic documents which dealt with such matters as private sales of slaves or houses, contracts for harvesting, and the like. This conclusion is supported by the discovery at Nineveh in the 1970s of similar economic documents in an area well away from the palaces.

However, most of the tablets in the Kuyunjik collection did belong to the royal palace and temple libraries at Nineveh. We know something about the origin of these libraries, which were mainly due to Ashurbanipal, although the nucleus goes back to his predecessors, some of whom made collections of tablets. As early as about 1100, Tiglath-Pileser I established a library in a temple at Ashur, of which over one hundred tablets can be identified from finds there. But without question it was Ashurbanipal who was the greatest royal collector of all. His activities in this connection are established not only by the presence of his name on a large proportion of the tablets from Nineveh, but also by a letter dealing with this. The letter reads:

Royal command to Kudurranu. May it be well with you; may your heart be glad.

On the day you see my tablet, take under your authority [various named persons and 'the scribal experts of Borsippa', a city near Babylon] and seek out such tablets as there are in their houses, and tablets deposited in Ezida [the major temple of Borsippa, whose god was the scribal deity Nabu].

The royal letter then goes on to specify by name some of the texts or series of texts which the king particularly wanted. These included 'as many series as there are about battle, together with additional tablets belonging to them, as many as there prove to be', rituals, texts of the type of prayer called 'raising of the hand', and texts called 'inscriptions about stones' and 'what is good for kingship'. The details of the king's instructions continue:

> Seek out and send to me any rare tablets which are known to you and are lacking in Assyria. . . . No one is to withhold tablets from you. And if there is any tablet or ritual which I have not mentioned to you, and you find by examination that it is good for my palace, then get it and send it to me.

Although this royal command does not contain the name of the writer (documents of this type never do), the mention of Assyria puts it beyond doubt that it was an Assyrian king writing. Features of the language show that this letter was written not long before the end of the Assyrian empire, and so the king concerned can only have been Ashurbanipal. The contents make clear why he was collecting these Tablets. The categories into which they fall are mainly omen series, rituals, prayers and incantations, and these texts had a practical function. Life on earth was overshadowed by the supernatural – the influences of which were thought of not straight-forwardly as the will of the great gods but rather in terms of some-thing as amorphous as our own concept of 'luck' – and there was no one as closely concerned with this as the king, the embodiment of the state. At any time disaster might loom. But if the signs were prop-erly read, forewarning would be given of danger ahead, and magical steps might be taken to avert it. The omen texts gave warning of potential danger to the state, and it was the rituals, incantations and prayers which could provide the means of overcoming it.

In this letter, Ashurbanipal was clearly commandeering tablets from the temple of Borsippa, and tablets which are originals from Babylonia (as distinct from copies made of Babylonian tablets) have been found in his library. There are others which he had had brought from the older Assyrian capitals, Ashur and Calah. But the greatest number of tablets in his library (or, more accurately, libraries) were specially copied for him. We know such details from the colophons. A colophon, when the word is applied to a cuneiform tablet, is a statement at the end giving certain details about the particular tablet. Those used by Ashurbanipal fall within twenty-three patterns. Three examples follow:

> Ashurbanipal, the great king, the mighty king, king of all, king of Assyria, son of Esarhaddon king of Assyria (who was) son of Sennacherib, also king of Assyria. I wrote this tablet in the

assembly of experts according to the wording of tablets and writing boards, originals from Assyria and Sumer and Akkad [i.e., Babylonia]. I checked and collated it, and placed it within my palace for my royal perusal. Whoever erases my name as written and writes his own name, may Nabu, the universal scribe, erase his name.

The second example represents the longest type found:

Written and collated according to its ancient form. I, Ashurbanipal, king of all, king of Assyria, on whom Nabu and Tashmetu [Nabu's consort] have bestowed keen intelligence [literally 'a broad ear'] and clear eyes to grasp the most precious parts of scribal knowledge, who amongst the kings who preceded me no one understood this matter, I wrote on the tablets the wisdom of Nabu, the pricking in of cuneiform signs as many as there are, and I checked and collated them. I placed them for futurity in the library of the temple of my lord Nabu, the Great Lord, which is within Nineveh, for my life, for the guarding of my soul, that I might not have illness, and for making firm the foundation of my royal throne. O Nabu, look with gladness, and ever bless my kingship. Whenever I call on you, take my hand. While I walk about in your House, guard my steps continually. When this work is put in your House, and placed in front of you, look on it and remember me with favour. . . .

This colophon is particularly revealing. It makes it clear that Ashurbanipal's concern for tablets was neither antiquarian nor a mere literary enthusiasm; it had a strong religious element. The texts were not so much literature as scripture, in the sense which that word has for biblical fundamentalists. They contained the wisdom of Nabu, and to preserve them and to be associated with them brought merit and reward from the god. These ancient texts were scripture also in the sense that their exact wording was considered important and unchangeable; canonical forms of the texts had developed and were officially recognized. That is why there is emphasis in the colophons upon checking and collation against the original tablets which bore the ancient form. Even when colophons were very brief, they still referred to the authority of an original text, as in the following example:

Written and collated according to the wording of a tablet, an original from Cuthah.

The concern shown in the colophons to guarantee the authenticity of these library tablets must surely have been reflected in a careful filing system; this view is reinforced by the existence of catalogues of text titles. Unfortunately, because of the failure of the early archaeologists to record the find-places of tablets and associated details, we have no first-hand knowledge of how tablets were originally stored in the Nineveh libraries. However, excavations at Nimrud in the 1950s have filled some of the gaps. The state letters found there came from the floor of a chamber in the building known as the North-West Palace, and the containers in which they must originally have been kept are still to be seen. These were in the form of boxes about a foot and a half square, made of large burnt bricks. It seems likely that the tablets in Ashurbanipal's libraries were stored in some similar way.

The types of texts found in Ashurbanipal's libraries give a good indication of the scholastic literature, mainly of Babylonian origin, in use in Assyria. The following does not set out to be an exhaustive list, but only to indicate some of the principal classes of texts. Classes already illustrated earlier in this book are generally not mentioned again unless there is some additional point to be made about them.

Omen Texts

The largest single category of texts from Ashurbanipal's libraries was concerned with omens; it has been calculated that over a quarter of all the estimated total of 1000 to 1200 tablets were of this genre. The observing of omens figured very prominently in Babylonian and Assyrian culture; it was regarded as a means by which the king or a private individual might be forewarned of any unpleasant eventualities ahead, so that steps might be taken to avoid the evil consequences. First-millennium Assyria specially developed one particular form of this technique – the use of astrological texts already mentioned. Babylonia had earlier produced many other types, of which the majority are represented in Ashurbanipal's library. Omens might be drawn from a vast number of circumstances: from the appearance or movements of ants, dogs, cattle, sheep or other animals, birds, snakes, scorpions; from dreams; from the appearance of fire or smoke; from the patterns of oil on water; from human sexual behaviour; from monstrous births. Such omens came to be arranged in long sequences, which in the course of time acquired a fixed official, or as we say 'canonical', form. Such texts were known technically as series, and the series would be designated by a name based on its first line, such as 'If a town is set on a hill'.

It would occupy far too much space to give even a few examples from each of the main classes, but the form is illustrated by the following:

If (in a dream a man) does the work of a seal-cutter, his son will die.

If he does the work of a fuller,
for a poor man (it means that) his misfortunes will leave him.

If water is poured out at the door of a man's house and it takes the shape of a snake, the man will experience evil.

If a man is covered with warts, he will have food to eat if there is a famine.

Scribal Education Texts

This was the next largest group of texts. Essentially these were compilations incorporating the basic technical knowledge required for scribal proficiency in the Akkadian and Sumerian languages. These included lists of cuneiform signs with explanations, synonym lists (in essence having similarities to *Roget's Thesaurus*), lists of Sumerian or foreign words with an Akkadian translation, and texts written bilingually in Sumerian and Akkadian.

Rituals and Incantation Series

These involved both direct appeals to deities and what we might broadly call religious rituals and magic to give protection from evil or to release a victim from its power. Some of these texts were for use in royal state rituals, others might be applied to any individual threatened with or suffering misfortune. Some extracts from this latter category have been given in Chapter 13. The texts in question include one series for use against witchcraft, and another against evil spirits, who were invisible and could attack humans anywhere. A third series bore a title meaning 'Burnings', from the rituals associated with its incantations. These last were used to treat a man suffering from an illness thought to result from some evil which had got into his body as the result of the breach of a taboo or the commission of some sin. A specimen group of possible causes of the affliction includes offences which in our categories might be designated superstitious, religious, social and ethical. The man's trouble might have come

> By the evil taboo that he ate,
> By the many misdeeds that he sinned,
> By the assembly that he scattered,
> By the tight-knit group that he dispersed,
> By his disregard of god and goddess,
> By his promising in heart and mouth but not delivering.

Another section of this series points more consistently to socio-ethical offences as the cause of the man's trouble. This section seeks release for

> So-and-so, son of so-and-so, whose god is so-and-so, whose goddess is so-and-so, [The terms translated 'so-and-so' are present in the text, and at the recital of the incantation for a particular patient would have been replaced by appropriate names]
> who is . . . ill, worried, wretched, troubled,
> . . .
> who separated son from father,
> who separated father from son,
> who separated daughter from mother,
> who separated mother from daughter,
> who separated daughter-in-law from mother-in-law,
> who separated mother-in-law from daughter-in-law,
> who separated brother from brother,
> who separated friend from friend,
> who separated companion from companion,
> who did not set free a captive, did not release a man in bonds,
> who did not let the man in the prison-house see the daylight.

The treatment used in this magical series involved purification rites employing sympathetic magic. The central feature of it was that the *ashipu* (see pages 212ff.) took something such as an onion, a date or a piece of wool, and pulled it to pieces and threw it into the fire whilst he recited an incantation. As the layers of onion (or whatever) were peeled away and burnt, so the evil in the man's body was peeled away and disposed of. One typical section reads as follows:

> Incantation. As he peels this onion and casts it into the fire,
> and the flame consumes it utterly,
> (so that) it will not be cultivated in a bed,

it will not stand up by a ditch or irrigation channel,
it will not take root in the ground,
it will not make shoots, it will not see the sun,
it will not get to the table of a god or king,
so may . . . the illness that is in my body, my flesh, my veins be
peeled away like this onion;
let the fire utterly consume it this day.

Myths and Epics

These are the class of Babylonian and Assyrian texts which most
appeal to the average reader today, but there is no reason to suppose
that the people of ancient Mesopotamia shared this preference;
certainly myths and epics were well behind omen texts and scholastic
literature in the number of tablets represented in the Kuyunjik libraries. There are about forty texts which come into this category.

The formal distinction between myths and epics is that myths
treat of activities on the divine plane, whereas epics are concerned
with the deeds of heroes which, although they may contain a good
deal of the supernatural, are essentially on the human plane. The
origin and purpose of myths has given rise, and continues to give
rise, to a vast amount of speculation, into which it is not proposed
to enter here. But it is clear that in ancient Babylonia (from which
Assyria received its myths) two essential features of myths may be
recognized: one was to explain the origin of the world order, and
another was to resolve tensions which might arise on the social or
political or even the personal level. Particular themes which were
often found within these areas included: the origin of the universe;
conflicts between gods; the creation of man; the social order.

The most important myth in first-millennium Mesopotamia was
the Myth of Creation on which the New Year Festival in Babylon
centred. This incorporated fragments of a number of much older
myths, cleverly combined and transformed with the purpose of
glorifying Marduk, the god of Babylon. The myth presented him
– a junior but powerful god – as the deity who had defeated the
primeval powers of chaos, in the form of the female dragon Tiamat
and her cohorts. For this, the assembly of the gods had granted
Marduk a supremacy in the pantheon which had originally belonged
to others. This had the consequence and object of transferring to
Babylon – a city which was an upstart in comparison with many
others whose origins could be traced back to the beginning of
Sumerian times – the religious prestige of much more venerable
cult-centres. The Assyrians took this myth over, but this in turn

gave them a theological problem. They claimed that their national god Ashur held world dominion, a claim manifestly incompatible with the Babylonian theology of Marduk's supremacy. The Assyrians dealt with this problem by substituting Ashur for Marduk throughout the myth.

The most important epic in both Babylonia and Assyria was the Epic of Gilgamesh. There is good evidence that there actually was a person Gilgamesh, who was a ruler of the city of Uruk (Erech) in the early third millennium. A number of separate epics developed about him and were written down by Sumerian scribes in the third millennium. In the early second millennium some great Babylonian poet took these separate Sumerian epics, translated them into Akkadian, and welded them together in a masterly fashion to create one great epic; he even cleverly managed to work in the Flood story, which originally had had nothing at all to do with Gilgamesh. There are many sub-themes in this epic, but the main strand which runs through it is the problem of human mortality – man's attempt to make himself the equal of the immortal gods, and the inevitable failure of this goal in his decline into old age and death. Yet at the end Gilgamesh, and mankind for whom he stands, is left with the consolation of human creative achievement. This epic was very widely known throughout the ancient Near East, as we know from pieces of the text having been found in several places, including Palestine, well outside Mesopotamia. It is therefore not surprising that it is represented by several copies (none complete) in the Kuyunjik collection.

We do not know what practical purpose the Epic of Gilgamesh may have served in Assyria. There is no reason to suppose that it was used in the cult, and it would not lend itself to dramatic representation. One may guess that it was recited for entertainment and edification at court ceremonies, but there is no positive evidence to support this.

The Kuyunjik texts include most of the other epics known from Babylonia. There were also two epics which were actually composed in Assyria, but these were in no way comparable with the Epic of Gilgamesh in depth or literary merit. Both commemorated triumphs of Middle Assyrian kings; the circumstances of their composition is mentioned on pages 47 and 52. In this case we do know their purpose; it was propaganda. They had the politico-religious object of showing that the action taken by the Assyrian kings against Babylonia was in accordance with the will of the gods.

Wisdom Literature

This is a category of ancient Near Eastern literature well known to Western readers from such biblical examples as Proverbs, Job and Ecclesiastes. We know of no work of this type which provably originated in Assyria, but most of the Babylonian Wisdom literature is attested in Assyria. Except for an occasional proverb quoted in letters, there is no indication that such texts played any significant part in Assyrian life and thought, and the examples which occur in Assyria were probably not current outside very limited scribal circles. There are, however, three works of sufficient intrinsic interest to merit mention.

The first is a composition called 'I will praise the Lord of Wisdom'. In this the speaker is a person of princely status who finds himself deserted by the gods, expelled from office and estates, and stricken with illness and pain. Yet he insists that he has never neglected his duties to the gods. The text thus constitutes an examination, as in the biblical book of Job, of the problem of evil, though at a much lower level. The conclusion reached is that conflict may arise because humans cannot know the hidden will of the gods:

What is proper to oneself is an offence to one's god,
What in one's own heart seems despicable is proper to one's god.
Who knows the will of the gods in heaven?

A second work of this class, known as 'the Babylonian Theodicy', is in the form of a dialogue between a sufferer and a friend. The sufferer complains of the injustices with which life is beset, and the friend offers the trite answers of conventional Babylonian piety. When the sufferer points out instances of those who have always served the gods but yet suffered hardship, the friend asserts that in the fullness of time piety will be rewarded with prosperity. And when the sufferer instances wicked men who prosper, the friend blandly assures him that in the end these will undoubtedly suffer the penalty for their misdeeds.

A third composition, the 'Dialogue of Pessimism', has similarities with the foregoing; again the form is a dialogue, this time between a master and his slave. There is a regular pattern to it. The master proposes a course of action, whereat the slave fulsomely endorses it. The master then immediately changes his mind, pointing out the folly of what he had proposed, and at this the slave turns right round and offers arguments in support of his master's latest point of view. The whole trend of the poem is to point out the vanity of all human activity.

287

Other Classes of Texts

There are many other texts found in Assyria – some from the Kuyunjik collection and some from other Assyrian sites, though not necessarily originating in Assyria – which do not easily fit into any of the main categories. One such is the story known as 'the Poor Man of Nippur', a tale about a poor man who had been cheated by a mayor and used ingenious means to obtain his revenge; this has been touched upon elsewhere in a different connection (see page 232). There are at least two specifically Assyrian texts from the eighth or early seventh century which had the function of political propaganda against Babylonia, under religious guise, and a corresponding pro-Babylonian text is also known. One striking text, again of Assyrian origin, contains a verse account of a campaign of Sargon, from which some lines have been quoted (see pages 93f.), in the form of a letter to the god Ashur; other such letters are known. Other texts of which we have only one example or a small group from Assyria include treaties with vassals, a charter of special privileges for the city of Ashur, and a text about horse-training (see pages 169f.). But this list is far from complete. Even a complete list would not be final, for it is one of the fascinations of Assyriology that amongst the hundreds of thousands of cuneiform tablets still unread in the world's museums, and the still greater number yet to be excavated, any one may introduce us to something entirely new from ancient Mesopotamia.

18

The Rediscovery of Assyria

When Assyria collapsed at the end of the seventh century, its place as the centre of world empire was taken first by Babylon and then, from 539, by Persia. Assyria's buildings did not long survive the society which had created them. Even in the heyday of Assyria, major temples and palaces cannot have continued long in their pristine splendour, and, to judge by records of rebuilding, their extreme life as usable structures seldom exceeded three centuries. Often it was much less.

Ancient Mesopotamian buildings, embellished though they might be with stone and baked brick, commonly had much of their structure in mud-brick; and mud-brick is very susceptible to the effects of water. Although the total rainfall of Assyria is low, such rain as there is often falls in a few very heavy and prolonged storms, and in ancient Assyria the water would soon find out any cracks in the flat mud roofs which were the usual covering of buildings.

After the fall of Assyria, the situation was worse; there had been deliberate sacking of buildings by fire, and disintegration was correspondingly more rapid. Within two centuries nothing at all was recognizable of the Assyrian capital cities other than the outline of their fortification walls. We learn this from the description by Xenophon, a Greek soldier-historian who in 401, as the leader of a harried mercenary army fighting its way back from Persia to Greece, encamped with his men at places unknown to him but which we can recognize from his account as Calah and Nineveh. It seems that both of these cities had already become examples of what we commonly know by the Arabic word *tell* (or Kurdish *tepe*). A *tell* is an artificial mound resulting from ancient human occupation. The first settlers at a site would build their houses and temples on virgin soil, often on a slight natural rise. When these structures collapsed the next generation would level the debris and rebuild on top, thus raising the ground level, a process to which the accumulation of refuse would further contribute. In some cases temples and palaces would be deliberately raised on platforms, thereby accentuating the rise of level. This building-up of the mound would continue relentlessly, so that in the course of centuries or millennia a major settlement might grow high above the original plain; we know, for example, that part of Kuyunjik, the palace area of Nineveh, is ninety feet above virgin soil. When, because of war, disease or other reasons, the settlement became depopulated, soil deposits, laid down by the frequent dust-storms which blast Iraq, would gradually cover the ruins of most buildings and in time build up the top of the mound to a more or less level or smoothly curving surface, with only the remains of the ziggurat or any other exceptionally tall buildings projecting above the general level. Such *tells* (see plate 8A), ranging in size from well under an acre to something near three hundred acres in the case of Qal'ah Shergat (ancient Ashur), are sprinkled all over Mesopotamia, and there are places from which more than a hundred can be seen.

Had Xenophon been in the area of Calah and Nineveh in more favourable circumstances, he might have learnt the identity of these ruins from local inhabitants. The destruction of the Assyrian empire did not wipe out its population. They were predominantly peasant farmers, and since Assyria contains some of the best wheat land in the Near East, descendants of the Assyrian peasants would, as opportunity permitted, build new villages over the old cities and carry on with agricultural life, remembering traditions of the former cities. After seven or eight centuries and various vicissitudes, these people became Christians. These Christians, and the Jewish communities scattered amongst them, not only kept alive the memory of the sites of their Assyrian predecessors but also combined them with traditions from the Bible. The Bible, indeed, came to be a powerful factor in keeping alive the memory of Assyria and particularly of Nineveh. Nineveh was at the centre of one of the most fascinating of the Old Testament legends, the story of the prophet Jonah who attempted in vain to escape the God-given duty of preaching to the great pagan capital. On part of the ruins of Nineveh there was a sacred mound, and this – probably originally an Assyrian temple – Christians and Jews came to identify with the spot where Jonah preached. A church was built on the site. When the Muslims conquered Mesopotamia in the seventh century A.D., they adopted the local traditions of the Christians and Jews amongst whom they lived, and Jonah (Yunus) became significant to Muslims no less than to Jews and Christians. A mosque replaced the church but retained – and retains to this day – the association with Jonah. The tenth-century Muslim geographer Al-Muqaddasi, describing the Mosul district, wrote: 'Here God forgave the people of Jonah. Does (the district) not contain the mosque of Jonah, at Tell Taubah [Repentance Hill], to which seven visits are said to be equal to a pilgrimage?' Another Muslim visitor to Mosul in the same century,

Ibn Hawqal, spoke of the fertile land at Ninaway [Nineveh], where the prophet Jonah was buried.

Travellers' Tales

One factor contributing to Assyria's greatness had been its position on the major natural route constituted by the Tigris. This same factor ensured that in every century many pilgrims and merchants should pass the ruins of Assyria. The first such traveller known to us from Europe was a Jewish rabbi, Benjamin, from Tudela in Spain, who journeyed through much of the Near East in the eleventh century, noting Jewish communities and sites with biblical associations. Of Mosul he records:

It is Ashur the Great, and about seven thousand Jews live there. . . . It sits on the river Tigris. Between it and Nineveh is a connecting bridge. It [Nineveh] is in ruins but within its ruins there are villages and communities. And the extent of Nineveh may be determined by its walls, about forty Persian miles, as far as the city Erbil. . . . And in the town of Ashur is the synagogue of Obadiah, which Jonah built.

Here, alongside the accurate identification of the site of Nineveh, we find an enormously inflated assessment of the length of the walls of the city. This was probably influenced by the pious wish to secure agreement with the statement in Jonah 3:3 that 'Nineveh was an exceeding great city of three days' journey'. Benjamin was also at fault in identifying Mosul with the ancient city Ashur.

In fact, the correct identification of Ashur well to the south was traditionally known, as we learn from another Arab geographer, Abu'l-Fida, of the early fourteenth century. Referring to Mosul, he says: 'opposite, on the east bank, are the ruins of Nineveh. South of Mosul, the Lesser Zab joins the Tigris near the ruins of the town of Ashur.'

In the sixteenth century Mosul was visited by a certain Rauwolff, a German gentleman described as 'very famous for his skill in natural products, and in the practice of physic'. Describing his visit, he says:

In this place and thereabouts, stood formerly the Potent Town of Nineve (built by Ashur) which was the Metropolis of Assyria. . . . At this time there is nothing of any Antiquities to be seen . . . save only the Fort which lieth upon the Hill, and

some few Villages, which as the Inhabitants say, did also belong
to it in Former Days.

The absence of conspicuous remains was mentioned again in the
early seventeenth century by an English emissary to the court of
Persia, Sir Antony Sherley, who tells us that 'Niniwy (that which
God himself calleth, that great Citty) hath not one stone standing,
which may give the memory of the being of a Towne.' For all its
alleged lack of remains, Sir Antony had no doubt about the site of
Nineveh, for he adds that 'one English mile from it, is a place
called Mosul, a small thing; rather to bee a witnesse of the others
mightinesse, and Gods judgement, than of any fashion of Magnifi-
cency in its selfe.'

There was, however, a contemporary, John Cartwright, who
could see more in the ruins than did Sir Antony. Having described
his arrival at Mosul, he says:

Here in these plaines of Assiria, and the bankes of Tigris . . . was
Nineuie built by Nimrod, but finished by Ninus. . . . It seemes
by the ruinous foundation (which I throughly viewed) that it was
built with four sides, but not equal or square; for the two longer
sides had each of them (as we guess) an hundred and fifty furlongs;
the two shorter sides, ninety furlongs . . . which makes threescore
miles.

Cartwright guessed high, but had accurately identified the walls of
Nineveh. He had, however, been long anticipated in that by the
fourteenth-century Muslim traveller Ibn Baṭṭuṭa, who had stated of
the site of Ninaway [Nineveh] at Mosul: 'The remains of the encircling wall are still visible, and the positions of the gates which were
in it are clearly seen.'

A Frenchman, J. B. Tavernier, Baron of Aubonne, who visited
Mosul in the second half of the seventeenth century, improved on
Cartwright's estimate of the dimensions of Nineveh. In a contem-
porary translation of his account we read:

There is nothing worth a man's sight in Moussul. . . . But now
let us cross the Tigris, over a Bridge of Boats, to view the sad
Ruines of a City that has made such a noise in the World; though
there be now scarce any appearance of its ancient splendour.
Niniveh was built upon the left Shoar of the Tigris, upon Assyria-
side, being now only a heap of Rubbish extending almost a League
along the River. There are abundance of Vaults and Caverns
uninhabited; nor could a man well conjecture whether they were

the ancient Habitations of the people, or whether any houses had been built upon them in former times. . . . Half a League from Tigris stands a little Hill encompass'd with Houses, on the top whereof is built a Mosquée. The people of the Country say 'twas the place where Jonas was bury'd. . . .' Having pass'd the Tigris, we stay'd three quarters of an hours Journey from Niniveh [i.e., two miles or so]. . . . From the very banks of the River to the place where we lodg'd that Evening, we saw nothing but continu'd Ruines, which makes me believe, it was the place where the ancient Niniveh stood.

So far, tradition and travellers' reports had been unanimous in acclaiming the ruins opposite Mosul as ancient Nineveh. But now a dissenter appeared. Towards the middle of the eighteenth century, the Frenchman M. Otter inclined to the view that Nineveh was not opposite the major city Mosul, but was represented by ruins at a place called Eski Mosul (Turkish for 'Old Mosul'), about thirty miles upstream. He supported this view by what he said were local claims linking Eski Mosul with Jonah, although he was aware of the standard tradition transmitted by Abu'l-Fida and other Arab geographers. He concluded that either Abu'l-Fida or the local inhabitants were in error. But as no one else seems to have come across the alleged Eski Mosul tradition, it may well be that the muddle was due to Otter himself. When talking about traditions of Mosul in ancient times, people of north Iraq are still prone to use (in Arabic) an expression meaning 'old Mosul'. In Otter's time, Turkish was widely used in north Iraq and he spoke that language himself. If Otter used Turkish to question local people about their traditions, they could well have referred to the district of Mosul in ancient times as 'eski Mosul' (Turkish for 'old Mosul'), which he mistakenly took as the place-name Eski Mosul.

Otter's siting of Nineveh was an aberration. He should have known better, for by the middle of the eighteenth century Mosul was widely celebrated for its ruins, even amongst people who had never been there. We see this from Bartholomew Plaisted, an engineer and surveyor in the East India Company. In 1750 he made his way home from India overland from Basra, and although his own route onward from Baghdad was across the Syrian desert to Aleppo, he pointed out to other intending travellers that there was an agreeable alternative: 'If you should be tired of waiting in Bagdad, you may proceed to Mousul, and that will afford you a great deal of variety, for there are many remains of antiquity which will yield you an agreeable amusement, especially if you have a taste that way.'

Two decades after Otter, the scientific Danish explorer Carsten Niebuhr had no doubts at all that the ruins of Nineveh were near Mosul. He mentions 'a village called Nunia on a large hill, and a mosque in which the prophet Jonah lies buried. Another hill in this area is called Kalla Nunia, i.e. "the castle of Nineveh"; on the latter is a village Koindsjug [later spelt "Kuyunjik"].' He adds a sketch of the layout of the mosque, the village Nunia, and the city walls.

Decoding the Inscriptions

The rediscovery of Assyria involved not only the recognition and excavation of its sites, but also the decipherment of its script. From the beginning of the seventeenth century there had been reports of a strange writing of wedge-shaped signs engraved on bricks and stone at various ancient sites in the Near East. For example, an Italian gentleman, Pietro della Valle, writing to a friend in 1625, describes what he had found in some ruins in south Mesopotamia called Muqeijer, which we now know to be ancient Ur:

> I found on the ground some pieces of black Marble, hard and fine, ingraven with the same letters as the Bricks. . . . Amongst other letters which I discover'd in that short time two I found in many places, one of which was like a jacent [i.e., lying down] Pyramid thus, ▷, and the other resembled a Star of eight points.

But the area which attracted most attention for its examples of curious writing was in south Persia. At a place named Takht-i-Jamshid, now known as the site of ancient Persepolis, there are impressive remains of a marble palace, with many inscribed stones. Pietro della Valle published a discussion of the writing found here, with brief specimens, and several other people followed suit during the seventeenth and early eighteenth centuries; some copied and published quite long inscriptions.

The most important contribution came eventually from Carsten Niebuhr. Not only did he make some excellent copies of inscriptions at Takht-i-Jamshid, but also he recognized that they contained three different systems of writing, and that one of these was alphabetic. We know now that the Persian king Darius, who built Persepolis, had his inscriptions written trilingually in Babylonian, Elamite and Old Persian, each of these languages having its own form of cuneiform script, that used for old Persian being alphabetic. The publication of Niebuhr's copies in 1774–8 stimulated interest amongst scholars in Europe, and provided material and incentive for attempts at decipherment. The scholar who achieved the most notable early success was the German G. F. Grotefend, of Göttingen. The principles of his method have often been told and will not be repeated here; suffice it to say that in 1802 he was able to publish a paper assigning correct values to about a third of the characters of the Old Persian cuneiform alphabet. The credit for the complete decipherment must go to an Englishman, Henry Creswicke Rawlinson, whom we shall meet later.

Let us return to Mesopotamia. A number of travellers had sent inscribed bricks and other curios back to Europe, but there had been no scientific excavation. The first attempt at this began within a decade of Grotefend's researches, partly under their stimulus. The man concerned was Claudius James Rich. Born in France of English parents in 1785, he was in 1803 appointed to a cadetship in the East India Company on the strength of an exceptional facility in learning oriental languages. After travelling for several years in the Near East to perfect his Arabic and Turkish, he arrived in Bombay in late 1807, taking up residence with Sir James Mackintosh, Recorder of Bombay, a distinguished Scottish philosopher and a most cultured man. By the spring of 1808, Rich had both married Sir James' eldest daughter and been appointed – when still not twenty-four – to the prestigious post of Resident in Baghdad, which had just fallen vacant. Once settled in Mesopotamia, then part of the Ottoman empire, Rich did a great deal for British commercial and political interests and – more to the point in the present context – for archaeology. His father-in-law deserves some of the credit for the last, as we see from the advice given in a letter from Sir James to Rich:

> Notwithstanding the investigation in the neighbourhood of Hilla by Pietro della Valle, Niebuhr and Beauchamp, much remains to be done respecting the antiquities of Babylon. Major Rennell . . . says, that 'the position and extent of the city walls might probably be ascertained even at this day, as both the rampart and the ditch must have left visible traces. The delineation and description of the site and remains, would prove one of the most curious pieces of antiquity that has been exhibited in modern times'. This is an object worthy of your curiosity and talents. Your talent for drawing will be of important service. . . . What invaluable antiquities there would be if you could find any such!

In conformity with his father-in-law's suggestion, Rich undertook the first scientific excavations (as distinct from digging for mementoes) at Babylon, publishing in 1813 his *Memoir on the ruins of Babylon*, followed by a *Second Memoir* in 1818. This beginning of

Mesopotamian archaeology was immortalized by Byron, who wrote of

> *. . . some infidels, who don't*
> *Because they can't, find out the very spot*
> *Of that same Babel, or because they won't*
> *(Though Claudius Rich, Esquire, some bricks has got,*
> *And written lately two memoirs upon't).*

In the summer of 1820, to escape the appalling heat of Baghdad, Rich undertook a journey of exploration through the mountains of Kurdistan. Returning via Erbil and Mosul, he made some valuable observations upon Assyrian sites. Everywhere he recognized and recorded evidence of ancient remains, such as 'a high artificial mount [today we would say 'mound'] of ancient date' at Kermalis. (This Assyrian site, otherwise spelt Karamles, remains unidentified.) At Erbil, he ascertained that the vast ancient mound dominating the modern city contained masses of brickwork, although he associated this with the Persians rather than with the Assyrians. He also gave the most thorough examination and description of the ruins of Nineveh up to that time and, with the help of a Greek navigator, surveyed the area to produce a valuable plan of the site of Nineveh (plate 17).

The southernmost of the two principal mounds of Nineveh is named Nebi Yunus (Arabic for 'the prophet Jonah') and is by the local Muslims regarded as of such sanctity, because of the mosque which surmounts it and its association with Jonah, that to this day it has been impossible to undertake major excavations. Assyrian remains do, however, come to light in the course of building or repairing houses, and Rich took full advantage of this. He writes:

Nebbi Yunus . . . contains about three hundred houses, and is built on an ancient artificial mount, the whole of which it does not cover. Its antiquity is well ascertained by the remains found on digging into it very deep; when fragments of bricks, whole bricks, and pieces of gypsum, covered with inscriptions in the cuneiform character, are found. . . . Today we were shown some fragments built up in the foundations of houses. One of these, a broken piece of gypsum with cuneiform characters, was in the kitchen of a wretched house, and appeared to be part of the wall of a small passage which is said to reach far into the mount. Some people dug into it last year; but as it went under the houses, and they were afraid of undermining them, they closed it up again with rubbish. . . . A little farther on, in a small room occupied by the women of an inhabitant of the town, who very politely went out to allow us to inspect it at our leisure, was another inscription, in very large cuneiform letters, on a piece of gypsum. . . . This inscription is the more curious, as it seems to occupy its original position. . . . I doubt not but many other antiquities might be found in this mound; but the greater part of it is thickly covered with a labyrinth of small houses, and it is only on the repairing or falling down of these that such things are discovered.

Later, Rich made a thorough surface examination of the larger of the two principal mounds of Nineveh, Kuyunjik, describing it thus:

Its sides are very steep, its top nearly flat. . . . The perpendicular height is forty-three feet; the total circumference 7691 feet. . . . The top of the mount does not wear the appearance of ever having been greatly higher than it is at present; but it evidently has had building on it, at least round its edges. Stones and bricks are dug or ploughed up every where. . . . A piece of fine brick or pottery, covered with exceedingly small and beautiful cuneiform writing, was found while we were looking about the mount.

Rich was, of course, acquainted with traditions equating the ruins near Mosul with Nineveh, but had no scientific proof of the identification. He was content to say this of the remains he had seen at Nebi Yunus, Kuyunjik and the surrounding walls: 'Whether they belonged to Nineveh or some other city is another question, and one not so easily determined, but that they are all of the same age and character does not admit of a doubt.'

Rich also drew attention to the importance of the mound of Qal'ah Shergat, which we now know to be the site of the ancient capital city of Ashur, and provided a sketch (shown here) and description:

It is a mount of earth surrounded at the foot by a ruined wall, the whole elevated on a platform of ruins. Heaps of rubbish were scattered about, in which might be seen lines of stone-masonry with lime cement; on the surface, fragments of building, and large square bricks. . . . These ruins are well worth investigation. They form a mass of about twenty feet high, extending north and south along the west bank of the river for nearly two miles.

Later in the same year Rich was at Shiraz in Persia when a cholera epidemic broke out. 'The prince, with all his family, all the chief nobles, and the higher classes, and such of the lower as were able, deserted the town. Mr Rich refused to quit the place, and continued nobly to exert himself to quiet the alarm of the inhabitants, and to assist the sick and dying.' He himself contracted the disease and died, aged only thirty-five. His collection of Mesopotamian antiquities was acquired by the British Museum.

Botta, Layard and Rawlinson: the Fathers of Assyriology

Major excavations in Assyria began some twenty years after the death of Rich. Two factors in particular came into play to bring this about. The first, and the most significant, was the general interest in antiquities amongst the upper classes. This had begun as early as the sixteenth century; Henry VIII, for example, had given his Chaplain the title 'King's Antiquary'. During the eighteenth century this interest became widespread, and by the end of the century the fashion of collecting antiquities had developed throughout Europe. Charles Dickens pokes kindly fun at this in *Pickwick Papers* (published in 1836–7), with Mr Pickwick excitedly discovering a wayside stone inscribed

+

BILST

UM

PSHI

S. M.

ARK

on which he 'wrote a Pamphlet, containing ninety-six pages of very small print, and twenty-seven different readings of the inscription'. For this he was rewarded by election as 'an honorary member of seventeen native and foreign societies, for making the discovery'.

The other factor in the beginning of major excavation in Assyria was political. Various European countries, notably France and Great Britain, were interested in India and were looking for fast land routes for their communications with it. Therefore, both France and Great Britain took every possible means to increase their influence in the relevant areas, mainly Egypt, Mesopotamia and Persia. One such means, in the conditions of the mid-nineteenth century, was archaeology. Let it be said at once that there is not the slightest suggestion here that European archaeology in the Near East was at its beginning, or ever has been subsequently, a cover for espionage or subversion. It can, however, and often does, have the wholly honourable consequences both of gaining knowledge of local conditions and of forging local links of friendship. In the circumstances of the 1840s this was likely to contribute to the influence of the European country within the area concerned in the Near East.

In 1842 the French government established a consulate in Mosul, and appointed to it Paul Emile Botta, a remarkable man who was not only a good Arabist already experienced in the consular service, but who earlier, after being educated as a doctor, had gone round the world on a botanical expedition. Although his attitudes could be violently anti-British, this did not prevent him from making warm friendships with individual Englishmen, one of whom said that Botta had 'once or twice alarmed . . . the French Ambassador at Constantinople, by wonderful stories about our intrigues at Baghdad'. The Asiatic Society of Paris, impressed by Rich's collection of antiquities in the British Museum, promised Botta full support for any archaeological work he might undertake. He began excavations at Kuyunjik in December 1842, but with little significant result – because, as we now know, he was not digging to sufficient depth. In March 1843 he shifted his operations to the mound of Khorsabad, ten miles north-west of Mosul. Within days his workmen had come upon walls of stone slabs carved with scenes in bas relief. When news of this sensational find reached Paris, the French government put substantial funds at the disposal of Botta to continue the work. What he had found, though no one at that time knew it, was a palace built by Sargon II at his new capital, Dur-Sharrukin.

Now there comes on the scene another Englishman, one of the giants of Mesopotamian archaeology, Henry Austen Layard. His surname was pronounced as 'Laird', not – as Assyriologists usually mis-render it – bisyllabically as 'Lay-ard'. Born in Paris in 1817, and brought up until the age of twelve in Florence, he was eventually articled to his maternal uncle, a well-to-do London solicitor, and in June 1839 found himself a duly admitted attorney of Queen's Bench. At the advice of his father's younger brother, who had recently retired from high office in the Ceylon Civil Service, he decided to go out to Ceylon, where his qualifications would allow him to practise as a barrister, and where his family connection promised success. For his proposed journey he joined with a certain Edward Mitford, several years his senior, and the two set off in July 1839, travelling overland from Brussels. Layard's enthusiasm for travel was not unaccompanied by intelligent foresight. Before leaving he

299

took steps to learn something of navigation, routes, customs and peoples, received elementary instruction in medicine and first-aid, and learnt Arabic script and a little Persian. In addition, he read everything available to him on Mesopotamia and Persia, and, as he put it, 'such treatises as had then been published . . . on the cuneiform . . . writing'. By November the two men were in Aleppo, and – after detours in which Layard nearly lost his life from hostile tribes – reached Mosul in April 1840. There they were guests of William Francis Ainsworth, a much-travelled physician with antiquarian interests who had just published *Researches in Assyria, Babylonia and Chaldaea*, and of Christian Rassam, a native Christian who ably served as British vice-consul. Layard spent much of his time in Mosul upon the mound of Kuyunjik, 'taking measurements and searching for fragments of marble and bricks with cuneiform inscriptions'. Their hosts also took the travellers into the desert to see other ruined cities, and Layard describes the impression they made on him: 'The scene around is worthy of the ruin (the traveller) is contemplating; desolation meets desolation; a feeling of awe succeeds to wonder. These huge mounds of Assyria made a deeper impression upon me, gave rise to more serious thoughts and more earnest reflection, than the temples of Balbec and the theatres of Ionia.'

But the intended destination was still Ceylon. Layard and Mitford went on to Baghdad, where they joined a caravan travelling into Persia. There obstacles awaited them. They were prohibited from taking the particular eastward route they had proposed, as this led through disputed territory, but were offered alternatives. Mitford accepted, and the two separated. Layard, hoping eventually to get his way, went south to Isfahan, but on finding himself still baulked decided on a detour into Luristan – the mountains of the central Zagros. Part of the attraction was to locate the ruins of the biblical Shushan (A.V. of Nehemiah 1: 1, Esther 2: 8), known to be in that region although the site was in dispute. Layard spent ten months (September 1840 to July 1841) in those mountains with the Bakhtiari tribe, dividing his time between examination of ruins, gaining exact knowledge of the possibilities of the area for trade, and political intrigue in support of the tribe, which was on the brink of rebellion against the Shah. After the Shah's capture of the khan (chief) of the tribe, Layard was put under open arrest. In August 1841, having now abandoned the objective of proceeding to Ceylon, he escaped back to Basra, in Ottoman territory. He sent an account of his travels in Luristan to the *Journal of the Royal Geographical Society*, which published a summary in 1842. After further journeys in south Mesopotamia and neighbouring Persia, to examine both antiquities and trade prospects, he decided in summer 1842 to return to England. At this time Colonel Taylor, British Resident in Baghdad, was concerned that Sir Stratford Canning, British Ambassador in Istanbul (at that time known as Constantinople), should have full details of border disputes between the Ottoman and Persian empires which were affecting British interests. Layard was to travel via Istanbul, and so, in view of his first-hand knowledge of the disputed area, Taylor took the opportunity of entrusting him with letters for Canning, with the understanding that he should put himself at Canning's disposal to provide supplementary information if required.

Layard set out on horseback under the protection of a Tatar (government dispatch-bearer). A fortunate three-day wait in Mosul resulted in his becoming acquainted with the newly appointed French consul, Botta, who treated him with great consideration, escorting him over the ruins at Kuyunjik and Nebi Yunus.

In Constantinople Layard made a good impression on Canning, who was glad to avail himself of his expert knowledge. Not wishing to lose the services of this potentially valuable young man, the ambassador devised an assignment for him, inviting him to go on a fact-finding mission into what is now Yugoslavia, where disturbances threatened European interests. Subsequently Layard served as the ambassador's private secretary, forming a useful front through which the ambassador could exercise influence, as in editorial involvement in a Mediterranean newspaper, the *Malta Times*.

When Botta made his spectacular finds at Khorsabad in March 1843, he generously sent Layard a private account of them. Layard used these to stimulate the interest of Canning – already known as a patron of antiquarianism – in excavation in Mesopotamia.

We now meet another Englishman, who shares with Layard and Botta the credit for the beginning of Assyriology. Henry Creswicke Rawlinson, a good classical scholar and a fine athlete, was an officer in the East India Company. Having acquired a good knowledge of Arabic and Persian, he was posted to the intelligence department, and in 1835 was seconded to Persia as military adviser to the Shah's brother. There he devoted his spare time to copying ancient inscriptions on rocks, the most extensive and important of these being a very large trilingual inscription high up on a cliff at a place called Bisitun (or Behistun), near Kermanshah.

In 1843 Rawlinson was appointed resident in Baghdad in succession to Colonel Taylor. This gave him time to work on the decipherment of the Bisitun inscriptions, and he soon effected a complete decipherment of the Old Persian alphabet, begun by Grotefend some forty years before. In early 1845, we find Rawlinson initiating a correspondence with Layard, prompted partly by articles Layard had written in the *Malta Times* about Botta's excavations, and partly by notes on inscriptions which he had left with Colonel Taylor. Rawlinson knew of some inscriptions that Layard had copied but requested details of any further examples, which might be of help in the analysis being undertaken by him.

Meanwhile Botta, after overcoming the opposition of the governor of Mosul which had caused delays, had been continuing his excavations at Khorsabad, with spectacular results. He closed his excavation in October 1844. A selection of the best preserved finds, including huge stone bull-colossi, were sent down the Tigris by raft and on by ship to France.

Botta's success gave a great stimulus to Mesopotamian excavation. Rawlinson was anxious that some British effort should be made, and he himself undertook some small-scale digging in south Iraq. Writing in October 1845, he told Layard:

> I should be exceedingly glad if the Ambassador and through him the Govt. could be induced to take an interest in the antiquities of this country. It pains me grievously to see the French monopolize the field, for the fruits of Botta's labour, already achieved and still in progress, are not things to pass away in a day but will constitute a nation's glory in future ages, when perhaps the Turkish Empire that we are now struggling so hard to preserve shall be but a matter of history.

By this time, however, Layard had already persuaded the ambassador to support him financially for a limited period of excavations in Mesopotamia. A memorandum, written in Canning's hand, with the date pencilled in (not by Canning) as 9 Oct. 1845, reads:

> I rely upon Mr Layard's obliging attention to the following points
>
> 1 To keep me informed of his operations, and of any objects of sufficient interest and curiosity which he may see or discover.
> 2 To keep clear of political and religious questions, and as much as possible of missionaries, or native chiefs in tribes regarded with enmity or jealousy by the Turkish authorities.
> 3 To cultivate the goodwill of the Pashas and others of the Sultan's functionaries by all becoming means.
> 4 To bear in mind that his professed character will be that of a traveller, fond of antiquities, of picturesque scenery, and of the manners peculiar to Asia.
> 5 Not to start on his return without a previous communication

with me subsequent to his first inquiries and attempts at discovery.

6 In case of success to give me early and exact information as to the nature of the objects discovered, and the best means of removal etc. with an estimate of cost, doing what he can to obtain the necessary permission on the spot.

Besides the allowance of £200 a year, which still continues and the P[iastres] 3,000 already received for outfit, Mr Layard will take from Mr Hanson another sum of P[iastres] 3,000, on account of travelling expenses, and the accompanying letter to Mr Rassam of Moussul, which, besides a general recommendation to kindness and assistance, contains a credit on me for 10,000 turkish piastres. . . .

I reckon on Mr Layard's reaching Moussul towards the end of October, and being able to complete a fair experiment of discovery in the most probable spots during the two ensuing months. Should he have reasons for adding another ten days or fortnight, he is at liberty to follow his own discretion.

Rawlinson was delighted when he heard of Layard's arrival in Mosul (27 October 1845), and ready with advice. Layard already had a clear idea of what he wanted to do. After presenting his credentials to the tyrannical governor of Mosul, though without telling him his objective, he proceeded at once to put his plan into operation. Caution was essential, as he had no formal permission from the Ottoman authorities to undertake excavations. Giving out that he was going to hunt wild boar, he set off down the Tigris on a *kelek*, accompanied by his friend Henry James Ross, a British merchant in Mosul, and by a guard, a servant and a mason, with tools made in Rassam's workshop. His destination was Nimrud, a spectacular *tell* about twenty miles south of Mosul, standing forty feet above the plain, and covering some sixty acres, with the remains of its ziggurat as a prominent hill at the north-west corner (see plate 9A). He describes how, on an earlier occasion, when travelling to Baghdad by *kelek* in April 1840, he had seen Nimrud from the Tigris (he had already had a distant view from the desert) and resolved one day to excavate it:

I again saw the ruins of Nimroud, and had a better opportunity of examining them. It was evening as we approached the spot. The spring rains had clothed the mound with the richest verdure, and the fertile meadows, which stretched around it, were covered with flowers of every hue. Amidst this luxuriant vegetation were partly concealed a few fragments of bricks, pottery, and alabaster,

upon which might be traced the well-defined wedges of the cuneiform character. A long line of consecutive narrow mounds, still
retaining the appearance of walls or ramparts, stretched from the
base of the ruins, and formed a vast quadrangle.

Layard found the village nearest to Nimrud almost deserted in
consequence of the depredations of the rascally governor of Mosul.
The only man present was a sheikh whose tribe had also been
plundered and dispersed and who had taken refuge in a hovel there.
Layard used him to organize labour from nearby settlements to assist
in the excavations.

Digging began on 9 November 1845. Success was immediate. A
week later Layard was able to write to Canning:

> Having opened a trench . . . I came at once upon a chamber 25
> feet long and 14 broad, formed by slabs of marble 8½ feet in
> length, also each slab containing an inscription in the cuneiform
> character. . . . After four days's labor a slight fever . . . compelled
> me to return to Mosul. I left the excavations under the charge of
> my cawass [guard], with orders to clear the chamber.

Layard took the opportunity of his return to Mosul to come to
an understanding about his operations with the governor. He told
Canning: 'I called upon the Pasha, who had already been informed
that I had discovered treasures, and explained to him the nature
of my researches. He offered no objection, and I avoided asking
permission to continue the excavations.'

The problem was not only the governor. Layard knew that the
French consul, M. Rouet, Botta's successor, was stirring up local
prejudice to get his excavations stopped. With a view both to establishing priority and to completing as much as he could before steps
were taken to interrupt him, he had agents open trenches at six
other Assyrian mounds, for which Canning commended him. He
himself continued at Nimrud. There at the end of November he
found stone slabs bearing a splendid series of bas reliefs of scenes of
Assyrian warfare. He had just reported this success to Canning when
the French machinations resulted in the governor bringing his work
to a halt. But this was a very temporary setback, which Layard
managed to circumvent through his friendship with the officer in
charge of the pasha's local troops. He was hoping to find large
sculptures, and soon did so, on 19 December being able to report to
Canning the finding of 'two winged bulls of great size' – limestone
monsters some fourteen feet high. Botta had found similar colossi,

the reports of which had made a great noise in Europe, though the sculptures themselves had not yet reached France.

Layard continued to suffer intermittent interference with his excavations, for which he still had no formal permission. But one of his gifts was skill in overcoming opposition, and he continued to excavate and to record and interpret his finds – bas reliefs, inscriptions and colossal stone bulls and lions. But dirt-archaeology was not enough for him: he also occupied himself in attempting to decipher the Assyrian inscriptions. Down in Baghdad, Rawlinson was doing the same, and although he was at this time well ahead of any competition (he had already completed his decipherment of the Old Persian script), he treated Layard's views on the Assyrian inscriptions with respect, and sought his opinions.

Canning was enthusiastic about Layard's results and the public interest they were likely to attract. So far he had financed Layard privately, but he planned, on his return to England shortly, to take up with the prime minister, Sir Robert Peel, the question of governmental support comparable to that given by France to Botta. Meanwhile he exerted himself to obtain (May 1846) a vizirial letter giving Layard authority to excavate in the Mosul district. It reads:

Letter of the Grand Vizier to the Pasha of Mosul. 5th May, 1846.

There are, as your Excellency knows, in the vicinity of Mosul quantities of stones and ancient remains. An English gentleman has come to these parts to look for such stones, and has found on the banks of the Tigris, in certain uninhabited places, ancient stones on which there are pictures and inscriptions. The British Ambassador has asked that no obstacles shall be put in the way of the above-mentioned gentleman taking the stones which may be useful to him, including those which he may discover by excavations . . . nor of his embarking them for transport to England.

The sincere friendship which firmly exists between the two governments makes it desirable that such demands be accepted. Therefore no obstacle should be put in the way of his taking the stones which . . . are present in desert places, and are not being utilized; or of his undertaking excavations in uninhabited places where this can be done without inconvenience to anyone; or of his taking such stones as he may wish amongst those which he has been able to discover.

It was not only Canning who was impressed by Layard's finds. English and American society had at that time a deep vein of Old Testament piety, and the history of the ancient Hebrew kingdoms of Israel and Judah was a living thing, as generally known as British history. There were many people at that time who were like the lady of whom Matthew Prior wrote:

Some parts of the Bible by heart she recited,
And much in historical chapters delighted.

Everyone knew that the Assyrians had led away into exile the ten tribes of the northern kingdom of Israel, and that Sennacherib, through his general Rabshakeh, had vainly besieged the holy city of Jerusalem; these things were part of British and American cultural consciousness. For the minority learned in ancient history, the finds of Botta and Layard might have an importance for human culture generally, but for most people the impact was biblical. Here were monuments directly illustrating the Word of God. A pious American friend spelt this out to Layard: 'You can scarcely dream of the importance which your solitary labors may have upon the right understanding of the Historical and Prophetical parts of the Holy Word.' Others saw the same point but were more cynical. A close friend of Layard, writing from Constantinople, told him: 'If you can . . . attach a Biblical importance to your discoveries you will come the complete dodge over this world of fools and dreamers: you can get some religious fellow to inspire you with the necessary cant, for which I won't think a bit the worse of you.'

In addition to his major finds of bas reliefs and colossi at Nimrud, Layard had had successes in his soundings elsewhere. 'Several trenches', he wrote, 'had been opened in the great mound of Baasheikha;* and fragments of sculpture and inscriptions, with entire pottery and inscribed bricks, had been discovered there. At Karamles a platform of brickwork had been uncovered, and the Assyrian origin of the ruin was proved by the inscription on the bricks, which contained the name of the Khorsabad king.'

Clearly, Layard was now able to understand the cuneiform script sufficiently for him to be able to identify which groups of signs were the king's name, and to interrelate names at different sites.

So far Layard had abstained from digging in the great mound of Kuyunjik, just across the Tigris from Mosul, as, in the absence of formal permission for excavations, he feared interruptions from the people of Mosul. Now, armed with the vizirial letter, he could begin there with impunity. The only opposition he met was from

---

*This was the name of the village. The mound, more extensively excavated by an American expedition in the 1930s, is called Tell Billa, which represents ancient Assyrian Shibaniba.

he French consul, who claimed prior rights there, a claim Layard
disregarded.

Since the supersession of Botta by Rouet, there had been unplea-
ant rivalry between French and English. This had already found its
way into print. A friend writing to Layard from Constantinople on
3 June 1846 told him: 'A few months ago there appeared in the
Literary Gazette a letter from Constantinople, speaking in somewhat
extravagant terms of the labours of Rouet and depreciatingly of
yours. I should like therefore to be enabled to write something
authentic to the Editor as to the comparative results of these
excavations.'

There was another aspect of this rivalry – to be the first to get
Assyrian finds on display in Europe. Botta had already sent specimens off, but these had been delayed at Baghdad. Knowing this,
Layard had written to Canning as early as December 1845: 'I think
we might manage to transmit our sculpture to Europe as soon if
not sooner than the French. This will be very important for our
reputation.' Rawlinson keenly seconded this idea, and wrote to
Canning to offer the use of an East India Company steamer stationed
on the Lower Tigris. He elaborated on this to Layard:

If you could have a chamber or two cleared out by the beginning
of March and the rafts ready, I would send up the steamer at that
time with tackles. . . . They might be in England in the Autumn,
before the French . . . have time to look about them. The priority
of European exhibition would I think be a great triumph for
us. . . . I have written to the Ambassador on the subject of the
steamer's ascent of the river, pointing out the political advantage
of showing our flag on the upper Tigris.

But rapids prevented the steamer's getting up the river as far as
Nimrud, and in the event Layard's antiquities were (as those of
Botta had been) floated down to Baghdad by raft. The French finally
won the contest by three months, putting Botta's finds on display
in the Louvre Museum in May 1847, whilst the first twelve stone
slabs of bas reliefs found by Layard went on show in the British
Museum in August.

The work for which Rouet had received commendation in the
Literary Gazette was, in fact, little more than the fag-end of what
Botta had done at Khorsabad, although he had reported some reliefs
on a cliff face at another site. Layard visited Khorsabad in high
summer of 1846 and reported: 'Since M. Botta's departure the chambers had been partly filled up by the falling in of the trenches; the
sculptures were rapidly perishing; and, shortly, little will remain of

307

this remarkable monument.' He adds the interesting statement tha early Arab geographers describe Khorsabad as occupying the site o an ancient city called 'Saraghoun' – further evidence of the reliability of oral tradition, inasmuch as 'Saraghoun' is manifestly a form o 'Sargon', which had been an element in the city's ancient name.

Layard spent a month or more from the end of August 184(travelling in the mountains north of Mosul. He returned to Mosu to find that Canning, back in England, had obtained official suppor for the excavations. Canning wrote:

> The British Museum undertakes Nimrood in my stead. Th(Treasury allows £2000. You are the agent. You will have £50(for yourself, besides £100 for your expenses home. My outla) will be repaid. A sum between £1000 and £1100 will be applicabl(to the continuation of your works, including the embarkation o the spoils. You are to finish all by the end of next June.

But Layard considered this financial provision niggardly:

> The grant was small, and I was doubtful whether I should be abl(to fulfil the expectations which appeared to have beer formed. . . . The sum given to M. Botta for the excavations a Khorsabad alone, greatly exceeded the whole grant to th(Museum, which was to include private expenses, those o carriage, and many extraordinary outlays inevitable in th(East. . . . I determined, however, to accept the charge . . . anc to economise as far as it was in my power – that the natior might possess as extensive a collection of Assyrian antiquities as considering the smallness of the means, it was possible to collect

Layard went on to outline his difficulties. 'Many of the sculptures' he said, 'were in too dilapidated a condition to be removed. Photography was not yet available, and a record could only be mad(by drawing. Layard pointed out: 'There was no inclination to senc an artist to assist me. . . . I had therefore to superintend the excava tions; to draw all the bas-reliefs discovered; to copy and compar(the innumerable inscriptions; to take casts of them; and to presid(over the moving and packing of the sculptures.' He also had tc build houses for himself and his workmen, and to organize defenc(against raiding Arab tribes. Further, it was to him that the Arab preferred to bring their private disputes and domestic quarrels fo decision, so much so that in one case it fell to him to find a husbanc for a girl who had invoked his protection.

He resumed large-scale excavations at Nimrud in November 1846 when his finds included more bas reliefs of the highest interest. He gives some graphic descriptions of the various groups; for example:

The lower series of bas-reliefs contained three subjects – the siege of a castle, the king receiving prisoners, and the king, with his army, crossing a river. The besiegers have brought a battering-ram (attached to a moveable tower, apparently constructed of wicker-work) up to the outer wall, from which many stones have already been dislodged and are falling. One of the besieged has succeeded in catching the ram by a chain, and is endeavouring to raise or move it from its place. . . . Another is throwing fire (traces of the red paint being still retained in the sculpture) from above, upon the engine. The besiegers endeavour to quench the flame, by pouring water upon it from two spouts in the moveable tower. Two figures, in full armour, are undermining the walls with instruments like blunt spears; whilst two others appear to have found a secret passage into the castle.

In addition to the bas reliefs, Layard also found iron and copper scale-armour and helmets, vessels of alabaster and of glass, a further colossal winged bull, and a black marble obelisk six and a half feet high. The best description of this last is by Layard himself:

It was sculptured on the four sides; there were in all twenty small bas-reliefs, and above, below, and between them was carved an inscription 210 lines in length. The whole was in the best preservation; scarcely a character of the inscription was wanting; the figures were as sharp and well defined as if they had been carved but a few days before. The king is twice represented, followed by his attendants; a prisoner is at his feet, and his vizir and eunuchs are introducing men leading various animals, and carrying vases and other objects of tribute. . . . The animals are the elephant, the rhinoceros, the Bactrian or two-humped camel, the wild bull, the lion, the stag, and various kinds of monkeys. Amongst the objects carried by the tribute-bearers, may perhaps be distingui-shed the tusks of the elephant, shawls, vases of the precious metals, fruit, and bars of metal, or bundles of rare wood.

Nimrud contains a number of palaces of different periods within the ninth and eighth centuries. Most of the major finds so far mentioned were from the north-west palace, but Layard was also working on a palace in the south-west corner of the mound. Here he found antiquities of similar type, with differences which he carefully recorded, recognizing them as indications of a different date. One

THE MIGHT THAT WAS ASSYRIA

of the factors which gave Layard's work unique importance in the recovery of Assyria was his art expertise, the consequence of his upbringing in Florence, which enabled him to see at once, as others could not, the sequence in time of comparable pieces of sculpture.

Nowadays it is regarded as almost an indecency to ask an archaeologist what he has found; as likely as not he will answer primly that he is looking for answers to problems, not for objects. But Layard had a more robust attitude and was rewarded with considerable tangible success. He was able to send off another large cargo of finds for its destined final home in the British Museum. As he reports:

> On Christmas Day [1846] I had the satisfaction of seeing a raft, bearing twenty-three cases, in one of which was the obelisk, floating down the river. I watched them until they were out of sight, and then galloped into Mosul to celebrate the festivities of the season, with the few Europeans whom duty or business had collected in this remote corner of the globe.

After his Christmas break, Layard continued his excavations at Nimrud, mainly in the north-west palace, for the first three months of 1847. One of his most interesting finds was a chamber full of carved ivories; and there were also rooms with wall paintings in red, blue, black, and white, which unfortunately he was unable to preserve. There were many other important discoveries, which there is no space to mention here, but which are fascinatingly described in Layard's own writings. He sums up his work at Nimrud:

> The ruins were, of course, very inadequately explored; but with the very small sum at my disposal I was unable to pursue my researches to the extent that I could have wished. . . . I have left a great part of the mound of Nimroud to be explored by those who may hereafter succeed me in the examination of the ruins of Assyria.

As we shall later see, the challenge thrown down was taken up a century later, with great success, by M. E. L. (later Sir Max) Mallowan, husband of Agatha Christie.

When he eventually published his results, Layard incorrectly identified Nimrud with Nineveh, which is in fact represented by Kuyunjik and Nebi Yunus. The mistake did not originate with Layard, who left the question open for a long time; it was due to Rawlinson, who wrote to Layard on 10 December 1845:

> I have lately examined with some attention the geographical and

historical questions connected with Nimrud, and I can come to no other conclusion than that it is the original Nineveh which was destroyed under Sardanapalus, the ruins at Nebi Yoonus being those of the second Nineveh, that of the lower Assyrian dynasty.

Rawlinson was not as far out as might appear. If one simply substitutes 'capital of Assyria' for 'Nineveh', what Rawlinson said is correct. His idea that Nimrud was an older capital, subsequently replaced by one of which Nebi Yunus was part, is accurate, although the name 'Nineveh' belongs only to the later capital.

Layard was not content with excavating Nimrud and Kuyunjik. He had heard tales from visiting Arabs of the site Qal'ah Shergat (Arabic for 'castle of earth') on the Tigris about sixty miles south of Mosul. He tells us: 'An Arab, from the Shammar [the principal tribe of the Jazirah], would occasionally spend a night amongst my workmen, and entertain them with accounts of idols and sculptured figures of giants, which had long been the cause of wonder and awe to the wandering tribes, who . . . pitch their tents near the place.' The site was, he says, 'notoriously dangerous, being a place of rendezvous for all plundering parties', but tribal movements now presented circumstances whereby he could hope to dig there in comparative safety. He found it a wild spot: 'We started for the ruins in the afternoon, and rode along the edge of the jungle. Hares, wolves, foxes, jackals and wild boars continually crossed our path, and game of all kinds seemed to abound. . . . Lions are sometimes found near Kalah Shergat. . . . As I floated down to Baghdad a year before, I had heard the roar of a lion not far from this spot.' He had sent a party of workmen some days in advance to begin digging. A headless statue of a sitting figure in black basalt had already been found. Layard's excellent progress in understanding the cuneiform script enabled him at once to place it in relation to the finds at Nimrud:

The block, upon which the figure sat, was covered on three sides with a cuneiform inscription. The first line, containing the name and titles of the king, was almost defaced; but one or two characters enabled me to restore a name, identical with that on the great bulls in the centre of the mound at Nimroud. On casting my eye down the first column of the inscription, I found the names of his father (the builder of the most ancient palace of Nimroud), and of his grandfather, which at once proved that the reading was correct. An Arab soon afterwards brought me a brick bearing a short legend, which contained the three names entire. I was thus

311

enabled to fix the comparative epoch of the newly-discovered ruins.

We know now that the king he called the 'grandfather' was Tukulti-Ninurta II (890–884), the 'builder of the most ancient palace of Nimroud' was Ashur-nasir-pal II (883–859), and the statue in black basalt his son Shalmaneser III (858–824). The sitting figure now graces the Nimrud Central Saloon of the British Museum.

Deteriorating security at Qal'ah Shergat deprived Layard of the opportunity of further work there beyond a quick survey, and the main excavation of the site had to await a German expedition in the years immediately before the Great War. Layard returned to Nimrud to complete his principal excavations and to arrange the transport of a colossal winged bull and lion. This he did by means of rollers and a specially made cart, which was dragged by about three hundred men, encouraged by musicians and shrieking women, the mile or so from the mound of Nimrud to the bank of the Tigris. There they were left to await a rise in the river which would enable the colossi to be slid on to a *kelek*.

In consequence of a severe drought, the inhabitants of all the villages around Nimrud had gone to the hills, where they might hope to be able to raise a little grain; the pastoral Arab tribes had also moved northwards. There were thus no Arabs around other than Layard's own workmen. As soon as a rise in the river made it possible to embark the sculptures, these workmen, supposing that Layard was now wholly dependent upon their assistance, went on strike for higher wages. Layard was not a man to be brow-beaten. He let them go, and off most of them went, although some families refused to desert him. But a nomadic tribe, with whose chief Layard was on very friendly terms, was still within reach, and on receipt of a message by horseman, he provided Layard with sufficient men to complete the embarkation. The strikers then returned, offering their services on any terms, but Layard was able to manage without them.

After the sculptures had gone off, Layard, in accordance with the instructions of the British Museum Trustees, reburied such antiquities as were still exposed. He left Nimrud in the middle of May 1847. As he still had a small sum of money left from his grant, he determined to apply this to excavations at Kuyunjik. What he was really doing was staking a firm British claim there, to forestall the most recently appointed French consul, M. Guillois, who was making an application to excavate. Layard was quite explicit about his object when he wrote to Canning on 14 June 1847:

I have carried on the excavation in Kouyunjik during the last fortnight and the experiment has been now fairly made. Eight chambers have been partly uncovered. . . . The discovery of this building and the extent to which the excavations have been carried out, I conclude establish our claim to the future examination of this mound should the Trustees be desirous to continue the researches in this country.

The main practical problem in excavating at Kuyunjik, and the one which had frustrated Botta in his attempts there, was the very great depth of soil above the Assyrian level. Layard recognized this, and dug trenches twenty feet deep to reach the Assyrian floors of un-dried brick. Here again he found both bas reliefs and colossal winged bulls. His knowledge of cuneiform told him that the king to whom they belonged was the son of the king who had built Khorsabad; as we know now, the Kuyunjik palace, which represented Nineveh, was built by Sennacherib, whose father was Sargon, builder of Fort Sargon (Khorsabad). He also recorded 'several small oblong tablets of dark unbaked clay, having a cuneiform inscription over the sides'. These were the first indications of the presence of the vast wealth of cuneiform tablets at Kuyunjik, so important subsequently for our detailed knowledge of ancient Mesopotamia.

Layard had been intermittently assisted at Kuyunjik and elsewhere by Henry James Ross (see page 303). As Layard prepared to leave Mesopotamia, the British Museum requested Ross to continue small-scale excavations at Kuyunjik; the primary object was, of course, to retain British rights over the site. Layard left for Constantinople in June 1847, and arrived in England in time for Christmas, after showing his drawings of the Assyrian sculptures to antiquarians in Italy, and spending some days discussing finds with Botta and his colleagues in Paris. His work was already becoming well known in England. As early as November 1846 there had been a meeting at the Royal Institute of British Architects, chaired by Earl de Grey, on Layard's 'description of an Ancient Structure existing at Al Hather, in Mesopotamia, and of some Antiquities recently discovered . . . at Nimroud (the site of Nineveh)'. The first of Layard's finds had been on display in the British Museum since August 1847, and had made a considerable stir with the public. His friends were anxious that he should receive all the credit due to him. Canning wrote: 'You must make the most of the Assyrian antiquities. Do them justice, and do yourself credit, and make the public understand that they have got a prize.' Honours began to come his way. Shortly after his return to England he was elected to the Athenaeum, and in July 1848 was given the honorary degree of D.C.L. by the

University of Oxford. The general public interest in the Assyrian antiquities persuaded the Trustees of the British Museum that excavations should continue in Mesopotamia, preferably under Layard but he was disposed to decline. There were two reasons for this One was financial, since the scale of funds offered by the British Museum was once again niggardly. The other was that, despite his considerable success in archaeology, this remained a hobby for him his real objective was a career in the diplomatic field. He had achieved one step in the latter direction, by appointment as attaché (though unpaid) to Sir Stratford Canning in Constantinople. He left to take up that appointment in November 1848 – as he told a friend 'an unpaid attaché without a sixpence'.

Meanwhile he had been preparing his results for publication There was a volume of drawings of the monuments, which came out in 1849 under the title *The Monuments of Nineveh*. A second publication, which finally appeared in 1851, was *Inscriptions in the Cuneiform Character from Assyrian Monuments* – plates of copies of cuneiform inscriptions so excellently done that they are still of value to scholars over a century and a quarter later. But his masterpiece was *Nineveh and its Remains*, a book in two volumes giving a lively account not only of his excavations mainly at Nimrud (mis-identified in the title as Nineveh), but also of his travels. This book came out at the beginning of 1849. It was not only a success; i was a sensation. Layard was as surprised as pleased. Writing from Constantinople on 5 February, he told a friend: 'I am lost in wonder at the puffs I see of my humble work, and half suspect someone has been hoaxing me. . . . Murray [his publisher] . . . talks of a second edition.' This was an underestimate on the part of the publisher: by early May the book had gone into a third edition, and by July into a fourth. Edwin Norris wrote to Layard from the Foreign Office on 19 February: 'I believe I may congratulate you on having published *the book* of the season. Certainly none is so much spoken of and wherever I go, the question is "what do you think of Layard's book?" No body asks, "Have you read it", that is taken for granted. Everyone who mattered, from Prince Albert down, visited the Assyrian antiquities in the British Museum. Samuel Birch of the British Museum, writing to Layard on 28 March, told him: 'All the world is mad to see the monuments – and the cry is "the bulls – the bulls". . . . I have been daily harassed with the streams of Lords and Ladies who come to see Nimroud.' There was an occasional sour dissenter from the general praise. Rawlinson wrote from Baghdad on 17 January to say: 'What do you mean by the attack on you in the Athenoeum calling you a vandal of the 19th Century Does Bonomi take Nimrud for Athens?' Bonomi, twenty years

314

older than Layard, was an authority on sculpture, with some reputation for drawing Egyptian monuments. He followed up his attack by publishing a very successful work, *Nineveh and its Palaces*, subtitled 'The Discoveries of Botta and Layard, applied to the elucidation of Holy Writ', which was essentially a more wordy and less elegantly written adaptation of Layard's *Nineveh and its Remains*.

In Constantinople Layard still had doubts as to the wisdom of his taking any further part in excavations in Mesopotamia. He now heard, however, that the government had instructed Canning to make his services available for that purpose, and shortly afterwards he learned that he was to be appointed a paid attaché with a salary of £250 per annum, as a mark of the government's 'recognition of his important services to ancient history'. Canning congratulated him: 'I wish you joy of being a *paid* attaché – with your £250 per an. – a little plain pudding after the snap-dragon of glory is no bad thing after all.' Parliament voted £1500 a year for two years for further Mesopotamian excavations, and provision was made for a small staff of an artist, a doctor, and Hormuzd Rassam, younger brother of the vice-consul in Mosul. The British Museum sent him a memorandum, dated 14 July, summarizing the terms of the excavations:

The expedition of which Mr Layard is about to take charge is designed to obtain the amplest and most accurate Information respecting the early Antiquities of Mesopotamia which the means at the disposal of the Trustees can procure.

This information will be supplied to the Museum partly in the form of selected specimens from the sculptured and inscribed Remains and partly in the form of plans of the Buildings discovered Drawings of the Sculptures Copies of the Inscriptions and detailed statements of the several objects and appearances which may present themselves. . . .

The Trustees do not think it expedient to fetter Mr Layard's discretion by any specification of the localities in which his Researches are to be made. His own large experience of the Country and of its monumental sites will be the best guide.

Layard considered the funds placed at his disposal 'miserably small and inadequate', and wrote to a friend: 'I cannot say that the trustees of the B.M. have behaved handsomely – on the other hand I must admit that I have been far too well treated by the public and the one makes up for the other.' He was more specific in his complaint in the following year:

The worst is that the funds are doled out and I am expected to dole out my time too – whereas had a proper sum been given me at once I could have finished in 2 years what under the present circumstances cannot be accomplished in 5 or 6. . . . I am altogether very badly provided – The artist who was sent out to me is far from equal to his work and will not do justice to the discoveries made.

Layard left Constantinople for Mosul in late August 1849. His excavations in his second expedition were more far-ranging than in his first, extending into Babylonia as far south as Nippur, though with little success there because of unsettled conditions. In Assyria his work was mainly divided between Kuyunjik and Nimrud, with some time spent at Qal'ah Shergat and other sites. His method of excavation, where it was practicable, as at Nimrud and Kuyunjik, was to dig down until he had reached the floors of Assyrian chambers, and then work along the walls to find further examples of the slabs of bas reliefs which lined Assyrian palaces. But in the course of clearing floors there were other interesting finds, which at Nimrud included an important collection of bronze objects – bells, weapons, cauldrons, vases and a throne. He also discovered a full-size statue of Ashur-nasir-pal in almost perfect condition. At Kuyunjik, he recovered a huge collection of bas reliefs and some further colossal winged bulls. But his most important find at the latter site was the first large group of cuneiform tablets from Ashurbanipal's library, which, once Babylonian and Assyrian cuneiform writing had been deciphered, was to give the key to the literature, religion, medicine and way of life and thought of the people of ancient Mesopotamia.

Layard's excavations during his second expedition lasted from October 1849 until April 1851. But he was in poor health and had become so depressed at the provision made for his work by the British Museum – 'The expedition has been got up in a scurvy way and I have neither proper funds nor proper assistance. The results will consequently be far from what I anticipated' – that by the spring of 1851 he had resolved to give up archaeology for good. He told a friend: 'I think it almost time to finish with excavations and to turn to the more sober duties of life, to try to make some permanent position for myself.' He maintained this resolve despite efforts to persuade him to undertake a third expedition, and when he returned to England in July he had finally finished with field archaeology. He did, however, fulfil his obligations by publishing two further books – a second series of *The Monuments of Nineveh*, and an account of his second expedition, under the title *Discoveries in the ruins of*

Nineveh and Babylon, which was almost as successful as *Nineveh and its Remains*.

Meanwhile Rawlinson had remained in continual correspondence with Layard, particularly on questions of chronology and of reading the cuneiform script. It would be too long and complex to chronicle here the steps and stages in Rawlinson's progress. We have seen that he had already completely solved the Old Persian cuneiform alphabet by 1845, and by 1849 Layard was satisfied that Rawlinson could read the Assyrian form of cuneiform. He wrote to a friend in England:

Rawlinson has just been here – spending two or three days with me. I gave him a letter to the Guests – a liberty which I should not have taken had not Rawlinson been a real lion. . . . He is a first rate fellow and certainly the first in his line. He will astonish the good people in England with his cuneatic [i.e., cuneiform] discoveries. . . . There is no doubt that he is now in possession of all the preliminary matter in the decypherment of the inscriptions – and the work which he intends to publish whilst in England will give an approximate if not a literal translation of the inscription of the obelisk and most of the important records of Assyria hitherto discovered.

Place and Rassam

During his second expedition, Layard had had as assistant Hormuzd Rassam, a native Christian of Mosul, younger brother of the gentleman who served as British vice-consul, whom Layard had earlier had sent to Oriel College, Oxford to complete his education. When Layard declined to undertake the third expedition planned by the British Museum, he proposed to the Trustees that Rassam should be appointed. This was done, Rassam being sent out in 1852 to excavate under the direction of Rawlinson in Baghdad.

However, at the beginning of January 1852, a new French consul had arrived in Mosul, Victor Place. He informed Rawlinson of his intention of digging at Kuyunjik, and Rawlinson, supposing that Layard had substantially cleared the site from the point of view of objects of major archaeological interest, made no objection. On the arrival of Rassam, who well knew that there was much more to be done at Kuyunjik, this became a source of dispute. Eventually both Place and Rassam were digging simultaneously on different sectors of the site. Rassam had the greater success, discovering not only the splendid series of bas reliefs depicting a lion hunt by Ashurbanipal,

317

which is one of the glories of the British Museum, but also the bulk of that king's library of cuneiform tablets, which, as a representative of the British Museum said afterwards, 'form the foundations of the science of Assyriology'.

Place and Rassam also came into competition for excavating Qal'ah Shergat; neither of these pioneers had any major success there. There was a more satisfactory situation at Nimrud, where Rassam continued Layard's work to good effect, and at Khorsabad. There Place uncovered a hundred and eighty-six further chambers of an Assyrian palace, in addition to the fourteen found by his predecessor Botta. Place had different objectives from Botta and Layard; instead of concentrating on portable finds, he was concerned to recover detailed plans of buildings, and what he uncovered at Khorsabad is still the best example of an Assyrian palace. Place also produced some interesting drawings of restored façades of buildings. Despite the friction over excavation rights, relations between Rawlinson and Place were good, and these two representatives of their nations effected an exchange of monuments from Kuyunjik, Nimrud and Khorsabad for their respective museums. But disaster overtook the French antiquities on their way down the Tigris in 1855. They were sent by *kelek* in the usual way, but a few miles north of the junction of the Tigris with the Euphrates the convoy was attacked by rebellious Arab tribes. Two of the four *keleks* foundered, and their precious cargoes of antiquities disappeared into the waters of the Tigris, where they remain, awaiting such a combination of funds, technology, political stability and luck as will enable them to be recovered.

Both Place and Rassam finished their excavations in 1854. After Rassam's departure a little further work was done at Kuyunjik by another representative of the British Museum in Mesopotamia, W. K. Loftus, whose main work was excavation further south in Babylonia. Interest was in fact now shifting, in terms of archaeology, from Assyria to sites further south, and field archaeology itself was beginning to be overshadowed by the importance of cuneiform tablets. In 1855 Rawlinson resigned from his post of consul-general in Baghdad, and returned to England, where he devoted himself to the decipherment and publication of cuneiform texts. A number of other scholars were also working on decipherment, but there was some scepticism amongst the public as to the reliability of the translations offered. Eventually the Royal Asiatic Society arranged that Rawlinson and three other scholars prominent in decipherment should independently prepare translations of a long new inscription. When the results were compared in 1857, the four translations showed sufficient similarity to prove that the decipherment of the

Babylonian and Assyrian system of cuneiform writing had been substantially effected.

Rawlinson was given overall responsibility by the Trustees of the British Museum for preparing a series of volumes of cuneiform texts, though most of the work of copying was done by other people. Perhaps the most notable of these assistants was a young man, George Smith. He was apprenticed as a bank-note engraver at the age of fourteen, but his considerable interest in biblical history and the relevance of Assyrian antiquities and inscriptions to that subject led him to spend most of his spare time in the British Museum. His interest was noticed and, as he proved to have considerable knowledge of the subject, he was offered employment to make joins to broken pieces of the clay tablets from Nineveh. In doing this, he taught himself to read and to understand the cuneiform script, and in 1866 he was appointed an assistant in the Department of Oriental Antiquities, where he henceforth worked copying tablets for publication.

In 1872 George Smith made a major discovery; he recognized that one of the broken tablets from Kuyunjik on which he was working contained an Assyrian counterpart of the biblical Flood story. England was still a Christian nation with a deep interest in the Bible, and here was, it seemed, proof of the truth of a major Old Testament story. Consequently, when he announced this discovery to the Society of Biblical Archaeology in December, it created a sensation. There were calls for the resumption of excavations at Kuyunjik to find the missing parts of the Flood tablet, and the *Daily Telegraph* offered 1000 guineas for the purpose, with the proviso that George Smith should be sent out to undertake the excavations. He went out in early 1873, and after obstruction from the local governor, began to dig in May. Within a week he found a text fragment with a missing section of the Flood story. Smith returned to England in July, but was sent out a second time, arriving in Mosul at the beginning of 1874. He found several hundred further tablets at Kuyunjik, but his inexperience in dealing with Oriental bureaucracy resulted in the confiscation of some of them. An account of his travels and work, filled out with translations and discussions of cuneiform texts, was published in 1875, under the title *Assyrian Discoveries*. In 1876 George Smith was in the Orient again, but died of dysentery without being able to undertake further excavation.

By this time there was considerable public interest in cuneiform writing in England, reflected in Gilbert and Sullivan's *Pirates of Penzance*, first heard at the end of 1879, where the Major-General's song contains the boast: 'I can write a washing bill in Babylonic cuneiform.' Cuneiform was in fashion, and George Smith's success in finding further tablets at Kuyunjik was a good argument for continuing work there. The obvious person was Hormuzd Rassam, who was sent out in the middle of 1877. After the usual bureaucratic delays he was able to recommence excavations in January 1878, and undertook further campaigns in 1878–9, 1880 and 1882. His success in the matter of collecting texts from Assyrian sites was marked by two groups of tablets, totalling about sixteen hundred texts, bearing his name in volume IV of the British Museum *Catalogue of the Cuneiform Tablets in the Kouyunjik Collection*. One of his more striking finds, at a mound called Balawat twenty miles from Mosul, was a great Assyrian double gate, of wood (which had of course rotted away) overlaid with bronze panels with scenes of warfare in *repoussé* work. These bronze panels, remarkably well preserved, are to be seen in the British Museum. But the greater part of Rassam's efforts was devoted to sites in southern Mesopotamia, not Assyria. There was a general shift of interest: sites in Babylonia were yielding texts in thousands, and for twenty years after Rassam completed his operations in 1882 nothing was done in Assyria.

International Expeditions

Scholars in countries other than England and France had been working on the cuneiform texts and related monuments. An important work published in 1883, which did much to make the significance of Assyriology widely known in German-speaking countries, was E. Schrader's *Keilinschriften und das Alte Testament* [*Cuneiform Inscriptions and the Old Testament*]. This was one of the factors leading to the founding in 1898 of the *Deutsche Orient-Gesellschaft* [*German Oriental Society*] under the patronage of the Kaiser. This society now sponsored excavation at Babylon, which went on continuously from 1899 until 1917, and, of more importance for Assyria, at Qal'ah Shergat, the ancient city Ashur. The work, under W. Andrae, was continuous from 1903 until 1914. Andrae's work was very markedly not a search for tablets or other portable antiquities but a meticulously executed operation in scientific archaeology, with the attempt to recover the plan of the city, its walls and buildings, and their interrelation, at different periods. Earlier Assyrian excavations had concentrated upon the period of spectacular remains from the first half of the first millennium; Andrae took the archaeological history of Assyria back to the third millennium. And although the objective was not primarily tablets, a considerable collection of tablets was found, of the highest importance for Assyrian history, religion, and law.

After the Great War, the British mandate over Iraq gave archaeology there a new dimension. Under the stimulus of Gertrude Bell,
a Department of Antiquities was set up, and in 1924 the Baghdad
Museum was instituted. In the same year, an Antiquities Law was
promulgated, of which the most significant provision was that in
future excavations the Iraqi Department of Antiquities should
receive all unique finds made by foreign expeditions, and one half
of the remainder.

The years between the two world wars were a time when the
most striking results in Mesopotamian archaeology were coming
from Sumerian sites in south Mesopotamia; from this period were
Sir Leonard Woolley's spectacular finds at Ur (1922–34). However,
excavation was once again also going on in Assyria. In 1926–31 an
American expedition dug at sites near Kirkuk, opening a new vista
of second-millennium Assyrian history, generally subsumed under
the name of its best-known city, Nuzi (see page 40). Many thousands
of tablets were found, important for our understanding of ancient
Near Eastern society, including that of the biblical Patriarchs.
American excavations were also undertaken between 1930 and 1938
at two sites about twelve miles north-east of Mosul – Tell Billa,
where Layard had made soundings, and Tepe Gawra. Both sites
were important, in that successive periods of occupation were traced
back to a very early phase, in the case of Tepe Gawra to the Neolithic
period.

Ignoring long-established French excavation rights, between 1929
and 1935 an expedition from the University of Chicago dug at
Khorsabad. The main importance of their results was to make some
corrections to the plans of the city and buildings which Place's team
had published seventy years before. An interesting offshoot of this
was the survey and excavation of a huge aqueduct built by Sennacherib as part of his provision for Nineveh's water supply.

During the same period the British Museum and its associates re-
opened excavations at Kuyunjik (1927–32). The main development
here for the rediscovery of Assyria was that for the first time there
was an attempt to investigate the prehistory of the site, by means
of a deep sounding which traced occupation back to the fifth millennium. This was technically very difficult, as the depth of deposits
meant that the assistant in charge of this sounding, M. E. L.
Mallowan, had to dig a pit to a depth of ninety feet to reach virgin
soil. To obtain further information about the prehistoric levels of
occupation in this area, Mallowan therefore, in 1933, excavated a
nearby site, Arpachiyeh, where the early levels had not been covered
by considerable later occupation.

The wide international aspect of Assyrian research between the two world wars was seen in the participation of an Italian expedition, which in 1933 had a season of excavation at an Assyrian city Kalizi (formerly read Kakzu), south-east of Erbil. Political circumstances prevented a continuation of the work; this was unfortunate from the scientific point of view, as subsequently local inhabitants, digging illicitly, found cuneiform tablets which are now in private possession, unpublished and unread.

The boundaries of ancient Assyria were not precisely co-terminous with those of the northern part of the modern state of Iraq. Consequently there are sites in north-east Syria which are relevant to the history of Assyria, and some of these were also dug, with important results. The most significant of these was Tell Halaf, near the source of the Habur river, dug by Baron Max von Oppenheim just before the Great War and in the late 1920s. This site was important in two main respects, firstly as providing cuneiform documents bearing upon an Assyrian provincial centre, Guzanu (Gozan of 2 Kings 17:6, etc.), and secondly as a site of one of the most important prehistoric cultures of the region which became Assyria. Other major mounds in the Habur area, potentially important for Assyrian history, were being investigated by Mallowan from 1934 until the Second World War brought a suspension of archaeological activities.

The last phase to date of the rediscovery of Assyria began when M. E. L. Mallowan, on behalf of the British School of Archaeology, decided to re-open the excavation of Nimrud in 1949. The work continued intermittently until 1963, directed by him personally or by younger archaeologists under his wing. Most British archaeologists in Mesopotamia seem to model themselves consciously or unconsciously on Layard, but Mallowan filled the mould better than most. He also had, in terms of finds, success comparable with that of Layard and, although few completely new aspects of Assyrian life were opened up (one exception was the quay wall; see page 182), depth and detail were added to our knowledge of Assyria at many points. His very successes have, three decades after his excavations, become a stumbling-block to some later archaeologists who owe much of their scholarly opportunities to his efforts. One lady reviewer, writing in 1981, sniffily referred to Mallowan's approach as 'an unfortunate nineteenth century hang-over . . . perpetuating object-orientated rather than knowledge- and behaviour-orientated goals', and took offence at his thinking of the splendid collection of carved ivories which he discovered as 'treasures'. But the only justification for devoting public funds to archaeology is to enrich the lives of the non-archaeologists who eventually pay for it, and the beauty of Assyrian carved ivories surely has its part to play towards that end at least as much as knowledge of the details of such matters as Assyrian land tenure.

Mallowan's dig at Nimrud represented the last major excavation in Assyria in the old style, that is, on lines which produce results likely immediately to capture the interest of the general public. *Sic breviter transit gloria mundi.* Subsequent archaeological work in northern Iraq has been on a smaller scale and has been dominated by different objectives. A number of factors have contributed to this. One was the revision of the Iraqi Antiquities Law after the revolution of 1958, abolishing the right of foreign expeditions to a half of all duplicate finds; this has removed any incentive to give preference to the kind of archaeological site most likely to yield museum-worthy antiquities. A second factor is finance; labour costs in Iraq have risen steeply since 1958 and are now (1983) at about the level of Western countries. This puts a premium on small sites in which the occupation levels of interest are not heavily overlaid with later debris. A further factor is that the Iraqi authorities, recognizing archaeological sites as tourist attractions, now press the excavator to accept responsibility for restoration of monuments as a sequel to excavation, and this can be expensive if the site is one with major buildings and sculpture. There is also the question of which periods are most urgently in need of further elucidation. In consequence of this combination of factors, almost all excavations in Assyria since the campaigns of the British School at Nimrud have been at sites earlier than the Assyrian empire.

Assyrian imperial sites have not, however, been entirely deserted; a Polish team undertook some investigations at Nimrud, attempting to solve some of the problems left over from the excavations by Layard and Mallowan. The Iraqi authorities themselves, who have produced some archaeologists of very high calibre, have undertaken important work both at Sherif Khan (ancient Tarbisu, just north of Nineveh) and at Kuyunjik. The work at the latter principally involved conservation of monuments and restoration of buildings, whereby the fortification walls and gateways of Sennacherib once again stand for all to see. Above all, the world owes a debt to the Iraqi archaeologists for saving Nineveh from speculators who planned to build over the site.

Bibliography

Very detailed bibliographies of books and articles dealing with all aspects of ancient Mesopotamia will be found in 'Keilschriftbibliographie', published annually in the periodical *Orientalia* (Rome). What follows is a limited selection of suggestions for readers who may wish to follow up particular topics; the services of a good library will be necessary.

Publications relevant throughout this book are entered under 'General'; others are placed under the chapter for which they are mainly relevant.

General

Translations of Assyrian royal inscriptions

GRAYSON, Albert Kirk: *Assyrian royal inscriptions* (2 vols., 1972, 1976, Harrassowitz, Wiesbaden). Very reliable translations of inscriptions of all Assyrian kings down to Ashur-nasir-pal II.

LUCKENBILL, Daniel David: *Ancient records of Assyria and Babylonia* (2 vols., 1926, 1927, University of Chicago Press, Chicago). Less reliable than the foregoing, but the only comprehensive English translation available for inscriptions of Assyrian kings after Ashur-nasir-pal II.

Translations of Assyrian letters

WATERMAN, Leroy: *Royal correspondence of the Assyrian empire* (4 vols., 1930–36, University of Michigan Press, Ann Arbor).

SAGGS, Henry W. F.: 'The Nimrud Letters, 1952', in *Iraq* (London), vols. 17 (1955), 18 (1956), 20 (1958), 21 (1959), 25 (1963), 27 (1965), 28 (1966), 36 (1974).

Standard encyclopaedic work on Assyriology

EBELING, Erich and MEISSNER, Bruno *et al.* (eds.): *Reallexikon der Assyriologie* (in progress, 1932–   , Walter de Gruyter, Berlin).

Archaeology of ancient Mesopotamia

PARROT, André: *Archéologie mésopotamienne; les étapes* (1946, Albin Michel, Paris).

Chapter 1

OATES, David: *Studies in the ancient history of northern Iraq* (1968, British Academy, London).

OATES, David and Joan: *The rise of civilization* (1976, Elsevier-Phaidon, Oxford).

LLOYD, Seton: *The archaeology of Mesopotamia* (1978, Thames and Hudson, London).
ANDRAE, Walter: *Die archaischen Ischtar-Tempel in Assur* (1922, Hinrichs, Leipzig).

Chapter 2

KRAUS, F. R.: *Könige, die in Zelten wohnten* (1965, Amsterdam).
GARELLI, Paul: *Les Assyriens en Cappadoce* (1963, Adrien Maisonneuve, Paris).
LARSEN, Mogens Trolle: *The Old Assyrian city-state and its colonies* (1976, Akademisk Forlag, Copenhagen).

Chapter 3

KLENGEL, Horst: *Geschichte Syriens im 2. Jahrtausend v.u.Z*, 1–3 (1965–70, Institut für Orientforschung, Berlin).
DIAKONOFF, I. M.: 'Die Arier im Vorderen Orient: Ende eines Mythos', *Orientalia* (Rome), vol. 41 (1972), pp. 91–120.
GRAYSON, Albert Kirk: *Assyrian and Babylonian chronicles* (1975, J. J. Augustin, New York).

Chapter 4

WEIDNER, Ernst: *Die Inschriften Tukulti-Ninurtas I. und seiner Nachfolger* (1959, *Archiv für Orientforschung*, Beiheft 12, Graz).
FREYDANK, Helmut: 'Die Rolle der Deportierten im mittelassyrischen Staat', pp. 55–63 in J. Herrmann and I. Sellnow (eds.), *Die Rolle der Volksmassen in der Geschichte der vorkapitalistischen Gesellschaftsformationen* (1975, Berlin).
HINZ, Walther, *The lost world of Elam* (1972, Sidgwick and Jackson, London).

Chapter 5

WEIDNER, Ernst: 'Die Feldzüge und Bauten Tiglatpilesers I.', *Archiv für Orientforschung*, vol. 18 (1957–8), pp. 342–60.
MALAMAT, A.: 'The Aramaeans', pp. 134–55 in D. J. Wiseman (ed.), *Peoples of Old Testament times* (1973, Clarendon Press, Oxford).

Chapter 6

ANDRAE, Walter: *Die Stelenreihen in Assur* (1913, reprinted 1972, Otto Zeller Verlag, Osnabrück).
TADMOR, Hayyim: 'Azriyau of Yaudi', *Scripta Hierosolymitana* 8 (1961, Jerusalem), pp. 232–71.

Chapter 7

THUREAU-DANGIN, François: *Une relation de la huitième campagne de Sargon (714 av. J.-C.)* (1912, Paul Geuthner, Paris).
LUCKENBILL, Daniel David: *The annals of Sennacherib* (1920, University of Chicago Press, Chicago).

PARPOLA, Simo: 'The murderer of Sennacherib', pp. 171–82 in B. Alster (ed.), *Death in Mesopotamia* (1980, Copenhagen).

Chapter 8

BORGER, Riekele: *Die Inschriften Asarhaddons Königs von Assyrien* (1956, *Archiv für Orientforschung*, Beiheft 9, Graz).
STRECK, Maximilian: *Assurbanipal und die letzten assyrischen Könige bis zum Untergange Ninivehs*, 1–3 (1916, Hinrichs, Leipzig).

Chapter 9

DRIVER, Godfrey Rolles and MILES, John C.: *The Assyrian Laws* (1935, Clarendon Press, Oxford). This is the basic publication, but is updated by the following work.
CARDASCIA, Guillaume: *Les lois assyriennes* (1969, Du Cerf, Paris).
DIAKONOFF, I. M.: 'Agrarian conditions in Middle Assyria', pp. 204–34 in I. M. Diakonoff (ed.), *Ancient Mesopotamia* (1969, Nauka, Moscow).
FALES, Frederick Mario: *Censimenti e catasti di epoca neo-assira* (1973, Rome).
WEIDNER, Ernst: 'Hof- und Harems-Erlasse assyrischer Könige aus dem 2. Jahrtausend v. Chr.', *Archiv für Orientforschung*, vol. 17 (1954–6), pp. 257–93.

Chapter 10

MALLOWAN, Max E. L.: *Nimrud and its remains*, 2 vols. (1966, Collins, London).
MAXWELL-HYSLOP, K. R.: *Western Asiatic Jewellery c. 3000–612 B.C.* (1971, Methuen, London).
SALONEN, Armas: *Die Möbel des alten Mesopotamien* (1963, Helsinki).
SALONEN, Armas: *Die Hausgeräte der alten Mesopotamier*, 2 vols. (1965–6, Helsinki).

Chapter 11

SALONEN, Armas: *Agricultura Mesopotamica* (1968, Helsinki).
OPPENHEIM, A. Leo: 'Essay on overland trade in the first millennium B.C.', *Journal of Cuneiform Studies*, vol. 21 (1967), pp. 236–54.

Chapter 12

OPPENHEIM, A. Leo et al.: *Glass and Glassmaking in ancient Mesopotamia* (1970, Corning, New York).
PLEINER, Radomír and BJORKMAN, Judith K.: 'The Assyrian Iron Age; the history of iron in the Assyrian civilization', *Proceedings of the American Philosophical Society* (Philadelphia), vol. 118 (1974), pp. 283–313.
PLEINER, Radomír: 'The technology of three Assyrian iron artifacts from Khorsabad', *Journal of Near Eastern Studies* (Chicago), vol. 38 (1979), pp. 83–91.
WERTIME, Theodore A. and MUHLY, James D. (eds.): *The coming of the age of iron* (1980, Yale University Press, New Haven and London).

Chapter 13

SAGGS, Henry W. F.: *The encounter with the divine in Mesopotamia and Israel* (1978, Athlone Press, London).
DRIEL, G. van: *The cult of Aššur* (1969, Van Gorcum, Assen).
ANDRAE, Walter: *Das wiedererstandene Assur* (1977, second edition revised by B. Hrouda; Beck, Munich).
OPPENHEIM, A. Leo: 'Divination and celestial observation in the last Assyrian empire', *Centaurus* (Copenhagen), vol. 14 (1969), pp. 97–135.

Chapter 14

LABAT, René: *Traité akkadien de diagnostics et pronostics médicaux* (1951, Brill, Leiden).
OPPENHEIM, A. Leo: 'Mesopotamian Medicine', *Bulletin of the History of Medicine*, vol. 36 (1962), pp. 97–108.
RITTER, Edith K.: 'Magical-expert (= āšipu) and physician (= asû); notes on two complementary professions in Babylonian medicine', *Assyriological Studies* (Oriental Institute of the University of Chicago), no. 16 (1965), pp. 299–321.

Chapter 15

FRANKFORT, H.: *The art and architecture of the ancient Orient* (1954, Penguin, Harmondsworth).
MOORTGAT, Anton: *The art of ancient Mesopotamia* (1969, Phaidon, London).
KING, L. W.: *Bronze reliefs from the gates of Shalmaneser, king of Assyria B.C. 860–825* (1915, British Museum, London).
LLOYD, Seton: *The art of the ancient Near East* (1961, Thames and Hudson, London).
FRANKFORT, H.: *Cylinder seals* (1939, Macmillan, London).

Chapter 16

SAGGS, Henry W. F.: 'Assyrian warfare in the Sargonid period', *Iraq* (London), vol. 25 (1963), pp. 145–54.
ODED, Bustenay: *Mass deportations and deportees in the Neo-Assyrian empire* (1979, Ludwig Reichert, Wiesbaden).

Chapter 17

WEIDNER, Ernst: 'Die Bibliothek Tiglatpilesers I', *Archiv für Orientforschung* (Graz), vol. 16 (1952–3), pp. 197–215.
OPPENHEIM, A. Leo: *Ancient Mesopotamia* (1964, University of Chicago Press, Chicago and London). The relevant part for writing and literature is chapter V.
SPEISER, E. A.: 'Akkadian myths and epics', pp. 31–86 in James B. Pritchard (ed.), *The ancient Near East*, vol. I; *an anthology of texts and pictures* (1973, Princeton Paperback, Princeton University Press).
LAMBERT, Wilfred G.: *Babylonian Wisdom literature* (1960, Clarendon Press, Oxford).

Chapter 18

RICH, Claudius James: *Narrative of a residence in Koordistan and on the site of ancient Nineveh*, 2 vols. (1836, James Duncan, London; republished 1972, Gregg International, Farnborough, Hants.).

LAYARD, Austen Henry: *Nineveh and its remains* (first edition, 1849; abridged edition with introduction by H. W. F. Saggs, 1970, Routledge and Kegan Paul, London).

ROSS, Janet (ed.): *Letters from the East by Henry James Ross*, 1837–1857 (1902, Dent, London).

BUDGE, E. A. T. W.: *The rise and progress of Assyriology* (first edition, 1925; reprinted 1975, AMS Press, New York).

CURTIS, John (ed.): *Fifty years of Mesopotamian discovery* (1982, British School of Archaeology in Iraq, London).

Indexes

Proper Names

Adad 104, 201f., 204
Adad-apla-iddina 66, 68
Adad-narari I 44, 46ff.
Adad-nerari II 71
Adad-nerari III 78f., 81ff.
Agade (city) 19
Agade (dynasty) 19f., 26
Agade (empire or period) 19ff.,
   26ff., 37
Akhlamu 50
Akitu 68, 91, 208f.
Akkad (city) = Agade (city), q.v.
Akkad (land) 5, 27, 35, 220, 222,
   276, 281
Alalakh 38
Aleppo 81, 85, 293, 300
Al Hather = Hatra, q.v.
Alshe 41
Amel-Marduk 117
Amid 75
Amorites 25ff., 35ff.
Amurru (ethnic group) =
   Amorites, q.v.
Amurru (state in Syria) 50, 63
Anu 201, 203
Anzu 203, 235
Arabs 107f., 115, 252
Aramaeans 50f., 62, 65ff., 74, 81f.,
   89, 100, 127, 129, 178,
   243f., 255, 262
Arbail = Erbil, q.v.
Arik-den-ili 44
Arpachiyeh 13f., 321
Arpad 81, 88, 92
Arrapkha 3, 36f., 40, 91, 126, 131,
   148
Ashur (city) 3, 5, 19ff., 25ff.,
   35ff., 40f., 47, 50ff., 54f.,
   79, 92, 98, 113, 119, 126,

131, 148, 162, 176, 187,
   189, 194, 197, 208, 222, 241,
   243, 277ff., 291, 297, 320
Ashur (deity) 21, 44, 50, 65, 93ff.,
   104, 114, 125f., 129f., 148,
   201ff., 208ff., 214, 237,
   246ff., 258, 272, 275
Ashurbanipal 79, 106, 108ff., 130,
   147, 174f., 181, 186, 217,
   229, 237f., 242, 245, 250,
   279ff., 316f.
Ashur-bel-kala 65ff.
Ashur-dan I 56
Ashur-dan II 69ff.
Ashur-etillu-ili 117f.
Ashur-nadin-apli 55
Ashur-nadin-shum 101
Ashur-nasir-pal (son of Tukulti-
   Ninurta I) 55
Ashur-nasir-pal II 72ff., 86, 128,
   163, 165f., 184, 203, 234ff.,
   249, 251, 255, 262, 267,
   272, 312
Ashur-nerari V 83
Ashur-rabi II 70
Ashur-resh-ishi I 57f.
Ashur-uballit I 41ff., 50, 176
Ashur-uballit II 120f.
Aššurayau 124, 131
Azariah 89
Azriyau 89

Baasheikha 306
Babylon (Babel, Babil) 5, 22, 24f.,
   36, 52, 55, 57, 91, 97, 102f.,
   105ff., 113, 115, 118, 121,
   134, 178, 188, 208, 222,
   248, 289

Balawat 236, 320
Baltil 22
Bel 104, 113, 148, 212
Bel-ibni 100f.
Berossus 181
Beth Eden 71
Bit-Adini 71f., 74, 128
Bit-Amukkanni 89, 100
Bit-Dakkuri 100
Bit-Sa'alli 100
Bit-Yakin 91, 100
Borsippa 113, 167f., 222, 279f.
Botta, Paul Emile 298ff., 304f.,
    307f., 313
Byblos 107, 240

Calah 5f., 78, 80, 83, 93, 98f., 128,
    131, 165, 182, 189, 194,
    197, 234, 236, 240, 249,
    252, 267, 275, 278, 280, 289
Cappadocia 28ff., 33, 36, 176, 275
Carchemish 62, 72, 74, 81, 83, 88,
    95, 120f., 127, 247
Çatal Hüyük 11f.
Çayonu 12
Chaldaea 74, 99f., 192
Chaldaeans 77, 88ff., 99ff., 106,
    113f., 117ff., 247f., 258
Cilicia 14, 39, 72, 77, 81, 91, 107
Cimmerians 97, 106f., 109, 111,
    119, 218
Cuthah 100, 113, 203, 281
Cyprus 77, 107

Damascus 75, 81f., 87, 89, 115
Daughter of Anu 138
Der 92, 102
Diyala 18, 38, 47, 57, 71, 73, 88,
    102, 131
Diyarbekr 12, 14, 46, 75, 196
Dur-Sharrukin 98, 129, 163, 185,
    189, 237, 299

Ea 201f.
Egypt 39ff., 58, 87, 91f., 101,

108ff., 119ff., 178, 196, 240,
    244, 252, 266
Ekallatu 25, 35
Elam, Elamites 56ff., 92, 97,
    100ff., 111ff., 171, 199, 238,
    248, 253, 258
Enlil 47f., 64, 188, 201ff., 235, 250
Enlil-narari I 44f.
Erbil 3, 5, 11f., 20ff., 27, 36f, 41,
    45, 70, 72, 78, 126, 131,
    148, 203, 208, 252, 291, 296
Erech 5f., 18, 118, 222
Eresh-kigal 214ff.
Eridu (culture) 15
Erishum I 28, 33, 35
Erishum II 25
Esagila 105
Esarhaddon 100, 104ff., 113, 149f.,
    152, 219, 245, 247, 251f.,
    254, 260, 266, 275, 280
Euphrates 5, 7, 11, 17ff., 35f.,
    38f., 46f., 52, 54, 58, 62,
    65f., 69, 71f., 74, 80, 82,
    86, 88f., 102, 119, 128, 131,
    166, 176, 237, 255, 318
Ezida 279

Fort Sargon (see also Dur-
    Sharrukin) 97, 129, 174, 313

Gasur 26
Gaza 92, 107, 120
Gilgamesh 286
Gozan 275, 322
Grotefend, G. F. 295
Guti 26
Guzanu = Gozan, q.v.
Gyges 109, 111

Habha 60f., 77, 83, 166f.
Habuba Kabira 17
Habor, Habur 3, 6, 17, 31, 38, 66,
    68, 71f., 74, 105, 263, 268,
    322
Hadad-ezer 75

Hajji Muhammad 15
Halaf (culture; for the site see 'Tell
Halaf') 12ff., 127
Hamath 81f., 89, 92f.
Hammurabi 24f., 36, 230, 276
Hanigalbat (or Haligalbat) 39, 41,
47, 49f.
Harran 66, 120, 127, 137, 203
Hassuna 12ff., 127
Hatra 5, 11, 313
Herodotus 78, 111
Hezekiah 91, 101, 256f.
Hittites 38f., 41, 47, 50, 54, 56, 58,
60, 83, 176, 184
Hurri 39, 41
Hurrians 37ff., 127, 132

Ilu-kabkabi 24f., 35
Ilushuma 27f., 35
Imdugud 235
Inanna, Innin 26, 159
Ishme-Dagan 37
Ishtar 21, 114, 159, 201f., 203, 227
——of Bit-kitmuri 202
——of Erbil 21, 104, 112, 202,
245, 275
——of Nineveh 21, 104, 202
Itu'a 243f.

Jarmo 9
Jazirah 3, 5, 11f., 21, 63, 161, 311
Jebel Bishri 62, 66
Jebel Hamrin 3
Jebel Makhul 2
Jebel Sinjar 5, 11, 19
Jemdet Nasr 15, 18
Jericho 11
Jeroboam II 82
Jerusalem 2, 52, 91, 93, 101, 131,
249, 257, 264, 305
Jonah (Jonas, Yunus) 290f., 293

Kadmukh 45, 49, 59f., 72f.
Kalizi 131, 147, 252, 322
Kandalanu 114, 117f.

Kanesh 28f., 31ff.
Karamles 296, 306
Kar-Tukulti-Ninurta 54
Kashiari 44, 73
Kassites 42, 44, 46, 57
Kermalis = Karamles, q.v.
Khorsabad 98, 185, 189, 206, 234,
299, 302, 307, 313, 318
Khosr 99, 120, 190, 193
Kirkuk 3, 7, 9, 26, 29, 36f., 40,
46, 73, 91, 132, 143, 321
Kish 19
Kultepe 29
Kummukh 88
Kuyunjik (also spelt 'Kouyunjik')
240, 275, 277ff., 286f., 290,
294, 297, 299, 306, 310,
313, 316ff., 323

Lachish 158
Lamashtu 139, 224
Layard, (Sir) Henry Austen [On
some publications he used
his Christian names in
reversed order] 299ff., 322f.

Mallowan, M. E. L. (Sir Max) 21,
310, 322f.
Manasseh 107
Manishtusu 19
Mannaeans 80, 94, 119, 129, 218,
249f.
Mannai = Mannaeans, q.v.
Marduk 52, 91, 105, 108, 139,
201f., 204, 221f., 248, 260,
275f., 285
Marduk-apil-iddina = Merodach-
baladan, q.v.
Mari 35f., 64, 83
Medes 77, 80, 89, 106, 115, 119ff.,
129, 218, 263, 267
Melid 60, 80f., 88
Merodach-baladan 91f., 97, 100f.,
118, 248
Midas = Mita, q.v.

333

Mittanni, Mittannians 39ff., 46f., 49, 196, 241, 246
Mita 95, 247
Musasir 95
Mushki, Muski 59f., 95, 128, 247
Musri 44

Nabataeans 115
Nabonidus 117
Nabopolassar 117ff.
Nabu 104, 147, 168, 201, 276, 278f.
Nairi 49, 51, 60f., 73, 77
Naram-Sin of Assyria 25
Nebuchadrezzar (Nebuchadnezzar) 117, 121, 263
Necho I 109, 111
Necho II 120
Neo-Babylonian dynasty 117
Nergal 201, 203, 272
Neriglissar 117
Nimrud 74, 131, 183, 206, 233, 240, 275, 282, 303ff., 318
Nineveh (see also 'Kuyunjik') 3, 14, 17, 19ff., 26, 36f., 41, 43, 45, 51, 56, 65, 72f., 78, 88, 98f., 102, 106f., 109, 115, 120, 126, 131, 148, 163, 174, 182, 186, 188ff., 197, 203, 207, 217, 234, 251, 255, 275, 279, 281f., 289ff., 297, 311, 313f., 319, 321, 323
Ninlil 203
Ninshiku 250
Ninurta 202f., 227, 229, 235, 250, 272
Nippur 100, 118, 222, 232, 288, 316
Nuzi 26, 40, 143, 321

Papkhu 59f.
Persian Gulf 91, 100, 102, 169, 199, 256
Persians 77, 80, 114f., 267

Pharaoh (title used as quasi-proper name) 108, 111, 120
Philistines 58, 184
Phoenicians 72, 102, 107, 129, 199, 255, 266
Phrygians 128
Psammetichus 111
Pul 83, 88

Qal'ah Shergat 5, 29, 275, 290, 297, 311f., 316, 318, 320
Qarqar 75
Qumani (form of 'Uqumani, Uqumeni', q.v.) 71
Qutians 45f., 51

Rawlinson, H. C. 295, 301ff., 305, 310, 314, 317f.
Rich, Claudius James 295ff.
Rusa (also spelt 'Ursa') 94, 259

Sam'al 85
Samaria 92f., 263
Samarra 13, 127
Sammurammat 78f.
Sarduri I 80, 83
Sargon of Agade 19, 29
Sargon II 92ff., 100, 129, 162f., 169, 174, 178, 185, 189, 237, 247ff., 253, 259, 265, 267, 288, 299, 313
Scythians 106f., 119
Semiramis = Sammurammat, q.v.
Sennacherib 79, 86, 98ff., 104, 138, 158, 163, 169, 171, 182, 188ff., 197f., 203, 209, 245, 248f., 250, 253ff., 266, 280
Shalmaneser I 48ff., 54, 74, 184
Shalmaneser II 70
Shalmaneser III 75ff., 86, 184, 235f., 252f., 312
Shalmaneser IV 82
Shalmaneser V 92, 189
Shamash 104, 158, 201f., 218, 275
Shamash-resh-usur 83

Shamash-shum-ukin 106, 109, 112f., 115, 117
Shamshi-Adad I 23ff., 28, 33, 35ff., 147f.
Shamshi-Adad IV 68
Shamshi-Adad V 78f., 81
Shinar 5f.
Shubat-Enlil 36f.
Sidon 81, 107
Sin 104, 138, 202ff., 275
Sin-ahhe-eriba (more exact transcription of name 'Sennacherib', q.v.) 138
Sin-shar-ishkun 118, 120
Subarians 44, 46
Subartu 19
Sultantepe 278
Sumer, Sumerians 5f., 15ff., 22f., 29, 127, 180, 203, 234, 280
Şupite 69
Susa 102, 114, 119
Sutu 161

Tadmor (Palmyra) 62
Tarbisu 119, 203, 223
Tarqa 108f.
Tell Billa 306 footnote, 321
Tell Brak 17f.
Tell el-Rimah 50, 160
Tell Halaf (see also 'Halaf') 275, 322
Tell Sotto 11f.
Tell Taya 19
Tepe Gawra 17f., 194, 321
Teumman 112ff.
Tiamat 208f., 285
Tiglath-Pileser I 58ff., 70, 74, 162, 184, 196, 247, 255, 266, 279
Tiglath-Pileser III 84ff., 95, 98, 107, 129, 177
Tigris 2f., 5, 17, 20f., 27, 35, 45, 47, 49, 55, 59f., 66, 71ff., 82, 88, 91, 93, 99, 102, 119f., 166f., 175, 189f., 192f., 197, 236, 252, 255, 291, 305ff., 311f., 318

Tukulti-Ninurta I 50ff., 56f., 125, 189, 196
Tukulti-Ninurta II 71f., 312
Tur Abdin 38, 41, 44f., 49, 59, 61, 66, 70f., 73, 82, 196, 246
Turushpa 80, 94
Tushkhan 73
Tuthmosis III 39
Tyre 75, 81, 107, 177

Ubaid 15f., 127
Ugarit 176
Ukin-zer (read 'Mukin-zer' by some scholars) 89, 91f.
Uqumani, Uqumeni 51
Umm Dabaghiyeh 11, 15
Ummanmanda 120
Ur (city) 27, 203, 294, 321
Ur (dynasty) 27, 35, 38
Urartu 48, 77, 79ff., 85, 87ff., 93ff., 102, 106, 169, 185, 249ff., 252ff., 259f.
Urbilum (old form of name 'Erbil', q.v.) 27
Urmia, Lake 79f., 93ff., 169, 249
Ursa = Rusa, q.v.
Uruatri 48
Uruk (city, = Erech, q.v.)
Uruk (culture) 15, 17f.
Ushukani = Washukanni, q.v.

Van, Lake 10, 14, 48f., 60, 77ff., 95

Washukanni 40, 47

Y'dy 87

Zab rivers 3, 160, 167
 Great (Upper) 3, 74, 93
 Lesser (Lower) 3, 47, 52, 57, 71, 73, 93, 291
Zamua 128
Zawi Chemi 9
Zobah = transcription of Hebrew form of name 'Şupite', q.v.

General Index

administration 36, 57, 70, 85, 126, 148, 150, 210
agriculture 3, 5, 7ff., 11ff., 20, 49, 131ff., 162ff., 174, 193
amulets 14, 138, 155, 228
animal husbandry 162, 166ff.
annaku 30
anthropomorphism 212f., 218, 235
aqueduct 99, 161, 192f., 321
archers 80, 154, 236, 253, 260
armour 154, 184, 309
army 243ff.
art 233ff.
ashipu 212ff., 224
Assyrian King List 23ff., 35, 37, 68
Assyrian royal inscriptions 48, 55, 65, 68, 86, 115, 189, 271ff.
astrology 149, 164, 175, 217, 220ff., 274
asu 226ff.
atrocities 248ff., 261f.

baru 215, 217ff.
bas reliefs 113, 152, 154, 167, 197, 199, 233ff., 242, 260, 263, 305ff., 313, 316
beds 22, 142, 158, 166
bee-keeping 83, 266
bread 165, 172, 207f.
Broken Obelisk 63, 65f.
bronze reliefs (on gates) 80, 236, 320
building inscriptions 189, 271ff.
burial (see also 'tombs') 17, 113f., 149, 157, 195

canals 68, 74, 95, 103, 163, 192f., 199, 211, 260

cannibalism 113, 261
caravans 29ff., 97, 176, 178, 196f.
castration 145f., 166
cavalry 72, 75, 94, 169, 192, 196, 253f., 259
chariotry, chariots 39, 41, 59f., 62, 72, 94, 113, 147, 149, 169, 192, 195ff., 209, 236, 242ff., 251, 253, 255, 258f.
chemical technology 186ff.
cities, beginning of 16f.
clothing 142, 149, 152ff., 207, 209
colophons 229, 277, 280ff.
colossi 170, 182, 191, 197, 239, 272, 305ff., 312ff., 316
communications 85f., 102, 111, 168, 196f., 255ff.
contraception 144f.
cosmetics 159
cotton 163, 166, 192, 265
cuneiform (see also 'tablets, clay') 23, 105, 129, 147, 156, 186, 218

decipherment of cuneiform 294f., 301f., 305, 316ff.
demons 138f., 155, 201, 213ff., 223f., 226, 230
deportation 48f., 62, 125ff., 134f., 263f.
divination, diviners (see also '*baru*') 148ff., 164, 167, 202, 210, 217ff., 226
divorce 143
domestication of animals 7ff., 196

Early Dynastic period 16ff., 22

336

eclipses 150, 211, 222f.
economic documents 117, 277, 279
education 129f., 146f.
epics 47f., 52, 285f.
eunuchs 145f.
extradition 112

famine 103, 112f., 163f., 171, 261
farmer (as title of the king) 276
fauna and flora, interest of
  Assyrian kings in 63f., 193
flood 64, 147, 170, 319
flooding 55f., 120, 175, 190, 223,
  245
food 74, 168, 170, 176, 207
furniture 72, 95, 156ff., 181,
  233ff., 261

ghosts 187, 215, 227f., 230
glass 186f., 309
graves: see 'burial', 'tombs'
uffa 198

harvest 163f., 172, 175, 251
headgear 156
homosexuality 144f.
horse-breeding 43, 77, 169
horse-training 39, 169f., 251, 267,
  390
hostages 75, 129f., 148
houses, private 193ff.
hunting 7ff., 63f., 202f., 234, 238,
  241f.

il as place-name element 22
incantations 116, 138f., 181, 208,
  213, 227f., 230, 280, 283ff.
infant exposure 140, 145
infant mortality 138ff.
intelligence system 85f., 93, 102,
  119, 256f., 276f.
interpreters 148, 257
irrigation 15, 20, 55, 99, 131ff.,
  162f., 175, 180, 192f.

ivory 72, 152, 157ff., 178, 239ff.,
  309f., 322f.

jewellery 49, 141f., 155f., 207, 233

kalu 211f., 218f., 226
kelek 62, 167, 198, 244, 255, 303,
  312, 318
kingship (see also 'Farmer (as title
  of the king)', 'substitute
  king', 'succession, royal')
  44, 50, 147ff.

land tenure 117, 126, 131ff., 171f.,
  277, 323
languages 22, 125, 127ff., 148
  Akkadian 23, 37, 131, 179,
    273
  Aramaic 129, 179
  Assyrian dialect 48, 129
  Babylonian dialect 48
  foreign languages, difficulty of
    writing 185
  Hebrew 249, 257
  Hurrian 37, 59, 126
  Indo-European languages 38
  pre-Sumerian language 16, 22,
    44, 127
  Sumerian 16, 37
  Urartian 273
lapis lazuli 18, 42, 77, 81, 178, 240
laws 64, 124, 130, 132, 136, 140ff.,
  181, 199, 230, 277
letters 218, 243, 262, 275ff.
library 116, 181, 186, 217, 229,
  277ff., 316, 318
locusts 163, 176, 221, 258, 260

magic, magicians (see also '*ashipu*')
  138f., 146, 148, 213ff.,
  224f., 227ff.
marriage 33, 140ff.
medicine 226ff.

merchants, merchant colonies
  28ff., 36, 50, 69, 127, 129,
  133, 173, 176f., 246
midwives 139
military campaigns 37, 44, 58ff.,
  72ff., 93ff., 238, 243ff.
moneylenders 132
monogamy 137, 140
monotheism 203f.
month names 65
monumental architecture,
  beginning of 15ff., 21
music 148, 208, 211f.
myths 285f.

New Year Festival: see 'Akitu' in
  Index of proper names

omens 116, 139, 149f., 157, 175,
  181, 187, 245, 282f.
oracles 105, 116, 254, 275

paintings 11, 234, 237, 265, 310
palaces 21, 29, 40, 81, 86, 99, 104,
  148, 150, 182, 190ff., 206,
  218, 230, 233, 251f., 318
pantheon 200ff.
papyrus 152, 154, 179, 244
parks 98, 165, 193
physicians 148, 226ff.
plaques 144, 152, 240
ploughs 62, 70, 162f., 166, 195
polytheism 201ff.
prayers 181, 208, 211, 280
prices 103, 174
priests (see also 'ashipu', 'kalu',
  'shangu') 148, 156, 210ff.
prisoners of war 17, 49, 51f., 59f.,
  62, 115, 128f., 134ff., 152,
  190, 236f., 256f., 261ff.
prostitutes 140f., 145, 153
punishment 141, 146, 150, 250

quay 182, 197, 322

Rabshakeh 91, 257, 263, 306
racial mixing 88, 125ff., 190
racialism, Assyrian freedom from
  72, 125, 128, 244
reliefs: see 'bas reliefs', 'bronze
  reliefs (on gates)'
religion 148, 200ff.
rituals 138f., 146, 149, 207ff.
roads, routes (see also 'trade
  routes') 31, 81f., 87, 94f.,
  192, 196f., 252, 254, 292

Sacred Marriage 208
Sacred Tree 235, 241, 265
sanctions: see 'trade sanctions'
schools 147
scribes 129, 146, 181, 244, 252
sculpture 233, 239, 308ff.
seals 17f.
  cylinder seals 144, 152, 155,
    233, 241f.
  stamp seals 13, 18
sexual behaviour 144ff.
shangu 210ff., 218
siege warfare 37, 260f.
slavery, slaves 17, 131, 133ff., 143
social organization 8, 13, 17, 130ff
spies 93, 256
statues 22, 95, 103, 191, 205, 239
substitute king 149, 276
succession, royal 104ff., 114
suicide 94, 113
šulmanu 42f.
surgery 230

tablets, clay (see also 'texts,
  cuneiform') 23, 29, 36,
  38ff., 50, 57, 116, 179, 217,
  241, 244, 269f., 319f., 322
taboos 135, 149, 168, 340
taxation 28, 31, 54, 92, 97f., 126,
  137, 148, 177f., 189
temple personnel 209ff.
temples 16ff., 21f., 26, 28, 36, 50,
  52, 81, 92, 98, 103, 105,

114, 145, 167, 171, 182, 188, 204f., 219
xtiles 14, 30f., 33, 72
xts, cuneiform (see also 'Assyrian King List', 'Assyrian royal inscriptions', 'building inscriptions', 'cuneiform', 'economic documents', 'incantations', 'prayers', 'tablets, clay'):
astrological reports 220ff., 274
astronomical texts 181
Flood text 319
letters 275ff.
lexical texts 152, 181
limu lists 273f.
literary texts 181
magical texts 138, 214ff., 283ff.
medical texts 181, 227ff.
mythological texts 217
myths and epics 271, 285f.
Nuzi texts 132
omen texts 282f.
oracles 275
Penitential Psalms 116
rituals 279f., 283ff.
synonym lists 159f., 271, 283
Wisdom literature 271, 287

•mbs (see also 'burial') 114, 190, 194
•nsure 156, 232
•ols 183ff., 195, 244
•wn-planning 98f., 187ff.

trade 10, 12, 14, 16, 18, 20, 27ff., 42f., 50f., 56, 58, 72, 77, 85, 97, 107, 111, 162, 170ff., 246
trade cycles 175
trade routes 47, 56, 77, 81, 107, 115, 183
trade sanctions 50, 92, 177f., 184
transport (see also 'water transport') 30f., 72, 107, 172, 195ff., 255
treaties 78, 83, 106, 119, 124, 149
tribute 47, 51, 71ff., 80f., 85, 88f., 177f., 236

underworld 159, 202, 204, 227

wagons 192, 195, 197, 244, 255
warfare 17, 37, 51, 243ff.
warfare, theology of 246f.
water supply 99, 107, 160f., 192f., 252
water transport 63, 74, 167, 169, 190f., 197ff., 244, 255f.
waterproofing 182, 192, 198
witchcraft 225
writing, beginning of 16, 23, 269ff.
writing boards 270
writing systems 129, 179, 294

ziggurat 206
zoos 63, 267

Biblical References

Genesis
  10:8, *51*
  10:10–11, *5*
  10:22, *56*

Deuteronomy
  7:3, *124*

1 Samuel
  13:19, *184*
  14:47, *69*
  28:7–14, *219*

1 Kings
  22:10–12, *219*

2 Kings
  14:25–8, *82*
  15:19, 20, *89*
  16:7, *177*
  17:3–5, *92*
  17:6, *263, 322*
  17:24–8, *263*
  18:12, *91*
  18:17–36, *91, 101*
  18:21, *101*
  18:26, *257*
  18:32, *264*
  18:33, *249*
  18 and 19, *243*
  19:37, *103*
  20:12, *101*
  23:12, *117*

23:15–20, *117*
23:29, *120*

2 Chronicles
  33:11–13, *107*

Ezra
  4:9–10, *115*

Isaiah
  5:8, *134*
  10:5–6, *264*
  10:12–13, *264*
  36 and 37, *243*
  46:6–7, *200*
  49 to 55, *200*

Jeremiah
  1:13–15, *118*
  2:28, *201*
  46:5, *121*
  46:10–12, *121*
  47:1, *120*

Amos
  1:5, *71*

Jonah
  3:3, *291*

Nahum
  1:8, *120*
  3:8–10, *109*
  3:16, *246*